HITLER'S COSMOPOLITAN BASTARD

HITLER'S COSMOPOLITAN BASTARD

*Count Richard Coudenhove-Kalergi
and His Vision of Europe*

MARTYN BOND

MCGILL-QUEEN'S UNIVERSITY PRESS
Montreal & Kingston | London | Chicago

ISBN 978-0-2280-0545-2 (cloth)
ISBN 978-0-2280-0701-2 (ePDF)
ISBN 978-0-2280-0702-9 (ePDF)

Legal deposit first quarter 2021
Bibliothèque nationale du Québec

Printed in Canada on acid-free paper that is 100% ancient forest free
(100% post-consumer recycled), processed chlorine free

Library and Archives Canada Cataloguing in Publication

Title: Hitler's cosmopolitan bastard : Count Richard Coudenhove-Kalergi
and his vision of Europe / Martyn Bond.
Names: Bond, Martyn, author.
Description: Includes bibliographical references and index.
Identifiers: Canadiana (print) 20200384228 | Canadiana (ebook) 20200384295 |
ISBN 9780228005452 (cloth) | ISBN 9780228007012 (ePDF) | ISBN 9780228007029
(ePUB)
Subjects: LCSH: Coudenhove-Kalergi, Richard Nicolaus, Graf von, 1894-1972. |
LCSH: Internationalists—Austria—Biography. | LCSH: European federation. |
LCSH: Europe—Politics and government—1918-1945. | LCSH: Europe—
History—1918-1945. | LCGFT: Biographies.
Classification: LCC D1075.c68 B66 2021 | DDC 320.54092—DC23

Set in 10.5/13 Adobe Caslon with Rama Gothic E and New Century Schoolbook
Book design and typesetting by Lara Minja, Lime Design

*I dedicate this book to my wife, Dinah,
whose infinite patience and generous welcome
into our lives of my growing fascination with
the story of Richard Coudenhove-Kalergi
made this work possible.*

CONTENTS

Illustrations

Vittorio Pons with Otto von Hapsburg present the RCK Prize
to Helmut Kohl in 1991. *Cantonal Archives of Vaud, Lausanne,
File P.1000.* 376

Every reasonable effort has been made to trace copyright holders of material reproduced, but if any have been inadvertently overlooked, the author
would like to hear from them for correction in subsequent editions.

Acknowledgements

IN THE FIVE YEARS that this book has been in preparation, I have been helped by over eighty people in half a dozen countries who either knew Richard Count Coudenhove-Kalergi personally, knew others who knew him, or came across him professionally. They gave of their time freely, and I thank them all, not only for the insights they gave me, but in several cases also for illustrative material they made available. On consulting my notes, I realize that they fall into three groups.

First, members of the Coudenhove-Kalergi family and close friends. Barbara, the Count's niece (daughter of his brother Gerolf), told me much about her uncle, whom she remembered well from her childhood. Over breakfast meetings in her favourite café near the Hofburg, she explained several details which she had not included in the chapter on the Coudenhove family in her very readable memoir, *Zuhause ist überall* (*Home Is Everywhere*), which was published in Vienna in 2013. Then his nephew Jakub (Gerolf's son) and his wife, Monica, kindly received me in 2017, not long before Jakub died, and their wide-ranging reminiscences over tea in their villa in Vienna considerably enlarged my view of Richard Count Coudenhove-Kalergi, especially his later years. Katharina, the daughter of Jakub's brother Michael, the Count's great-niece, was also generous with her memories when we met on two occasions, also in Vienna. Alongside his family, I also include Karl Schwarzenberg, for whom Katharina worked as a personal assistant. He knew Dicky well enough to call him by this familiar name, and much admired him, and I had the pleasure of hearing his reminiscences when I sat beside him at a dinner in Prague in 2017, which had been arranged by the English College there, of which he is a patron.

Second, there were others who either knew Count Richard personally or knew of him and were associated in some way with his life and his work. Stephan Jaggi, architect in Gstaad, was the first to give me background information about the family grave and showed me press cuttings about his funeral. Adrian Frischknecht in Frutigen confirmed details from the Grundbuch about Idel's purchase of the house and adjoining land in Gruben in the 1930s. Vivienne Perreten of the *Anzeiger von Saanen* opened the local newspaper's archives to reveal not only articles by the Count himself, but also reports on the progress of the Second World War that he read in 1939 and 1940. Werner Genahl, registrar of births and deaths in Schruns, kindly pointed to the anomaly in his death certificate of 1972, confirming that it was signed by the undertaker, not the doctor, Ernst Albrich, who was the specialist in charge of the clinic. Subsequently, Dr Albrich's son kindly allowed me to inspect the notes his father made about the Count's several visits to the Kurhotel.

Marco Pons, son of Vittorio Pons, his literary executor, was most helpful in illuminating his father's work with the Count, and in providing a number of excellent photos of their time together. With André Poulin, former co-president of the Pan-Europa Union in Switzerland, he provided excellent company at convivial evenings at restaurants in Lausanne and Geneva. Dr Heinz Wimpissinger of the European Society Coudenhove-Kalergi offered his continuing encouragement, and Hanne Dézsy, RCK's former secretary and author of an insightful 2001 memoir, *Gentleman Europas* (*Gentleman of Europe*), contributed illustrative details about RCK's character when we met in Vienna. Adolf and Christine Zottl welcomed me into their house in the suburb of Mödling, in which Mitsu, Richard's mother, spent her final years, cared for by her daughter Olga. Lacy Milkovics, the former secretary-general of the Pan-Europa Union in Austria, who knew both the Count and Otto von Hapsburg well from the 1960s, also filled out the picture of his later years.

Third, as any biographer knows, the god of helpfulness has poured out his blessings generously on the world of libraries and archives. In those I have visited I have always been made welcome by professional staff whose lives are devoted to maintaining the record of the past. The Count's papers and those of his literary executor, Vittorio Pons, are housed in the Regional Archive of the Canton of Vaud, where Gilbert Coutaz, Christian Gilliéron, and Claudia Margueron were unstinting in offering their professional assistance, preparing dossiers on my numerous visits to Lausanne. Lubor Jilek, academic adviser to the European Society Coudenhove-Kalergi, has been generous with his wide-ranging advice, especially his interpretation of the Czech dimension to the Count's life and of academic research on Pan-Europa in that language. Matthias Walter, Philippe Klein, and Régis Clave of the Jean Monnet archives at the Ferme de Dorigny in Lausanne kindly prepared for me a meticulous dossier of correspondence between Jean Monnet and the Count.

Jana Jankovcová went out of her way to arrange a visit to the family castle at Ronsperg. Masumi Schmidt-Muraki, who has done so much to nurture the Japanese links with the story of the Count, generously shared her insights, both when I visited her in Munich and in subsequent correspondence. Dr Christian Matzner, director of the museum of Mödling, which houses a small exhibition of material relating to the Count's mother, Mitsu, was enthusiastic about him, and Anton Hubauer kindly guided me though the vast collection of the Austrian Mediathek to the key recordings involving him, in particular the dramatic speech he delivered at the funeral of the assassinated Chancellor Engelbert Dollfuss.

Allen Packwood and Sophie Bridges at the Churchill College Archives also guided me to the key files that reveal much about the Count's relationship not only with Winston Churchill but also with his son-in-law Duncan Sandys. Jean-Pierre Humm, retired archivist from Nyon, went out of his way to research the history of the hotel at Prangins on Lake Geneva where Idel died in 1951. Marie Gentilhomme, in charge of the parish archives of St Pierre de Chaillot in Paris, researched the marriage register for details of his second marriage there in 1952, and Dom Maurizio at the Monastery of Saint Benedict Sacro Speco di Subiaco kindly directed me to the archive that housed the records of the ceremony at which, in 1970, he lit a votive lamp in the name of Pan-Europa at the shrine of St Benedict.

Alun Drake of the Council of Europe Secretariat has on several occasions brought extra details to light about the Count's reception in the European institution where he was seen as one of the founding fathers. Dr Ruth Meyer and Nastos Pandelis at the European University Institute in Fiesole, Florence, made my brief visit most productive by their judicious preparation of key material from the historical archives there. John Fell and Kieron Goron have both kindly ensured the quality of the photos that illustrate this biography.

The sheer volume of research for this book is more than one person could manage alone, and, in this work, I have been helped more than I can say by Claudia Hamill. She alone knows how difficult it has been to steer a reasonable course between the partial image of the man as he presented himself in his published writings and the full picture that emerges from this extensive research. She shared my enthusiasm about the importance of this charismatic Count, discussed the results of many of the meetings we attended together, and researched and helped assemble much of the material on which I have relied. I am indebted especially to her organizational skills and editorial acumen, which have materially contributed to the final shape of this, the first English biography of the Count.

While I take full responsibility for any errors or omissions, I trust that this biography will prove a useful contribution to understanding the life and times of this passionate and controversial character, as well as the enduring cause that he promoted.

Hitler's 'Cosmopolitan Bastard'
Why This Title?

IN 1928 HITLER WROTE a third volume to *Mein Kampf,* in which he damned Richard Coudenhove-Kalergi as a 'cosmopolitan bastard' (*Allerweltbastard*). As an insult, 'cosmopolitan' implied both international and Jewish, and the Count, who was half-Japanese and half-Austrian, had a Jewish wife. And 'bastard' was equally true. His diplomat father married his geisha mother after he was born in order to secure a family inheritance.

Why was Hitler so concerned? Because the Count offered thousands of Europeans who flocked to his rallies a peaceful pan-European alternative to the Nazi creed of *Deutschland über alles*. This charismatic, cultivated, and intellectual young man knew all the anti-Nazi leaders across the continent, was the model for Victor Laszlo in *Casablanca*, and – for a while – was a rival for Hitler.

As Hitler wrote: 'At first sight, the Pan-European Movement might really appear to have a lot in its favour. Indeed, if you could judge world history from an economic angle, it could well be right... But in the life of nations, what is decisive is not numbers, but values.'

After the destruction of the Second World War, when Europeans were starting to get their act together again, it was to Richard Coudenhove-Kalergi's ideas that they turned. Today, we are a long way down the road to translating his utopia into reality.

HITLER'S
COSMOPOLITAN
BASTARD

INTRODUCTION

THIS FIRST ENGLISH BIOGRAPHY of the controversial and charismatic Count sets out to describe clearly just who he was, what he did, and what other people thought about him. And opinions differed. During his lifetime he was for some the apostle of European unity, but for others – Hitler among them – he was a 'cosmopolitan bastard', whose plans for Europe ran counter to the Nazi view of a German Europe. Even after his death, his legacy continues to divide opinion. Some see him as the founding father of the Council of Europe and a powerful influence on the development of the European Union, while others see him as the originator of a plot to drown the European race in a sea of multicultural immigration.

Why has Richard Coudenhove-Kalergi, well remembered in political circles in continental Europe, remained such a shadowy figure, unknown to a wider public, particularly in the English-speaking world? His extraordinary background and upbringing, his three marriages and lasting friendships with leading statesmen and cultural leaders, make his story a political and personal adventure that amply deserves to be retold. Born in Japan to a diplomat father and a geisha mother, he led a charmed life, growing up with his six siblings in a castle in Bohemia and then being taught at an elite boarding school in Vienna. He married young, against his family's wishes, the leading Viennese Jewish actress, twelve years his senior, already divorced with a five-year-old daughter, and a will of steel.

She helped him promote his vision of Europe, which brought him lasting friendships with cultural leaders and statesmen of the time. He counted among his friends Jan Masaryk and Aristide Briand, Gerhard Hauptmann and Thomas Mann, William Bullitt and Otto von Hapsburg. Twice he escaped from the Gestapo – in 1938 and again in 1940 – and he served as the model for the Czech resistance hero, Victor Laszlo, in

Casablanca. The Count could be a man of action when he had to be, with an adventurous aspect to his character that he otherwise concealed with aristocratic *politesse.* The full story of his life reveals a highly nuanced picture of an extraordinary figure, who helped to shape the fate of Europe, content sometimes to influence the thinking of the great and good, and at others striving to play a political role himself in the full glare of publicity.

I first stumbled upon the grave of this passionate Count some years ago when walking in Switzerland near the tiny hamlet of Gruben, close to Gstaad in the Bernese Oberland. Up a few shallow steps from a bend in the road, a small gate opens onto a triangular plot of ground at the bottom of a sloping meadow below an imposing Alpine chalet. There, in a small, neglected private cemetery, lies the Count, with his second wife immediately beside him, and his first wife – the love of his life, I later discovered – in a small wooden mausoleum nearby that looks rather like a dilapidated woodshed. The Count's gravestone records just his name, his dates of birth and death, and – in French – the simple phrase: *Pionier des Etats Unis d'Europe.*

A Japanese admirer of this pioneer of the United States of Europe was so distressed by the lack of respect shown for his neglected grave that she designed a Zen garden around the tombstones, a fitting gesture to the part-Asiatic origins of this political pioneer. His exotically beautiful Japanese mother, now an icon of women's liberation in her homeland, converted to Catholicism to marry his handsome and dashing diplomat father, *chargé d'affaires* in the Austro-Hungarian embassy in Tokyo in the 1890s. He then brought her and their two sons back to the family home, his castle at Ronsperg in Bohemia (now Poběžovice in the Czech Republic). Richard was her second child.

This handsome young Count – a courtesy title that Richard Coudenhove-Kalergi chose to maintain throughout his life, even though aristocratic titles were abolished in the new Austrian Republic in 1918 – never stood for public office, and yet he had a marked effect on European politics in his own lifetime, and that effect still echoes in the European debate today. He was the first European who not only believed in the common future of the continent, but also tirelessly worked to bring about the union of its many disparate states in practice during the years between the two world wars. Through his charismatic personality as much as through his political writings, he and his famous actress wife attracted support from the great and the good in European society. His connections continued beyond the Second World War to include Winston Churchill, General de Gaulle, and President Truman – and so did his influence.

He launched his enduring big idea – the peaceful federation of all the nations of Europe – with a political bestseller in 1923. On the back of this manifesto he built two political movements – Pan-Europa between the wars and the European Parliamentary Union after 1945 – headed by cross-party groups of politicians and leading national figures from business and the arts. A European flag, a common currency, a single passport, and a European anthem were all his ideas, later adopted and built on by the Council of Europe and the European Union.

Pan-Europa's interwar congresses in Vienna, Berlin, and Basel attracted thousands of supporters, crowding elegant hotels and restaurants for days on end, while renowned speakers elaborated on the prospects for international peace and harmony on the basis of the Count's political programme. His ceaseless propaganda for the cause of Pan-Europa ensured him fame across the continent, his richly cultured voice well known on radio, his photograph in newspapers and magazines, his articles and books translated into almost every European language. This passionate European, his popular movement, and his political programme were one: the Count and Pan-Europa stood for uniting the continent, the peaceful transformation of more than two dozen states into the United States of Europe.

The Count galvanized elite opinion and influenced government policy, often persuading considerably older and more experienced political leaders, both in and out of office, to take up his proposals and run with them. He was both an éminence grise and also someone who enjoyed the limelight. Hitler was his sworn enemy, and in the third volume of *Mein Kampf* referred to Coudenhove-Kalergi as an *Allerweltsbastard*, best translated as 'cosmopolitan bastard'. He banned Pan-Europa in Germany and made sure that the Count's books were among those publicly burned in May 1933. The Count fell back on Vienna, rallying opposition to the Nazis and nurturing support for Austrian policy under both Chancellors Dollfuss and Schuschnigg among all the states along the Danube, while the old continent slid again towards war, the second time within a generation.

Hitler annexed Austria in 1938. The Count and his wife escaped just in time, thanks to the Swiss ambassador, who lent them his car and his chauffeur for the occasion. Narrowly avoiding arrest by the Gestapo, they nonetheless took their two pet dogs along with them as they fled across northern Italy to Switzerland, courtesy of a safe-conduct pass and a posse of outriders supplied by Mussolini. There the Count carried on the struggle against Hitler throughout the phoney war, trying to rally London and Paris to his ideas of post-war European federation. He fled again with his family when Germany finally invaded France, this time escaping via Spain and Portugal to exile in New York. When Hollywood made *Casablanca*, Victor Laszlo was modelled on the Count, the handsome Czech hero who knew all the Resistance leaders across the continent and was at the top of the Nazis' hit list.

In the United States, he preached American involvement in the war on the side of Britain against the Nazi menace, and equally against the threat of Bolshevism. After the Second World War, he influenced both Marshall and Truman, ensuring American post-war support for his vision of Europe. In 1946 Churchill publicly acknowledged his debt to the Count in his Zürich speech on the future of Europe. President de Gaulle awarded him the Légion d'honneur and Konrad Adenauer awarded him the Bundesverdienstkreuz for his work in promoting Franco-German understanding. Still in his fifties, the Count was the first recipient of the Charlemagne Prize, awarded for his outstanding contribution to European integration, and he was subsequently received in audience both by the pope and by the emperor of Japan.

This charismatic Count did not lack self-belief. He was nothing if not opinionated – often right, but also often controversial. All his life he was unambiguous in his views on communism and Russia, seeing both as everlasting enemies of the Christian and classical roots of the European culture that had nourished him. During the 1920s and 1930s he was ambivalent about the role of Great Britain. At that time, he saw it as totally committed to its world-wide empire, regarding Europe and his efforts to encourage European unity as a distraction, rather than the major issue it was soon to become.

Like his father, he deeply admired the concept of the English gentleman as the epitome of a cultural development that had brought the values of the West to a new height. RCK discovered, however, that in practice this high code of personal behaviour was not demonstrated by some of those with whom he had to deal, notably by Churchill's son-in-law Duncan Sandys. He used the Count's contacts, given to further their joint European vision, and at the same time tried to exclude him from the growing movement for a united Europe. But this did not stop Churchill from writing a preface to one of his many books, or the Count from speaking immediately after the great war leader at the opening of the 1948 Congress of Europe in the Hague.

Jean Monnet, the first president of the European Coal and Steel Community, kept him at arm's length, borrowing what suited him from the Count's ideas, but pointedly failing to acknowledge this in his *Mémoires*. In the 1960s, the Count drew close to de Gaulle, himself a controversial figure with his opposition to Britain joining the European

Community and his own lukewarm support for the growing supranational power of Brussels. The Count was frequently nominated for the Nobel Peace Prize by the great and the good from numerous countries, but was never awarded it.

Long after his death, he has been maligned by members of the Far Right as the author of the supposed 'Plan Kalergi'. According to this conspiracy theory, the Count recommended the destruction of the white European race through mass immigration and cross-breeding, producing a passive society of racially impure helots, forced to serve the wickedly selfish purposes of a plutocratic Jewish elite under laws dictated to national member states by a conspiratorial European Union, based in Brussels and bent on world domination. This conspiracy theory enjoys some currency in contemporary White Supremacist circles, spread world-wide though the Internet, which carries wildly exaggerated elaborations and interpretations of one of the Count's early essays.[1]

In researching this biography, I have visited streets and squares named after the Count in France, Germany, and Austria. In 1994, on the centenary of his birth, the Austrian postal authorities issued a memorial stamp with his portrait, and he has also figured on the curriculum in schools and universities across Europe. The family castle in Ronsperg had long been a ruin, but is now structurally restored, the work largely financed by Japanese sponsors. In Vienna, the headmaster of the Theresianum, considered the Eton of the Austro-Hungarian Empire, recounted how the Count is proudly remembered at that elite boarding school from his time there before the First World War.

Vienna was also the location of his first Pan-Europa Congress in 1926, held in the magnificent Konzerthaus and attended by over two thousand of Europe's intellectual and cultural elite. 'For three days,' Coudenhove-Kalergi proudly wrote of that event, 'Vienna was the capital of Europe.'

The Count lived for his political vision, and in their different ways his three wives each helped him fulfil this role. Before the First World War, Ida Roland, a Jewish divorcée and highly successful star of the German stage, twelve years older than her young husband, spotted the potential of this talented, handsome, aristocratic student. She shaped him into the passionate leader of a political movement that would unite the continent. Their shared concern for peace and their mutual emotional dependence tied them tightly throughout their lives, and she lived on in his memory long after her death in 1951.

Coudenhove-Kalergi always appreciated the company of women, and he was not a widower for long. Alix, his second wife, came from Switzerland

and had first married a rich Silesian landowner. For her, the political aspirations of her new husband seemed self-evident. Why should not the states of Europe organize their affairs politically as the Swiss Federation had done so successfully? However, after eight years of mutually supportive marriage, she fell ill, and for the next eight years, until she died, the Count found himself supporting an increasingly dependent invalid.

His third wife, Melanie Benatsky, was several years younger than the Count and came from a totally different background. A dancer with celebrity status as the widow of Ralph Benatsky, the successful composer of the operetta *The White Horse Inn*, she rejuvenated her new partner with her gaiety and relieved him of some of his financial worries. She paid no attention to the world of politics, in which she was sublimely uninterested, but actively widened the aging Count's circle of younger friends and acquaintances and reconciled him with his previously neglected family.

On my travels I have followed him and his wives to Paris and the stylish hotels that they frequented there, the Meurice and the Raphael, as well as the fashionable church where he celebrated his second wedding in 1952. Finally, I visited the Kurhotel Montafon in Schruns in the Austrian Vorarlberg. It was here that he often stayed in the 1960s to socialize with Austrian and Bavarian politicians. He was there with his third wife when he died in 1972. I heard from the aged local undertaker how the doctor in charge of the clinic, who was also the owner of the hotel, told him to wait until nightfall and to go in through the staff entrance to attend to the corpse, as any indication of a death on the premises might tarnish the spa-hotel's reputation.

My journey has also led me to numerous archives across Europe: to Pilsen, Vienna, Florence, Lausanne, London, and Cambridge, as well as several sources now more conveniently on the web. There I have inspected the Count's personal letters as well as the official papers of his political movement, a treasure trove of material containing gems about the man and his milieu and the Europe that he knew and loved – and tried to save from its demons, some of which still haunt the Europe we know today.

The Count lived in interesting and dangerous times, and this is the story of a man with a mission, whose life was a grand adventure. His biography reads like fiction, with obstacles and triumphs for the dashing young protagonist, wild chases and narrow escapes, looming disasters and unexpected recoveries. He and his first wife possessed prodigious networking skills, and he knew all the great and the good of the political world. This charismatic figure met, charmed, cajoled, and persuaded innumerable public figures to support his cause. At the same time, he clashed with a few, whom he failed to convince and who broke with him. These he rarely referred to publicly again, airbrushing them out of his history as if they had never existed.

Richard Coudenhove-Kalergi wrote fluently in three languages – German, French, and English – and he published incessantly. But not everything he wrote about himself should be taken at face value. The more I explored beyond his published works – 'All propaganda for the cause', he once wrote with unusual candour – the more my task has been to place the Count in the context of his times, not just in the context he defined for himself. He wrote several versions of his autobiography, but memory can be selective, and not everything was actually as he would have us believe. In that larger picture, which includes much that he neglects to mention, he often shines, but he also sometimes appears in a slightly less-attractive light. His flawed personality on occasion frustrated the success he craved for his grand and ambitious vision. But he was the man who created and publicized that vision, which many followed then, and which culminated in the Europe we know today.

In *The Long Pursuit*, Richard Holmes wrote that every biographer is torn between 'the scholarly drive to assemble facts as dispassionately as possible and the novelistic urge to find shape and meaning within the apparently random circumstances of life.' Through empathy, the author invites his readers 'to enter imaginatively into another place, another time, another life'.

In this biography, readers are rewarded with the picture of a multi-faceted character, with both determination and intelligence, who in his twenties declared what he intended to do and went on through the changing circumstances of his long life to do just that. With his forceful-yet-charming personality, he single-mindedly pursued his long-term objective, the practical unification of the continent, both as an intellectual project and as his heart's desire. He was a passionate European, who never gave up, as well as a charismatic character, sometimes on stage himself and sometimes behind the scenes, pulling the strings of more prominent political actors. And the cause that RCK promoted remains a cause that is at least as relevant today as it was in his lifetime. He was, as his gravestone records, the *Pioneer of the United States of Europe*.

1

EUROPEAN FATHER, ASIAN MOTHER

TO UNDERSTAND THIS EXCEPTIONAL MAN, one needs to know his origins and his childhood. Richard Count Coudenhove-Kalergi had extraordinary parents. Heinrich, his intelligent and aristocratic Austrian father, and Mitsuko, his strikingly beautiful Japanese mother, were an oddly matched, but uniquely powerful, pair. Richard was only eleven in 1906 when his father died prematurely, and he idolized the memory of the man for the rest of his life. But Mitsuko lived on until 1941, and for all his adult years, Richard's relations with her were strained.

His father – Heinrich Johann Maria Coudenhove-Kalergi – led a life packed with interest and action. He served as a diplomat representing the Austro-Hungarian Empire in South America, the Middle East, and Asia, learnt languages for a pastime, and was a keen sportsman. For many years he held the record for the largest pair of black jaguars ever shot on a single hunt in South America. He was a dashing young man with an excellent singing voice, a powerful intellect, and overwhelming self-confidence.

Lord of Ronsperg, Stockau, and Muttersdorf in Bohemia, of Opathegy and Agyagos as well as Sokut and Rudlyo, his hunting estates in Hungary, on his death Heinrich was buried in the local Catholic cemetery of Ronsperg in the Sudetenland, now Poběžovice in the Czech Republic. Carved into the side of the monumental stone sarcophagus is simply his name – Heinrich Coudenhove – along with his noble status and his dates of birth and death. Everyone knew the rest, his own and his family's history. His children were taught, as he had been, to look back over more than five hundred years of unbroken service to the Hapsburg emperors by the men of the Coudenhove family, beginning in the fourteenth century.

In 1857 Heinrich's father, Franz Coudenhove, was visiting Paris – as young diplomats did – and was introduced there to Marie Kalergi, a beautiful young Polish heiress. Just seventeen years old, Marie fell in love with the dashing, but relatively impecunious, Austrian diplomat, and after a short courtship he took her back as his bride to Vienna.[1]

The couple spent Marie's dowry acquiring a castle at Ottensheim on the Danube, near Linz, and estates in Hungary and in Bohemia. Franz and Marie's first child, their son and heir, was born in October 1859 and christened Heinrich. With the Coudenhove-Kalergi line well established, they went on to have six more children, and all seemed set fair for an aristocratic idyll at the heart of the Austro-Hungarian Empire.

But fate intervened to mar this all-too-happy story. In 1877, when her eldest son was eighteen, Marie died unexpectedly, aged only thirty-seven. Heinrich was very close to his mother, and at her death he was left with an increasingly difficult and aging father, whose opinions and moods were no longer moderated or softened by her understanding and charm.

Educated at a Jesuit College in Kalksburg, near Vienna, Heinrich served briefly in the army before beginning his legal studies at the university in the capital. Aged just twenty-one, he fell in love with a beautiful French drama student at the Conservatoire, Marie Dalmont. When she became pregnant and Heinrich wanted to marry her, his father refused to hear of his son's union with a relatively penniless commoner, who was also a foreigner and already pregnant. He confined Heinrich, who was still a minor under Austrian law, in the family castle at Ottensheim. Marie bore Heinrich a son, who was immediately taken back to France to be brought up by Marie's parents. With a female student friend, she tracked Heinrich to his father's castle. Refused admittance by an irate Franz, the two young women committed suicide, shooting themselves in a rose-bed in the garden beneath Heinrich's window.

As news of the scandal broke, Franz sent Heinrich to finish his legal studies at the University of Czernowitz, close to the Russian border, as far as possible from Vienna. Franz then compounded the scandal by writing a short pamphlet defending his own and his son's behaviour as excusable on the basis that females from the lower orders, like horses, offered 'sport' for the aristocracy. Intended for only a limited and private circulation, the pamphlet leaked to the Viennese press, which made the Coudenhove-Kalergi affair into a *cause célèbre*.[2]

As soon as he graduated, Heinrich was packed off abroad to start a career in the diplomatic service. First, he was posted to Athens, where some members of the Kalergi family could keep an eye on him, then in quick succession to Rio de Janeiro, Constantinople, and Buenos Aires. Heinrich may have been emotionally damaged, but he was highly intelligent, learnt quickly, and was gifted at languages, later being credited with speaking sixteen, including Japanese, Russian, Turkish, and Hebrew. He became a reliable pillar of the embassies where he was posted, a safe pair of hands, hard-working and physically brave, as shown by his rescue of an Armenian who was being hounded by a group of bloodthirsty Turks in one of the sporadic pogroms that plagued Constantinople. Babik Kaligan swore life-long fealty to the man who had saved his life, subsequently accompanied Heinrich on all his diplomatic postings, and served as his bodyguard and general factotum to the day his master died.

THE AUSTRO-HUNGARIAN CONSULATE GENERAL in Yokohama was moved to Tokyo in 1891 and upgraded as the new embassy of the Austro-Hungarian Empire to the Empire of the Rising Sun. Heinrich was posted there in February 1892, a handsome and energetic young diplomat, *chargé d'affaires* at just thirty-three. He was required to set up the embassy from scratch, with all the practical and material issues this entailed, including furnishing the new premises. Early in the course of his duties, he made the acquaintance of Kihachi Aoyama, an astute, self-made merchant, who was building up the family fortunes trading, especially with foreigners, in oriental furniture. It was on a visit to buy furniture at Aoyama's emporium in the Tokyo suburb of Azabu, not far from the Austro-Hungarian Embassy – perhaps his first visit, since it was barely a fortnight since he had arrived in the city – that Heinrich met Mitsuko, one of the merchant's daughters.

Family history relates how, one freezing March day, Heinrich's horse slipped on ice outside Aoyama's establishment. Heinrich was thrown, and Mitsuko came running out to help the fallen foreigner. He was evidently struck by the kindness and youthful beauty of this innocent seventeen-year-old as she tended his sprained ankle. She in turn was impressed by this imposing and assured foreign diplomat, fifteen years her senior. After that, love found its true course, they married and raised a happy Austro-Japanese family. That's the story. Reality, however, was somewhat different.[3]

Mitsu (as Mitsuko was called by family and friends) was the third daughter of Kihachi Aoyama by his wife, Tsune, and was born in 1874. When she was twelve, Mitsu was placed by her father in an up-market Tokyo restaurant and place of entertainment called Koyokan, to be trained in a wide range of arts and skills. This was not formally a training as a geisha, but it gave her skills as a hostess who could dance and sing, recite poetry, and converse intelligently with educated clients, attributes which

His parents, Mitsu in Japanese dress and Heinrich as a young diplomat.

might well fit her to partner, if not marry, a man of substance and status in a society where polygamy was still commonly practised. Her father had effectively bought her back from the Koyokan when she was sixteen and considered to be of age. A few months later, she served tea to her father and his rich foreign client that afternoon in March.

There is no evidence to suggest that her father introduced her to his client with intent, but, suffice to say, there was no ice on the cobbles in Tokyo at that time of year, and the daughter of a respectable merchant would not have rushed out into the street to tend anyone, let alone a foreigner. Nonetheless, on 16 March 1892, within a fortnight of their meeting and less than a month after arriving in Japan, Heinrich had come to an arrangement with her father, and Mitsu moved into a job at the embassy, technically as a housekeeper, or more correctly as Heinrich's maid.[4]

At this stage, there was no question of marriage. Heinrich treated Mitsu with great respect and was evidently much attracted to her, but she was in effect his concubine. She was a dutiful daughter of a traditional family and lived with this foreign barbarian because that was what her father demanded of her. Over time she came to realize that she was better treated than was any woman of her acquaintance in a Japanese marriage, and that the partner imposed on her was considerably more loving and committed than she could have expected. He even went out of his way to obtain official permission for her to accompany him on his travels to Korea and to the Russian port of Vladivostok, an exceptional gesture at that time towards a Japanese woman in her position.

A few months after her first son, Johannes ('Hansi' to the family, though given Mitsutaro as his Japanese name), was born on 15 September 1893, Heinrich learned that his despotic and obdurate father, Franz, had died at the age of sixty-eight. Franz Coudenhove had not owned the capital that Marie brought from the Kalergi side of the family, but simply enjoyed a life interest in the income produced by his deceased wife's estate. According to Marie's will of 1877, on the death of her husband ownership of her estate would pass to Heinrich's eldest legitimate son, as soon as that child reached the Austrian age of majority, then twenty-four. Until that date, Heinrich himself could manage the estate on her grandson's behalf. In light of that, it became imperative for Heinrich to legitimize Hansi, the heir, as soon as possible, and that would require him to marry Mitsu formally, both in the eyes of the Church and according to Japanese and Austro-Hungarian law.

The first step was to christen Hansi, and he was baptized when just nine months old, on 18 June 1894. Then Mitsu had to convert from her Buddhist faith to Christianity. She was prepared for this step by a Jesuit priest in Tokyo, Father Ligneul, and subsequently baptized and given first communion in the Catholic cathedral there, all on one day, 23 July that same year. On that occasion, her union with Heinrich was blessed by the Archbishop of Tokyo, Monsignor Pierre-Marie Osouf, who had come as a missionary priest to Japan some twenty years before and knew the ways of Japanese society well.

So much for the ecclesiastical aspect of the affair, but it required somewhat more time for the civil arrangements to be completed, and Mitsu was now visibly pregnant. To ensure no loss of face before that could happen, Heinrich let it be known among the diplomatic corps in Tokyo that he would challenge to a duel anyone who dared to show his new wife less respect than that shown to other diplomatic wives.

Mitsu gave birth to her second child, another boy, on 17 November 1894. He was nearly eight weeks premature, a sickly baby, hard to feed, and his parents were uncertain whether he would live or die. Because of his precarious state of health, Richard Nikolaus Edjiro (known as Dicky to the family) was baptized just two days later. However, a friend of Mitsu, Baroness Ushida, the wife of a Japanese diplomat, who was considered to have second sight, reassured his mother. Not only would her child survive, but one day he would be famous.[5]

Formal marriage as opposed to concubinage between a foreigner and a Japanese subject was an extremely rare occurrence in the nineteenth century and required the personal permission of the emperor of Japan. In this case, the value of such an intelligent and successful young woman as an unofficial ambassador for Japan inside the Austro-Hungarian legation was not lost on the authorities, and after a short delay, the necessary imperial permission was granted. The whole business needed to be regularized in the eyes of Austrian law as well and, despite the formal impropriety of the original arrangement, the Austrian Foreign Ministry and Emperor Franz Josef himself were not inclined to object. That left only Mitsu's father to be won over, and a generous cash gift ensured that he did not oppose the marriage of his daughter with a *gaijin*, a foreigner.[6]

The church wedding was solemnized on 8 July 1895 in the neo-Gothic cathedral in Tokyo by Monsignor Osouf. He was authorized to do so through a general papal indulgence, which permitted marriages between Catholic westerners and members of oriental races at the discretion of the local church hierarchy, so long as the children were brought up in the Catholic faith. A document subsequently issued by the office of the governor of Tokyo on 7 October 1895 confirmed the earlier date of 16 March 1892 as the date of the couple's engagement and served as a certificate of legitimation for the children in Japanese law.[7]

Family history later suggests that Heinrich and Mitsu's marriage took place on that earlier date, but this smacks of retrospective correction of the record. It may, however, have marked the day, three years before, when Mitsu first moved from her father's house into the Austro-Hungarian legation.

Dicky and his elder brother, Hansi, were the only children born to Mitsu in Japan. They were her 'Japanese boys', the centre of their mother's affection, loved well above her subsequent five children, who were all born in Europe. But being at the centre of her affection may not have made much difference in practice, as one of her daughters later wrote that there was very little *Nestwärme*, or maternal warmth, in their home at all. Although Japan was modernizing, formality, obedience, and tradition were still cardinal virtues in the country of Mitsu's birth, and she was unemotional with her children. In later life she recalled the hard job she herself had adapting to Western customs, not the least of which was seeing her newborn children dressed and wrapped in white, the traditional colour of mourning in Japanese culture.[8]

As Heinrich's official wife, Mitsu's status in society changed considerably. She became a member of the diplomatic community, indeed the only Japanese wife of a foreign diplomat in Tokyo at that time. She was received at court along with the other diplomatic wives, whom she helped with her knowledge of the local language and customs. She was a natural bridge at social gatherings between the relatively small diplomatic community of little more than a dozen embassies and the Foreign Ministry, as well as members of the court. In that environment, she made friends easily, and for the eighteen months that she was living in Tokyo as Countess Coudenhove-Kalergi, the young and beautiful wife of the handsome Austro-Hungarian *chargé d'affaires* enjoyed what was perhaps the most exciting and socially enriching period of her life.

HEINRICH'S DECISION to accept the inheritance on behalf of Hansi and return to Europe to run the Coudenhove-Kalergi estates until his son came of age, however, posed a major problem for her. Heinrich had earlier promised her that he would give up his diplomatic career rather than be posted anywhere other than Japan. While Heinrich could now speak Japanese well and was comfortable within her culture, she could hardly string a sentence together in German, and she feared she would be lost back in Europe, a world so far away from her traditional home. Mitsu felt – in true Japanese style – a duty of obedience to her father, as well as to her husband, and her father also had no wish to see his daughter leave the country, unless it involved some pecuniary benefit for himself. But Heinrich would not change his mind; he had decided to return to Bohemia and run the family estates. As a concession, he suggested that this might simply be an interim solution until he rejoined the Foreign Ministry at a later date and was given another posting elsewhere in Asia. He requested a two-year leave of absence from the Foreign Ministry and set about planning the journey home.

As far as Mitsu's father was concerned, money again played a role in facilitating an acceptable solution. He received a generous sum on their departure, and regular monthly remittances later from Europe, which kept him and his wife in a manner well above what they might have expected in Tokyo, even as a successful merchant family. It amounted to one hundred Yen a month, roughly ten times a teacher's salary or double that of a government official in Tokyo. Heinrich wanted Mitsu, and Kihachi evidently drove a hard bargain, but equally evidently Heinrich was happy to pay. It was an arrangement that Mitsu continued after Heinrich's death, until her father died, two years after her mother, in 1910.

Heinrich's young family, together with their Japanese nursemaids and Armenian manservant, set off for Europe at the end of January 1896, travelling first class on a steamer of the Austrian Lloyd line called *Gisela*. First, they called in at Hong Kong, where the weather was already spring-like. Then it was Singapore, where it was as warm as summer in Japan. There they visited diplomatic contacts of Heinrich and were entertained on an Austro-Hungarian cruiser that happened to be in port. From there they sailed on to Ceylon and India, the captain showing Mitsu on the ship's atlas the route they had taken thus far. It was at this point that for the first time she lost her composure and broke down, weeping uncontrollably, realizing just how far she had left Japan and her family behind her, and probably realizing – as was the case – that she would never return or see them again.

In Bombay, the *Gisela* stayed for ten days. Heinrich left his manservant Babik with the nursemaids and the children on board, while he and Mitsu travelled by rail to Hyderabad, where for a few days they were guests of Prince Nizam, whose acquaintance Heinrich had made earlier in his diplomatic career. Mitsu was mightily impressed by the pomp and power of the British Raj, and in particular by the magnificence of the Maharaja's exotic palace. When they left Bombay, the ship sailed to Aden and then Port Said, where again Heinrich and Mitsu left the children on board ship with their servants while he took his young wife on a tour of the Middle East, starting with Jerusalem.

For the rest of the journey, first by ship to Trieste, then by rail to Vienna and on to the castle at Ronsperg, Babik was in charge of the two baby boys, their two Japanese nursemaids, and all the family baggage. He had never been to Europe before, but he was not only strong, but also practical and resourceful. All went according to plan, and at the end of March the party was met inTrieste by Heinrich's younger brother Johannes (Hans), and together they travelled by train to Vienna. There the two baby boys were briefly inspected by their grand-aunt Marietta, now aged nearly seventy and a spinster, the youngest sister of Heinrich's father, Franz. She pronounced herself satisfied that they looked as healthy as was to be expected and was pleased that they were now in their proper country and could be brought up as Catholics.

Hans subsequently accompanied the babes, their nursemaids, and Babik on another long train journey to the family home in Bohemia. Dicky – although much too young to remember it personally – imaginatively recreated the scene in colourful detail fifty years later in his first autobiographical memoir, *An Idea Conquers Europe*. He describes the odd procession of carriages and carts carrying two small babies (one of them himself), the Japanese nurses, their Armenian bodyguard, and all the luggage of their Eurasian diplomatic family, travelling in early summer 1896 from the nearest country railway station in western Bohemia along the dusty road to the family castle in Ronsperg. Tellingly, however, he omits any mention of Uncle Hans, who accompanied them on that journey, perhaps because Hans subsequently quarrelled with Heinrich about the inheritance.[9]

In Jerusalem, Mitsu had presented Heinrich with a talisman, a small wooden cross encased in silver, and he was so moved by the gesture that he carried it with him for the rest of his life. By now it was early April, and before following the others to Bohemia, Heinrich took his new bride to Rome for an audience with Pope Leo XIII, whose progressive social views on the role of labour and capital broke new ground in Catholic teaching at the end of the nineteenth century. However, that would not have been the subject of the pontiff's conversation with this strangely assorted couple, Heinrich tall and imposing in his official uniform, and Mitsu, shorter and slender, wearing a black veil especially purchased for the occasion. It was an intensely moving moment for Mitsu, who once more broke down and wept, kneeling before the pope and sobbing. He stroked her hair before raising her to her feet and giving her his personal blessing, a blessing that gave Heinrich's foreign wife a status in the staunchly Catholic Coudenhove clan that lasted throughout her life.

They stayed five days in Rome, visiting the Sistine Chapel and the ruins of the Forum, the Villa Borghese, and the Catacombs, and spending an evening at the opera, where they were entranced by a lavish production of *La Traviata*. The next day they travelled north by train to cross the Alps at the Brenner Pass and on to Innsbruck. There they were met by Marietta, Heinrich's youngest sister, named after her elderly aunt, and the first member of the wider family to meet Mitsu. The two women liked each other at first sight, Marietta later remarking in a note to another sister that she was pleased to see that Mitsu looked roughly like women in Europe: she had two arms and two legs and no ring in her nose. The papal blessing impressed her as well, since she herself had never visited Rome, let alone been received in the Vatican.

The final rail station was Taus in Bohemia, now Domazlice in the Czech Republic, and as they climbed down from their train, Mitsu found the weather decidedly cool. Dressed for what she expected to be early summer, Mitsu had to search in the luggage and unpack her fur wrap to keep warm. Before moving off in their open carriage, they were greeted by the local priest and officials from the town hall as well as enthusiastic

Sketch of Ronsperg Castle, his childhood home, remembered by Dicky as 'paradise'.

schoolchildren who had come to see the new lord of the manor and his exotic Asian bride.

An hour later, in Ronsperg, everyone turned out to greet the couple and celebrate. People stood two and three deep on the roadside as they entered the little town, which Mitsu discovered was really hardly more than a large village, with about two thousand inhabitants. Rustic celebrations were in full swing, with speeches and toasts, singing and dancing, which lasted until late into the evening. Heinrich and Mitsu were exchanging the sophisticated life of diplomacy and a capital city for the provincial pleasures of their country estate and the parochial concerns of the locality. While that suited Heinrich, as he was coming home to his castle, to Mitsu it must have seemed a painful narrowing of her horizons.

HOWEVER PICTURESQUE the Bohemian countryside, life in the antiquated castle could have offered Mitsu few attractions. She did not speak German well enough to show she was in command of the household. The local populace was predominantly German-speaking, but their dialect was incomprehensible to a foreigner who had learned a little high German, and the smattering of Czech and Yiddish that she also heard meant nothing to her. She sensed that, as she walked down the corridors of the damp castle, doors would open behind her and unknown faces would scrutinize her every move, perhaps sniggering and sneering at her strangeness in their eyes. Commenting later to one of her daughters, Ida, on her early married life at Ronsperg, she said, 'It was worse than death. But Japanese daughters know how to obey.' She was clearly lonely, far from home and far from the diplomatic social life that she had tasted briefly in Tokyo, or the privileged, exotic experiences of travel. She had stepped backwards into rural Austro-Hungarian society and felt increasingly depressed.[10]

Her isolation in this foreign land drew her ever closer to her husband, whom she revered with near-idolatrous worship. She knew no greater satisfaction than to kneel beside Heinrich as he was reading or writing and to watch his every movement, or to dress in a traditional kimono for special occasions and to serve him tea, as she had done when they first met. She also loved to retire to her private quarters and write to her parents in her own language, or nostalgically to paint in the Japanese style. Sometimes they would travel to their hunting lodge, the Dianahof, a few miles west of Ronsperg, well into the forest and close to the German border. There the family could relax, life was simpler and less formal, and there were fewer servants.[11]

MITSU'S DEVOTION suited Heinrich perfectly. He had, as Dicky judged later in life, an 'oriental' view of the weaker sex. Women were to be decorative and obedient. He loathed the idea of a bluestocking in principle, let alone as a wife. But he did at least go through the motions of delivering on his promise to consider a new diplomatic posting to the Far East. He negotiated with the Foreign Office in Vienna and was offered the post of ambassador to Thailand, with additional responsibility for Singapore. After some hesitation, he declined even this and decided – as he had probably intended all along – to stay in Bohemia and live his life as a country gentleman, the lord of the manor, managing his extensive estates.

Mitsu may well have been disappointed at this decision, but it renewed her desire for more sophisticated company than Ronsperg could offer. With Heinrich she visited the family's Hungarian estates in the Western Carpathians (now Slovakia) and met the neighbouring families, including a branch of the extremely wealthy Pállfy ab Erdöd family, one of whose daughters would subsequently marry Mitsu's third son, Rolfi. She accompanied Heinrich to Prague and to Vienna on several occasions, and further afield as they extended their travels in spring and autumn of most years. They visited Munich and Hamburg, London, Riga, Moscow and St Petersburg, Venice and Padua, with Mitsu often pregnant They also attended the Wagner Festival in Bayreuth, just over the border in Germany, where Heinrich could proudly show off his exotic Japanese wife as they socialized with the cream of European society.

The family had close links with the Wagners. More than fifty years earlier, Maria Kalergi, Heinrich's wealthy grandmother, who had at one time been a pupil of Chopin, bankrolled Richard Wagner when he was a struggling young composer in Paris, long before he achieved fame and made Bayreuth the centre of his operatic cult. He did not forget, nor did his widow, Cosima, and members of the Coudenhove-Kalergi family were always welcome there. A little glamour must have gone a long way to lighten the depressive aspects of provincial life, and Mitsu knew that Heinrich enjoyed opera. He had an excellent tenor voice and had sung to local acclaim the role of Mephistopheles in Gounod's *Faust* in an amateur production by the diplomatic corps while they were still in Japan.

Heinrich and Mitsu conversed most often in Japanese, which Heinrich spoke well, rather than in her broken German. At his behest, however, she successfully learned some elementary English, shown clearly in her later correspondence with Dicky, which was conducted on both sides partly in English and partly in German. Heinrich also pressed her to learn other languages, specifically Hungarian and French, but there is no evidence that she made progress in either of them. To him, she remained essentially the decorative princess from Asia, though, as the same daughter to whom she confessed the pain of her early married years tartly commented later, 'She was always more a geisha than a princess.'

Her attraction for Heinrich was very clearly her striking oriental beauty and her dependent devotion. She was far from unintelligent and learnt informally every day by observing others around her. She must have been endowed with inexhaustible reserves of patience and of common sense, which enabled her to assimilate new experiences and adapt to the circumstances of her new life, so far removed from anything she could have imagined before she met Heinrich. She formed close relationships with the abbess of the nearby St Borrominer Convent and with Sister Leontia, who helped to teach her German, while imparting religious instruction and caring for her soul.

Her growing family became her main preoccupation. Her third son, Gerolf (Rolfi to the family), was born in 1897. Thereafter she bore three girls – Elisabeth, Olga, and Ida Friderike – in less than six years, followed by her last child, Karl (Ery), in 1903.

Shortly after Ery's birth, she contracted tuberculosis, probably brought on by the damp conditions in the castle at Ronsperg, and early the following year she went for treatment to a sanatorium in Arco, near Lake Garda in the South Tirol. The whole family decamped and followed her, staying there for several months before all travelling on to Todtmoss, not far from Freiburg in the Black Forest, where Mitsu attended the renowned Wehrawald clinic. They returned to Ronsperg only in May 1905, by which time Heinrich had made sure that the castle was modernized, at least to the point of installing better heating and warmer flooring, adding wall hangings, and renovating windows.

Mitsu had preferences among her children, and she did not hide them. She clearly loved her Japanese boys most and treated the others with notably less affection. Perhaps this explains Ida's later claim that there was precious little *Nestwärme* about their home in Ronsperg. Only for Rolfi did she make some exception when he went on to study Japanese and could converse with his mother in her native tongue. Equally importantly, there was his good marriage to the daughter of the aristocratic Pálffy family, who was considerably more acceptable to Mitsu than the women her two elder boys chose to marry. Much later in life she grew closer to Olga, the daughter who stayed with her as her companion and carer.

Heinrich also had favourites among the children. He related best to the three older boys, especially Hansi and Dicky, and could fulfil a role in laying the foundations of their education. While they were still very young, he set them an imposing example, developing their mental as well as physical strength and skills with cold baths, physical exercise, and long walks in all weathers, interspersed with extended – if one-sided – educational conversations. Their father's physical asceticism and his intellectual curiosity not only developed their bodies, but also opened their young minds and gave them all, especially Dicky, a role model for life. Dicky later commented that, in the first few years of a young boy's life, his father is like a god and can do no wrong. Only later does he reveal weaknesses, and the boy then learns to doubt his father. Heinrich's early death meant that he never reached the age when his sons grew disillusioned with him. He lived on vividly in Dicky's memory, and he later said that he always weighed up his own actions to see what his father would have done in similar circumstances.

While there was little enough conversation between Heinrich and Mitsu personally, there were always guests and others in residence at Ronsperg: visiting Austrian and Japanese diplomats, officers from a regiment stationed nearby, travelling clerics, often including Jesuits, as well as the rabbi from Pilsen and the local Catholic priest, who were frequent visitors. Some stayed just a day or two, many several weeks. Summer was always the busiest season for guests, but even in winter there were the resident English and French governesses, the Hungarian female companion for Mitsu, Heinrich's Bavarian secretary, the Czech director of the castle, a Russian teacher, a Muslim Albanian who was there to teach Heinrich Turkish, and Abdullah Al-Mamun Suhrawardy, who claimed to be a learned descendant of Abu Bekr, the first caliph. He stayed several months, studying German and reading ancient Arabic and Indian texts with Heinrich. From four years of age, the boys were allowed to eat at table with their parents and guests, listening – in silence – to the conversation. The Coudenhove-Kalergi castle in Ronsperg was a cosmopolitan and intellectual oasis in the deeply provincial Bohemian countryside. As Dicky wrote half a century later:

Home, or Heimat, is the land of your childhood. Born in Tokyo, I lived in Ronsperg from the second year of my life, and I loved Ronsperg. It was in Ronsperg I learned to walk, in Ronsperg I learned to talk. It was in Ronsperg that I learned to read and write and to do my sums, all taught by dear Sister Leontia of the Borrominer Cloister there in Ronsperg. I think back and dream of that ancient castle, of the shady castle park, of the high surrounding wall, the chapel, the theatre, and the gym, the painting studio of my dear mother, and the library with its ten thousand tomes, where the writing desk stood at which my father wrote his book. All around the room on dark wooden columns stood life-sized busts of great thinkers: Socrates and Plato, Marcus Aurelius and Aristotle, Kant and Schopenhauer. Among them also were a mediaeval statue of Christ and a copy of Michelangelo's Moses. Smaller busts stood on the tables: Goethe and Schiller, Homer, Apollo and Napoleon. Over the main door hung a rare picture of Zarathustra, and in the window niches glowed ornately calligraphic texts from the Koran.[12]

During his first years in Ronsperg, Heinrich enrolled as a mature student at Charles University in Prague, studying for a doctorate in philosophy. He produced extensive notes for an unpublished work on Schopenhauer's philosophy entitled *Das Reich der Verneinung* (*The World of Denial*). Heinrich's admiration for Schopenhauer gave him a deep understanding of asceticism, and a profound insight into Buddhism, which had already impressed him during his years in Japan. Even fifty years later, Dicky would recall the words of a prayer their father taught the children to recite each evening before going to bed. After stressing Jesus' commendation of the first commandment, to love the Lord your God, and the second, to love your neighbour, it went on to stress denial of self and subjugation of personal desire and ambition: 'Teach us to deny ourselves and our will.'

Heinrich's published works reveal an inquiring mind that was tolerant of all world religions and intolerant of prejudice wherever he found it. His first pamphlet – written in French and published in 1897 – was a defence of Freemasonry in the face of a distorted critique that had found some popular resonance in Austrian Catholic circles. In 1900, he published a short essay extolling the virtues of the Austro-Hungarian Empire as a potential cultural bridge between the Germanic and Slav worlds. In 1901, he published a study of the nature and history of anti-Semitism entitled *Das Wesen des Antisemitismus* (*The Essence of Anti-Semitism*) and distanced himself from the widely held anti-Semitic views of his generation. Every Easter, Heinrich would ostentatiously leave the celebrations in his local church when the priest recited the Catholic prayer blaming the 'perfidious Jews' for the crucifixion of Christ, an astonishingly bold gesture by the lord of the manor in such a conservative society.

In 1903, Dicky's father also published a tract in which he considered, from ethical, religious, and legal viewpoints, the still-widespread custom of duelling. He lent his support to a growing movement against the practice among officers and gentlemen, even resigning his commission in a reserve regiment to free himself from any conflict of interest in the matter.[13]

Heinrich's admiration for Schopenhauer's philosophy and his lasting interest in Buddhism led him in his later years to give up hunting and become a vegetarian. But he did not force his opinion on others and continued to visit the Dianahof, the family's hunting lodge, where he enjoyed the company of foresters and huntsmen, being close to nature rather than dealing with the everyday demands of the estate in the castle at Ronsperg. Dicky later followed in his footsteps, doubtless a reflection of his admiration for his father, though he was never a strict vegetarian. He did it, he asserted, because as a precocious teenager he worked out the principle of vegetarianism philosophically, reaching the logical conclusion that killing animals and birds for sport was indefensible. Later, when as a young man he wanted to escape what he increasingly felt were the absurdities of high society in Vienna, he would also retreat to the rural simplicity of the Dianahof.[13]

'I have always studied and will continue to do so as long as I live,' wrote Heinrich in the preface to a short book entitled *Los von Rom* (*Free from Rome*) that he published in 1906, only a few weeks before his death. He criticized the 'Free from Rome' movement, a contemporary German nationalist campaign to convert Roman Catholic Austrians to Lutheran Protestants, the better to integrate them culturally into a potentially enlarged Prussian Reich. In his preface, Heinrich claimed that as a life-long, loyal Catholic he had always sought truth with an unbiased and unprejudiced mind. Indeed, Heinrich was so impressed by the Cistercian Order, which had only recently been readmitted to Austro-Hungary in 1902, that he became an 'adept', the first step towards lay membership, a step which also reinforced the ascetic aspect of his style of life, further restricted his diet, and possibly damaged his health.

Shortly before his forty-eighth birthday, he looked back on his life, remarking that he had served as a diplomat for eleven years, had himself partly educated his own children, and personally administered large estates both in Bohemia and in Hungary. He was independent, blessed with an abundance of worldly goods, and was able to indulge in writing for the sole purpose of serving the truth. Dicky both admired and was in awe of his father, whom he remembered 'half as a myth and half as a man'. But sadly, the personal example of this influential man, who only punished lying, stealing, and cruelty to animals, was short-lived.

In May 1906, Heinrich's youngest brother, Richard, stopped at Ronsperg with his new wife for a few days on their way to Africa for their honeymoon. He planned to visit his brother Hans, the one who had quarrelled with Heinrich about the inheritance some years earlier and had emigrated to Nyasaland. Heinrich and Mitsu prepared a festive weekend for the new couple, culminating in a celebratory dinner on Sunday evening. Dicky commented later that he had seldom seen his father so happy: 'He sang Wagner; his laughter reverberated from the castle walls.'

On the morning of Monday, 14 May, Heinrich rose as usual at five and took his energetic daily walk around the castle park. On his return, he complained of chest pains, and Babik asked if he should call the countess. 'No,' said Heinrich, 'do not disturb her.' 'Perhaps the doctor?' asked Babik. 'No,' replied Heinrich, 'but call the priest.'

By the time the local priest arrived, Heinrich had lost the power of speech. When Dicky was called to his father's room, he found the family already gathered around his deathbed, praying and in tears. It was the first time he would see a corpse. Heinrich's talisman cross, Mitsu's gift, was in his hands, and Dicky was amazed by the peaceful aura of his dead father's face. He had died of heart failure, aged just forty-seven. Dicky was only eleven years old.

That same day Babik, as usual wearing his fez on his head and his curved dagger at his belt, followed his master's final instructions. He carried Heinrich's notebooks and diaries into the castle yard – over thirty years' worth of accumulated records and reflections – and burned them all. The family watched silently from the windows of the castle as the smoke from the bonfire rose slowly into the summer sky. The Lord of Ronsperg had died, the world of his family was changed utterly, and a new phase of young Dicky's life began.

2

SIBLINGS, SCHOOL, LOVE, AND MARRIAGE

NOT EVERYONE IN RONSPERG shared the enlightened attitude to world religions and cultures that Heinrich Coudenhove-Kalergi had tried to impart to his children. Every Monday, the day of the week on which his master died, Babik Kaligan tended Heinrich's grave in the local Catholic cemetery. Years later, on his deathbed, he would ask to be buried near his master, but the local Catholic priest objected, informing him that only true believers could be buried in that cemetery. Distraught, Babik was persuaded to renounce his Armenian Apostolic creed and be baptized a Roman Catholic before it was too late, jeopardizing in his eyes his lifetime's faith and practice in favour of a local custom in what must have seemed to him – without his master – a benighted cultural backwater of a foreign empire. Fortunately, the local priest then kept his word, and Babik was buried as he had wished, close to Heinrich.[1]

Mitsu was widowed with seven young children and, according to Heinrich's will, she was to manage the estates until the eldest son, Hansi, came of age. That was still more than ten years away, and it is clear that Heinrich did not trust the rest of the Coudenhove-Kalergi family. He feared they might recall Johannes, his 'hermit' brother from Africa, the one who had initially expected to manage the estates while Heinrich was abroad, and ask him or another of his brothers to run them until Hansi came of age. But Mitsu was determined to carry out her deceased husband's wishes – the more so as the rest of the wider Coudenhove family did not trust her. They feared she might sell everything and return to Japan with the children and the family fortune, or fall in love and marry an unsuitable man. In either case, the estates would be lost to the family. They formally challenged Heinrich's will, demanding that the children should be placed under the authority of a male member of the family, and that Mitsu should accept the tutelage of an attorney in all financial matters, since as a woman and a foreigner she was 'not competent'. They expected her, the delicate, widowed, foreign woman, meekly to accept this clearly sensible and responsible plan.

They were astonished when she refused, challenged them at law, and mastered the legal details of the case herself. On her day in court, she dressed in her best, charmed the judge, and won on every point. She had retained her figure despite repeated pregnancies, and boasted that she could still reach around her waist with her two hands. It was not only a legal, but also a personal triumph, an assertion of her will which none of her family had ever seen before. Indeed, it was the first dramatic and public display of a change of personality that turned the meek and docile Mitsu into the dominant and difficult widow who would rule her household with severity for the next twenty years.

She paid attention to every detail of business and of behaviour, was long on correction and short on praise, and punished disobedience immediately. She was sharp and precise. Advisers, managers, teachers, or servants who could not explain themselves to her satisfaction were instantly dismissed. Nobody deceived her twice. Hansi would inherit the Ronsperg estate when he came of age, but until then she would manage the family fortunes even more carefully than Heinrich had done before her.

Her children also felt the change, especially her daughters. From them she demanded and expected Japanese obedience. As for the boys, she was strict on their behaviour but, given her own lack of a formal European education, she was at a loss to know how to educate them. Initially she simply gave them free access to Heinrich's library, imagining that what had been good for him must be good for the boys. They could choose their reading as they wished, climbing the library ladder to select books from whatever shelf took their fancy. Dicky remembered there were commentaries on the Bible, books on other religions and on necromancy, science and history, geography, philosophy, and world literature. In that time, he asserted, he and Hansi learned far more in free study than their tutors taught them in their formal lessons.

For the school year of 1907 to 1908, however, Hansi, Dicky, and Rolfi, then aged thirteen, twelve, and eleven respectively, were sent to Brixen in the South Tyrol to stay with a former companion of Mitsu's who had married a Count Wurmbrand. There they attended the Augustiner-Gymnasium, the local grammar school run by the Catholic Church. But of much more interest than their lessons at school were the stories and *séances* they enjoyed with the count and countess, who were both spiritualists, devotees of the occult. They introduced the boys to horoscopes, second sight and sixth sense, turning tables, palm reading, and the judging of character by handwriting. Dicky was fascinated and retained an interest in the occult until he died, a compensation for the otherwise severely rational intellectual heritage of his earlier years with his father. He never employed staff without first taking a professional graphologist's advice.

The small town of Brixen was pretty, but barely less provincial than Ronsperg. Mitsu had no intention that her children – or she herself – should miss the opportunities presented by living in the capital, and in 1908 she would sell the Hungarian estates and rent an apartment in a fine house in Hietzing, near the imperial palace of Schönbrunn, a fitting residence in Vienna for the wealthy widow of a cultivated diplomat and aristocratic landowner. It was also a springboard from which to fulfil the ambitions she held for her children.

During the year when the boys were in Brixen, Mitsu also decided to move the family from the castle in Ronsperg to what she felt were more pleasant quarters in Stockau, a small hamlet on the estate, some five kilometres to the west. There the family owned a former Augustinian monastery, which at modest cost could be adapted to provide more acceptable living quarters than the castle, still damp and cold despite Heinrich's improvements. It would be somewhere to bring up the younger children without the unhappy memories associated with the old home in which her husband had so recently died. As the estate-management offices remained in the castle, the family move to Stockau also meant that Mitsu and the children had greater privacy in their daily life.

DICKY'S RELATIONS WITH HIS SIBLINGS were initially formed in the early years in Ronsperg before his father's death and during the years in Stockau afterwards. He was only ever close to those nearest to him in age, in particular to his elder brother, Hansi. The two of them were after all their mother's 'Japanese boys'; the rest of the children were 'Bohemians' and belonged to a foreign land. Dicky looked up to Hansi at this stage, but it would become increasingly clear that he outstripped his brother considerably in raw intelligence. Their relationship shifted in their teens, as Hansi played the role of a worldly-wise older brother to compensate for being outshone at school by the younger and more intellectual Dicky.

Dicky was somewhat less close to Rolfi, his younger brother, until Hansi left school and just the two of them were there together for one year. Rolfi

Mitsu with her three eldest sons – Hansi, Dicky, and Rolfi.

was certainly more academic than Hansi and, judging by his performance
at school and later in his professional life, possibly as intellectually gifted
as Dicky. Rolfi learnt Japanese in addition to Hungarian, which helped his
personal relations with Mitsu, and he was described by an acquaintance of
the family as the nicest of Mitsu's sons. One of his sisters later described
him as mother's *Paradesohn*, the one she could be proud of and show off

to her friends and acquaintances. Rolfi's wife was later heard to complain within the family that her husband was as intelligent as Dicky and worked even more diligently, and it was unfair that he did not get the public recognition that Dicky apparently effortlessly received. Dicky clearly had charisma and could naturally charm.

Elisabeth (Elsa) was the eldest of Dicky's sisters, and Dicky was somewhat closer to her than to the others. She was described by one acquaintance as a young woman with an insatiable hunger for life, curious and intelligent, and she grew up a modern, emancipated woman. Like all her sisters, during her teenage years she boarded at the Mary Ward convent school run by the English Sisters at St Pölten, near Vienna, and she subsequently studied law and economics at university in the capital. She corresponded with Dicky about family financial interests at the end of the Great War, when Mitsu was considering how best to improve the copper mines on a small nearby estate at Muttersdorf. She also acquired secretarial skills and worked in the private office of Austria's Chancellor Dollfuss.

Elsa struck out on an independent course and the only one of her siblings to whom she was really close was her youngest sister, Ida. The pair of them formed an intense relationship, described as a 'union of souls', a *Seelenverwandtschaft*, by an intelligent contemporary observer who went on to become the local teacher and later edited a book of reminiscences about Ronsperg.[2] Many years later, an admiring friend who knew Elsa in her last years in Paris called her 'the wisest human being he had ever met'.[3]

Apart from some brief letters and cards from their early school years, there is little evidence of Dicky being close to his two youngest sisters – Olga and Ida – or to his youngest brother, Karl Heinrich (nicknamed Ery), who was only three when their father died. The age gap between them was probably too great for that. The local teacher in Ronsperg described Olga as 'lovable', but also 'somewhat simple', and it is unclear whether or not her adult years were spent in protracted mourning for a teenage suitor, a young man killed at the start of the Great War. In any case, she never married, but lived as companion to her domineering mother, reading to her, often for several hours a day, until Mitsu died in 1941.

Despite the convent education of all three daughters, only Ida, the youngest, initially thought she might have a religious vocation. Realizing in her twenties, however, that she did not, she declined to take vows and went on instead to study history and economics at the University of Vienna and later also in Freiburg. She became a social worker and then a teacher. Like Elsa, she too was independent and had an inquiring mind. She would marry Carl Joseph Görres, an engineer from Leipzig, and under her married name of Ida Görres went on to be a well-known Catholic writer. Her close relationship with Elsa, however, was at the expense of their other sister, and she later commented that the deed for which she felt most guilt was her neglect of Olga.[4]

The youngest son of the family, Ery, was sent to boarding school in Vienna like his brothers, but did not overlap with them there. He showed little academic flair and broke away from any conformist influences to follow an artistic calling and to frequent bohemian circles. He became a painter and married a Jewish artist, Anita Neuber. Together they travelled to Australia, later returning to Europe to lead an itinerant and creative life in several different cities.[5]

In September 1908, Mitsu enrolled Hansi and Dicky in the leading school in Vienna, the Theresianum. Rolfi joined them a year later. The Theresianum was the elite boarding school for sons of the nobility and ambitious bourgeois families, training them for leading posts in government, including the diplomatic service and the army. In attending this school, the Coudenhove-Kalergi boys were following a family tradition. Their grandfather Franz had been there briefly from 1839 to 1840, as had two relatives from an earlier generation – Paul Coudenhove for just two years from 1822, and Ludwig Coudenhove for ten years from 1829. Its exclusively aristocratic status was not modified until 1848, when it first opened its doors to the children of bourgeois families, but despite this, it maintained its cachet as a socially select establishment.

Students at the Theresianum wore a dark-blue uniform modelled on that of officer cadets, senior students wearing a dress sword. Education was traditional in style and laid particular emphasis on natural sciences and languages, with French a compulsory subject throughout the school. Apart from his formal classes, Dicky was also taught to swim and to fence, neither of which he enjoyed, as well as to dance. Groups of senior students also visited the Burgtheater to see productions of the classics, visits which left a deep and lasting impression on Dicky. Historical drama in particular stimulated his imagination, bringing together, he said, 'world events and the most exalted thoughts that determine the best actions in noble characters'. As a serious young man, he saw the theatre – as Schiller and Goethe had done in their day – as a school for moral education.

Dicky does not mention any teacher by name in his memoirs, and probably the most important influences on his intellectual development were his classmates. They were exceptionally international. In his class year of nearly fifty students, there were no less than fourteen different nationalities: Bohemian, Moravian, Galician, Croatian, Slovenian, Bosnian, Herzegovinian, Serbian,

German, Russian, Turkish, and Japanese, as well as Austrian and Hungarian. In other classes in the school at that time were students from Poland, Italy, Romania, Ukraine, India, Persia, Egypt, and China. One went on to be Austrian minister of finance, another the director of the private office of the president, others to be heads of banking houses, army officers, university professors, lawyers, and politicians. The Theresianum was cosmopolitan, and its students were socially from the top echelons of society.

In his memoirs, Dicky declared that he did not particularly enjoy his years at school, but looked on them as a necessary apprenticeship for life. He pointed to the two great lessons the Theresianum taught him: self-discipline and tolerance for diversity, both learnt from living among this heterogeneous selection of other young men of his generation and his class, some very bright, but others, in his eyes, very stupid. However, he failed to mention that *he* must have made an exceptional impression on *them*, and that he also kept in touch with many of his classmates – as they did with him – for many years afterwards.[6]

Dicky briefly recounts his impressions of school in his memoirs:

Honesty and a decent attitude were respected, lying and breaking your word were scorned; most pupils at the Theresianum became decent and useful members of society. The most important thing that I learned was understanding other people and how to handle them, rejecting any national ideology. At that time Vienna was the international capital of the world. Being cosmopolitan was valued as being superior; being nationalist was seen as petty bourgeois.

His formal education confirmed the attitude of tolerance and respect for linguistic, religious, and racial differences that his father had inculcated in him from an early age. But with a European father, an Asian mother, and cosmopolitan influences from visitors to the castle while he was still a young boy, his world was already larger than many of his contemporaries could imagine. From his formative years, he later wrote, he had a global perspective on life, learning to think in terms of continents, not countries.

He was an intelligent young man with an independent turn of mind. From the age of fifteen he organized his reading systematically to cover in chronological order the main works of the great philosophers, starting with Heraclitus. Later he acknowledged his special debt to Plato, Schopenhauer, and Nietzsche. As an illustration of his thoroughness in his schoolwork, he read the main works of Seneca in the original Latin when preparing a presentation on Marcus Aurelius, since Seneca had been an important influence on the Roman emperor. Somewhat to his surprise, he was required to repeat some of his final year's subjects, since he had spent so much time writing an extended essay entitled *Objektivität als Grundprinzip der Moral* (*Objectivity as the Basic Principle of Morality*). Although this may have been a slight scholastic setback, the essay later formed the basis for his university doctoral thesis. Dicky's reports consistently show a cerebral and diligent student, achieving well when his mind was set on it, but obstinate enough to seek his own way. It comes as no surprise to learn that his favourite sport was chess.

Mitsu lived in Vienna not more than a couple of miles from the school, but only on Sundays were her sons allowed to return home. Dicky likened his school years to the experience of living a double life: weekdays in the Theresianum on the school bench with his contemporaries, listening to lessons from teachers of a social rank well below his, and then Sundays in Viennese high society alongside his elegant and exotic mother, to whom all doors were open.

Wickham Steed, a foreign correspondent in Vienna who later became editor of *The Times*, recalled meeting Dicky's mother there in 1912 and being introduced to Dicky, along with his brother Rolfi. He described them as 'two well-groomed boys wearing the uniform of the famous Theresianum Academy', accompanied by 'a lady who looked as though she might be their elder sister. As I passed them, this lady, Countess Coudenhove-Kalergi, turned and presented to me her sons.' The boys were, as expected, well mannered, and Dicky charmed the foreigner, reviving this acquaintance, much to his advantage, in London in the 1920s.[7]

The social elite of Vienna clung to their belief in the permanence of the cosmopolitan Austro-Hungarian Empire, mirrored in the tolerant, cosmopolitan atmosphere of the Theresianum. But, as Dicky later put it, 'The walls of the city had long been undermined by nationalism.' In response to an earlier threat from Prussia, the German-speaking political elite of Austria had co-opted the Hungarians into the imperial establishment through the historic compromise of 1867, which created the Dual Monarchy. Now Slav nationalism was on the rise. Thomas Masaryk, professor of philosophy at Charles University in Prague, was planning independence for the Czech nation. Josef Pilsudski, the Polish revolutionary then living in Vienna, was planning the creation of a Polish state. Theodor Herzl, a former journalist at the right-of-centre liberal-minded *Neue Wiener Presse*, had organized the Zionist movement that would later establish the state of Israel. And a powerful Pan-German backlash was also under way, both in the capital and in the country.

Just a few years before Dicky left school, Houston Stewart Chamberlain, the Anglo-German son-in-law of Richard Wagner, lectured at the university and published the first volume of his *Grundlagen des neunzehnten Jahrhunderts* (*The Foundations of the Nineteenth Century*), the seminal work that rejected a liberal and multicultural interpretation of European history in favour of Aryan racial supremacy. And here the mayor of Vienna, Karl Lueger, made his political career on the back of specifically anti-Semitic propaganda. Cosmopolitan high society in Vienna was dancing on the edge of this nationalist volcano.

With his final school certificate, the Matura, Dicky, aged eighteen, left the Theresianum in July 1913 to go on to the University of Vienna that autumn to study philosophy and history. His mother assumed that he would follow in his father's footsteps and choose a career in the diplomatic service, but Dicky had in mind a career as a university professor, or perhaps as an independent writer or a journalist – a more prestigious profession then than now. He was a somewhat introverted, intellectually curious, hard-working, and wilful young man on the cusp of adulthood, although under the Austrian legal code he would not reach the age of majority for another six years. Only then would he gain access to his portion of the family fortune and enjoy for the first time a degree of financial independence.

Mitsu was proud to introduce her adolescent sons into glittering Viennese society at the highest level. After all, she had been received in all the best salons when she first visited Vienna with her husband, and she now had access to the most fashionable and exclusive circles again. In early 1913, in the salon of one of her friends, Countess Caroline Hadik, the wife of a leading Hungarian politician, she met the actress Ida Roland, then making a powerful impact on the Viennese stage and on society, and this acquaintance would play a decisive role in Dicky's life.[8]

IDA ROLAND had just arrived in Vienna from Munich for the new season at the Deutsches Volkstheater. She was playing the lead role of Catherine the Great in *Die Zarin* (*The Czarina*), with a plot that centred on a palace revolution in St Petersburg, full of politics, scandal, and intrigue.[9] It opened on 4 December 1912 to enthusiastic reviews, and was such a success that it ran for sixty-one performances, with Ida engaged for the princely fee of six hundred gold kroners for each performance. She was the talk of the town for her powerful interpretation, and nearly fifty years later, Dicky described in glowing terms his first sight of her in this role.

I shall never forget her first entrance: through a series of doors thrown open for her by lackeys, she hurries to her enormous Baroque writing desk and stands motionless, facing the audience directly, every inch an empress, every inch a desirable, a lovable woman. Her delicate form, dressed in a wide crinoline, makes a bold impression of size running up to her small, delicate, and narrow head, giving her the proportions of a Japanese Tanagra figure. Her half-shut, light-blue eyes gaze into the distance under her long lashes. After a pause she issues her orders in an unforgettable voice that reminds you of dark velvet – one of the essential secrets, part of the magnetic power, that her personality projects.

He left the theatre that night in thrall to this 'incomparable artist'.

Mitsu and Ida initially struck up a mutual friendship, and the actress invited the aristocratic widow to the opening night of her next play, a dramatization of Dostoyevsky's novel *The Idiot*. In this, Ida's role was as a modern young woman, Natashya Filippovna, a passionately divided soul who alone is able to recognize through her love for him the value of the princely hero, Prince Myschkin, who appears to everyone else to be an idiot. The 'unforgettable portrait of beautiful, hungry, wounded, and predatory Natashya', as one distinguished critic of Russian literature later described it, was the closest that Dostoyevsky ever came to creating what might be called 'carnal dignity'. It was a new experience for Dicky.[10]

Ida invited Mitsu to supper after the theatre, along with a small group of friends, to celebrate the troupe's new play. Hansi, Mitsu's eldest son and his mother's first choice as her companion for that evening, was then out of town visiting Ronsperg, so she asked Dicky to take his place and escort her both to the theatre and to supper. Dicky agreed to accompany his mother. It proved to be the turning point of his life.

That evening the young man sat next to the leading lady at dinner. He later described her as

a child-like creature, of impressive simplicity and incomparable charm, with no trace of conceit. She had a fair and almost transparent complexion. The oval of her face with its delicately moulded features was surmounted by an alabaster white forehead and temples framed in lightly waved red-blonde hair. Her mobile expression was lit by light-blue eyes and a full, beautiful mouth with dazzling teeth. The nose was that of a lioness or sphinx, and her hands were delicate and most beautiful.

They spoke about many things that evening, including, of course, her role as Natashya and Dostoyevsky's novel. 'I was deeply moved,' Dicky later wrote, 'and felt in my innermost soul that within this great actress there hid a fine human being.' To his mother's surprise, Dicky, often taciturn in society, was unusually talkative.

Just five days later they met again at the Volkstheater annual ball, to which Dicky, much to Mitsu's delight, suggested he accompany his mother. It was a masked ball, or rather 'half masked,' in that the ladies wore masks but the gentlemen were in simple evening dress. Dicky and Ida sought out each other's company and were together much of the time, arm in arm, 'like children in the primeval forest,' Dicky later wrote, 'happy to have found each other.' He accompanied his mother back to the apartment in Hiezing knowing he was in love, and sure that he was loved in return.

For him, it was love at first sight and this *coup de foudre* was mutual. Thirty years later he wrote,

> Since childhood my dreams had been to find someone who was like a twin sister, someone who was my other self, yet a woman; someone with whom I could share my thoughts and longings; who would understand me without words. Suddenly this dream had come true. In these hours spent together, in the midst of the hubbub of Viennese society, I had revealed my most intimate thoughts and dreams, and she had spoken as if we had known each other since early childhood.

Throughout the summer of 1913, Ida and Dicky saw each other in Vienna almost daily, and on several occasions went together to the country – to Traunsee in the Salzkammergut or further afield to Starnberg in Bavaria. Despite their age difference – Ida was thirty-two and Dicky not yet nineteen – they decided to spend the rest of their lives together. But knowing that a decision to marry would raise strong opposition in his family, in particular from his mother and from his uncle Max, governor of Bohemia and head of the wider Coudenhove clan, they agreed to keep their intention secret for as long as they could.

Their mutual involvement, however, was apparent for all to see, and Mitsu soon discovered Dicky's plans. She roundly condemned them, above all his choice of an actress as his wife. Despite her early friendship with Ida, she bluntly expressed her traditional Japanese prejudice against actors. 'No better than beggars living in holes in the mud of the riverbank' was her damning description of their social and economic status. That the first of her sons to wish to marry, barely himself out of school, had chosen a woman of dubious status, of uncertain fortune, many years older than himself, divorced, already with a child, and above all Jewish: what could have possessed him? His uncle Max was equally forthright and forbade the marriage.

But Dicky could be as stubborn as his mother, and on this issue he would not change his mind. He might still be in his teens, but he and Ida had chosen each other. His mother saw it differently. She was convinced that Ida was seeking to marry into a title and had preyed on an innocent young man.

Ida opened the doors to a new life for Dicky beyond the confines of his family and his class. She was a professional success and inhabited a world that was less class-bound and more democratic, more modern and more bohemian, than his. According to Dicky she was, 'a happy mix of Jewish and Slav bloodlines', the daughter of a moderately successful Viennese Jewish businessman who had married a Slovak wife, and she introduced Dicky to a completely new circle of friends and acquaintances. For him it was as if Ida had opened the windows of a musty house and let in fresh air along with all the noise and bustle of a more creative world. Between them they bridged both the artistic and the social circles of Vienna, groups that ranged politically from monarchists to democrats, from conservatives to republicans, even communists. Ida – whom Dicky always called Idel to distinguish her from his own younger sister Ida – was born, he romantically declared, 'on a Sunday under the sign of Venus, for a life dedicated to love, to art, and to beauty'. But Mitsu condemned Idel as a witch, and never forgave her for seducing her son.

Against the odds, Dicky and Idel embarked on their journey together just as the world engaged in a cataclysmic war that within four years would totally change the map of Europe, destroying the Russian, Ottoman, German, and Austro-Hungarian empires. The student and the actress would both survive the slaughter and the destruction to play distinctive roles in the subsequent new drama of rebuilding Europe, alongside statesmen and revolutionaries as yet unheard of. So would Adolf Hitler, who also experienced, as they did, the last years of the Hapsburg Empire in pre-war Vienna.

3

THINKING IN CONTINENTS, NOT COUNTRIES

WHILE DICKY WAS STILL A STUDENT at the Theresianum, Hitler spent several unhappy years, lonely and hard-up, in Vienna. He came there from Linz initially in 1907 and again in 1908 to take the entrance exam for the Vienna Academy of Fine Arts, but on both occasions he failed the test and went back home. After the death of his widowed mother in December 1908, he came again to try to make his name as an independent artist. It did not work out well for him. When he left the city in 1913, disillusioned and penniless, the twenty-four-year-old was still not clear in his own mind what he wanted to be or to do.[1]

Dicky was then preparing for university, destined for the diplomatic service, or perhaps academia, or even journalism. Dressed in his smart school uniform on his way to a tryst with Idel, he may have passed the bedraggled Hitler in the street, but there would have been no reason for them to notice each other. Later they would each draw lessons about the future of Europe from their years in Vienna, and these lessons would set them off on political careers that took diametrically opposed directions. Their experiences of the same city over the same years could not have been more different: one in the comfort and privilege of the Theresianum and his mother's apartment near the royal palace in up-market Hiezing, the other in a men's hostel in a down-market district, barely earning a living as an artist and odd-job man and facing ever-diminishing prospects.

In *Mein Kampf*, Hitler describes at some length the impression Vienna made on him. 'Vienna was and remained for me the hardest, though most thorough, school of my life. I had set foot in this town while still half a boy and I left it a man, grown quiet and grave. In this period there took shape within me a world picture and a philosophy which became the granite foundation of all my acts. In addition to what I then created I have had to learn little; and I have had to alter nothing.'

He was a close observer of the political scene, where politicians were coming to grips with both the ethnic diversity of the population and an intensifying class struggle which reflected the grossly uneven distribution of wealth. He particularly admired the Pan-German Nationalist Party, led by Georg Ritter von Schoenerer. Above all, it stressed the ethnic identity of a greater Germany that should include all Austrian Germans; hence 'Anschluss'. But von Schoenerer's movement was not at that stage a dominant force in Austrian politics, and Hitler diagnosed the reason for its failure. He criticized the party's anti-Catholic stance and argued that to enjoy political success it would be wiser to ensure the support of the churches – like mass media, one of the great myth-making powers in any state – and to co-opt them in support of the political aims of the party. The Pan-German Nationalists' failure to understand the force of religion, he argued, condemned von Schoenerer to perpetual political opposition, when with greater insight and flexibility, he could have gained power and achieved the union of Austria with Germany.

Hitler admired the organization and tactics of the Social Democratic Party much more. It battled with the Christian Social Party for control of the city, and he witnessed the Social Democrats' mass rallies, admiring in particular their strength as a mass movement that efficiently organized the working class. He praised the spiritual terror that the sheer size of the crowd of their supporters on the street could generate, as well as their more carefully aimed attacks on specific political enemies. 'The barrage of lies and slanders against whatever adversary seems most dangerous ... until the nerves of the attacked person break down ... reflects a tactic based on a precise calculation of all human weaknesses,' he wrote. He gave the Social Democrats high praise for their 'equal understanding of the importance of physical terror towards the individual and towards the masses', even if he viscerally disagreed with the way the German leaders of the movement pandered to the ethnic diversity of the populace, to the Slavs and Hungarians – and, worse still, the Jews.

His greatest praise was reserved for Karl Lueger, leader of the Christian Social Party, whose power of oratory impressed Hitler as much as his overt anti-Semitism. Hitler went several times to hear him speak in public before Lueger's death in 1910, and admired his skill in playing on the emotions of his audience. Little by little, the anti-Semitism that Lueger made acceptable in political circles converted Hitler to the same point of view. He claimed that he did not arrive in Vienna with an anti-Semitic attitude, but that it grew on him during those years of stress, of failure and self-doubt. 'In Vienna I gradually began to hate the Jews ... For me this was the time of the greatest spiritual upheaval I have ever had to go through. I had ceased to be a weak-kneed cosmopolitan and became an anti-Semite.' This specific attitude went along with his general dislike of anything non-German: 'The longer I lived in this city the more my hatred grew for the foreign mixture of peoples which had begun to corrode this old site of German culture.'

In May 1913, at just about the same time as Dicky and Idel were deciding their future together, Hitler finally turned his back on Vienna and moved to Munich. Disinclined to fight for the mongrel Austro-Hungarian Empire, this fanatical young nationalist had dodged military conscription by leaving Vienna. Less than a year later, however, he petitioned King Ludwig III of Bavaria to be allowed to volunteer (still as an Austrian citizen) for a Bavarian infantry regiment. Fighting for Germany was altogether different. His petition was successful, and he spent what he later described in *Mein Kampf* as the most memorable period of his life fighting for the German Empire on the Western Front.

DICKY'S EXPERIENCE could not have been more different. On 28 June, the day that Archduke Ferdinand and his wife were assassinated in Sarajevo, Austrian high society was enjoying the Vienna Derby. Idel and Dicky were at the racecourse, planning their future together as a recently married couple. As a leading lady, Idel was idolized by Viennese society and was earning record fees. She received sixty thousand gold kroners that summer for a two-month tour with George Bernard Shaw's comedy *Great Catherine*, an unrivalled sum, worth close to £200,000 in today's money. The leading painters of the art-besotted city all wanted to paint her portrait.[2]

As a young student, Dicky had read a recent book by Aurel Popovici, a highly respected Romanian lawyer and politician, entitled *Vereinigte Staaten von Gross-Österreich* (The United States of Greater Austria). Popovici proposed empowering the ethnic minorities that made up the Austro-Hungarian Empire by striking a bargain with them similar to the historic deal that the German-speaking Austrians had made with the Hungarians fifty years earlier. Popovici's idea for a stable future for the heterogeneous empire was to allow home rule for the other minorities and to hold them together in a federal union. The reform-minded Archduke Ferdinand agreed with him, but the aging Emperor Franz Josef did not. He was not in favour of any constitutional change at all. The archduke's

Ida Roland as
Catherine the
Great, the role
in which Dicky
first saw her.

assassination on Derby Day in Sarajevo by a Serb nationalist decided the issue. It blocked that prospect of peaceful reform of the empire and opened instead the road to the First World War.

On 20 July, the day of the Austrian ultimatum to Serbia, Russia's closest Balkan ally, Dicky and Idel were in Bayreuth for the Wagner Festspiele. Dicky had no real interest in music, but he introduced Idel to the Wagner family. She learnt not only how Marie Kalergi, Richard's grandmother, had supported Richard Wagner financially in his early years in Paris, but also that she had embroidered a sofa as a present for Wagner and his wife, Cosima. The stage of the Festspielhaus was also made of timber from the forests of the Coudenhove estate at Ronsperg. Wagner had died in 1883 in the Vendramin-Calergi Palace on the Grand Canal in Venice, a property that also belonged to another branch of the Kalergi family. The widowed Cosima introduced Dicky to her son, Siegfried, the forty-five-year-old artistic director of the festival, a darling of the *beau monde* and a notorious bisexual. She also introduced him to her son-in-law, the philosopher and historian Houston Stewart Chamberlain, a man whom Dicky found personally charming, but whose racist views he found intellectually repulsive.[3]

With Serbia's failure to reply to the Austro-Hungarian ultimatum, the die was cast. As the Russian, German, French, Ottoman, and British empires mobilized, the members of the *beau monde* at Bayreuth dispersed to their own countries. After a few more days together on the Alpsee in Bavaria,

Idel went to her villa in Munich, while Dicky went on alone to Stockau to console his mother. Japan had declared war on both Germany and Austro-Hungary, and his mother was now no longer an exotic and admired member of Viennese society, but a lonely, ostracized enemy alien. Mitsu, however, had already thought through her personal strategy. Descriptions of the Japanese in the Viennese press as 'yellow monkeys' might hurt this proud woman, who had been enjoined by her empress to always act as an ambassador for her country, but Europe was now at war, and she prayed, or so she somewhat paradoxically told Dicky, for an Austro-Hungarian victory.

Her practical response to the outbreak of war was to demonstrate her loyalty to the Austro-Hungarian Empire in traditional Japanese style by encouraging her sons to enrol in the army. Rolfi did not object; indeed, he was later heard to say that it was better to be at the front for a couple of weeks than to have a quarrel with his mother. He enrolled straight after leaving school. Hansi held out a little longer against her wishes, since he was at that time courting his future wife, the famous Jewish-Hungarian aviatrix, Lilly Steinschneider-Wenckheim, the first female aviator in the Austro-Hungarian Empire. But in the case of Dicky, it appears that his mother made no effort to override a decision by the local recruitment office that he was not fit to serve. He had simply pre-empted her decision by ensuring he had an exemption on account of weak lungs.

His illness is not something mentioned earlier in the family history, and was hardly justified by Dicky having shared the experience of staying as a boy with the rest of the family in the South Tyrol and the Black Forest while Mitsu was treated for tuberculosis. But the decision of the local recruitment office on the basis of a doctor's certificate, which was not difficult for a rich young aristocrat to obtain, was enough to ensure that he was exempt from military service and had a 'home ticket' for the duration.

This allowed him to stay with Idel in Vienna when she was acting there, or in Munich in her villa at Romanstrasse number 16, near the Nymphenberg Schloss. It also allowed him to pursue his university studies throughout the hostilities, and he did not miss a single semester. He switched to Munich University for the summer semester of 2015, when he was living with Idel for some months in the city, but otherwise registered in Vienna for his studies from 1913 to 1917.

In April 1915 he pre-empted any further obstacles placed in the way of his marriage to Idel by the Coudenhove-Kalergi clan. He made use of a wartime dispensation, introduced by the emperor, that allowed young men to marry without parental permission if aged twenty-one, rather than having to wait until twenty-four, for the peace-time age of majority. He persuaded an acquaintance of his, Count Franz Walderdorff, the court curate of Schloss Nymphenberg in Munich, to officiate at a simple church wedding for the couple in the Baroque Chapel there on 22 April. It would be four years before this was written into the Austrian republic's civil register in Salzburg, but the private ceremony sufficed for the couple and for them to appear together in public as man and wife.

He commented on his position in his autobiographies, notably in the last, where he wrote, 'I hated the war from the bottom of my soul and in that I was at one with Idel who, as a real woman, was a pacifist throughout her life. It was hard to bear the tension between our personal happiness and the tragedies around us. We lived socially a very retired life, since most of our acquaintances were caught up in the enthusiasm for the war and there was no point in trying to bridge the irreconcilable differences between us.' Instead they pursued a family life with little Erika, Idel's daughter by her first marriage, who was just five years old when they first lived together. He recalled 'her big, deep blue eyes, her long, blond hair, her red cheeks and her bright laughter as clear as a bell. She was for us both a permanent source of unmitigated pleasure.'

AT THIS POINT we shall no longer refer to Dicky by his family nickname, although he was known by this to those close to him throughout his life. We shall simply use his initials – RCK – which he occasionally used to sign off informal correspondence. By this time he was old enough to be called up to fight for his country (though he refused), and he had already found himself a life partner, and had decided to marry (despite his family's objections). He was no longer a child.[4]

His friends and family were now faced with a *fait accompli*. They had warned RCK and Idel independently against their plans, and yet their warnings had no effect on the lovers.

Observers for the most part thought of RCK and Idel as an oddly assorted couple, and not just because of the more than twelve years' difference in their ages. RCK himself admitted that their interests initially lay far apart, as he knew little about acting and she had neither a taste for nor an interest in politics and 'had not gone far into philosophy'. As a serious and somewhat introverted student, possibly even an aspiring university professor, RCK was extremely cerebral and rational, but in relation to Idel intensely emotional. RCK noted that they fortunately shared a number of practical likes and dislikes that laid the everyday basis for their happy marriage. 'Neither of us smoked, played cards, or hunted; we both drank sparingly, preferred country to town life, loved animals, and disliked large parties.'

Contemporaries, however, cannot have failed to note some similarities between the relationship of Idel with RCK and that of the Marschallin with Count Octavian in the latest fashionable opera in Vienna, *Der Rosenkavalier.*[5] Richard Strauss and his librettist, Hugo von Hofmannsthal, had just put on stage a wealthy older woman with a younger aristocratic lover, but whereas the older Marschallin reluctantly gives up Count Octavian in favour of her young rival, Idel and RCK stayed together, formalized their relationship, and made an extremely happy match.

She organized and controlled the relationship and was as used to leading in their personal sphere as he was in his professional field. An anonymous commentator wrote an appreciation of their relationship, in the Vaud regional archives: 'He honoured and admired not only the artist but above all the human being in her; so she is the perfect completion of his soul and brings to him the deepest understanding of his moral structure. Seldom have I ever seen such a high degree of respect for a wife.'[6] RCK was evidently acting on his father's precept that the best way to judge a man's character was from the way he related to women, and he was fond of recalling Plato's allegory of a man and a woman being two halves of an accidentally divided pair, only fulfilled when the halves found their original partner again. 'Our temperaments were as different as they could be, but fundamentally we were akin. Our life together altered our two characters and adapted them to each other.'

With the emotional blossoming and personal liberation of this, his first love, RCK also experienced the first serious challenge to his adolescent view of the world, a wide-ranging intellectual upheaval that undermined the view of the political and social order that he inherited from his family and their circle. Received ideas about state and nation, about class, race, and identity, loyalty, and political legitimacy, about economic development and technological innovation, about the past and the future, finally about the war itself, its aims, its ends and means, its human and the material costs, and the combination of idealistic sacrifice and pragmatic profiteering that accompanied it, all were nowhere more hotly debated than in Vienna. RCK was open to this at a particularly sensitive time. Idel's circle of acquaintances exposed RCK's mind to a wide range of opinion – liberal, bohemian, pacifist, even socially subversive – that contrasted starkly with the traditional caste-bound attitudes of his aristocratic background. His marriage freed him at a stroke from the ties of the conservative milieu from which he had already in his later years at the Theresianum been growing both politically and intellectually estranged.

Given the views that he expressed in a letter to Idel in August 1914, it was perhaps wise of the Austrian authorities that they did not draft some-one with such markedly anti-war opinions into the army. 'The saddest thing about this whole World War,' he wrote, 'is not so much the frightful killings and cruelty in all corners of the globe. That is all merely tempo-rary. What is the worst of the horrors, and will perhaps last for several hundred years, is the aggressive tendency of national consciousness that has been aroused. It is no more than another form of the religious fanati-cism which we thought was dying out.'

He went on to blame Houston Stewart Chamberlain, whose racial the-ories led to the notion that the Germans should lead all the Germanic peoples, that the Germanic peoples should be leaders among the Aryan race, and that the Aryans were the superior race in relation to all others. 'Writers glorify war,' he added, 'and the cruelty of people is inspired by such hatred as has never existed since the end of the wars of religion. And the basic reason is simply that people speak different languages and on that basis are grouped together as different nations!' Blaming first the false prophets of racial theories, and then the laziness of people who fail to learn other languages, he lamented to Idel that there were 'no cosmo-politans left now in Europe'.

He underlined the task of 'all objective people in all countries to struggle against this hatred, these lies and these illusions – above all by enlightening the peoples about the lie of nationhood ... And I will do my bit in this struggle. And you too, Idel,' he demanded of his wife. 'Otherwise this war will not be the end of war, but the beginning of innumerable subsequent slaughters.' The letter could hardly offer a more exemplary demonstration of his concern for peace, his international per-spective, his historical awareness, and a young man's desire to make his mark on the world in order to leave it a better place. 'Even more than the warmongering statesmen, it is teachers like Gobineau and Chamberlain who are responsible for all this. My father must have known this when, in conscious opposition to Chamberlain, he fought against anti-Semitism. I intend to carry on his work.'[7]

RCK and Idel found themselves uncomfortably between two camps that developed as Europe stumbled and slid into the Great War. They were loyal for reasons of class and self-interest with their cultural and personal roots in Austro-Hungary, but strongly anti-war for intellec-tual, as well as emotional, reasons. All those who thought like RCK and

Bertha von Suttner and Hermann Fried, leaders of the peace movement in Austria and Germany.

Idel about pacifism would have read *Die Waffen Nieder* (*Lay Down Your Arms*), the best-selling novel by Bertha von Suttner, the *grande dame* of the Austrian Peace Movement, published twenty years earlier. In 1905 Bertha von Suttner was awarded the Nobel Peace Prize, and six years later, while RCK was still at the Therasianum, Alfred Hermann Fried, a young Viennese writer who founded the German Peace Movement with her, was also given the same honour. They were the two important points of reference, both for Idel and RCK, giving them the moral framework and practical direction for their own work, which would culminate in their proposal to bring all the states of Europe into a peaceful union. Von Suttner would die just before the outbreak of the First World War, but Fried would become a key contact for RCK, both in the peace movement and in Masonic circles, when they met after the end of the war. But by the beginning of the war, the peace movement was already a well-established network of non-governmental organizations in most of the countries of Europe, and Idel was a life-long supporter.

RCK's thinking was also strongly marked by the peace movement, but he did not automatically accept all it stood for. He could see that its central flaw was that it was organized in national chapters, which then co-operated internationally. When hostilities broke out, the various organizations and societies that made up the peace movements in each country split into opposing sides, often in line with their nations' alliances. The moderate and bourgeois groups tended to support their national governments – albeit with reservations – in what each considered a justifiable and defensive war. Only the more fundamentalist and radical elements, a much smaller group, underlined the class character of what they saw as capitalist belligerence in all the warring nations and called for neutrality, and even sabotage of the war effort, as the true expression of pacifism.

Somewhat to her surprise, Idel's sympathy for pacifism did not curtail her popularity as an actress. Nor did the theatres close down when war was declared. Indeed, they attracted audiences keen for entertainment or distraction, for the experience of a world far removed from their increasingly sombre daily lives, where the officially positive news offered in the newspapers was inevitably undermined by economic hardship and the reality of casualties returning home.

RCK helped Idel professionally by discussing the characters and plots of the plays she appeared in, commenting on rehearsals, discussing the context in which the plays had been written, and encouraging her to assume the roles in their daily life that she was to play on stage that evening, dressing and speaking the part at home in order to immerse herself fully in the character. RCK commented that she was happier in the light-hearted roles, and found herself weighed down in daily life at home when she was playing serious and tragic roles. As the war progressed, she preferred to play lighter parts in comedies, which were in any case more in demand.

If the theatres offered distraction from the war, newspapers and journals offered more immediate reportage. To keep up morale on the home front, the Austrian War Ministry quickly established an exemplary system of 'embedded' correspondents writing about the war, fighting with their pens rather than with guns. These included writers of experience and reputation such as Hugo von Hofmannsthal, Richard Strauss's renowned librettist, Rainer Maria Rilke, the world-famous poet, and Stephan Zweig, whose reminiscences in *Die Welt von Gestern* (*The World of Yesterday*) describe this period so evocatively. They were enlisted and given uniforms, training, and junior-officer rank, and based in the military archives in Vienna. From there they visited the front, briefly, to report positively on the progress of the war. The authorities imposed censorship, and as casualties mounted and success eluded the generals, newspapers and journals appeared with more and more blanked-out columns. In this situation, a steady supply of well-written articles, sometimes perceptive, sometimes informative, but always positive, sent 'from the front' by 'writers in uniform' was increasingly welcome to fill the gap.

Mitsu kept up with news of the war as reported in Austrian newspapers, read to her by her growing children. She had a strong sense of social responsibility, reinforced by her desire to prove her loyalty despite her Japanese, and hence alien, status. She volunteered for elementary first-aid training, and in response to the authorities' need for more hospitals to cope with the rising number of casualties, she transformed part of Stockau into a convalescent home for a small number of wounded officers, at the same time continuing to run the estate as best she could.

But it was no easy task. Two of her grown sons were away in the army, and Idel and RCK were not welcome at Ronsperg or Stockau as a couple, since the quarrel over their marriage was not resolved. As all able-bodied men were conscripted, she had to manage an estate workforce made up of the very young and the very old, the semi-sick and the convalescent, and more and more of women. Iron railings were collected to be smelted down into weapons, and extra land was dedicated to growing vegetables. Inspectors arrived to assess the acreage in the autumn of 1916 and imposed an even higher quota of grain to be collected from the following year's harvest. Without her competent Hungarian estate manager, who had been conscripted for military service, Mitsu knew she would have no hope of sowing enough wheat to meet the target.

Mitsu refers to the estate manager in her memoirs only as 'D', and her first request to the military authorities for his release on long leave, to allow him to return to his duties at Ronsperg, met with a formal refusal. Not one to give up easily, she armed herself with a letter of recommendation from a highly placed friend in Vienna, and, with just one female servant, undertook the difficult journey from the Sudetenland to Budapest in mid-winter to petition the minister for war personally. Despite his sympathy for her case, he felt he could not countermand the written refusal she had already received. But he advised her that, if she went on to Teschen in Silesia (now Cieszyn in Poland), where the General Staff headquarters then was, she might personally petition Archduke Ludwig, the emperor's brother. The minister for war himself rang the archduke's personal adjutant, Count Herberstein, a family friend, to announce the imminent arrival of Countess Coudenhove-Kalergi.

Despite her strong sense of aristocratic entitlement, even Mitsu and her maid needed new passports to travel farther than Budapest, and it took all day to obtain them – with photographs and police authorization – as well as to find a train and reserve seats. The train journey through the night brought them to Teschen at three in the morning. In the overcrowded little town in deepest January, she and her maid could not immediately find any lodging, and when eventually they did find a bed, it was so filthy that Mitsu slept fully dressed. Next morning, she hired a pony and trap, drove to the General Staff headquarters in a nearby castle, and begged the emperor's brother to release D for six weeks 'for the sowing'. Her request was immediately granted, and the archduke, regretting that he could not invite her to lunch, advised her that she should leave Teschen as soon as possible. In just a few hours the railway station would be closed, as the General Staff was expecting the German emperor that day for discussions on the course of the war. Travel for any civilian would be impossible.

Several days later, back in Ronsperg, she learnt that three Hungarian detectives had been detailed to follow her and her maid on their journey to the archduke, because, as a Japanese woman – an enemy alien just behind Austrian lines in the middle of the war – the police felt she looked suspicious. But, despite all difficulties, she achieved her goal. Shortly after this adventure, D was released on six weeks' leave, enough to ensure the fields on the Ronsperg estate were fully sown and Mitsu was able to fulfil the estate's grain quota for the following year. D's subsequent fate is unknown.

RCK CAME FACE TO FACE with the impact of war on the home front while pursuing his studies in the university in Vienna. Quite apart from food being in short supply, everyday life was disrupted in many other ways. The university was transformed into a military hospital for over a thousand wounded soldiers, with the Ceremonial Great Hall serving as a dining room and the neighbouring Small Hall adapted as an operating theatre. Many students served part-time as nursing or auxiliary personnel. Funds were drastically cut for both teaching and research; there was a shortage of books, and international contacts were broken off. Nonetheless, RCK persevered, and although he accompanied Idel on her professional engagements away from Vienna to theatres in Budapest, Prague, Berlin, and Munich, he was also single-minded enough to study through the many privations and distractions. By dint of hard work and application, he completed his dissertation and successfully defended his thesis at the university in the summer of 1917.

The argument of his thesis is complex, even abstruse. It concerned the nature of ethics, and in particular the relation of ethics to aesthetics, issues he had first dealt with in his final essay at the Theresianum. He argued for a higher form of ethics (hyper-ethics), which would encompass and super-sede less all-embracing systems or frameworks. Instead of the traditional religious opposition of good and evil, or the secular, materialist opposition between desire and disinclination, he postulated on the one hand 'noble' and 'common' and on the other 'beautiful' and 'ugly' as ethical opposites to be applied when judging behaviour. For him, nobility – developed from the classical concept of virtue – and beauty represented the key aspirations of human experience, the key values informing both objective thought and personal behaviour. Virtue he called human, but beauty, divine.

Although the ideas – much influenced by Plato and by Nietzsche – are more complex than this summary may suggest, RCK's style is clear, and this well-presented thesis by a twenty-three-year-old student earned him his doctorate, despite some dispute among his examiners. The first two professors awarded him the mark 'satisfactory', but he was not content with this, and pressed for another opinion. The second set of assessors found the work 'excellent', and that was the grade finally awarded him. Doctor of philosophy was a title of which he was justly proud, and it served as a springboard for him to publish in various intellectual journals of the day, both in Austria and in Germany. It also opened the door to an academic career, should he wish to go on to be a professor, as had been an ambition from his school days.[8]

Obtaining his doctorate also helped to heal the breach with some of his family caused by his marriage. Countess Marietta, his father's youngest, unmarried sister, had stayed in contact with the couple after their marriage out of admiration for Idel's dramatic talent, and, along with RCK's sister Elisabeth, she was the only relative to attend the award ceremony for his doctorate. She even persuaded her widowed older sister Thekla to be rec-onciled with the couple, since her nephew had shown that he could study soberly and deliver an impressive doctoral thesis in close-to-record time. Marrying an actress had evidently not softened his brain or otherwise ruined him as far as his intellectual capacity was concerned. RCK had even con-firmed the permanence of his arrangement by adopting Idel's daughter; little Erika now became Erika Coudenhove-Kalergi. Thekla offered the couple a vacant house that she owned in Pöstlingberg, near Linz, which they used for the better part of the last two years of the war – rent free – as their home.

Until then, Idel and Dicky had been living an itinerant life, staying partly in Idel's villa in Munich and partly in hotels when he accompanied her on tour. In its romantic setting of dark fir trees climbing the steep slopes of the hill, and with its quaint local mountain railway running down to Linz on the Danube, the Pöstlingberg house was their first real home together. It was designed in the style of a Swiss chalet and located high enough up the hill to overlook the river, not far from the castle of Ottensheim, where RCK's father – aunt Thekla's brother – had discovered his fiancée's suicide nearly fifty years earlier. RCK must have reflected somewhat ruefully on his father's experience then and his own situation now: his father, as a minor, forcibly separated from his young French love and disinherited, and RCK himself, also still a minor, but happily married, academically successful, and approaching the age of majority at which he would have access to his inheritance.

In their house in Pöstlingberg, RCK and Idel were to some extent insulated from the great events taking place on the world stage. But they were not quite out of sight of the family. Idel's three younger sisters, having finished their training for the stage, joined them there for a while, and neighbours reported to Thekla that they were tarnishing the family name by their riotous behaviour in the town, using the name of Coudenhove as credit and leaving bills unpaid. She wrote to RCK asking him to restrain them.[9]

Two of RCK's brothers were in uniform, but only Rolfi saw action, most dramatically in the final year of hostilities. When Lenin and the Bolsheviks pulled out of the war,[10] Austro-Hungary switched troops to the southern front and concentrated on Italy, where they captured the Italian headquarters at Udine and pushed the enemy back towards the River Po. Rolfi was serving as a junior artillery officer and described with wonder the sudden breakthough, as his unit emerged from the mountains and for the first time he saw the great North Italian plain bathed in sunlight below him.[11]

When the lines stabilized, Rolfi was granted a three-month furlough to see his family in Ronsperg and to study briefly in Vienna. There he obtained his first qualification in law, awarded to him, he modestly wrote, largely because of his war service rather than because of his knowledge of the subject. He returned to his unit in the summer of 1918, happy to leave behind him the 'disconsolate atmosphere of the capital' and to be back in the 'simple, clean world of the soldier' at the front again. But it did not last long.

On 25 October, a direct mortar hit on their mountain position killed his long-serving batman, Stromsky. Three nights later, Rolfi saw Stromsky, with his arm outstretched, marching on clouds that filled the Brenta valley that separated his unit from the Italian lines. Stromsky's apparition seemed to want to report something, and Rolfi, who like RCK believed in second sight, was sure that Stromsky was telling him that the war was about to end. The very next day, Czech nationalists declared independence from the empire, over-interpreting Emperor Karl's promise – similar to Popovici's earlier proposal – that after the war all the nationalities of the Austro-Hungarian Empire would achieve home rule. In the light of this proclamation, desertions from the army by different ethnic groups escalated. Two Hungarian divisions pulled out of their nearby positions and returned to Hungary to fight Romanians, rather than staying in the Tyrol to fight Italians. With the Austrian line now broken, Rolfi's unit – part of a Viennese regiment – was immediately ordered to retire. They destroyed their howitzers so that they did not fall into enemy hands, as there were no mules or horses available to pull them back. Trudging northwards, his unit encountered the staff car, flying a white flag and carrying General Weber and Prince Liechtenstein south to negotiate an armistice with the Italian commander.

In the confusion of the retreat, Rolfi and his company only narrowly escaped capture by taking forced marches as far as Bolzano (Bozen). There the Czechs in his regiment decided to take the route through the mountains to Bohemia, soon to become part of independent Czechoslovakia, and the Austrians to march on an alternative route towards German-speaking Innsbruck. From there, Rolfi found his way back to Vienna, riding on the running plate of a train. When he arrived on 12 November, mutinous soldiers at the railway station stripped him of his money, camera, and service revolver, but left him physically unharmed. He walked on to the house of his father's brother, Richard, where he lodged during the tempestuous days of the early republic in Vienna. His first painful task was to report Stromsky's death – his unit's last casualty before the armistice – to his batman's distraught mother.

Unlike Rolfi, RCK's elder brother, Hansi, did not record his memories of the war. In 1915 he had married Lilly Steinschneider-Wenckheim, the daughter of a wealthy Hungarian Jewish businessman, and had been reluctant to enrol. He was finally given a junior staff post in the army, and spent much time in Budapest. Lilly was more combative. She was barely five feet tall and very slight – an advantage for an aviatrix – and had wanted to fly as a fighter. But the War Office would not allow a woman in the front lines, so she became a nurse instead. Mitsu approved neither of Lilly, nor of the marriage. Hansi, a burly, thick-set man, well over six feet tall, had also not yet reached the age of majority and, like RCK, had also chosen a Jewish woman – though in this case only slightly older than himself. In addition, as several people noted, throughout his romantic engagement and as the war progressed, Hansi's personality had grown ever more eccentric.

RCK asserted much later in life – when negotiating Hansi's release from a Czech internment camp after 1945 – that he had tried to persuade the wider Coudenhove family not to allow Hansi as eldest son to take over their father's estate when he came of age towards the end of the First World War, because he was not of sound mind. He did indeed prepare a legal case at that time to challenge Hansi's inheritance, not on grounds of insanity or incapacity, but rather through a re-interpretation of his grandmother's will. Whatever the reason, disqualifying Hansi would have placed RCK conveniently next in line to inherit and, not surprisingly, relations between the brothers were never as good again after the end of the Great War as they had been earlier, when as young boys they had been taught together by their father.[12]

Hansi came into his inheritance in 1917 and, following their marriage, Hansi and Lilly took over the estate and set up home in Ronsperg castle. Despite not getting on well with her new daughter-in-law, Mitsu maintained her residence at Stokau, just a few kilometres away, and continued to maintain her apartment in Vienna, since her youngest son, Ery, was by then attending the Theresianum.[13]

One of Hansi's first acts was to petition Emperor Karl to upgrade his title. He asked to be allowed to add a 'von' to his name, and on 24 April 1918, in the final months of the war, he received imperial permission to style himself Count *von* Ronspergheim. Doubtless he and his wife were pleased and proud of their upgraded title. RCK and Idel, however, had more important matters on their minds: the prospect of the world they knew collapsing around them.

THE ARMISTICE – on the southern front on 7 November and on the western front on 11 November – shattered the Austro-Hungarian and the German empires. It was called an armistice, but in reality it was a defeat. The fighting was over, but neither Germany nor Austria-Hungary would have any say in the terms of the settlement. The four victorious leaders – Woodrow Wilson for the United States, Georges Clemenceau for France, Lloyd George for Great Britain, and Vittorio Orlando for Italy – convened in Paris to translate into reality the war aims of the Allies. They would dictate the peace.

While RCK gained his doctorate and considered the issues of the Great War from his intellectual refuge on the Pöstlingberg, Hitler had been in the thick of it on the Western Front, fighting for Germany, wounded, gassed, and twice awarded medals for bravery. It took both men a year or more to articulate their plans with any clarity, but their responses to the situation were diametrically opposed.

RCK wanted to ensure peace in Europe, and his plan was to bring all European countries together, the old states and the new, irrespective of their size and strength, in a peaceful association that would take away the causes of war and allow them to mutually guarantee peace on the continent. With peace at home, Europe would then be a force in the world again. Hitler, however, demanded revenge against those who had defeated Germany, both her foreign enemies and those politicians and fellow travellers on the home front – in particular the Jews – who had stabbed the German army in the back. Hitler was determined to make Germany strong again, to ensure a new order in Europe. This time it would be dominated by Germany, the largest state geographically, and the most populous.

These two visions were diametrically opposed to each other, and sooner or later would inevitably clash.

4

EUROPE ANSWERS HIS QUESTION

RCK'S VISION that Europe's future lay in reconciliation and co-operation between states rather than in German domination of the continent did not come to him in a blinding flash. There was no existential moment of revelation associated with the end of hostilities and the return of peace. It gradually took shape in his mind as he diligently worked through the evidence brought to him by newspaper reports of contemporary political events, especially the reports from the Paris Peace Conference, where the Allies were negotiating the terms of the Versailles settlement that would shape the face of Europe for another generation.

RCK was well aware of President Wilson's widely reported speech to the US Congress in January 1918, which set out the war aims of the United States in a series of Fourteen Points, including the game-changing principle of self-determination for the oppressed people of the defeated European empires.[1] Just how that would be worked out in practice was the subject of exhaustive negotiations among the victorious Allies in Paris, where Wilson's high-minded principles met the entrenched interests of France, Great Britain, and Italy in the persons of their representatives – Clemenceau, Lloyd George, and Orlando – in a struggle between American idealism and European *Realpolitik*.[2] After more than six months of complex negotiations, the outline of the main settlement was eventually agreed upon in June 1919.

The Versailles settlement changed the map of Europe, as new states were created out of the old empires. Germany, Austria, and Hungary, the losers in the Great War, were cut back in size. Estonia, Latvia, Lithuania, and Czechoslovakia were established as new states, and Poland re-established as an independent republic after well over a century of suppression by its larger neighbours. For the first time the south Slavs were brought together

Lloyd George, Orlando, Clemenceau, and Wilson: the Big Four at the Paris Peace Conference.

into one state, the future Yugoslavia, then called the Kingdom of Serbs, Croats, and Slovenes. Romania was much enlarged, and Alsace-Lorraine reverted to France. Italy was rewarded with the Austrian province of South Tyrol for having joined the winning side half-way through the war.

The last of Wilson's Fourteen Points was the creation of a new international organization, the League of Nations, established to hold the ring, police the new settlement, and prevent further wars from breaking out. It had a global, not just a European, remit, and its international administration had to be created from scratch, with civil servants drawn from all the participating states, including the new European ones. Britain provided the first secretary-general, Sir Eric Drummond, and one of his deputies was a French civil servant, Jean Monnet. It took time for the organization to build up both the legal expertise and the political clout for the League to play a positive role in policing the peace, let alone creating confidence that could lead to reconciliation between former foes.

Meanwhile, across the continent the collapse of traditional values followed hard on the heels of military defeat. A few days after the armistice, Emperor Karl withdrew from all government responsibilities in Vienna, but his studied ambiguity in not formally abdicating gave hope for many years to a loyal group of Hapsburg monarchists. A fierce debate ensued between supporters, who wanted to maintain the monarchy, and detractors, who wanted to arrest the former emperor and put him on trial. After protracted negotiations, Karl Hapsburg agreed to leave the country, and was escorted into political exile in Switzerland, not far from the Austrian border, under British protection. As the train passed through stations along the route, supporters silently lined the platforms to bow and curtsy as their emperor passed. Karl's departure symbolically confirmed the end of the old dynastic order, but left residual sympathy for monarchy, coupled with enduring nostalgia for the defunct Austro-Hungarian Empire in many loyal subjects' hearts. RCK was not completely immune to this, although he recognized rationally that republicanism represented the future.[3]

AS PART OF THE VERSAILLES SETTLEMENT, the Treaty of St Germain made RCK and Idel citizens of Czechoslovakia, not Austria, since RCK's family home was in Ronsperg in Bohemia, territory now within the new Czechoslovak state. Living in Pöstlingberg, however, he and Idel were more concerned with what was happening in Vienna than in Prague, and Austrian society was in turmoil, coping as best it could with the dramatic losses of war, followed hard by the debilitating ravages of the Spanish flu pandemic that caused almost as many deaths as the fighting.

Elections for a constituent Austrian assembly in February 1919 returned Karl Renner as head of the largest party, the Social Democrats. The son of a peasant farmer, he had gone on to read law at the University of Vienna, had been a progressive MP for ten years and, like RCK, had avoided being called up in the Great War. RCK admired his political skills and experience, and up to a point sympathized with his progressive ideas. To maintain order until the Versailles settlement would fix the conditions for future political life in Austria, Renner formed a coalition with the other major party, the Social Christians, a national government to run the country while the Versailles negotiations proceeded. But RCK was suspicious of how far to the political left Renner's socialist leanings might take him, and whether the Bolshevik example of Russia would infect the politics of the new Austrian Republic, as they would soon infect Hungary under the short-lived Soviet republic headed by Bela Kun.

Like all young intellectuals of the time, RCK was politicized by the war. He read widely and corresponded with other intellectuals, not only about the progress of the war but also about the philosophical questions to which war and peace gave rise. His response to the war, and to the peace which followed, was to mark the rest of his life profoundly. He had not put on a uniform or served at the front, as his brothers had, and the nearest that he and Idel had come to any physical danger was an incident which in retrospect might appear trivial. They had been forced to move from Pöstlingberg into the centre of Linz to stay with friends for a few nights, because a band of former Russian prisoners of war was plundering isolated houses and murdering farmers in the surrounding countryside. Apart from that, neither of them was ever near any 'action' during the hostilities. RCK's approach to the questions of war and peace was intellectual, and he started with a blank sheet of paper, considering fundamental issues to do with the nature of the state and society, government and international relations. He saw contemporary issues through the academic lens of philosophy and history, and he began to write about them from that perspective.

In early 1919, RCK's first published article appeared in *Die Erde* (*The Earth*), a short-lived political journal recently founded in Breslau (now Wroclaw in Poland) by Walter Rille, the husband of one of his wife's sisters, Theresa.[4] It was on Plato and the nature of contemporary government: 'Platons Staat und die Gegenwart' ('Plato's State and the Present Day'). Other articles soon followed on the confused state of international relations, especially contemporary European politics. Slowly he gained a readership in intellectual circles concerned with public affairs, partly because his arguments were clear and partly because he had a good turn of phrase. For instance, he described the conflicting ideologies of socialism and nationalism following the success of the Bolsheviks in Russia and the creation of new states through the Versailles settlement as 'Lenin and Wilson battling for the soul of Europe.'

In his intellectual approach, RCK much admired Kurt Hiller, who was ten years older, a liberal pacifist and political activist living in Berlin. Hiller was also an original stylist, and his elegant and powerful essays influenced RCK considerably.[5] In 1916, Hiller published *Das Ziel: Aufrufe zum tätigem Geist* (*The Aim: Appeals for Active Intelligence*), which demanded that intellectuals make their thinking practical in the sphere of politics. At the end of the Great War, he founded a group entitled Der Politische Rat geistiger Arbeiter (The Council of Working Intellectuals), with what was for the times a radically libertarian programme. The council's programme was in favour of peace, the League of Nations, abolition of the death penalty and of compulsory military service, separation of church and state, and an economic position that was neither capitalist nor Marxist. Hiller was both liberal and homosexual and, unsurprisingly, it was also against discrimination on grounds of sexuality. The manifesto was signed by twenty-eight writers and academics, some aleady prominent and some yet to make their names. Among them were Walter Benjamin, Otto Flake, Max Brod, Heinrich Mann – and the young Count Richard Coudenhove-Kalergi.[6]

RCK had sent Hiller his first essay on Plato in manuscript form, and Hiller appreciated his assessment of the role of Plato's 'guardians', the elite who ruled the state, and how he applied the concept to contemporary society. RCK did not argue in favour of democracy, although that was a popular call throughout Europe at the end of the war. Democracy, he argued, merely opened the door to government by plutocratic, financial elites. Instead he called for a socialist organization of society, but under the guidance of an intellectual or spiritual aristocracy, based on what he called the 'neo-aristocratic principle'. The wise use of material resources – as the Platonic 'guardians' decided – would strengthen, not undermine, those qualitative aspects of society whose value could not be measured in financial terms.

With his public association with Hiller's Council of Working Intellectuals and his first publishing foray, RCK had thrown his hat into the ring as a promising young author prepared to write for serious journals that dealt with contemporary social and political issues. Several editors invited him to contribute, and he struck up a particularly good rapport with Max Harden, the editor of *Die Zukunft* (*The Future*), perhaps the most influential and progressive political weekly at that time in Berlin. Several of his early essays would appear there.[7]

What drew the two men together was a shared belief in the need for intellectual leadership and a concern for how to reconcile this with popular democracy, an issue they realized affected every state in Europe, old and new, victors and vanquished alike. They both rejected as false the argument that simply extending the franchise would improve the quality of government. RCK's insistence on *quality* rather than *equality*, his neo-aristocratic principle, led him to suggest a separate, additional electoral franchise for journalists, authors, artists, and other intellectuals. That would ensure that the intelligentsia played a greater role in guiding the political life of the nation. Intellectuals were for him the contemporary equivalent of Plato's guardians.

RCK was also much impressed by the analysis, though not by the conclusions, of an older contemporary author who similarly dealt with politics in philosophical terms. Oswald Spengler's *Der Untergang des Abendlandes* (*The Decline of the West*) was an immediate best seller when it appeared in 1918. It caught the pessimistic mood of the times and painted an unremittingly critical picture of the hollowing out of European civilization. For Spengler, the ruins that were apparent to everyone at the end of the war – not just the material damage and loss of life and limb, but also the collapse of ethical values – were just another example of the fall of civilizations, the latest in a long historical line. The spirit of the countries of Europe was failing, according to Spengler, because materialism, symbolized by the power of modern machines, had overwhelmed all other values in society. And behind this abnegation of spirit before the power of materialism lay the unknown forces of international finance. The only thing that now could save Europe from 'some mysterious Caesarism', he wrote, was to hold on to the traditional values of identity and community, race and blood.

Whether intended or not, the effect of Spengler's book was to stoke the fires of nationalism, xenophobia, and in particular anti-Semitism. It empowered majorities and endangered minorities in all the nations of Europe, old and new alike.[8]

In vain did Spengler later qualify his argument by explaining that he did not mean 'blood' in any vulgar, ethnic sense, but more as the 'vital force' of any community united in the values, such as patriotism, or its close cousin, nationalism, for which it was prepared to make sacrifices. But by the time Spengler qualified what he had first written, the damage had been done. 'Blood' in the popular sense of race had been made widely *hoffähig* – acceptable in society – and was popularly thought to define the nation. Purifying the nation or the race – whether that meant through war, persecution, or sacrifice – was a way for the people, the *Volk*, to assert themselves against the decadence of the age.

RCK recognized the evidence of decadence and failure within society, but for him it was not materialism or money alone that was to blame for the decline of values. It was what people did with the fruits of material progress. RCK interpreted the same evidence that Spengler considered, but in a different way. For him, what really made a civilization great was not the purity of its racial bloodline, but the quality of its intellectual leadership and the moral choices that its leaders made. It was neither material development nor money that determined the quality of a culture, but how its elite thought and acted. This left its traces in the richness of a people's history, its art and culture, and the narrative by which it lived, as much as the values for which it fought – by soft power as much as by military might. It showed itself at its best in contemporary political and cultural leadership, which could come from individuals of any race at any time. It was not *Blut* – blood or race – that mattered, but *Geist* – intelligence or spirit.

RCK argued that if only Europeans of all nations would seek reconciliation instead of revenge, see the larger picture, organize efficiently, embrace the advantages of modern technology, and adapt their political system to the demands of the modern age, Europe could yet be saved from itself. Decline was not inevitable. On the contrary, Europe had all the values needed for survival in a potentially hostile world. Even more than that, Europe could grow strong again and flourish.

BUT THE EXCHANGE of ideas in the rarefied intellectual world in which RCK was operating was far from the dominating force determining day-to-day events in the immediate aftermath of the First World War. While the intelligentsia was debating alternative forms of government in theoretical journals, political agitators were working in the real world to impose their will in one city after another, one country after another, across the defeated empires. Social and political conditions in Berlin and Vienna were tense, and in Munich, where RCK and Idel also spent some time, they were even more unstable.

Munich was a hotbed of political radicalism, both from the left and the right. In November 1918, the Wittelsbach dynasty abdicated, and the Social Democratic leader Kurt Eisner, a charismatic Jewish journalist, declared the Bavarian Republic. His government lasted only until new elections late in January the following year, when he was assassinated by a right-wing nationalist. A coalition of Social Democrats and Communists then controlled government, but within a few weeks the Communists organized a putsch to take power alone, establishing the Bavarian Soviet Republic, or *Räterrepublik*.

RCK was with Idel in Munich at that time, as she was playing the lead in Mikhail Artzybashev's *Eifersucht* (*Jealousy*) in the Münchener Kammerspiele. In the febrile political atmosphere of the city, the play opened in April 1919 to surprisingly good houses, audiences hungry for diversion from the violent politics of daily life. One evening, however, the violence followed RCK and Idel back to where they were lodging in the elegant Park Hotel, close to the Maximilian Platz, not far from the Communist Party headquarters. To secure their hold on government, the

Communist militia were on the search for counter-revolutionaries, and that night they targeted the Park Hotel.

Around midnight, there was a knock on their door. Militiamen were searching for class enemies. They demanded their passports, discovered that RCK was an aristocrat, a count, and were about to lead him away, when Idel – imitating the local Bavarian dialect to the guards – asked what they had against counts? Tolstoy, she pointed out, was also a count, and he had paved the way for Lenin and the Bolsheviks. To prove that RCK was likewise more progressive than reactionary, she had the presence of mind to show the corporal a copy of *Die Erde* with RCK's article on Plato, fortunately signed not with his title, but as plain Richard Coudenhove-Kalergi. Unconvinced, the corporal left two guards in their room while he took the copy to his commanding officer. After three tense hours, he returned, gave them back the journal, saluted, and wished them good night.

RCK was fortunate. A few doors further along the corridor in the same hotel, the militiamen found Prince Gustav von Thurn und Taxis, took him away for questioning, and held him as a hostage with several other aristocratic suspects. When the regular Bavarian army recaptured the city a few days later, one of the final acts of the rebels was to shoot their hostages, including the young prince.

Initially, RCK had been an enthusiastic supporter of President Woodrow Wilson and sympathetic to the war aims of the Allies. But Allied insistence on pinning the guilt for the Great War on the defeated enemy and demanding high reparations soured public opinion, both in Germany and in Austria. As the negotiations dragged on and details of the new settlement leaked out from the Paris Peace Conference, many Wilsonians – including RCK – moderated their enthusiasm. He was soon describing himself as a 'disappointed Wilsonian' and feared, like many other commentators, that the compromise resulting from the clash of Wilson's idealism with French, British, and Italian self-interest would carry the seeds of its own destruction. The international settlement dictated by the peace conference would be unjust and unstable.

In September 1919, after nearly a year of negotiations following the Armistice, the victorious Allies were finally ready to dictate terms to Austria.[9] Karl Renner, the first post-war prime minister, had no option but to sign the Treaty of St Germain. Austria became a mere rump of a state, banned forever from uniting with Germany. Only in some minor details did Renner succeed in softening the terms of the treaty. He pressed for and was granted a plebiscite in Klagenfurt, with the result that the city and surrounding countryside stayed Austrian rather than being allotted to Yugoslavia.

A small strip of territory on the Hungarian border was likewise reat-
tributed to Austria, and Vienna was permitted to retain many of the artistic
treasures that had graced the galleries and museums of the old empire.
Vienna did indeed have cultural pretentions to rival Paris and London,
but without its old markets, Austria's inflated capital of two million people
was economically unviable, short of food and fuel, and politically explosive. Austria became a small, agrarian country, with less than a tenth of
the population of the empire it had lost.

The coalition that had steered Austria since the Armistice now fell
apart. The right blamed the workers, bolshevism, and the Versailles settlement for the economic and social mess that the truncated country was in.
The left blamed capitalism, the middle class, and the old Establishment.
Everyone sought to blame any scapegoat they could find, including the
Jews, for defeat and for Versailles. RCK and Idel found themselves now in
the thick of the political struggle, targets as well as players in the popular
and the intellectual debate.

———————

WITH LIVING CONDITIONS in Vienna so difficult – some of the theatres were
open for only one night a week, short of energy for heating and lighting –
the couple seized the opportunity to explore the rest of Europe that peace
had opened to them. Over the next few years, RCK and Idel organized
their lives so that they could leave the city for up to two months each year,
usually in spring, to set off with Erika and their chauffeur, together with
their dogs. With a copy of Baedeker on the dashboard and their list
of personal contacts in their luggage, they undertook European voyages of
exploration.

In 1919, they travelled across Switzerland and France into Spain and
Portugal, staying often at modest inns in the smaller towns. They took the
ferry from Algeciras to Cueta and explored northern Morocco, visiting a
local Arab sheik. Idel and Erika were entertained by his wives and children, while RCK engaged in political discussion with the sheik himself.
It was here that Idel bought a dramatic, all-encompassing white burnous,
or hooded cloak, that she loved to wear. Later she would leave instructions that she was to be buried in it. Another year, they journeyed north
through Germany and Poland as far as Estonia, exploring the Baltic, visiting Gerhart Hauptmann at his rural retreat on Hiddensee. Yet another
long holiday exploration took them through the Balkans and Greece as far
as Turkey. Idel always bought examples of local folk art when she travelled

and brought them back to display in their flat in Vienna. En route, RCK, Idel, and Erika would combine the experience of the simplest of lodgings in remote rural places with the comfort of luxury hotels in the capitals – Madrid, Belgrade, Istanbul, and Athens, for instance.

They travelled slowly in their chauffeur-driven Bentley, at Idel's insistence never going more than sixty kilometres an hour. She loved to stop from time to time in the country to pick armfuls of flowers which would subsequently adorn their rooms in the inns they stayed in. In the cities, RCK looked up friends made during his school and university years, as well as family contacts, particularly those in the diplomatic service who had known his father, men who could give him insights and contacts in the countries in which they were now serving or had served previously.

In an effort to clarify further his basic political ideas, in 1920 and 1921 RCK also published three articles, first a general argument about Vienna and its contemporary role as a capital city: 'Wien als Hauptstadt'('Vienna as a Capital'). It was followed by two more, one about the racial clash in Czechoslovakia, 'Czechen und Deutsche'('Czechs and Germans'), and a final one about modern society and democracy, 'Plutokratie'('Plutocracy'). All three appeared in Harden's journal, *Die Zukunft*, and with them RCK established his name as a leading young contributor to the intellectual debate about politics and society, a member of the contemporary commentariat.

'Vienna as a Capital' made him friends in the Austrian government, setting out the case for Vienna rather than Geneva as the headquarters of the newly established League of Nations. Vienna's generously planned infrastructure as the large capital of a now-much-reduced state made it an obvious practical choice, he argued, and its multinational and multilingual history offered the prospect of uniting the member states of the League of Nations more easily there than anywhere else. In addition, its long experience as the co-ordinating centre of a far-flung network of nations assured it the human capital and the collective memory necessary for making a success of the new international organization. However, the League ignored this unofficial offer and remained in Geneva.

'Czechs and Germans' made him friends in the Czechoslovak government. In this article he argued by analogy that, just as the peace of Europe in the West depended on friendship between France and Germany, so too Czechs and Germans needed to establish friendly relations to permit the countries of central Europe to live in peace. This implied security for minorities, tolerance and a search for common interests, and a common concern when viewing the geopolitical situation from either a Slav or a German perspective. RCK always asserted that he identified with the whole continent rather than a single country, and was European rather than belonging to any single nationality, and so he called on the new president of Czechoslovakia,Thomas Garrigue Masaryk, whom he described as a convinced European, to take the first step. Masaryk may have been open to the idea, but no concrete action ensued.[10]

The third, 'Plutocracy', gained RCK friends among intellectuals who formed the mainstay of the readership of Harden's journal. In this essay, RCK attacked the illusion of democracy as a goal in itself, arguing that elected representation was no more than a façade through which the value of money – owned by the plutocratic minority – spoke louder than ethical or aesthetic values. For RCK, formal equality was a chimera and a cruel deception, as it ignored intellectual and educational distinctions. He argued that in any state there should be a chamber of intellectuals, with membership based on educational achievement. He clearly expected to be a member of the latter chamber himself, but, however interesting the idea, no country then adopted it as an element of its constitution.

With these articles already to his credit, he wrote to the new president in Prague to request an audience. He wanted to explain to the great man another of his ideas: how to create a grouping of European states within the League of Nations. This, he suggested, would allow Europe to solve its problems without interference from outside the continent. Climbing the steep road up to Prague Castle in spring 1920, RCK had ample time to calm his nerves before this, his first interview with Masaryk. In conversation, he soon discovered a straightforward character who put him at his ease, someone he later likened to one of his former professors at university. Masaryk had read the short essays that RCK had sent him in advance, and the two men quickly moved on to discuss the state of European politics. RCK outlined his idea for a peaceful association of all the countries of the continent as a way of laying the ghosts of nationalism and solving the issue of minorities. After some discussion, Masaryk replied: 'I believe your idea is correct, and the United States of Europe will one day come into being. But I fear the time is not yet ripe.'

He then described how he had tried in the early stages of the Versailles Conference to form an association of East European states from Finland to Greece, including Czechoslovakia, to act as a buffer between Germany and Soviet Russia. But he had failed in the face of the ardent nationalism of the leaders of several of those countries, who would not consider putting their new-found independence into an alliance that would constrain their national sovereignty.[11] Hence he did not now feel able to support RCK's initiative publicly, but he was personally sympathetic and would encourage him unofficially. True to his word, he introduced him to Edvard Beneš, the Czechoslovak foreign minister, who also supported the thrust of RCK's argument. More importantly, Beneš gave him a Czechoslovak diplomatic passport to facilitate his future travel around the continent to propagate his political programme of closer integration.

This political programme was slowly taking shape in his mind, and RCK called it 'Pan-Europa', the title he would give two years later to the book that brought it to widespread public attention. Essentially it implied bringing together the new states of Europe that had been set up by the Versailles Settlement with the old states of the continent – both victors and vanquished in the Great War – in a joint political structure that would ensure peace among them all.

On that basis, they would harmonize and reduce tariffs to form an internal common market, which would enable them all to grow rich much faster than if they individually protected their own small, national markets. The states of Pan-Europa would also act as one in international affairs, eventually having a single diplomatic service and a single army to defend their role in the world. Thus Pan-Europa would become one of the world powers, alongside Communist Russia, the British Empire, the United States of America, and the growing power centre in East Asia.

RCK was much disappointed that the statesman whom he thought best able to realize his idea for the peaceful development of this embryonic United States of Europe had declined to take leadership of the project. He knew that Masaryk agreed with him, but he had to come to terms with the fact that, aged seventy, the Czech president had not the strength to take on the task.[12] Who now, RCK asked himself, could take on leadership of this project?

Like many Wilsonians, RCK had initially been enthusiastic about the proposal to create the League of Nations. But, in the way it was set up, he could see the problems that prevented it working as intended. He claimed it was 'neither truly global nor really European'. Bolshevik Russia and defeated Germany, for instance, as well as states from farther afield, such as Argentina and Mexico, were not members. Even the United States had failed to join, because its Senate blocked ratification of its accession, a dramatic first step along the road of American isolationism. RCK knew what he was talking about, since, as an observer, he attended the annual meetings of the foreign ministers at the League's Assembly in Geneva each September, partly to be able to write about discussions there, and partly to use the occasion to promote his ideas for greater co-operation in Europe.

The League of Nations incorporated procedures for international negotiation and judicial arbitration as alternatives to going to war, and it could recommend economic sanctions. But beyond that, its powers were limited. The League in many ways reinforced the power of the big states, since it was able to act only when they agreed, and therefore left these states – individually – with an ultimate veto on joint action. It was unthinkable that the League would commit armed forces, for instance, to keep the peace against the interests of a major state, but it could intervene with sanctions, and even with peacekeepers if need be, in quarrels between smaller members. Mussolini would later describe it disdainfully but accurately, as 'good when the sparrows twitter, but no use when the eagles scream.'[13]

RCK considered that a relatively simple adjustment to the League's membership rules could solve the problem constructively. Instead of *individual* states being members, he proposed that *regional* groupings should join the League to discuss world problems, leaving regional issues to be decided within each regional group. To function effectively, he argued, the states of the Americas, East Asia, and Europe needed to form clusters or regional groups that could both settle issues within their own region and speak with one voice for their region within the League, rather like the co-ordination of the British Empire's voice through Great Britain. 'If a world organization is to replace global anarchy, so states should form regional groupings first. As the unification of Germany, Italy and Poland were necessary stages in the unification of Europe,' he wrote, 'so will the unification of Europe be a necessary step towards the unity of mankind.'

This idealistic solution might also help the United States to join the League through its membership of the Pan-American Union, he pointed out, allowing the Administration to persuade Congress that it was not the United States itself but the regional grouping which was joining this international body. Recognizing a regional group for the Americas would also give moral support to RCK's plan for Pan-Europa, which he envisaged as the European grouping within the League. With the optimism, perhaps the arrogance, of an intelligent, handsome, and aristocratic young man, not used to contradiction, he boldly drafted a memorandum designed to persuade the member states to reform themselves and the League. He sent his memorandum to the Sir Eric Drummond, the secretary-general, and travelled to Geneva in 1921 to press his case in person.[14]

The meeting was not a success, as even the enthusiastic RCK was forced to admit in his memoirs. Sir Eric listened politely and attentively, but did not express any definite opinion, and RCK realized that he had not succeeded in convincing him. He left Geneva with his parting words echoing in his ears: 'Please don't go too fast!'

On reflection, RCK concluded that 'although Sir Eric attempted to be the impartial head of an international body, he never was an internationalist, but remained British to the core. And he knew only too well that the British government did not wish to support anything that might weaken Britain's role and power on the Continent, certainly not anything that might promote a continental European union.'

RCK realized his own political impotence, and felt he needed to persuade someone much closer to power actually to deliver what he was starting to formulate in his mind about the future of Europe. In 1920, Masaryk had turned him down; in 1921, Drummond had shown him the door. By 1922, RCK felt he needed a strong political leader, preferably from a major state, one who had the energy to take on the European task that he would happily outline. He needed a strong man who had political authority and whom he could influence. As he heard the news from Italy late that year, he convinced himself that the best country could well be Italy, and the right candidate Benito Mussolini.

5

BETWEEN HITLER AND MUSSOLINI

MUSSOLINI'S RISE TO POWER was swift and dramatic, and to outside observers seemed a phenomenal success. Not yet forty, he was the youngest prime minister of any major European state, propelled into power by a surge of popular support as an alternative to an impotent succession of liberal-dominated coalitions in government that were characterized by blatant corruption. Mussolini presented a young and vigorous alternative to the status quo, spear-headed by a popular demonstration of force, a threatened march on Rome by thirty thousand of his black-shirted fascist supporters. Expecting them in the capital in October 1922, the political establishment panicked. The prime minister asked for emergency powers, but King Victor Emmanuel III refused, fearing this might lead to civil war. Instead, he invited Mussolini to form a government, but insisted it should be in coalition with several other parties represented in parliament that opposed him, and hence would balance the administration.

Mussolini had begun his political life before the Great War as a member of the Socialist Party, which strongly supported the peace movement. However, the practical challenge of war changed his opinions radically. He enlisted in the infantry, spent nine months at the front, was wounded and – like Hitler – promoted and decorated for bravery. He was expelled from the Socialist Party for joining the army, and in response founded his own Nationalist Party, leading a movement for social regeneration that embraced all classes. His propaganda gave the impression that his movement was the legitimate heir to the Risorgimento, reviving the tradition of Mazzini and Garibaldi, and aiming for a new Italy with youthful leadership. Policy detail was in many cases left vague, but the energy and dynamism of the man and of his followers was distinctive. Fascism stood for change and was characterized by energy. Like Hitler, Mussolini was also enthusiastic about modern technology and grasped the role of public relations and propaganda intuitively. He had built a paramilitary organization, the Blackshirts, but his route to power was – formally at least – within the democratic and legal structures of the Italian state.

RCK had not met Mussolini, but he believed Mussolini's propaganda and admired the image of the strong, young leader. Here was a man who, if RCK could persuade him to make the idea of a European confederation into the foreign policy of his nation, would be able, he felt sure, to persuade other European leaders to follow him. Based on no personal knowledge, RCK persuaded himself that Mussolini would be the right man to federate the continent. It was a decision taken in an enthusiastic moment, but when he mulled it over, he found several arguments to support his choice.

First, Mussolini's fascist philosophy was critical of parliamentary democracy. Mussolini was keen to balance the voice of the people, as expressed through parties and elections, with other power centres, such as chambers representing the professions, employers, and unions. RCK sympathized with this dilution of parliamentary democracy, seeing in it some echo of his own insistence on a 'spiritual aristocracy', with a strong role for intellectuals, experts, and the more-educated classes of society.

Second, Mussolini was actually in power. RCK wanted a strong man who had already arrived at a point where he could be useful, not someone who still had to achieve power. For RCK, the issue of uniting Europe was urgent, and he did not have time to waste betting on an outsider.

Third, as one of the victorious powers from the recent war, Italy had a foreign policy that strongly supported an independent Austria as a buffer between Germany and Italy. Despite the continuing problem of South Tyrol, where Italy ruled a formerly Austrian province with a German-speaking majority, Italy made common cause with the rest of the international community in opposing German claims to absorb or annex Austria.[1]

Fourth, Mussolini was an intelligent man, considered by many as an intellectual, who could quote Plato and Nietzsche. Despite his humble origins, he appeared to be a cultivated leader who, while asserting Italy's rightful place in the world, was unlikely to do serious harm to other nations' legitimate interests. Even when Mussolini later flexed his military muscles – as with his intervention in Libya during the twenties, or later still the invasion of Abyssinia in 1935 – RCK continued to give Mussolini the benefit of the doubt.

And lastly, although Italian fascism would subordinate Arabs and Africans on grounds of race, it did not – initially target Jews. One reason may well have been that, from 1911, Mussolini had enjoyed a long-standing relationship with Margharita Sarfatti, a prominent Jewish journalist, known subsequently as the 'Jewish mother of fascism'. For Mussolini, she was only one of many mistresses, but her Jewish identity and her influence on Il Duce were an open secret, and they ensured that Italian fascism was free from anti-Semitism until the late 1930s. Happy and secure in his own relationship with Idel, RCK must have counted this much in Mussolini's favour.

Since he had no direct contact with Mussolini at that time, RCK took the bold, impractical, and somewhat naïve step of publicly inviting him through an Open Letter to lead his proposed movement for European unity. The tone of the letter was not dissimilar to Mussolini's own bombastic speeches, and it was published in February 1923 in *Die Neue Freie Presse*, the leading Viennese liberal daily, less than six months after Mussolini had come to power.

He appealed to Mussolini in the name of the Youth of Europe to save the continent by calling a conference in Rome of all the democratic states of Europe. Mussolini could set an agenda that would not only settle outstanding issues among the great powers, but also map out the future of the continent. It would be a European conference to determine European affairs, without any outside interference such as the League of Nations might bring with it.

'The threat to Europe's safety does not lie in the north; economically, it lies in the west – politically, in the east', wrote RCK. He argued that a dismembered Europe would be defenceless against American competition and Russian expansionism. 'Only by means of full economic union, based on a firm political alliance and a general readiness to submit disputes to arbitration, can the prosperity, the peace, and the independence of the Continent be guaranteed in the long run.'

He then added, somewhat pompously, 'As heir to Marius and Caesar, you, sir, have the power to postpone this new upheaval for many centuries. For it will depend largely on your attitude in this present crisis whether Europe is in future to confront Eurasia on the line of the Dniester and the Rokitno Swamps – or on that of the Rhine and the Alps.' RCK took an uncompromisingly broad and long-term view both of the past and of the future of the continent but, unsurprisingly, Mussolini was much too preoccupied with matters in hand in Rome to take note of RCK's naïve appeal in the Viennese press. He did not deign to reply.[2]

Mussolini led the March on Rome in 1922; Hitler led the Beer Hall Putsch in Munich in 1923.

BARELY SIX MONTHS EARLIER – just after Mussolini had come to power in Italy – Hitler attracted the attention of the US embassy in Berlin. The ambassador sent Truman Smith, the assistant military attaché, to Munich to report on this man and his new party. 'Less a political party than a popular movement,' reported Smith confidentially, 'the Bavarian counterpart to the Italian *fascisti*.' He attended party events and asked for an interview with Hitler himself. Hitler gave him more than two hours. 'His ability to influence a popular assembly is uncanny,' wrote Smith. 'In private conversation he disclosed himself as a forceful and logical speaker which, when tempered with fanatical earnestness, made a very deep impression on a neutral observer.' Hitler was clearly a man on the make, with a political party that certainly needed to be taken into account in the politics of Bavaria, and soon perhaps also in the politics of Germany as a whole.[3]

That diplomatic report was not for public consumption, and at that stage RCK was not aware of Hitler. Indeed, he had made even less of a public name for himself than RCK, who already enjoyed a reputation among a small circle of intellectuals and politicians as an independent thinker and writer. Hitler, while serving his last months in the army, had reported the aims and organization of the Deutsche Arbeiter Partei (The German

Workers' Party), or DAP, to the military authorities. The total membership of the DAP in early 1920 was less than two hundred, but Hitler so
impressed the small number who turned up to their meetings that, within
a few months, they co-opted him onto the steering committee. After his
army discharge in March that year, Hitler the poacher then turned game-
keeper by taking on the full-time role of managing this fledgling DAP
himself. His new role suited him well, and he grew more sympathetic
to the core aims of this group. It was anti-Semitic and also adamantly
opposed to the Treaty of Versailles, and so was he. He quickly took charge
of propaganda, branded the DAP with a new symbol, the swastika, and
rewrote its manifesto. He highlighted the first two demands of the party:
revision of the Versailles settlement and denial of all citizenship rights
to Jews, and renamed it the National Socialist German Workers' Party
(NSDAP), or Nazi Party, aiming to make it a power-broker in Bavaria. At
this stage, however, this was still wishful thinking, as it had made no
impact at all outside of Munich.

Like RCK, Hitler had received his first political impressions before the
war in Austria, watching the struggle between the political parties there.
Hitler had large ambitions for his little party, and he now put into practice in
Munich the lessons he had learned in Vienna. RCK might aim to influence
a select group of potentially important people already close to power, but
Hitler planned to lead a mass movement and seize political power himself.

First, he set about enlarging the NSDAP's membership. To do so he
applied the elementary principles of propaganda and public relations that
he had grasped intuitively, and his methods were straightforward. He
kept his core messages simple, and he repeated them over and over again.
Within less than a year his rallies were attracting audiences of a thousand
or more, as opposed to the couple of dozen when he first joined the party.
Audiences came to hear his rabble-rousing incitements to restore German
dignity after the disgrace of Versailles, and how German patriots should
renew the soul of Germany by expelling the Jews. Party membership grew
from just a couple of hundred to nearly two thousand during the first year
he was in charge. In December 1920, the Nazi Party bought an ailing
newspaper, the *Völkischer Beobachter*, a twice-weekly anti-Semitic gossip
sheet with a circulation between seven and eight thousand. Hitler quickly
built this valuable new asset into a daily political newssheet, incessantly
supporting the Nazi line with simple slogans and repetitive propaganda.[4]

In September the following year, Hitler and his followers tried to dis-
rupt a meeting of a rival political association, the Bauernbund, or Farmers'
Union, but they were badly beaten up in the ensuing brawl. Jailed for a

few months for disrupting the peace, he decided that in future he needed a paramilitary organization to intimidate the opposition and physically dominate his rivals. On his release in July, he set about organizing gangs of semi-uniformed Nazi volunteers, registered in the Gymnastic and Sports Division of the party to avoid contravening public-order regulations. From a few dozen storm-troopers he quickly built this unit into a powerful force with a reputation for silencing opposition through intimidation and violence.

Barely eighteen months after taking over a small political party, Hitler had fashioned it to suit his programme and made it a local power to be reckoned with, both politically and on the streets. He had done this essentially through dedicated and detailed work of organization, active public relations, ruthless propaganda, and successful fund-raising. He still lived alone – frugally, in a small two-room flat – and had few personal friends. In or out of jail, he was starting to make an impression on the local political scene.

Over the same period, RCK had clarified his ideas on state and society, published several articles in small-circulation political magazines, supported Hiller's manifesto of the Council of Working Intellectuals in Berlin, and had put his name about with several editors of political journals looking for intelligent contributions on contemporary politics. He had also married and assured his emotional happiness, with his financial position secured essentially through his wife's fees as an actress. He had also tried twice to persuade a political leader of influence – in Czechoslovakia and in Italy – to take up his political ideas on Europe, but he had failed on both occasions, as he had when he tried to interest the League of Nations in regional reform.

Hitler and RCK both saw the possibilities of the new mass media – mass-circulation newspapers, photography, radio, and film – but used them very differently.[5] In *Mein Kampf*, Hitler drew obvious, if cynical, conclusions about their propaganda value.

> All propaganda must be popular and its intellectual level must be adjusted to the most limited intelligence among those it is addressed to. Consequently, the greater the mass it is intended to reach, the lower its purely intellectual level will have to be … The more modest its intellectual ballast and the more exclusively it takes into consideration the emotions of the masses, the more effective it will be.

Hitler kept his propaganda simple for the masses, and he gave no space to any opposition views. 'The function of propaganda is not to weigh and ponder the rights of different people, but exclusively to emphasize the one right which it has set out to argue for. Its task is not to make an objective study of the truth, in so far as it favours the enemy, and then set it before the masses with academic fairness; its task is to serve our own right, always and unflinchingly.' For him, the end clearly justified the means. Bias, lies, and propaganda could all serve the cause, since the cause was what mattered.

RCK was also working out his basic political ideas, but from a totally different angle. He was an intellectual, and the target audience for RCK's articles was essentially other politically engaged German-speaking intellectuals and the political class that he and they could influence. RCK also had a high opinion of the value of propaganda – on one occasion noting that all his writing was 'propaganda for the cause' – but he brought to his cause all the sophisticated baggage of historical study and cultural tolerance that his upbringing and academic training had inculcated in him. While RCK appealed to the intelligent reader's reason and understanding, Hitler reached for the heart and the guts, stirring the basic emotions of the man in the street. The one built from the top down; the other built from the bottom up.

In the articles that he published in the early 1920s, RCK posed several pertinent and interesting political questions. Was Vienna better suited than Geneva to be the seat of the League of Nations? Was it up to the Czechs or up to the Germans to improve relations between the two communities in the new Czechoslovak Republic? Was democracy in any country worth striving for, if it meant that public opinion could be bought by those with the deepest pockets? However, his voice was just one among many speaking to the intelligentsia, one voice in an unorganized campaign to inform as much as persuade those who held political power in a variety of countries. He was in no position to take decisions. He had no party or organization with which to put solutions into effect. He simply put ideas into circulation, trying to influence political opinion: the state of mind of the political class across a whole continent. Hitler, on the other hand, attempted to gain political power initially in just one city, Munich, as a stepping-stone to a national goal, power in one country, Germany.

RCK had attempted to persuade political leaders in Prague and Rome and the international secretariat of the League in Geneva to adopt his ideas, and he had failed on each occasion. Since no suitable leader would take on the political role he was offering, RCK came to the conclusion that he would have to set up and lead his embryonic Pan-Europa Movement himself. His wife encouraged him in this. Idel had always seen him as a young man with a great future. She sensed that, with her support and encouragement, he could make his mark as a political leader. To do that with any hope of success, she knew he needed a higher public profile than simply as an academic commentator on political affairs within a small circle. He needed a more important status and a full-fledged political programme. He needed to establish his own political movement – something between an international party and a Europe-wide think-tank. And he needed to write a comprehensive manifesto that laid out his ideas on Europe simply and clearly. That would be Pan-Europa. Together, she was sure that they could succeed.

6

PACIFIST AND FREEMASON

IDEL HAD LONG BEEN A SUPPORTER of the peace movement with its goal of universal peace. There was obviously common ground between that and RCK's goal of European peace, and they both saw its potential to act as an amplifier of Pan-Europa's message. RCK also appreciated that the Freemasons – whose central ideal was the brotherhood of all men – could serve as an amplifier of his ideas. At first sight it might seem utopian, he conceded, but to make his dream of Pan-Europa a reality, he needed only a few hundred active supporters who would then persuade thousands and finally millions of people to translate his ideas into practical action. The united continent of Europe would be a stepping-stone towards wider global brotherhood. 'All good ideas start as Utopias,' he wrote, 'before they become reality.' This task required not only intellectual application, however, but also financial muscle. Even more, it needed his personal engagement in the political centre he knew best – Vienna.

On 16 November 1920, RCK reached the age of majority – twenty-four – and received his modest portion of the Coudenhove-Kalergi inheritance. The value of the proceeds from the sale of the Hungarian estates before the war had been seriously reduced by wartime and post-war inflation, but nonetheless it was a small boost for the couple's fortune. As soon as the influenza pandemic that followed the war had faded, he and Idel moved back from Pöstlingberg to Vienna permanently. They rented an apartment in a prestigious building, Schmerlingplatz 8, close to the Ring, near the parliament and the university, just a short walk from the Burgtheater and the town hall. It brought them into the centre of the progressive social scene, where they easily made contacts in the capital among artists, actors, journalists, academics, diplomats, businessmen, and politicians.

Vienna, with its population of nearly two million, was by far the largest city in Austria. No other town had more than one-hundred-thousand inhabitants. Despite having lost its vast empire, Vienna still considered itself culturally and socially comparable to London and Paris, and superior to Berlin or Munich. Politically, the city was dominated by the Social Democratic Party, with nearly two-thirds of the popular vote. That gave the party control of the town hall, and Vienna was admired internationally as a model of left-wing city government.[1] The main opposition came from the Christian Social Party, which drew most of its electoral strength from the deeply Catholic countryside, and also relied – as did two smaller parties, the Agrarian Party and the Peasant Party – on anti-Semitic propaganda to maintain mass support. The Communist Party had no more than a few thousand active members, but the German Nationalist Party had considerably more, and some of their followers were well organized in a paramilitary 'home guard'. Some financial support already flowed to them from German sources, and German nationalists advocating Anschluss with Germany posed a problem, which, though not yet critical, could easily become so.

RCK felt that a continent-wide vision of peaceful neighbourly relations between all states was precisely what was lacking in Europe after the Versailles settlement. Instead of creating European unity and peace, the Versailles settlement had simply created a dozen new, competing nation states on the old model, encouraging division and even opening the prospect of war again at a later stage. What peace there was in Europe at any moment was simply a brief intermission between periods of unceasing war.

Indeed, wars continued or flared up again almost immediately between smaller neighbours for several years after the end of the Great War. Civil war rumbled on in Russia until 1921, as did intermittent wars in the Baltic States. In 1918, the newly established state of Poland was immediately at war with the Soviet Union, with Germany, and later with Czechoslovakia, and throughout the 1920s never established good neighbourly relations with its neighbours. Turkey and Greece were at war from 1919 to 1922, as were the Soviet Union and Finland briefly from 1921 to 1922. France occupied the Ruhr and the Rhineland in 1923 in retaliation for German failure to pay reparations.

RCK wrote in the early 1920s, 'Europe is currently on the way to a new war.' The war he had in mind was not just a limited and local clash between two countries, but another general conflagration like the First World War. He prophesied that such a war would exceed the Great War in barbarity by a factor as great as that war had exceeded the horror of the Franco-German war of 1870. As with the destruction of Carthage by the Romans, he declared, any future war would lead to the total extermination of the defeated nation. He added, 'The recent World War has weakened Europe, but the next will kill it.'

In a short pamphlet in 1921 he highlighted the high level of war preparations among the twenty-six nations of Europe, and drew five succinct conclusions: European states needed to replace armed anarchy with peaceful organization; to institute a system of compulsory arbitration; to disarm rather than compete in an arms race with each other; to offer mutual guarantees of solidarity instead of pursuing economic self-sufficiency; and to co-operate economically instead of competing. Already he was setting out the core articles of his faith in a united Europe.

From this state of continuing warfare, RCK drew the conclusion that any European empire built on conquest by a temporarily dominant nation would be inherently unstable. Only a peacefully united Europe would be in a position to defend its interests against other powers at a global level. To those who dismissed this as unrealistic or utopian, he pointed to the example – in miniature – of the Swiss Confederation, which brought together three languages, several cantons of diverse sizes, and both Protestant and Catholic believers in a single political and economic whole, with a light central government and a high level of cantonal autonomy. It was a small-scale model for the peaceful and prosperous union that RCK strove for as he increasingly focused his thinking and writing on European issues.

His family was aristocratic, albeit from a part of the world where aristocratic titles had recently been abolished, and he could find no common ground for compromise with communists arguing in favour of one class, least of all the proletariat. Equally, he came from a multinational empire, now also abolished, and he had no common ground with nationalists who argued in favour of one nation. He wanted a regional political settlement for the continent as a whole, one that favoured neither one class nor one nation. In RCK's view, the idea of bringing European states closer together into a common political home desperately needed support from as wide a spectrum of political forces as possible, since nationalist resentment or class rivalry had the potential to spark armed conflict at any moment.

In Vienna at that time, many ideas were circulating about the future political and economic organization of the continent. They were all part of the intellectual turmoil that characterized the German-speaking world, in particular after the Great War. RCK had no specific political party allegiance, and in the struggle between parties of the left and the right, he remained ambivalent. His vision of Europe was, he claimed, überparteilich, above parties. Indeed, as a young man he was initially not unsympathetic to a socialist redistribution of wealth, so long as it was under the supervision of a select body of informed intellectuals, an aristocracy of the spirit. But the example of the Russian Revolution and subsequent Bolshevik rule pushed him more towards the conservative wing of politics. When RCK dispassionately reviewed the debate, he distinguished three divergent viewpoints that dominated all contemporary commentary – communist, nationalist, and pacifist – and he did not agree with any of them.[2]

Communists vehemently opposed the idea of European unity unless it was under the guidance of the Bolshevik vanguard of the working class, since a united bourgeois Europe would be in a position, they feared, to confront and contain the fledgling Soviet Union. To guard against that, and to go on the offensive, Lenin set up the Russian-dominated Comintern in 1919, with the aim of spreading proletarian revolution throughout the world. RCK was fundamentally opposed to atheistic Bolshevism, which he saw as antithetical to the Judeo-Christian inheritance of Europe, and he had no common ground with thinkers from this corner.

Nationalists were also hostile to any European framework, unless it was one which their own country dominated. Given its size and central geographical position, that meant Germany would dominate, and for Austrians, Anschluss with Germany implied subordinating the easier-going Catholicism of Vienna to the tougher Protestant and Prussian tradition of Berlin. RCK opposed that on principle, as much emotionally as intellectually, since it negated the whole Hapsburg and Austro-Hungarian tradition from which his family came. The small Austrian state would be swamped in such a union, because it had now lost all its old empire, while Germany had lost only Alsace-Lorraine in the west, Silesia and the further reaches of Prussia in the east, and in terms of population was still far larger than any other state in Europe. All RCK's instincts were Austrian rather than Prussian, and a German-dominated Europe, he feared, would mean an end to Austrian identity.

Pacifists, the third group, were committed as a matter of principle to the concept of universal peace. RCK considered pacifism impractical when applied as a universal principle. Peace was vitally important, but for him it was a means to ensure a higher goal: the freedom of Europe from external domination The peace movement was a powerful association of national pacifist organizations whose origins predated the Great War by many years, and that cataclysmic event had made it incomparably stronger in the post-war world. It celebrated a Peace Day each year, with public demonstrations and parades, incessantly lobbied parliamentarians, made its voice heard in the growing mass media of the age, and exerted a powerful influence on political opinion in all the democracies throughout the 1920s and 1930s.

Given the disastrous experience of the Great War, the League of Nations seemed to most pacifists the best practical security solution for a world otherwise characterized by international anarchy. They occupied the moral high ground, where peace meant universal peace, necessarily involving both Bolshevik Russia and the United States of America. Hence, many of them were hostile to any suggestion of an alternative that was simply European and regional. The moral force of the peace movement had a powerful influence on public opinion in every country, and by far its strongest section was the German Peace Society, headed by Alfred Hermann Fried.

RELUCTANT THOUGH HE ALWAYS WAS to acknowledge his intellectual debts, RCK owed a great deal to the peace movement generally, and to Fried in particular. He had first been introduced to Fried by Heinrich Glücksmann, editor of the Masonic newspaper in Vienna, the *Wiener Freimaurerzeitung*, when the fifty-five-year-old Fried returned to Austria from wartime exile in Switzerland. As director at the Deutsches Volkstheater in Vienna, Glücksmann was acquainted with Idel, who had a star contract there, and was soon on visiting terms with RCK and his wife. He also knew Fried well from pre-war years together in Vienna.

Fried appreciated the intellectual capacity, the ethical concern, and the youthful energy of Idel's young husband, and invited RCK to join him in a small Austrian delegation to a regional peace conference in Brunswick in late autumn 1920, where the two of them became better acquainted. Despite their differences, Fried recognized in RCK a younger kindred spirit, a dynamic disciple who could carry the ideas of the peace movement to wider circles, while RCK saw in his association with Fried the opportunity of harnessing the peace movement to disseminate his ideas about the future of Europe across the whole continent.

RCK admired Fried's clarity of thought and expression, and Fried's 1910 book on the Pan-American Union, *PanAmerika*, made a powerful impact on him. It demonstrated that economic co-operation, coupled with a degree of shared political sovereignty among nations, could lead to arms limitation and a system of international arbitration of disputes, the key precondition for peace. 'If we wish to substitute for war the settlement of disputes by justice,' wrote Fried, 'we must first substitute for the condition of international anarchy a condition of international order.' Pan-America was the model he cited. Disputes in America north and south were settled by a quasi-judicial procedure before an international bureau of the Pan-American Union, avoiding recourse to war. RCK could see the value of a comparable solution in Europe.[3]

Fried and RCK had much in common in their views of the contemporary political situation, but they differed in their assessment of pacifism itself as a principle. For Fried, peace was an ultimate value, while war was essentially a 'symptom of international anarchy'. For RCK, however, this was not necessarily so. War was simply to be abolished in Europe; that was RCK's more-limited aim. Only by maintaining peace among themselves, RCK argued, could the states of Europe rise again from the destruction of the First World War, restore their influence, and maintain their position in the world. 'States and peoples *should* arm against enemies,' he wrote: 'As a political programme, pacifism should in no way turn its back on the use of force: but it must use it only *against* war, not *for* it.' Not surprisingly, this was heresy to many in the peace movement and, temporarily at least, it distanced RCK from the leadership of the German movement, which reaffirmed the traditional universal principle of pacifism.[4]

RCK's personal friendship with Fried was also sadly brief. In May 1921, Fried unexpectedly died, aged just fifty-seven. He had been born into a poor Viennese family, had risen to fame through his work with the peace movement, and had been awarded the Nobel Peace Prize in 1911. His funeral was a major event in the city.

It may well also have been Glücksmann – like Fried, also a Freemason – who first encouraged RCK to join the Masonic brotherhood. In the autumn of the same year that Fried died, Glücksmann sponsored RCK's entry into the Viennese Lodge Humanitas. From his student years, RCK had much admired Plato and his concept of the Guardians, the self-selected group that ensured the right ordering of society, and his decision to become a Freemason was of a piece with his admiration for an aristocracy of the spirit. The notion of an all-male secret association, committed to self-improvement by progressing through degrees of knowledge and experience, and to the improvement of society by active social and political engagement, could not but appeal to this somewhat rootless young aristocrat.[5]

Writing in explanation of his decision to join the Masonic Lodge when he was just twenty-six years old, RCK set out his credo:

I wish to join a brotherhood in which many people together strive for the same ideals as those which move me. As a result of my parentage – my father was a European from the Flemish, Greek, Russian, Polish, German, and Norwegian nobility, my mother was a middle-class Japanese woman – I have no exclusive sense of belonging to any nationality, race, or class. I acknowledge a sense of belonging to the European, and in a narrower sense, to the German cultural community, but not in any national sense ... For all these reasons I can only call myself 'cosmopolitan' with the broadest possible degree of tolerance for foreigners and what is foreign, without the slightest national or social prejudice. My circle of acquaintances reaches into all social and professional spheres. I wish to join a community which is as international and cosmopolitan as I am, and whose central ideas contain the notions of international reconciliation and international brotherhood.

THE FOLLOWING YEAR the World Peace Conference took place in Prague, and it was well attended by Freemasons from Vienna, among them Richard Schlesinger and Wladmir Misar, from the Grand Lodge of Austria, and Dr Friedrich Hertz, a close colleague of theirs and a member of the Lodge Zukunft (Future). Hertz delivered a speech on the consequences for peace of the distressing economic situation in southeast Europe. On the strength of this, RCK invited him to work with him to develop his idea for a political movement that he hoped would grow from the manifesto he was planning. Hertz willingly accepted and was a pivotal figure in maintaining Masonic support for RCK's activities for many years, becoming secretary-general of the Pan-Europa Union when it was launched in 1924.

The support of other Freemasons was to prove invaluable for RCK in later stages of his life, but in all probability he was already acquainted with a prominent American Mason, Nicholas Murray Butler, who would later become one of his major benefactors. As early as October 1914, Murray Butler was interviewed by Edward Marshall, a well-known war correspondent, in the *New York Times*. In the interview, he singled out two key American experiences that Europeans, he argued, should take to heart when the war was over. First, just as north and south in the United States had been reconciled after the Civil War, so different races in Europe – Celts, Latins, Teutons, and Slavs – could live together in amity, once social and political conditions encouraged peaceful coexistence rather than exacerbated traditional hostility. Second, America demonstrated 'the great example of success of the principle of federation in its application to unity of political life regardless of local, economic and racial differences.' RCK would hold onto those two principles – reconciliation and federation – throughout his life.[6]

RCK contributed actively to debates both within the peace movement and among Freemasons, for instance with a public lecture on the first anniversary of Fried's death, entitled 'Nation als Kirche' ('The Nation as a Church') – subsequently printed and highly commended by the Grand Lodge of Austria as reading for fellow Masons – and a long article on 'Die europäische Frage' ('The European Question') in the Zürich journal of the Peace Society, *Die Friedenswarte*. But he was also learning fast from his wider reading and other personal acquaintances. Kurt Hiller and Maximilian Harden were in Berlin, but closer at hand were Rudolf Kassner, Graf Keyserling, Rudolf Pannwitz, and Klaus Haushofer, writers whose works RCK read and with whom he and Idel socialized on friendly terms.

Rudolf Kassner, despite being stricken with polio as a child, had already travelled the world when he settled in Vienna before the start of the Great War. A translator and cultural philosopher, he wrote an obscurely titled essay 'Zahl und Gesicht' ('Number and Face') in 1919. In it he propounded a conservative cultural revolution, arguing that analytic reason led to measurement and quantity, thus failing to grasp the importance of all that could be called quality. It was music to RCK's ears.

Hermann Graf Keyserling's massive tome, *Reisetagebuch eines Philosophen* (*The Diary of a Travelling Philosopher*), was written during the First World War and appeared to popular acclaim in 1920. Interspersed with traveller's tales of the many destinations he had visited in India, China, and the United States, as well as Europe, Keyserling's reflections on his travels attempted a reconciliation of Western and Eastern views on philosophy, between the development of an active personality and the passive acceptance of the individual's place – and limited relevance – in the vastness of all creation. In simple terms, it was a mixture of the philosophical traditions of Christianity and Buddhism, something very appealing to RCK, as in some ways it mirrored the philosophical concerns of his father, Heinrich. Keyserling returned the compliment of RCK's admiration by supporting the younger man's Pan-European ideas for the rest of his life.

RCK also maintained an extensive correspondence with Rudolf Pannwitz, a writer on cultural history, ten years older than himself, who lived on the Adriatic coast and was less often in Vienna. His main work *Die Krisis der europäischen Kultur* (*The Crisis of European Culture*) was published in 1917, and for RCK its particular attraction lay in its re-evaluation of Napoleon. For Pannwitz, as for RCK, Napoleon was the archetype of the Strong Leader, a progressive, classless innovator, the man who in his memoirs declared that all European wars were civil wars.[7]

RCK also learnt a great deal from Klaus Haushofer, a family friend and soon to be the first Professor of Geopolitics at the University of Munich. The term 'geopolitics' had been coined at the end of the nineteenth century by Rudolf Kjellen, a Swedish political scientist, and the geographical, political, military, economic, and demographic implications were much debated in intellectual circles. Like the notion of propaganda, it later acquired a bad name, because many of its concepts were exploited by the Nazis and used to justify the conquest of territory in Eastern Europe, *Lebensraum*, which ensured economic self-sufficiency for the German state. Whoever controls the heartland of Central Europe, wrote Haushofer, controls the whole continent. RCK borrowed several ideas from Haushofer's analysis of geopolitics, applying them to Europe as a whole, however, rather than to Germany.

In 1922, RCK published a long essay entitled 'Apologie der Technik' ('In Defence of Technology'), which explored the role of technology and innovation in society. Improvements in transport and communications, he argued, were daily becoming more apparent. Time and space were shrinking as information – as well as raw materials, industrial goods, and armies – travelled faster. Writing as early-twentieth-century globalization was gathering pace, he was particularly impressed by manned flight and predicted the serious implications of air power for international relations. The practical consequence, he argued, was that the states of Europe could no longer assure their citizens' security from aerial attack. They were no longer fit for purpose, and therefore had every interest in merging into a single federation that could effectively protect their common borders at the periphery of the continent. While the need to come together in this way might be dictated by technology and security, this should be seen as an opportunity rather than a weakness. European states, he argued, would inevitably gain additional influence in the world if they acted together.

Another of his publications that year was a shorter, but more controversial, essay entitled 'Adel' ('Nobility'). Characterized by RCK as 'more aesthetic than mathematical truth', it concerned social ideals. Through a series of stimulating comparisons or opposites, such as town and country, intellectual and Junker, gentleman and bohemian, pagan and Christian, he speculated about what he called the 'crisis of nobility' in contemporary society. He charted the historical evolution of human society from dominance by force of arms in feudal times to dominance by capital and by brain power in the contemporary world, and he contrasted the decline of the hereditary aristocracy with the rise of a plutocratic class. He pointed approvingly to Jews as examples of a new intellectual aristocracy in business, journalism, literature, and the arts, concluding with the prognosis that a generation led by noble individuals, the new 'aristocracy of the spirit', would arise from the progressive mixing of races and classes. He analysed the importance of the shift from rural to urban living in the developed countries of the continent, and saw that the less developed would inevitably follow suit, as economic innovation and modernization accelerated this trend.[8]

RCK's analysis of the forms of contemporary democracy that were actually developing in European states in the 1920s fundamentally questioned the ethical assumption behind democracy, the notion of equality for all before the law. He went so far along this Nietzschean road as to endorse eugenics, caring less about the elimination of weaker specimens than the survival of the fittest, the best. For him, 'the best' were the most intelligent, the most cultured, the noblest, and the most beautiful in society. The pursuit of equality, vulgarly interpreted as the extension of the franchise to all society, was contrary to this ideal. For him, cultures developed through the interaction of the thoughts and deeds of great men, with the admiration, support, and imitation of the masses. The former were indispensible, the latter simply offered complementary amplification of their leaders' originality.

This desire to preserve and cultivate the noblest and most highly developed minds and bodies – nobility both in body and mind – underlay his aversion to war, since in modern warfare, so he argued, numbers counted more than the quality of individuals, and force trumped intelligence. He callously remarked that the ten million dead of the First World War were replaceable, but not the ten among them who might have been geniuses. This line of thought brought him ever closer to the corporatist and fascist positions that his youthful ideal, Mussolini, epitomized. Little wonder that he wanted Mussolini to take the lead in promoting his ideas of European unity.

RCK CERTAINLY NEEDED an ethical compass as he charted the turbulent moral currents of political life in the post-war years. But it was ironic that, while he was clearly moving far away from traditional Christian values, he adopted a motto drawn from the writings of St Augustine, both for himself and for the Pan-Europa Union, his political movement for European unity. He chose 'In necesariis unitas, in dubiis libertas, in omnibus caritas' (In matters which are certain, unity; in matters which are doubtful, liberty; in all things, charity).

His Austro-Hungarian and aristocratic background, as well as the international ethos of his education, predisposed RCK to think in terms of continents rather than countries. That was the result of his upbringing with a European father and an Asian mother and of his select Theresianum education. But his big idea – the world organized around a limited number of centres of power – came to him one day, he said, when he was idly playing with a globe that stood beside his desk. Turning the globe under his fingers, he realized just how small Austria now was. Compared to the former Austro-Hungarian Empire, that was obvious, and compared to the European continent, even more so. Even big states like France and Germany were small when seen in the context of the whole globe. From that perspective, only extremely large actors had a role, and – regrettably – none of the continental European states were among them.

The United States had already started down the road that would make it a world power, drawing the states of Central and South America into a Pan-American Union (formally established in 1924), and applying the Munroe Doctrine that excluded other states from interfering in the affairs of that region. Great Britain, likewise, relying on the Royal Navy to control the seas, exercised its power in Europe, Africa, Asia, and North America, welding its far-flung empire together into a single political entity, Pan-Britannia. Russia, now organized across so much of the Eurasian landmass as the Soviet Union, unified by the Bolshevik ideology and backed by the vast natural resources of Siberia, was likewise a single power centre, keen to spread its influence wider still through the Comintern. In the Far East there was a growing Asian identity that, for all the differences between China and Japan, made it a fourth power centre. The globe showed clearly that continental Europe – from the borders of Russia to the Atlantic Ocean, and from the Arctic to the Mediterranean – was really also one geographic entity. Looked at as a whole, and not as the twenty-six separate states of his day, it too was potentially another power centre, especially if its colonial dependencies in Africa and Asia were included.

But, however culturally united and geographically contiguous its states were, Europe was still divided politically. To gain a role in the modern world, the states of Europe needed to co-operate and unite politically, and not compete and clash economically. Europe needed to catch up before it was too late, particularly before either America or Russia enclosed it within its own sphere of influence. Individually, European states would always be weak, but together they could become a mighty force, potentially a force for peace, both internally within their own continent, and externally in Europe's dealings with the rest of the world.[9]

This realization was for RCK a moment of truth. Europe must unite, both in order to ensure internal peace for its own citizens, and to restore the continent to its position as an arbiter of world affairs, the position its former great powers once filled before the disaster of the First World War cast them low. That was a vision to inspire his generation, the youth of Europe, and it was the Utopia that his political movement would make a reality.

This vision continued to haunt him through the early 1920s, as he published provocative political articles, promoting his ideas and raising his public profile. 'Europas technische Weltmission' ('Europe's Global Technological Mission') was an early article in the *Neue Merkur*, a leading monthly literary periodical, followed by 'Europas Erlösung' ('Europe's Salvation') in the *Vossische Zeitung*, the established newspaper of record in Berlin, and 'Pan-Europa: ein Vorschlag' ('Pan-Europa: A Proposal') in *Die Neue Freie Presse*, the popular Viennese daily. Disappointingly, he complained, the few dozen responses he received to all these attempts to rouse public opinion about the future of Europe – 'mainly from cranks and obsessives' – was quite inadequate for his purposes. He realized he needed something more than just articles and lectures to enthuse a generation and kick-start his political movement.

And RCK would not give up. His gifted and powerful wife supported him in this. They shared a peaceful vision of Europe's future that was fundamentally superior to any nationalist or class solution, and they were both confident that the wider public would appreciate this. They wanted to remain above party politics and outside state institutions, to preserve their independence at all costs. As an intellectual, RCK intended both to remain his own man *and* become an influential public figure. He resolved to write his manifesto as a political blockbuster, making a name for himself as Oswald Spengler had done with *The Decline of the West*. He would be both a thinker and a man of action, author of his own programme and leader of a continent-wide political movement.

7

PAN-EUROPA:
UTOPIA OR REALITY?

IN THEIR ACTIVE VIENNESE SOCIAL LIFE, RCK and Idel frequented a number of literary salons, including one hosted by Frau Andy von Zsolnay, the wife of a rich Hungarian tobacco merchant who was now honorary Austrian consul general to the new state of Czechoslovakia. The Zsolnay country estate, Schloss Oberufer, was a short journey downstream on the Danube from Vienna, not far from Pressburg (now Bratislava), and RCK and Idel occasionally attended weekend parties there. Paul von Zsolnay, Frau Andy's son, set up a publishing house in 1922 and went on to be the most influential Austrian publisher of the twenties and thirties.[1] When RCK's Leipzig publisher went bankrupt during the great inflation in early 1923, RCK received merely a few complimentary copies instead of the royalties that he was owed. RCK took Paul's advice to set up his own publishing house, Pan-Europa Verlag, so that in future he could ensure that he kept both editorial and financial control over all aspects of what he would publish for his grand new project, Pan-Europa.[2]

RCK and Idel also enjoyed the company of Willy Gutmann, a successful Viennese industrialist, and his wife, Stephanie. They had recently bought Schloss Würting, a Renaissance residence at Offenhausen in Upper Austria, halfway between Linz and Salzburg, and were now making it a meeting place for artists and writers. Knowing that RCK would not have peace and quiet to write his book in the social whirl of Vienna, the Gutmanns happily suggested that RCK and Idel should come and stay with them at Würting. It was there, over three weeks either side of Easter 1923, that RCK wrote *Pan-Europa*, the book that set out his vision for a united Europe and was to inspire a generation. It would determine the future course of his life – and influence the course of European history.

RCK wrote in the introduction, 'This book is designed to awaken a great political movement that at present is slumbering in all the peoples of Europe.' In barely one hundred and fifty pages, *Pan-Europa* offered historical analysis, geopolitical prognosis, and policy recommendations. The core of the *Pan-Europa* message was simple: Europe was weak because European states were divided among themselves. United, they would be strong. Their rivalry, which culminated in the Great War, destroyed their global hegemony, opening the door to the rivalry of Bolshevik Russia on the one hand and capitalist America on the other. Power now lay not with European nations but with two new players on the global scene. The present geopolitical situation, RCK argued, forced the states of Europe to 'unite or die'. Together, they could assure peace on their continent, and also exercise real influence on the world stage once more. He challenged his young readers to transform the 'Utopia' of his vision into the 'reality of tomorrow'.

Pan-Europa ranged widely, with chapters considering Europe's position in the world, continental Europe's borders, England and Russia (both of which RCK excluded at this time from his proposed continental union), and the League of Nations. The book also reviewed relations between Germany and France, the prospect of a future war, and what RCK called the 'National Question', the tangle of issues concerning sovereignty and identity – linguistic, historical, geographic, and economic. A final chapter indicated the way ahead: The Road to Pan-Europa.

Three simple tables completed the slim volume. One listed the states and micro-states that made up the Europe of his day, together with their African colonies, their relative size, and their populations. A second showed basic statistics – area and population – for the five dominant power centres in the world: Pan-Europa, Pan-America, the Russian Federation, East Asia, and the British Empire. The third was a map of the world – his globe laid flat on the page – that allowed readers to visualize the geopolitical structure in which he situated this international drama.

In an echo of Spengler's approach to the study of civilizations, RCK recounted how historically European powers filled the vacuum left by the collapse of earlier Asian empires – Chinese, Persian, and Ottoman. He illustrated the positive record of European influence world-wide, quoting as pluses the colonization of Africa, British control of India, and the recent populating of empty territories such as Australia and Canada. At the beginning of the twentieth century, major European states – England, Russia, Germany, Austria-Hungary, and France – ruled the world. Only the Americas, led by the United States, had escaped control by the great powers of Europe and asserted their own independence.

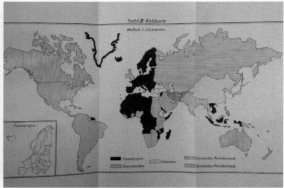

RCK published *Pan-Europa* in 1923, listing the five Pan regions of the world: Paneuropa, Panamerika, East-Asia, the Russian Federation, and the British Federation.

But the Great War had changed all that. Europe, he argued, was no longer the political, economic, or cultural power centre of a world which, by 1918, had 'emancipated itself' from European control. European states now ran the risk of themselves becoming the object of other states' policies, rather than independent actors on the world stage, with the United States chairing deliberations over the fate of Europe at the Paris Peace Conference a powerful reminder of Europe's weakness.

RCK explained that the progress of technology also worked against the individual states of Europe ever regaining their pre-eminent position in world affairs. The application of steam power, the internal combustion engine, electricity, and, most recently, manned flight had so reduced the importance of distance and time that individual states within the small European extension of the Asian landmass were no longer safe from the predations of each other or their larger neighbours in the rest of the world.

There were now five centres, which RCK called 'planetary force fields', around which world powers could be created: America, Britain, Russia, East Asia, and Europe. His message was clear. If Europe learnt nothing from its history, it would become – like the Holy Roman Empire in earlier centuries – politically and militarily the object of the policies of other powers, 'the chessboard of the world'.

After this warning, RCK disentangled the geographical and political definitions of Europe, distinguishing between *Weltteile* – continents (Eurasia, Africa, Australia, North and South America); *Weltreiche* – centres of political power (America, Europe, East-Asia, Russia, and the British

Empire); and *Weltkulturen* – world cultures (European, Chinese, Indian, and Arabian). Against the background of these distinctions, RCK then laid out the historical analysis which led to his Pan-European solution.

He claimed that Alexander the Great created the 'first Europe', a Eurasian empire, bridging geographical and ethnic divides within one pan-Hellenic culture. Ancient Rome created the 'second Europe', essentially around the Mediterranean. The division of the Roman Empire separated the Catholic West from the Orthodox East, and Constantinople then became the capital of a new Eurasian empire. The 'third Europe' was the result of the migration of tribes and reached its apogee with Charlemagne. However, the Europe that he ruled was smaller than the earlier Europe, as it excluded Moorish Spain and extended in the East only as far as the Elbe.

When Charlemagne's inheritance was divided, unified political control in Europe was lost. RCK argued that it fell to the Popes to maintain, rebuild, and extend the notion of Europe – the 'fourth Europe' – by spreading Christianity. In the east they brought Christianity to Hungary, Poland, and Lithuania, and in the west to Spain and Portugal. This Europe reached its apogee at the beginning of the thirteenth century under Innocent III, whose spiritual realm lent a sense of European religious unity to the many temporal rulers within it.

That sense of religious unity was shattered by the Reformation, which led to the 'fifth Europe' of the Enlightenment, characterized politically by absolute monarchies. It was during this period that, following the Mongol retreat, Peter the Great renewed the European credentials of Russia and fixed the Urals as a political frontier. The high point of this Europe, according to RCK's analysis, was the establishment of French continental hegemony under Napoleon. His empire renewed the idea of European unity and, despite military defeat, the idea lived on. Reactionary leaders might have brought him low, but the intellectual elite of Europe sympathized with much of what he and revolutionary France had represented.

After Napoleon, RCK posited that people in Europe could identify themselves as progressive Europeans as well as members of their respective nations. Throughout the nineteenth century, conservative nationalists were opposed by progressive Europeans, the spirit of Metternich opposed by the spirit of Mazzini. As the legacy of the French Revolution spread ideals of republican unity across all European nations, the struggle for supremacy between progressive and reactionary forces lasted right up to the First World War.

The late-nineteenth and early-twentieth centuries saw both Britain and Russia move away from Europe politically. Great Britain became the leader of an intercontinental empire, with interests that transcended Europe, and subsequently Russia turned its back on European values by establishing an atheistic, proletarian dictatorship within the new Soviet Union. Hence RCK restricted his vision of Pan-Europa to a continental union, excluding both Russia and the British Empire.

'Pan-Europa must be constituted without England,' RCK asserted, 'but not against England.' England, he noted prophetically, might join Pan-Europa later when the British Empire had dissolved, but meanwhile England would be an intermediary, a messenger, a link between Pan-Europa and Pan-America 'without belonging politically to the one or the other'.

He contended that Britannia might at the moment rule the waves, but given the advance of technology, planes and submarines could soon threaten the security of Great Britain and starve the Empire's homeland into surrender. In the light of this, friendly relations between Britain and Pan-Europa were essential, an *entente* to guarantee peace. That would assure England that Pan-Europa was the opposite of what historically had been England's enduring foreign-policy nightmare, a single power ruling the European continent. On the contrary, Pan-Europa was a peace project, bringing the continent together by agreement and mutual interest, not by force of arms, and with no desire for conquest.

As for relations with Russia, however, RCK's envisaged Pan-Europa as a mutual defence pact *against* the Soviet Union, the very opposite of the good relations Pan-Europa would pursue with England. 'The single greatest goal of all Europeans, of whatever party or nation,' he wrote, 'should be to prevent a Russian invasion.' He expanded this, explaining that Russia's relation to Europe was like Macedonia's relation to ancient Greece: both a source of strength and of danger, able to exploit disunity, to divide and to conquer. In order to prevent any further rapprochement between Germany and Russia – foreshadowed in the Treaty of Rapallo, signed in 1922, the year before he wrote *Pan-Europa* – RCK argued that 'it depends on the powers in the West, above all on France, whether Germany is saved for Europe – or is pushed away from Europe.'

Within the cluster of European states lying between the Soviet Union and the British Isles, the Great War, which he likened to a European civil war, decided the struggle of ideas in favour of Mazzini's progressive vision and against Metternich's reactionary ideal. As old dynastic empires fell across Europe, new nations gained their freedom, and modern Europe became essentially republican and democratic, opening the way for the 'sixth Europe', the Pan-European federation that, RCK declared, would usher in the United States of Europe.

RCK's vision of Pan-Europa at that time included twenty-six states[3] and a further seven small territories: the Saar, Danzig, Fiume, Monaco, San Marino, Liechtenstein, and Andorra. Together they covered roughly 5 million square kilometres and contained about 300 million people. If their dependent colonies were included, the figures rose to 26 million square kilometres and 431 million people, making Pan-Europa almost as large and as populous as the British Empire at that time, and double the population of Pan-America, his contemporary inspirational model. This alliance, he declared, could be independent in raw materials and in food, if only European states would co-operate, instead of competing with each other. Pan-Europa, together with its colonies, would become one of the five great powers of the world.

In a gesture towards the peace movement, RCK argued that securing internal peace within Europe would of necessity lead to peace externally. A united Europe would be obliged to conclude treaties with England, Russia, Pan-America, and East Asia. These would involve international arbitration instead of recourse to arms to settle disputes. European peace was the key that would open the door to world peace.

RCK could brook no neutrality in what he saw as a question of life and death for Europe. Whoever ignored or opposed this existential solution for uniting Europe, he wrote, and so indirectly lent succour to those who wanted to foment war among European states, 'commits high treason against his own people, against Europe, and against the whole of mankind.'

RCK was not a trained economist, and his analysis of economic issues was often painted with a broad brush, but it was no less persuasive for that. In *Pan-Europa*, he listed six main causes of monetary chaos, unemployment, and social misery in Europe: first, the wartime destruction of markets, manufacturing, manpower, and morale; second, the exclusion of Russia from Europe economically following the Bolshevik Revolution and the Allied blockade, leading to the country's economic collapse; third, the wasted expense of national rearmament programmes; fourth, the unsolved problem of reparations; fifth, indebtedness to foreign powers; and finally, the artificial segmentation of the Central European market as a consequence of the Treaties of Versailles, St Germain, Trianon, Neuilly, and Sèvres.

Despite these problems, for RCK there was no choice for any responsible statesman but to accept Versailles and the subsequent treaties. To open up the issue of the independence of new states again, or to try to change their borders now, would simply invite renewed fighting and political chaos. Five years after the end of the Great War, he suggested that reparations should be treated essentially as an economic, rather than a political, issue. Hand in hand with the negotiated reduction of reparations should go the reduction, if possible the elimination, of customs duties. Recognizing existing borders and working to eliminate tariffs, he argued, would lead to the United States of Europe, where 'state borders will lose their importance and sink to the level of mere administrative boundaries'.

RCK well knew that rivalry between Germany and France, the two largest powers in continental Europe, was the greatest obstacle to developing his vision of the United States of Europe. They were both now democratic republics, but the historic animosity between them was stronger than reason, stronger even than their mutual interests. France, he argued in *Pan-Europa*, had the choice between a foreign policy that would try to destroy Germany or a policy that would reconcile the two nations. Germany likewise had a choice between national imperialism or European engagement. Their joint choice was either to have a permanently armed frontier dividing them, or to sign a Europe-wide peace treaty that allied the interests of both states. National chauvinists in France and Germany were linked in an unholy alliance, he argued, determined to push each country's foreign policies towards war. All who wished Europe well needed to turn that vicious circle into a virtuous circle by working to frustrate the chauvinists' plans. All European states should therefore adopt Pan-Europa as their foreign policy.

Although writing in German, RCK was appealing to an audience in several nations at the same time, and his remarks in *Pan-Europa* on the 'National Question' were particularly revealing. Nations, he argued, were a symbiosis of great men and the wider populace. Through their different histories, each nation had developed a common language, a common culture, and often a common religion. What RCK recognized as a nation was a community of the spirit (*Geistesgemeinschaft*), created though noble actions and inspiring artistic creation and a shared narrative of its history. RCK argued that everyone who could master a second language could share, through conversation and reading, some aspects of the wider European community of the spirit, as could those who simply enjoyed music and the visual arts.

All that was great in European culture was interrelated, resting on a Greco-Christian base and sharing a common history from the time of the Romans to the rise of socialism. Whether from the Romance, Germanic, or Slav traditions, Europeans, he argued, were carriers of a civilization of global significance, which had achieved great things in all realms of human thought and action, and which had the potential to deliver even more in the future. For him, there was self-evidently a European identity, and hence a European nation, and all Europeans could aspire to join it. His vision was the very opposite of Hitler's idea of a community exclusively defined on the basis of race (*Blutgemeinschaft*), a nation from which lesser breeds were inevitably and explicitly excluded by heredity.

As a description and a prognosis, RCK's book was clear and succinct, but he was simply an author, not a political leader. He had no means to put his programme into effect. For that he still needed a statesman to take the initiative. So, in the concluding chapter of *Pan-Europa*, he invited contemporary leaders, any one of them who shared his vision, to call an international conference to establish as a first step a system of obligatory international arbitration – a Court of Justice – and then to prepare treaties guaranteeing mutual security.

He listed other key issues that needed to be debated and agreed upon together, including disarmament, minorities, transport, tariffs, monetary issues, indebtedness, and mutual respect for national cultures. This initial conference should not be just a single event, but should start a process of co-operation. It should create an institution, a central Pan-Europa secretariat, to co-ordinate future action and plan future decisions, moving on to create a customs union, a common economic area, and a common monetary zone – possibly several, he conceded, coming together in stages – on the way to creating a single currency. The apex of such a structure would be the establishment of a United States of Europe, loosely based on the model of the United States of America.

Inside such a federation, RCK proposed that each state would enjoy a maximum of freedom, while externally all would speak with a single voice. Its legislature would be structured, as in America, by a House of the People, with one representative for every million inhabitants, and a House of the States, with just one representative from each state. All national languages would be treated equally, but all schools would teach English, since English was already becoming an international lingua franca, 'the natural Esperanto'.

The advantages for each state in joining such a European federation would include guaranteed peace with its neighbours inside the federation, a neutral stance for Europe in world conflicts, protection from invasion by Russia, the benefits of disarmament, and increased prosperity through improved competitiveness against American and British industry. The security of all participating states' African colonies would be guaranteed by the federation, and the joint enterprise of all Europeans would develop these sources of food and raw materials. Major environmental and public-health projects – such as the transformation of the Sahara into agricultural land and the elimination of tropical diseases – would be better realized by the enhanced engineering and medical skills of a united Europe than by the efforts of any one country.

The consequences of carrying on as separate states would be disastrous, he argued presciently. Nationalism and competition would lead to a new European war, even more external interference – militarily and politically – in the internal affairs of the continent, quite possibly a Russian invasion, and the establishment of dictatorship in Europe. Nations would feel they must rearm to the point of financial exhaustion, and that would lead to diminishing competitiveness vis-à-vis Anglo-Saxon industry, with subsequent bankruptcy and economic enslavement.

RCK's final claim for his vision of Pan-Europa was that it would ensure the democratic future of participating states equally against Bolshevism and against Reaction. Communists on the left and chauvinists on the right wanted it to fail, he argued, the former in order to further the interests of the Soviet Union, the latter to secure unlimited sovereignty for their particular nation state. Elected democrats in all continental states, he argued, should oppose both Communists and chauvinists by supporting the creation of Pan-Europa as their common foreign policy. Pan-Europa as a European federation would maintain peace better than the looser, intergovernmental League of Nations, while also preserving internally in each nation political structures that were essentially democratic.

RCK could clearly see that his political federation needed to rest on the legitimacy of public opinion, which, he was sure, would quickly be convinced of its Pan-European identity. Publishing *Pan-Europa* was for him just the opening of an extensive public-relations campaign that would culminate in a shared sense of European patriotism. Public opinion in favour of Pan-Europa would then force governments down the necessary path of peaceful co-operation. European patriotism would take its place as the crowning complement of everyone's pride in their individual nation. At that point Pan-Europa would have moved from the realm of Utopia to become a practical reality.

ONCE HE HAD WRITTEN HIS BOOK, RCK set about getting for it as much publicity as possible. Before publication he sent advance copies to several newspaper editors, prominent among them Georg Bernhard, at the left-liberal *Vossische Zeitung* in Berlin, and Ernst Benedikt, at the more

conservative *Neue Freie Presse* in Vienna. He also distributed complimentary copies among his and Idel's circle of friends, and sent copies to
leading politicians across Europe. In September, he wrote an article himself for the *Vienna Masonic Newspaper*, entitled 'Paneuropa and Pacifism'.
Freemasons as well as members of the peace movement certainly could not
miss his book when it appeared the following month, and through them
he trusted that it would reach into an even-wider discerning public.

RCK had written well and judged correctly. When it appeared in
October 1923, *Pan-Europa* struck a chord in intellectual and political circles, with enthusiastic reviews both in Vienna and Berlin. The first edition of five thousand copies sold out immediately, and a second edition
appeared within a month. Each copy contained a prepaid reply card, asking readers if they agreed with the idea of Pan-Europa. With no further commitment, sending back the card automatically made the reader a
member of the Pan-Europa Union, the not-for-profit foundation RCK had
set up to further the campaign in favour of his programme. RCK received
over a thousand signed replies within the first month. By the end of the
following year, *Pan-Europa* had sold over twenty-five thousand copies, and
in 1925 sixteen thousand more. It was a political best seller, and the Pan-
Europa Union now had members. His name and his brand were publicly
recognized at last.

Idel had a large hand in the organizational preparation of the Pan-
Europa Union, as had Friedrich Hertz, RCK's fellow Mason, who became
its secretary-general. They devised the reply cards and sent out the complimentary copies, discussed together how its members would be the shock
troops, the spearhead, of a popular movement across the continent. RCK
gave himself the title of 'President for Life' of the Pan-Europa Union. He
needed little encouragement in this direction, and wags in the Viennese
press suggested that he and Idel were angling to become the president and
first lady of the new United States of Europe.

Friedrich Hertz also encouraged the Grand Lodge of Austria to recommend *Pan-Europa* to fellow Masons internationally. Grand Master
Wladimir Misar wrote to Masonic Lodges around the world, comparing
the ideas of peace and brotherhood presented in RCK's book with the core
values of Freemasonry. The book and the author merited attention and
support, he added, by all brother Masons. Richard Schlesinger, an influential Mason in the Grand Lodge of Austria, also ensured that financial
as well as moral support for RCK was forthcoming from the Brotherhood.

8

TAKING EUROPE
TO THE CAPITALS

JUST AS EVENTS were taking this happy course for RCK in Vienna, politics took a very different turn in Munich. On 8 November 1923, Hitler and General Ludendorff, the highly-decorated commander of the German army on the Western front at the end of the Great War, led an armed putsch against the Bavarian government. The two of them planned to take control in Bavaria and then to march on Berlin, imitating the successful march of Mussolini's Blackshirts on Rome just twelve months before. However, their plans were frustrated by army units loyal to the Bavarian government. Hitler fled the scene of the first armed clash, only to be captured a few days later, hiding in the countryside. He was charged with high treason.

RCK had no cause to know the name of Hitler before this failed putsch, but the media coverage of his trial early in 1924 gave Hitler such publicity that RCK could not then fail to form an opinion about the man and his politics. Hitler used his trial as a platform to promote what he claimed was his patriotic cause against the treachery of the leaders of the Weimar Republic, who had accepted the unjust Versailles Treaty with the imposition of excessive reparations on Germany. While serving his relatively lenient jail sentence in comfortable conditions in the Landsberg prison, Hitler then set about putting down his own story by writing *Mein Kampf*.

While in detention, Rudolf Hess, another of the conspirators, who would later become Hitler's deputy in the Nazi Party, introduced him to Klaus Haushofer, then professor of geopolitics at Munich University. Hess and Haushofer were fellow officers in a reserve regiment, and Hess was also Haushofer's research assistant at the university. Haushofer made sure Hitler was well briefed on international politics, in particular the implications of the notion of 'Pan-regions'. He would certainly have drawn Hitler's attention to RCK's recent book on *Pan-Europa*, and explained the

geopolitical concept of a peacefully united Europe between the opposing forces of communism and capitalism, of the Soviet Union and the
United States of America. That was not how Hitler envisaged the future
of Europe. Europe, he argued, needed German leadership and German
strength to stand up to these world powers militarily. Germany needed
Europe as its own backyard, as *Lebensraum*, a key economic region to be
conquered and dominated by the Aryan race.

In conversation with Klaus Haushofer a few years later, RCK would ask
him why Rudolf Hess, who seemed to him a reasonable man, had become a
Nazi and gone over so whole-heartedly to Hitler, even to the point of being
appointed his deputy. Why had not an intelligent man like Hess joined
Pan-Europa? In Haushofer's opinion, it was all a matter of timing. If Hess
had met RCK before he had met Hitler, he would certainly have joined Pan-
Europa. Hess simply wanted a charismatic leader whom he could follow.

The first volume of *Mein Kampf* was published in July 1925, about eighteen months after RCK published *Pan-Europa*. It sold just under ten thousand copies that year, and a second volume appeared in 1926. The third
volume (in which Hitler roundly condemned RCK as a 'cosmopolitan bastard') was written in 1927 and 1928, but not published then, since Hitler's
publisher thought it would hurt sales of the first two volumes, which were
not selling well at that time.[1]

Overlapping the publication dates of *Mein Kampf*, RCK also published
three volumes of his story, entitled *Mein Kampf um Europa*. They appeared
in 1925, 1927, and 1928, and reflected the early years of the Pan-Europa
movement with compilations of his articles and speeches. Although
RCK's and Hitler's books could hardly have been more different in tone or
in content, their titles are confusingly similar. Hitler and RCK were each
trying to build a political movement, to have readers and to have followers,
but each offered a different vision of Europe that he wished to turn into
political reality. For RCK, a Pan-European union was a step towards continental unity through international agreement in the common interest.
For Hitler, Europe's unity was to be achieved by way of German domination and territorial expansion across the continent.

Organizationally, they also approached their tasks from opposite positions. Hitler attempted to gain power by starting from the bottom, organizing a small band of followers through relentless propaganda work,
rabble-rousing speeches, street violence, and even insurrection. RCK
started from above, appealing to established statesmen with an intellectually demanding programme, now in the form of a book, and an international voluntary association that attracted a thinking elite, essentially

from the middle and upper classes. The two men were rivals, with aims that were mutually exclusive; appealing to different audiences, the one national and populist, the other international and liberal. With the vantage of hindsight, we know who 'won' – at least in the short term – but at the time it was by no means a foregone conclusion.

INITIALLY IT MAY WELL HAVE SEEMED as if RCK and Pan-Europa had the better chance. Just before Hitler went on trial in Munich in early 1924, RCK struck gold in Vienna. Baron Louis Rothschild, head of the prominent Jewish banking house and a fellow Freemason, told Max Warburg, a Hamburg banking colleague, about this promising young man and his political ideas. Early in January, Max Warburg phoned RCK in Vienna to say he had read *Pan-Europa*, agreed with much of what RCK had written, and wanted to meet him. The upshot of the meeting was an offer of sixty thousand gold marks, equivalent to three thousand pounds sterling then, or nearly a quarter of a million pounds at today's prices. The condition was that it was seed money to fund RCK's political movement, the Pan-Europa Union, for the next three years, and that it would not be repeated. Half would be for the movement's development in Germany and the other half for the rest of Europe.[2]

This game-changing financial support was all the more appreciated by RCK as Austria was just climbing out of a disastrous period of inflation, which, as in Germany, had undermined trust in the old currency. With the assurance of this financial backing, he was able to step up his propaganda activities. In April that year, he published the first copy of his movement's regular *Pan-Europa Journal* from the offices of the Pan-Europa Union's own new publishing house with its own printing presses.

Apart from Max Warburg's generous gesture, RCK was not without his own funds, thanks both to his modest inheritance and to the earnings of his actress wife. During the 1920s she was earning six thousand Austrian schillings per performance, which was only slightly less for one performance than the average income for a working man for a whole year. The productions with her most popular roles – in *Die Zarin* and *Die Rote Mühle*, for instance – ran for over sixty performances each, and a run of fifteen to twenty performances for other plays in which she starred was usual. Her income, if sometimes erratic, was considerable.[3]

Indirect financial support was also forthcoming from other sources. Ignaz Seipel, the Catholic priest and university lecturer who was Austrian

RCK and Idel's apartment
in Heiligenkreuzerhof, the
embassy of Pan-Europa.

In diesem Haus, in der Prälatur des Heiligenkreuzer Hofes,
lebte der Gründer der Paneuropa-Union
und geistige Vater der europäischen Einigung,

RICHARD GRAF COUDENHOVE-KALERGI.

Von hier aus floh er in der Nacht
von 11. auf 12. März 1938 vor den
Okkupationstruppen des nationalsozialistischen Deutschland.

Die Paneuropabewegung
Österreich

Anlässlich des 40. Todestages
am 27. Juli 2012

chancellor from 1922 to 1924 and again from 1926 to 1929, accepted the
chairmanship of the Austrian branch of the Pan-Europa Union, and
offered RCK a suite of rooms for the offices of the Pan-Europa Union very
close to his own office on the Marschallstiege in the Hofburg, the seat of
government in Vienna. RCK was more than glad to accept, as it gave him
the very best address in all Austria – simply 'Hofburg, Wien'. RCK held on
to this privilege of rent-free headquarters for the Pan-Europa Union, courtesy of successive chancellors, until the Nazis annexed the country in 1938.

RCK was less successful in his attempt to acquire a service flat in the
Hofburg. He pleaded with officials and petitioned ministers, using the
excuse that, given the number and status of international visitors, he and
his wife were now having to entertain, VIPs should not have to climb several
flights of stairs to reach their private apartment on the Schmerlingplatz.
However, his request was turned down, and he and Idel had to look

elsewhere for something prestigious where they could entertain important guests more appropriately. Through Chancellor Seipel's contacts, they eventually found just what they needed: the Cistercian prior's residence in the Heiligenkreuzerhof, the Court of the Holy Cross, a private square in the heart of the old city. As motor transport was now so much improved, the prior was returning to live in the main monastery a few kilometres away in the country and would no longer need such a magnificent lodging in town.

RCK and Idel moved into an apartment of very generous proportions, occupying the ground and first floor of an impressive eighteenth-century building on a corner site of the square. Given the prior's religious duties, an interior window in the drawing room looked down into an ornate Baroque chapel. It was in this beautiful apartment, leased to them at a very modest rent, that he and Idel entertained and networked with the great and the good from 1926 until 1938. Numerous politicians and ambassadors, church leaders and newspaper editors, university professors and distinguished foreign visitors called on them here. It served, said RCK, as the 'Embassy for Pan-Europa'. The couple's servants – cook, maid, butler, and chauffeur – used the ground floor, which was linked internally to the apartment above by a small staircase and a dumb waiter. For visitors, access to the *piano nobile* of the apartment was via the majestic main staircase of the house. All Vienna now knew that Pan-Europa had arrived as a young and dynamic political movement, led by an intelligent and charismatic Austro-Hungarian count with a famous Jewish actress wife, the German theatre's answer to Sarah Bernhardt.

BUT PAN-EUROPA was not the only show in town. Just a year earlier, Prinz Karl Anton Rohan had founded the Verband für kuturelle Zusammenarbeit, or League for Cultural Co-operation (more popularly known as the Europäischer Kulturbund, or European Culture Club), to boost cultural co-operation across the continent. Three years younger than RCK, Rohan was also an Austro-Hungarian aristocrat. His family came from near Melk in Lower Austria, a hundred miles or so west of Vienna. The family castle, the Albrechtsberg, lay on a tributary of the Danube and, socially speaking, Karl Rohan's early upbringing was, like RCK's, a traditional one as son of the lord of the local manor. But his father did not possess an intellectually liberal, tolerant, and inquiring mind like RCK's father. Karl Anton grew up in a staunchly reactionary Catholic family, steeped in national tradition rather than cosmopolitan modernity. When he left school in 1916, he enlisted in the army, served at the front in the Great War, and did not subsequently go on to study. Like RCK, however, he too was caught up in the intellectual and social turmoil of the dismembered Austro-Hungarian Empire. He found in Europe's common cultural history, its common religion, and the shared experience of literature, art, and music the glue that he felt would hold Europe together.

Prinz Rohan was an efficient organizer and a diplomatic operator, manoeuvring adroitly between conservative as well as – initially – social-democratic and liberal financial supporters. This was the same pond in which RCK was fishing. Even without the benefit of a university education, his imposing aristocratic title and his refined manners made him welcome in cultural circles. Who could not be in favour of better cultural understanding between European nations? For many artists, cultural exchange was the main purpose of peace, and for the nostalgic among the aristocratic elite, the Kulturbund brought to life again the best cultural aspects of the old Empire. The renowned novelist Thomas Mann, leading Austrian dramatist Hugo von Hofmannsthal, French poet Paul Valéry, and German Expressionist painter Max Beckmann all attended the Kulturbund's high-level congresses, as did Carl Jakob Burckhardt, the Swiss art historian, Karl Gustav Jung, founder of the psychoanalytical school that rivalled Freud's, Hermann Graf Keyserling, the popular conservative German philosopher, and Carl Schmitt, a prominent Austrian lawyer who went on to be a leading Nazi, known later as the crown jurist of the Third Reich. Some of these hedged their bets and joined RCK's Pan-Europa Union as well.

The Kulturbund held its first international congress in Paris in 1924, and the second the following year in Milan. For 1926, Prinz Rohan planned a congress in Vienna, and later he would organize others, in Heidelberg, Prague, Barcelona (in the context of the World Exhibition), Krakow, Zürich, and Budapest. He also quickly organized branches of the Kulturbund in other countries – by 1926 in France and Italy, and by 1930 in a dozen more, including Germany. The Kulturbund's congresses avoided overtly political debate by choosing neutral themes such as 'The Role of Intellectuals in Building Europe'. It encouraged discussion and networking among invited participants: artists and intellectuals on the one hand and representatives of big business and international finance on the other. Discussions about the spiritual and intellectual underpinnings of European culture were often enlightening, but equally often inconclusive. Many presentations were subsequently published in Rohan's *Europäische Revue*, a quarterly publication he set up in 1926 and which was for a few years held in high regard in intellectual and artistic circles. The first volume, for instance, contained contributions from artists of five different nationalities, including several previously unpublished offerings by the well-known poet Rainer Maria Rilke.

While Rohan's declared aim was cultural rather than economic and political, he and RCK were competitors not only when recruiting members for their respective organizations and readers for their journals, but also when looking for financial support, especially from the Austrian government. Rohan was first to succeed in persuading Chancellor Seipel, for instance, to become honorary chairman of the Kulturbund, but Seipel also hedged his bets and soon became chairman of the Austrian branch of RCK's Pan-Europa Union as well.

Rohan was initially strident in his criticism of Pan-Europa and of RCK personally. In an early edition of the *Europäische Revue* he tried to dissuade his members from supporting Pan-Europa, this 'upstart organization', since it was, he claimed, an artificial construct, without tradition and roots, lacking a spiritual dimension and merely rational. It was, Prinz Rohan wrote, 'a fascinating mixture of a correct and grand political vision with a remarkably thin and bloodless theory … a late hangover from the previous century, in which grand systems for the salvation of the world sprang up, unachievable utopias with theoretical plans for peace and plenty.'

RCK never mentioned Rohan or the Kulturbund in any of his published writings, denying his rival the oxygen of publicity. But in the light of RCK's subsequent success, Rohan later decided to follow the same tactic as his rival, and in his pre-war books of commentary and memoirs – *Umbruch der Zeit, 1923–1930* (*Turning Point of the Age, 1923–1930*) and *Schicksalsstunde Europas* (*Europe's Hour of Destiny*) – he made no mention of RCK and Pan-Europa. Jealous competition between their organizations would go hand in hand with life-long personal rivalry.[4]

RCK AND IDEL knew very well that the Kulturbund was the competition they had to overcome if the Pan-Europa Union was to achieve its goals. Publishing RCK's *Pan-Europa* was just the first step along the path towards making the Pan-Europa Union the leading organization in the field of European integration. Setting up the *Pan-Europa Journal* was the second step. Establishing branches of the Pan-Europa Union in other countries was to be the third. For RCK, Rohan's exclusively cultural agenda could not include politics and economics, while Pan-Europa's essentially political and economic agenda could – and did in his eyes – include discussion of cultural affairs. What was European patriotism if not an expression of identity? And that certainly included a cultural aspect, an argument underlined by Idel professionally as a living example.

RCK's book was not only a success in the German-speaking world. In 1926 it was translated into English (published in New York) and in 1927 into French. By 1928 it had appeared in Czech, Croatian, Spanish, Hungarian, Latvian, Greek, and Japanese as well. RCK became a best-selling author, something Prinz Rohan could not rival, nor Hitler at that stage. And the *Pan-Europa Journal*, which first appeared in 1924, had at least twelve months' head start on the Kulturbund's *Europäische Revue*. RCK planned to organize Pan-Europa committees not only in all the countries of the continent, but to go one better and establish support groups in England and America as well. These would spread the word, encouraging sales of his book as well as the *Pan-Europa Journal*, and contribute information and funds to the organization's headquarters in Vienna. Soon these national committees, he prophesied, would spread across the map of Europe 'as an ink blot on paper', and to realize this, he and Idel set out on a grand tour of European capitals.

First, he started in the country central to his plans: Germany. He and Idel travelled to Berlin in October 1924, intending to stay for three months. They installed themselves in the luxury of the Kaiserhof Hotel, surrounded by marble and gold leaf, close to the Brandenburg Gate, and set about making friends and influencing people.

When they arrived, the country was coming to terms with the consequences of stabilizing the currency after rampant inflation. Max Warburg's support opened doors for them in both business and political circles, in particular giving them an entrée to the man responsible for stabilizing the currency, Hjalmar Schacht.

The successful introduction of the new German Rentenmark in 1923 had been achieved by the Reichsbank, headed by Schacht, who backed the new currency initially with all the land and buildings in the entire country. It was a grand political gesture, a public-relations masterstroke, since the government did not own and certainly could not realize all the real estate in the country. But the gesture calmed the public mood almost immediately. In August the following year, Schacht introduced the new Reichsmark, this time backed by gold and a massive loan from the Rothschilds. As soon as the Reichsmark was considered sound, the government could borrow abroad again.[5]

Politically, three major issues were unacceptable for much of German public opinion at that time: the attribution of war guilt to Germany; the payment of excessive reparations; and the loss of territory both in the east and in the west. Would the nation seek peace and reconciliation with its neighbours, or try to rebuild its power and seek revenge and domination? And which relations would it prioritize: those with its eastern neighbours, or those with France? The answer would determine success or failure for RCK.

How Germany prioritized its foreign alliances was a vital concern for Pan-Europa. If Germany chose to look southwards and eastwards and expand its influence in central and eastern Europe – Poland, Czechoslovakia, Austria, Hungary, Romania, and the western Balkans – it would clash with the interests of France, which feared the growth of German power elsewhere on the continent before it had reached reconciliation with its ancient antagonist across the Rhine. If moderate German governments chose first the route of reconciliation with France, however, they risked alienating domestic opinion and being outflanked by nationalists and populists who wished to restore lost influence and territory in the east.

RCK wanted to strengthen the moderate body of public opinion that was prepared to accept the new state borders created by the Versailles Settlement and work for reconciliation with all Germany's neighbours, especially France. In Germany's foreign minister, Gustav Stresemann, he felt he had found someone who, with some reservations, would be prepared to take this route, both helping and being helped by RCK's Pan-Europa Union.

RCK was received by Stresemann and from their conversation he judged him to be an enlightened nationalist, keen to use the east-west choices open to Germany to leverage advantages from other European states. Stresemann in return was cautious, but offered RCK his unofficial support, essentially because Pan-Europa opened an alternative route for Germany to achieve a better understanding with France, potentially using a non-governmental organization as a back channel for informal contacts, in addition to the German Foreign Office. But Stresemann wanted to keep his options open to the east as well. He refused to recognize Germany's new border with Poland, for instance, since, if ever Poland was attacked by Russia, Stresemann knew his country could demand a territorial price for supporting its eastern neighbour. RCK noted succinctly, 'He was a European as far as he thought that Pan-Europa might serve Germany's national interest.'[6]

Stresemann for his part was happier to make compromises publicly in the name of European unity rather than because France asked for them, and he increasingly used the term 'Europe' in his speeches, helping to make the notion of Pan-Europa acceptable in those German business circles that formed his political base. In Stresemann's diaries – published after his early death in 1929 – he noted his first meeting with RCK: 'Coudenhove-Kalergi called on me today. His Pan-European ideas are making great progress. Whatever one may think of him, in any case he is a man of extraordinary knowledge and great energy. I am convinced that he is going to play a great role.'

To balance this unofficial support from the side of German government and business, RCK now sought support from the Social Democrats, then in opposition, and found it in the president of the Reichstag, Paul Loebe. From his powerful political position and his strong commitment to the peace movement, he could see enough common ground with Pan-Europa to accept the chairmanship of its German committee as soon as RCK offered it to him. RCK was also strongly supported by Rudolf Breitscheid, an outspoken Social Democrat MP, who explicitly backed the idea of the United States of Europe in a debate in the Reichstag, echoing RCK's words in *Pan-Europa*: 'What is today utopian will tomorrow be reality.' Together Loebe and Breitscheid ensured that the goal of a European federation was confirmed in the Social Democratic Party's official policy that same year, and through their influence many Social Democratic newspapers opened their columns to Pan-European ideas. Georg Bernhard, editor of the *Vossische Zeitung*, was already a good friend of RCK and Idel, and he continued to be an enthusiastic supporter of the Pan-European idea until he was forced to leave Germany in 1933.

RCK also secured a meeting with the minister of finance and future chancellor, Hans Luther, who surprised and delighted him by accepting that 'a European federation is the only way to save our peace and civilization'. But Luther added that he did not believe that it would come about, 'because no nation is powerful enough to take the lead within such a union. Germany, France, and Italy are too weak, the British will refuse to be involved, and Russia is basically non-European.'

RCK had interviews with many political figures in Berlin, among them Wilhelm Marx, the chancellor, and Joseph Wirth, who succeeded him the following year. Both were leaders of the powerful Catholic Centre Party. He also met other leaders of public opinion, including the president of the Supreme Court, Walter Simons, and the head of the Reichswehr, General von Seeckt. He clearly made a positive impression on them, which enabled him to stay in contact for many years afterwards.[7] Even more importantly, he set up a German branch of the Pan-Europa Union – Pan-Europa Union Deutschland, with the amusing acronym 'PUD' – and appointed Wilhelm Heile, a former member of the Reichstag, as its secretary-general. Heile was an efficient organizer and shared RCK's views on the need for European unity, having spoken publicly about the United States of Europe in a meeting held in Vienna as early as 1921.

From a standing start in October, RCK and Idel had, by Christmas, made many friends in influential circles in Berlin and established PUD. With their mission accomplished there, it was now time to take on Paris.

ON NEW YEAR'S DAY 1925 they travelled to France with letters of recommendation to four leading French political figures: Henri de Jouvenal, editor of *Le Matin*; Louis Loucheur, a former minister and currently proprietor of *Le Petit Journal*; Paul Painlevé, a former war-time prime minister; and Aristide Briand, another former prime minister. The French occupation of the Ruhr – in retaliation for Germany's failure to pay reparations – had not yet come to an end, and RCK thought it wiser to avoid recommendations from Germany, so tense were relations still between the two countries. The letters of introduction that RCK brought were not from his newly made Berlin contacts, but from the Czech foreign minister, Edvard Beneš.

The first three of his contacts – de Jouvenal, Loucheur, and Painlevé – all became firm supporters and helped form the French committee of Pan-Europa. As Briand was temporarily absent from Paris, RCK instead met Joseph Caillaux, leader of the left-of-centre Radical Party.[8] He had been prime minister before the Great War and a minister in several governments again in the 1920s and 1930s, and he gladly accepted the honorary chairmanship of the French Pan-Europa Committee, urging RCK to act with all possible speed. This new project, he argued, could improve Franco-German relations and strengthen links between progressive parties internationally, and he hoped this would find a receptive echo in French public opinion.

RCK knew he had the backing of Social Democrats in Austria, as well as in Germany, and he soon gained the enthusiastic support of the leader of the moderate wing of the French Socialists, Léon Blum, and also of Josef Paul-Boncour, a rising political star of the left. Each of them later became prime minister in the 1930s. RCK also persuaded Léon Jouhaux, leader of the moderate trade unions, to back Pan-Europa, and he remained a life-long supporter of the idea of a united Europe.

But it was Edouard Herriot, at that time combining the offices of prime minister and minister of foreign affairs, who was the closest and most influential of his new French supporters. Herriot received RCK in his office while dressing for dinner one evening, and told him straight away that he did not need a briefing on his ideas. He had received that already from his private secretary, R.R. Lambert, who had been so impressed on reading *Pan-Europa* that he himself had joined the Pan-Europa Union. Heriott declared that his own ideas on the future of Europe corresponded closely with those that RCK was proposing, and he would support Pan-Europa publicly.

He was as good as his word, and a few days later – on 29 January 1925 – he made a speech in the Chamber of Deputies in which he declared that his greatest wish was one day to see the United States of Europe become a reality. 'If I have been working with so much engagement for the League of Nations,' he continued, 'I have done so because I considered this great institution a first rough draft of the United States of Europe.'

Despite an enthusiastic reception given to this declaration in the French Assembly and a positive echo in the French press, there was no corresponding response from the German government. RCK took the matter into his own hands and caught the overnight sleeper to Berlin to speak to Chancellor Marx personally. The chancellor understood immediately that his country might be missing an important diplomatic opening being offered by France. He sent RCK to von Maltzahn, secretary of state for foreign affairs, who promised that the foreign minister himself would respond. A few days later, an article by Gustav Stresemann appeared in the *Frankfurter Generalanzeiger,* welcoming and endorsing Heriott's plea for a United States of Europe.

Back in Paris, RCK made sure everyone who needed to know was told how successful he had been on behalf of France. But a change of government only a month later brought the more conservative and nationalist Raymond Poincaré to power and appeared to put an end to this first Franco-German thaw. RCK was not able to meet the new foreign minister, Aristide Briand, during that visit, but some weeks later he was reassured when Briand declared that he intended to continue the same foreign policy as his predecessor, Heriott, thus at least keeping open this first small window of understanding across the Rhine.

AFTER FRANCE, RCK and Idel turned to Italy. Despite his earlier disappointment when Mussolini declined to respond to his appeal to lead Pan-Europa, RCK always consoled himself – without any convincing evidence – that the Italians as a people were somehow inherently more European in spirit than either the French or the Germans. At Easter 1925 he and Idel left Paris for Rome to promote Pan-Europa there. They were privileged to have introductions to Benedetto Croce, one of the greatest living philosophers, and Gugliemo Ferrero, the distinguished historian, as well as other political figures – the former prime minister, Giovanni Giolitti, the progressive journalist and politician Giovanni Amendola, and the reforming socialist Gaetano Salvemini – all intelligent observers but, now that Mussolini was firmly in the saddle, all distant from power.[9]

Until summer 1924, Mussolini could claim to have ruled Italy as prime minister of a multi-party coalition increasingly dominated by the Fascist Party. After the disappearance of the opposition deputy Giacomo Matteotti that summer and the discovery of his mutilated body some months later, Mussolini made a speech in the Chamber of Deputies on 3 January 1925, in which he stated, 'I declare before this Assembly and before the Italian people that I alone assume the moral, political, and historical responsibility of all that has taken place ... because I have deliberately created this atmosphere.' He reproached the opposition with failing to accept political leadership by the Fascists, adding, 'Italy wants peace and quiet, work and calm. I will give these things with love if possible, with force if necessary.' The chamber was then indefinitely adjourned, and Mussolini went on to ban all political opposition, censure the media, and politically control the judiciary.

Against this turbulent political background, RCK failed to achieve the breakthrough in Italy that he hoped for. But he did manage to gain a first-hand impression of Mussolini. His most active contact, Count Carlo Sforza, a former foreign minister and still a senator, invited him to a session of the Senate to observe Il Duce in debate. His first impression of Mussolini disillusioned him considerably. RCK wrote:

> I was struck at once by the strong contrast between Mussolini's pictures, giving the illusion of a modern imperator with features of bronze, and the actual man, who was nothing more than a vivid Italian, continuously fidgeting in his seat, visibly bored by long speeches, impatient, restless, nervous. This overexcited and obviously overworked man, who rolled his black eyes in an exaggerated manner, seemed utterly without balance, almost on the verge of insanity, driven by God only knew what internal furies. When I saw him, I understood why my open letter had been ignored. By his very nature, this man was seeking not rest but movement, not peace but war.

But these lines were written some fifteen or more years later, and with the benefit of hindsight. At the time of his Italian visit – indeed until the outbreak of the Second World War – RCK continued to believe and hope that Mussolini might not only keep Italy out of alliance with Germany, but might even lead a movement for European unity such as RCK was proposing. RCK never managed to establish a national committee for Pan-Europa in Italy, partly because of clerical suspicion of all things associated with the Freemasons, who were so clearly supportive of Pan-Europa in Vienna, and partly because Mussolini himself – and hence his government – was initially not interested in disturbing existing relations inside Europe while he was establishing his dominant role domestically. It was not until 1932 that Count Gravina, the Italian high commissioner in Danzig, in a letter to RCK, confirmed the Italian position in writing: 'He [Il Duce] is not particularly favourable to Pan-Europa; in fact he is quite sceptical about it.' An additional reason, although he did not admit it publicly, was that Mussolini was already supporting Prinz Rohan's Kulturbund, and that appeared a more useful and more amenable instrument for expanding Italian soft power across the continent.

Despite considerable evidence to the contrary, RCK persisted in deluding himself that Mussolini as a leader, and Italian fascism as a political movement, could be reconciled with his vision of Pan-Europa. A close associate of Mussolini, Asvero Gravelli, edited *AntiEuropa*, a journal consistently critical of Pan-Europa, and yet RCK interpreted his criticism as simply a tactical manoeuvre by Il Duce. He even wrote in 1930: 'The so-called Anti-Europeans (in Italy) are not really anti-European. They are simply the Fascist wing of the Pan-Europa Movement.'

RCK made a clear distinction between Nazism with its racial connotations and Italian fascism, which he saw as essentially neutral on racial issues. Just after Hitler's take-over of power in 1933, he appealed to Mussolini to form an alliance of Latin states as a counterweight to Nazi Germany. So desperate was he not to lose the prospect of Italian participation in Pan-Europa that he argued that it mattered little whether the internal organization of a state was democratic or fascist, so long as it worked together with others for common ideals of peace and prosperity. But in an article that Gravelli was invited to publish in the *Pan-Europa Journal*, Mussolini's spokesman put the alternative position clearly: 'A politically united Europe will not come about so long as it is partly fascist and partly democratic. The simple fact that two major European powers are now organized on fascist lines must inevitably have a decisive influence on the political developments in other European states.'

RCK still did not believe what he was reading and continued to hope that Mussolini would somehow accept the path of peaceful co-operation rather than the path of war and conquest in his European policy. As late as the summer of 1939, he launched a last-minute appeal to Mussolini 'to save Europe from Teutonic barbarism'. Mussolini did not deign to answer him. However, RCK's misjudgement of the man and of Italian fascism, though it may seem comprehensible when compared to Hitler and Nazism at the time, was later to cost him the sympathy of anti-fascists from Resistance circles and alienate him from their efforts at European unity after 1945.

Throughout his life, RCK's contacts in leading circles of European society were of the very finest, and it is no surprise to learn that, while in Rome in early summer 1925, he and Idel were received in audience by Pope Pius XI. The pope must have been briefed that a previous pontiff, Leo XIII, had received RCK's father, Heinrich, and his Japanese mother, Mitsu, more than thirty years earlier, and that Mitsu was a Catholic convert from Buddhism. The same briefing can hardly have omitted the fact that RCK's wife was Jewish and divorced. But despite this unconventional background, it did not prevent the pope from blessing the pair (if not the project of Pan-Europa explicitly) before they left his presence.

Although RCK failed to establish a support committee for Pan-Europa while in Italy that year, he drew some political advantage from his meeting with Cardinal Pietro Gasparri, the papal secretary of state. Though non-committal in the interview, Gasparri subsequently ensured that the Vatican's official mouthpiece, *L'Osservatore Romano*, took a consistently positive position on issues of European unity.[10]

RCK's efforts to establish national committees for Pan-Europa in other countries were unceasing. After Italy, he and Idel also visited Warsaw, Budapest, and Brussels, all in 1925, to establish local committees there. With help from the Austrian Foreign Office and contacts passed on from converts to the cause, they established fifteen national committees across the continent within three years of setting up the Pan-Europa Union. By 1927 their network included Austria, Germany, France, Belgium, Luxembourg, the Netherlands, Spain, Switzerland, Bulgaria, Yugoslavia, Poland, Latvia, Estonia, Czechoslovakia, and Hungary.

The Pan-Europa Union had spread, as RCK said it would, like ink on blotting paper. Each national committee was composed of leading politicians, together with other public figures sympathetic to the cause. The committees related directly to the central office of the Pan-Europa Union in Vienna, which took a proportion of their annual dues (at least twenty-five per cent) and whose authority the committees recognized in the person of its president, RCK.

9

NEW FRIENDS, NEW ENEMIES

RCK AND IDEL were never clear about the degree to which Pan-Europa should be an elite association or a mass movement. International membership of the Pan-Europa Union peaked at just over nine thousand paying members at the end of the 1920s. In Germany it was larger than in any other country; Hamburg and Dusseldorf branches had close to a thousand members each, and Berlin nearly two thousand. Conscious of their size and their importance at the centre of the European debate, the German groups were less inclined than others to accept the close control that RCK exercised over his growing movement. He published and broadcast, lectured and debated continuously – both in Austria and Germany and elsewhere –promoting the cause of Pan-Europa, as did a few leading members of the various committees in their own countries. But the Berlin group in particular objected to restrictions that RCK tried to apply to views expressed by its senior members. They argued that their own people could react to local developments more quickly, because they were closer to the political pulse of their country, especially in the capital. RCK feared that disparate voices would complicate and weaken the propagandistic thrust of Pan-Europa's message. He wanted the movement to speak with one voice, and that voice to be his.

It was with the German chapter of the Pan-Europa Union that the first, and perhaps the most damaging, of quarrels broke out as early as 1925. Wilhelm Heile, a Liberal MP, was head of foreign relations for the Reichstag's Special Interest Group for Relations with European Peoples (Interessengemeinschaft der Europäischen *Völker*) and, from January to April 1925, Heile was also in charge of the Pan-Europa Union (PUD) in Berlin.[1] From this dual vantage point, he suggested to RCK that the two aspects of his work could usefully be split, with the Pan-Europa Union concentrating on developing a wide public membership, a mass movement, while the Special Interest Group should concentrate on recruiting leading politicians to the common cause. RCK did not believe that these two bodies would pursue a common cause, since he was president of only one of them, while Heile was in both, and he told Heile in no uncertain terms that the best solution would be for Heile to stand down from his role in the parliamentary Special Interest Group. He, unsurprisingly, refused, where-upon RCK dismissed him from his role in charge of PUD in Germany, offering him in compensation two thousand Reichsmark (equivalent of one hundred pounds sterling at that time, or somewhat over five thousand pounds). Heile accepted, but he did not take his dismissal lightly.

He accused the young count of being intolerant of reasonable criticism. He described RCK as having 'a lust for power like Napoleon' and being 'a god who can tolerate no other gods in his vicinity'. RCK replied with youth-ful arrogance and a fully developed sense of entitlement, the effect of which he probably failed to appreciate: 'My personal views are quite objective and are based on the experience of all political mass movements,' he claimed. 'History teaches that one must personify political thoughts, and that such personification helps considerably to encourage, intensify, and accelerate the movement's propaganda. Without in any way wishing to make com-parisons, I would remind you of Garibaldi, Lenin, Ghandi, and Mussolini.'

But Heile was in a strong position on his home territory, and he responded by intriguing against RCK and Pan-Europa within the German govern-ment and the Reichstag, where he had powerful friends. He also teamed up with a well-connected, if unstable, Polish Jewish journalist, Alfred Nossig, who published what RCK considered a 'poor imitation' of *Pan-Europa* entitled *Neu-Europa* (*New Europe*). Together, Heile and Nossig founded and co-chaired the Verband für europäische Verständigung (The Association for European Understanding), which promoted a programme very similar to Pan-Europa's, except that it unambiguously stressed the inclusion of Great Britain in the process of European political and eco-nomic integration, and suggested that the powerful transatlantic triad of Pan-Europa, Pan-Britannia, and Pan-America should become the pre-cursor of the United States of the World.[2] RCK considered this fanciful futurology, but did not wish such ideas to take root in Britain or America.

So, after his extended visits to Germany, France, and Italy, RCK turned his attention to Great Britain, and he and Idel first visited London late in 1925. In his efforts to raise British awareness of the Pan-Europa Union, he was helped by several leaders of English opinion, in particular Henry Wickham Steed, the former chief editor of *The Times*, who had worked in Vienna before the Great War, where he made the acquaintance of the Coudenhove-Kalergi family. He wisely advised RCK that British opinion would be concerned with Pan-Europa only if it involved Great Britain and the British Empire as well: 'only if presented as a world problem, not as a continental one'.

***

RCK REGULARLY ATTENDED ministerial meetings of the League of Nations in Geneva, initially as an interested journalist and commentator, later as president of the Pan-Europa Union and editor of the *Pan-Europa Journal*, and there in 1925 he first met Leo Amery, who was attending the League meetings as UK secretary of state for the dominions and colonies. They enjoyed a long conversation at their first meeting, and RCK noted that his ideas and Amery's 'about world organization, about pacifism, about the League, and about the defence of Western civilization' were almost identical. Leo Amery continued throughout his life to be a close friend and adviser for RCK in all matters European, and would attend the first Pan-Europa Congress in Vienna the following year. Subsequently, Amery described it as 'the most important event of the year' in a polemical exchange in the House of Commons with Foreign Secretary Austen Chamberlain, who had failed to mention the Congress at all in his annual round-up of foreign-policy issues for 1926. Had he only known of the support that RCK had drummed up on his visit to America that same year, through the good offices of Nicholas Murray Butler, president of the Carnegie Endowment for International Peace, Chamberlain would doubtless not have been so cavalier as to omit to mention Pan-Europa.

It was through the good offices of Amery and Steed, on this first visit to London, that RCK and Idel met numerous leading figures in the British political elite. It was a steep learning curve for all concerned. Either Amery or Steed accompanied RCK to a host's office or club, sometimes with Idel also present, and in under two weeks they met an impressive list of the great and the good: Ramsay MacDonald (the first Labour prime minister); Lord Robert Cecil (Conservative free trader and chairman of the League of Nations Association in the UK); Lord Reading (former viceroy of India and Lord Chief Justice); Lord Balfour (pre-war prime minister, now president of the Privy Council), Sir Robert Horne (former minister of labour and president of the Board of Trade); Professor Gilbert Murray (Regius Professor of Greek at Oxford and a staunch supporter of the League of Nations); Philip Noel-Baker (politician, academic,

Leo Amery introduced RCK to Churchill; Nicholas Murray Butler financed RCK in America.

diplomat, former Olympic athlete, and later winner of the Nobel Peace Prize); Percy Molteno (Liberal politician, shipping magnate, and philanthropist); Sir Walter Layton (editor of the *Economist*); George Bernard Shaw and H.G. Wells (both famous socially engaged authors); Philip Kerr (Lloyd George's principal private secretary, newspaper magnate, and later, as Lord Lothian, UK ambassador to the United States); as well as Lionel Curtis (one of the founders of the Royal Institute of International Affairs – Chatham House – as well as a member of the UK delegation at the Paris Peace Conference, and later a proponent of World Federation).

This was an impressive array of influential figures for RCK to meet on his first London visit. He and his wife were after all not well known in London, he a minor Austrian count and she a successful actress in the German-speaking world. Their reception reflected the level of contacts and the conviction of the two figures who had introduced him into this select circle of high influence. The impression he and she made also spoke volumes for their charm and powers of persuasion, as well as for the quality, clarity, and novelty of RCK's vision of Europe's future. RCK later wrote, 'These were all outstanding men who sympathized with the ideas of peace, of armament reduction, and free trade,' but who, 'as soon as they were up against the alternative – either to have Britain join the European federation and face its dangerous consequences for the future of the Empire, or to allow the union to be organized along purely Continental lines – preferred not to commit themselves.'

British public debate then centred on issues of free trade and the future of the empire, hence Wickham Steed's earlier advice to RCK. Articles in the *Guardian*, the *Statist*, the *Economist*, and the *Round Table* at the time of RCK's visit point to the basic concerns of Pan-Europa under such general titles as 'Can Europe Prevent the Next War?' and 'Europe at the Crossroads'. In the *Free Trader*, Austen Chamberlain commented: 'Today, the alternatives are being pressed upon us with increasing urgency. We, in these islands, cannot stand by ourselves alone. If we do not think imperially, we shall have to think continentally.' But the business leader Sir Alfred Mond (later Lord Melchett) argued dramatically in *The Times*, in an article entitled 'Europe or the Empire?' that this was the question that would divide the nation as never before. 'Without doubt or hesitation,' he declared, 'we must place ourselves on the side of the Empire.' Melchett's views were in line with a large majority of political and public opinion at the time, which, despite – or perhaps because of – the trauma of the Great War, had barely begun to consider positive European alternatives. Britain was still the country of Kipling and of Empire.[3]

Not surprisingly, the visit of RCK and Idel to London did not pass unnoticed by the secret services, where Arthur Watts, a former captain who had been awarded the DSO and mentioned in dispatches in the First World War, seems to have been designated to check out the Pan-Europa Union and keep an eye on its leader. Ostensibly, he was now in the Royal Naval Volunteer Reserve, but used the revealing postal address of British Military Intelligence, c/o The War Office. He was one of the original members of Chatham House, the Royal Institute of International Affairs, at its foundation in 1920, and he would attend the Pan-Europa Congress that RCK was already planning in Vienna the following year. He remained interested in the project until his death in 1935.

Inside the Foreign Office, however, discussion of the issues that were on RCK's agenda was not far advanced. Alan Leeper, first secretary in the League of Nations and Western Department, was the only official in London of any standing who took RCK's efforts seriously, and he had an uphill struggle convincing his colleagues to pay them any attention at all. *Pan-Europa* had been reviewed in *Foreign Affairs*, the journal of Chatham House, in 1924, but, despite receiving occasional reports from embassies on the continent about Pan-Europa's activities, the Foreign Office purchased no works by Coudenhove-Kalergi for its library until

1930. Sir William Tyrell, permanent under-secretary at the Foreign Office, minuted in the margin of a report by the British ambassador in Vienna on the First Congress of Pan-Europa in 1926, 'I know Count Coudenhove: he is a thoroughly impractical theorist.' Three years later – when the French prime minister spoke to the League of Nations about the prospect of a federal link between neighbouring states in Europe – an internal note in the Foreign Office records that the issue had not yet been thoroughly thought through in London. Another note in 1932 suggests that, if ever the issue became pressing, then the Foreign Office would need to fix its position. In official London, European integration was not an option worth considering in the interwar years. The empire took centre stage.

RCK always considered the United Kingdom as a special case. For hundreds of years England had deployed its financial, intelligence, and diplomatic resources, and often gone to war, to prevent a single power dominating the continent. Even if a successful Pan-Europa was structured as a continental alliance of freely co-operating independent states, its potential size would make it appear as much of a threat to England as that posed by dominant continental leaders in the past – Philip II of Spain, Louis XIV of France, Napoleon, Nicholas I of Russia, or the Kaiser in the recent Great War. RCK realized that he needed to persuade British political opinion that Pan-Europa was a peaceful and democratic political movement with no expansionist goals which would clash with wider British interests, and hence posed no threat.

As Great Britain granted independence to the white Dominions, successive Imperial Conferences under prime ministers of all major parties – the Liberal leader Lloyd George in 1918 and 1921, the Conservative leader Stanley Baldwin in 1923 and 1926, and the Labour leader Ramsay MacDonald in 1930 – prepared the way for imperial preference as the trading policy of the empire. With the Statute of Westminster in 1931 and the Ottawa Conference the following year, a protectionist tariff barrier was created around the empire, providing for privileged access for empire products into Britain in exchange for privileged access for British goods in the markets of its empire. Britain might be a European as well as a global power in security terms, but British trading interests were predominantly imperial.

In his more enthusiastic and fanciful moments, RCK imagined resolving the dichotomy between British and continental interests by suggesting that Britain should lead his embryonic European grouping. The king of England, he thought, might be 'the hereditary President of the United States of Europe'. This was but a momentary dream, for the British question, he realized, 'was the most difficult and delicate problem of all the complicated problems confronting Pan-Europa.' In order not to create a rift inside the organization itself, the official programme of the Pan-Europa Union after 1926 left the issue of British membership open, deciding neither to include nor to exclude Great Britain from Pan-Europa. This was a step further than RCK himself had written originally in *Pan-Europa*, where he had excluded both Great Britain and Russia, if for different reasons. Now he worked to allay any British fears about the project and not to close the door on eventual membership. He argued that Britain should see Pan-Europa as a defensive continental alliance that would keep Russia in check. 'Pan-Europa is possible without England, but never against England', he wrote, since the security concerns of both should coincide. Demographic developments, he helpfully added, would also allow Pan-Europa to supply surplus population as migrants to help British colonial development overseas.

The situation was very different when viewed from Berlin and from Paris. There the two Foreign Offices were well informed about RCK, and each engaged directly with Pan-Europa. Both Foreign Offices subscribed to the *Pan-Europa Journal* and stocked RCK's books in their libraries. Ambassadors frequently reported on Pan-Europa's activities in the countries to which they were posted. It was in a note sent from the French embassy in Geneva to the Quai d'Orsay in early June of the same year that the French Foreign Office learned details about RCK's visit to London, for instance, including a full list of the names of people whom RCK and Idel had met. It clearly stated, 'He found everyone very open to the idea of a Pan-European group which he is planning. The British see in it the great advantage that they will not henceforth be required to intervene in European affairs and need no longer fear constant unrest from that quarter.'

Leo Amery remained RCK's closest British political contact throughout the interwar years and indeed until his death in 1955. He had been at school with Winston Churchill, who was a political colleague as well as a good friend, and, while Amery spoke several languages, Churchill did not, so he introduced him to the English translation of RCK's *Pan-Europa*. Churchill was impressed enough to have read it before he wrote his first notable article concerning moves towards European union five years or so later, since he refers to RCK and his work in some detail there.

Following his intense visit to London, RCK asked Henry Wickham Steed to set up a small preparatory committee to help the cause of Pan-Europa in Britain. However, despite Steed's role until 1930 as editor of the *Review of Reviews*, which gave him an unparalleled network among journalists, authors, and politicians, this committee developed no notable activity over the following years, and made little impact on public opinion. At that time British concerns simply lay elsewhere, in the British Empire on which the sun never set.

WHILE he was spending so much time away from his headquarters in Vienna, RCK was planning his next major public-relations exercise for Pan-Europa. In 1925 he sent a trilingual appeal, in German, French, and Italian, to several hundred leading cultural and political personalities of the day. In it he asked them two deceptively simple questions. First, did they think the creation of the United States of Europe was desirable? And second, did they think the United States of Europe could become a practical reality?

He published replies from one hundred of the most prominent respondents in a double issue of the *Pan-Europa Journal* in April that year. The roll-call of supportive names from the continent gives a good impression of the wide international reach that RCK had established for the new movement in so short a time.

Among those who answered 'yes' were many senior politicians: Graf Albert Apponyi, former Hungarian prime minister; Joseph Caillaux, the French finance minister; Hugo Celmins, the Latvian prime minister; Edvard Beneš, foreign minister of the Czechoslovak Republic; Edouard Herriot, the speaker of the French Parliament; H.A. von Karnebeek, Dutch foreign minister; Dr Liebermann, member of the Polish Sejm; Paul Loebe, president of the Reichstag; Andreas Michalakopulos, Greek foreign minister; Francesco Nitti, former Italian prime minister; Paul Painlevé, French prime minister; Karl Renner, former Austrian chancellor; Count Carlo Sforza, former Italian foreign minister and now senator; and Henri de Jouvenal, former minister and senator in Paris (and incidentally husband of the equally famous author, Colette).

Other Pan-Europa Union members who responded had made their reputations in cultural or scientific circles: Albert Einstein, then a professor in Berlin; Rudolf Goldschied, chairman of the Austrian Peace Movement; Gerhardt Hauptmann, the most famous German author of the day; Hugo von Hofmannsthal, acclaimed librettist of Richard Strauss's operas and a popular Austrian playwright; and Graf Hermann Keyserling, the much-travelled philosopher from Darmstadt.

Yet others were distinguished editors and journalists: Ernst Benedikt of the *Neue Freie Presse* in Vienna; Georg Bernhard of the *Vossische Zeitung* in Berlin; and Alfred Kerr, renowned theatre critic, who answered RCK's two questions from Italy, where he was on an extended holiday. From industrial and business circles there were also a number of replies, including from Edmund Stinnes, an influential German industrialist, who submitted a ten-page essay. And finally, of course, there was a reply from Max Warburg, RCK's banker patron from Hamburg.

RCK was wise enough to balance their overwhelmingly favourable answers with a few negative voices, who presciently pointed to enduring problems for European integration. Dr Heinrich Kanner from Vienna feared that Pan-Europa would be too large and too distant to win the hearts of its citizens, and that Britain would prevent any union between France and Germany. Graf Harry Kessler from Berlin insisted that Pan-Europa should be established only within the framework of the League of Nations, in order not to disturb wider international relations unduly. Other contributors warned that, while Pan-Europa might well secure peace within Europe, it ran the risk of becoming a military force in competition with other world powers, leading in the longer term to larger and worse wars at the global level.

Publishing these replies in the *Pan-Europa Journal* – the detail of the arguments as well as the names of the contributors – was a propaganda coup of which RCK was rightly proud. It confirmed to his wide circle of readers internationally not simply that Pan-Europa had now arrived on the public stage in Vienna, but that it enjoyed Europe-wide intellectual and political support. It was now a serious option to be reckoned with. His questionnaire, which was a rudimentary form of opinion polling, also provided him and Idel with a database of supporters, many of whom they hoped to attract to the first Pan-Europa Congress, which they were already planning to hold in Vienna the following year.

BEFORE ORGANIZING THIS CONGRESS, however, RCK intended to visit the United States to spread his message and encourage political circles there to back his plans. He and Idel sailed from Cherbourg on the SS *Berengaria* in October 1925 and stayed in the United States for three months. On the voyage out, they heard the encouraging news that Great Britain, France, Belgium, Italy, and Germany had signed the Locarno Treaty, mutually guaranteeing Germany's western border and securing the basis for peaceful relations between France and Germany. The treaty also confirmed understandings between Germany, Poland, and Czechoslovakia to refer important differences to international arbitration. It was a positive moment to be debating the future of the continent, commented RCK.

Arranging the visit had turned out to be easier than expected, thanks in particular to the good offices of Max Warburg, who contacted his two brothers Paul and Felix, who were both in America. Paul was a member of the first Federal Reserve Board and director of the Council on Foreign Relations, and Felix was a successful banker and prominent philanthropist. Together they set up a series of debates for RCK under the aegis of the American Foreign Policy Association, and also arranged meetings with leading members of the US Administration, including Frank Kellogg, secretary of state, and Herbert Hoover, secretary of commerce.

These debates – usually over lunch or dinner – were held in front of invited audiences made up of leaders of public opinion, business, and politics in over a dozen cities across the United States, and RCK made them into platforms from which he could profile his plan for Pan-Europa. He was opposed from a more global point of view by Christian Lange, the secretary-general of the International Parliamentary Union, a Norwegian academic who had written extensively on international relations and was credited with influencing President Wilson in planning the League of Nations. He had received the Nobel Peace Prize in 1921.

RCK commented in his autobiographical writings that Lange was already really convinced that Pan-Europa was the correct answer to the European problem of the time, and his support in the debates for the League's multilateral and global structure was merely pro forma, not heartfelt. But there is an alternative version of this lecture tour presented by Louise Weiss, the combative French journalist, in her *Mémoires*, and referred to also in a subsequent exchange of letters between her and RCK. She recalled that at least one of the dinner debates, specifically the one in Chicago, was a three-sided event, with her and RCK as well as Arthur Henderson junior, the son of Arthur Henderson, the first Labour home secretary. This young Arthur Henderson, a lawyer and former MP, later to be ennobled as Baron Rowley, represented a British point of view, while she presented the French angle on the project of Pan-Europa. She makes no mention of Christian Lange, but her *Mémoires* go on to enumerate various incidents during the American tour, including some disparaging remarks about Idel, the theatricality of her poses in public, how she missed her favourite dogs left behind in Vienna, and the superficiality of her conversation over breakfast. True to his habit of airbrushing out difficult moments in his story, RCK makes no mention either of Louise Weiss or Arthur Henderson.[4]

RCK and Idel's time in the States – whether it was with Christian Lange or, at least in part, with Louise Weiss and Arthur Henderson – was well spent. He and Idel achieved the goals they set out to achieve, anchoring Pan-Europa in the minds of many leading Americans. But it was not without its disappointments, chief among them the premature death of Frank Munsey, an extremely wealthy and influential publisher who might have become a major supporter of the Pan-Europa Union. At a luncheon party in Boston hosted by the American millionaire Vincent Astor and his wife, RCK gave a brief outline of Pan-Europa, and fellow millionaire Frank Munsey rose in reply to say: 'I am convinced that Count Coudenhove's idea alone can save Europe, and I am ready to back him with my papers, my money, and my personal influence.' RCK's travel schedule prevented him discussing the offer further with Munsey that day, but they fixed an appointment the following week to discuss details. Sadly, Munsey was operated on urgently that very week for appendicitis, and died in hospital. His will, made five years earlier and unrevised, left his fortune of forty million dollars to the Metropolitan Museum.

In recounting these sad events, RCK noted: 'His serious and intelligent personality had made a profound impression on me. I also regretted that his death prevented him from giving his promised support. Had he backed the Pan-Europa movement as he intended, it might have been able to triumph over the intrigues of political parties and leaders and perhaps even over Nazism.'

Before sailing home, RCK set up an American Co-operative Committee of the Pan-Europa Union, headed by Stephen Duggan, director of the Institute of International Education, and backed by a star-studded board that included the two Warburg brothers and Democrat and Republican members of both the House and Senate. RCK also arranged for an English translation of *Pan-Europa* to be published in New York, with a preface by Nicholas Murray Butler. In return, he ensured that RCK's views, expressed in a lecture entitled 'War Danger in Europe', were published in a pamphlet by the American Peace Society. But RCK failed to persuade the Warburg brothers to divert back to Europe three thousand dollars that they had earmarked for expenses connected with his tour of America and which remained unspent. RCK argued that the money would be much more usefully spent on preparations for the forthcoming Pan-Europa Congress he was planning to hold in Vienna, but that was not the view the Warburg brothers took. The Vienna congress was not on the American agenda.

Those weeks in America had been hard work, but they brought RCK and Pan-Europa considerable advantages, some appreciated immediately and others only later, when he and Idel would find themselves in exile in America during the Second World War.

10

EUROPEAN PATRIOTS ALL

IDEL AND RCK SAILED from New York to Cherbourg on the SS *Majestic* in mid-January 1926. As they sighted the coast of Normandy, buried deep in winter snow, they leaned together on the ship's rail and shared an intimate moment of insight and awareness. After three months in America, they realized they were returning not simply to France, but to Europe. 'We felt that this earth was our earth, the earth of Europe, stretching to the distant steppes of Russia and the shores of the Black Sea. Europe, for which we had pleaded all these years, had become our new and beloved fatherland – not only intellectually, but emotionally. We had become European patriots.'

Their chief task on their return was to prepare for the first Pan-Europa Congress, which they planned to hold in Vienna in October that year. RCK was well aware of Rohan's scheduled Kulturbund Congress also to be held in Vienna earlier in July, and realized that the first Congress of the Pan-Europa Union later that same year had to be bigger and better than the Kulturbund's event in every respect. Not a couple for half-measures, RCK and Idel intended to totally eclipse and crush their rival.

En route they stopped over in Paris for a few days, and it was there that RCK first met Aristide Briand, the French foreign minister, who was to play a major role in promoting his ideas over the next few years. RCK was still searching for a powerful national political leader who would adopt his cause and make it into a continental reality. He had asked Masaryk. He had written to Mussolini. Now he met Briand in his elegant study at the Quai d'Orsay and had the immediate conviction that this was the man he had been looking for. RCK described him as 'a little man with a broad face and unusually shining eyes. His smile was charming and ingratiating ... Briand was a high-bred Persian cat, graceful, keen, and shrewd ... a unique combination of wise philosopher and smart politician.' He needed little briefing, as he knew a lot about Pan-Europa. His private secretary, Alexis Léger, who was already a member of the Pan-Europa Union, had brought his minister fully up to date. At the end of the interview, Briand gave RCK words of encouragement: 'Go ahead, quick, quick, quick!' With some satisfaction, RCK compared this encouragement to the final words of his interview with Sir Eric Drummond at the League of Nations in Geneva four years earlier, when he was told not to go forward so quickly.

RCK certainly needed no urging. Over dinner that evening, to which he and Idel had invited Thomas Mann and his wife, Katia, he clearly gave a confident impression of his hopes for uniting Europe in the very near future. Thomas Mann recorded the event in his diary for 22 January 1926, subsequently published in his *Pariser Rechenschaft* (*Account from Paris*).

> Count Coudenhove-Kalergi and his wife Ida Roland (unforgettable, the Messalina-like majesty of her *Zarina*, commanding, with the star on her breast, erect behind her imperial writing desk) await us in the hall. Coudenhove, half-Japanese, half mixed from the breed of Europe's international nobility, really represents, as one knows, a Eurasiatic type of noble cosmopolitan, giving an average German the feeling of being somewhat provincial ... His personality and his words disclose unshakable faith in a political idea that I do not consider without defects, but that he is spreading throughout the world and propagating by his pen and his person with clearest energy. He had just had here a detailed talk with Briand who had listened to him very attentively. He expressed confidence that things were getting on and that his vision would be realised within two years.

Surprisingly neither writer's account of this dinner conversation mentions Prinz Rohan's Kulturbund. Thomas Mann was also a supporter of Rohan's initiative, and Rohan was RCK's main rival. They knew that both the organizations were holding congresses in Vienna later in the year. How could the two men – or their wives – not have mentioned it?

ROHAN'S KULTURBUND was not the only competition with which RCK had to contend. Wilhelm Heile and Alfred Nossig, RCK's erstwhile Berlin supporters, with whom he had quarrelled, were planning the first congress of their rival German organization in Geneva in September, coinciding with the foreign ministers' meeting at the League of Nations. Heile's good political contacts in Berlin ensured governmental support for his association, potentially scooping media interest and weakening RCK's chances of drumming up financial support in business circles.

In the light of these challenges, RCK conceived his Pan-Europa Congress in Vienna on an exceptionally impressive scale. It was not to be just a small, essentially German-inspired networking meeting on the margins of a larger event in Geneva – such as he imagined Heile's event would be – or a cultural event at which intellectuals and artists could debate and discuss issues, divorced from the realities of the political world – as he imagined Rohan's meeting would be. His Pan-Europa Congress was to be a high-profile, international political rally in favour of the political goal of a united Europe. The Congress was not called to discuss *whether* Pan-Europa was desirable or not, but to determine *how* and *when* to make it a reality. The goal, he confidently declared in the formal invitation, was already settled. The task of the Congress was to transform into political reality the vision that he had already set out.

But RCK also made clear that his Congress was not just for politicians. On the contrary, he expressly wanted the membership of his movement to encompass leading figures from business and the arts, as well as politics. For RCK and Idel, the elites of Europe spanned all three of these worlds, and he had scores of letters of support from leading figures in all three spheres to prove it.

He initially planned to have seven working groups or committees – to consider a customs union, economic and financial matters, the League of Nations, minorities, the Soviet Union and the British Empire, and conflict resolution. On reflection, however, this struck him as too heavily weighted towards politics and, in the end, he cut back the number to just three – political concerns, economic issues, and intellectual co-operation. That way he could widen the appeal of the programme and make even clearer his direct challenge both to Rohan and to Heile.

To strengthen his authority as convener of this first Congress, RCK established an honorary board for the event consisting of six highly respected European statesmen. First, he secured the support of Ignaz Seipel, the chancellor of Austria, who had already agreed to be honorary president of the Pan-Europa Union in Austria. From France, the Congress was endorsed by Joseph Caillaux, former prime minister and leader of the Radical Party, and from Germany by Paul Loebe, leader of the Social Democrats and Speaker of the Reichstag. That gave him political and geographical balance from the two most important countries on the continent, as well as cover at home in Austria with the chancellor himself.

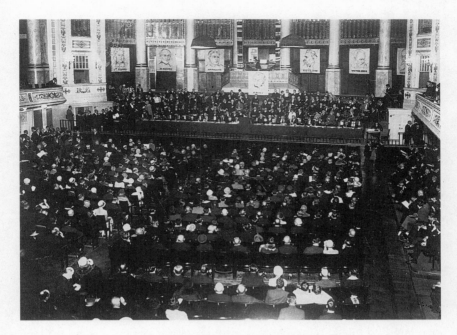

Europe's political and cultural elite attended Pan-Europa's first Congress in Vienna in 1926.

Then he invited Nicolaos Politis, a former Greek foreign minister, who was currently his country's representative at the League of Nations in Geneva, and – undiplomatically ignoring the affront this must have been to Mussolini – Carlo Sforza, former foreign minister and currently leader of the anti-fascist opposition in the Italian Senate. Finally, he persuaded Edvard Beneš, the foreign minister of Czechoslovakia and the man who had facilitated his work by giving him his diplomatic passport, to join this select company. It was a star-studded cast at the very highest level, and it set the tone for the rest of the programme.[1]

The international mailing list of leading figures that he and Idel had met on their travels, as well as the wide circulation of the *Pan-Europa Journal*, now proved their worth, giving them a continent-wide reach to already engaged and sympathetic supporters. But the time and effort that such organization required in the age before the Internet, without the advantages of email, text messaging, and social media, was inordinate. RCK and Idel had to work with the physicality of dictation and shorthand, typed top copies with carbon duplicates for filing, telegrams in several languages, international telephone calls requiring operator connections from exchange to exchange, and thousands of letters that needed a personal signature. RCK took care of the political content, the key speakers, and the media invitations, while Idel took over responsibility for ensuring that the number of participants and the administrative organization of the event were dramatically impressive. With the assistance of RCK's devoted secretary, Valerie Benedikt, the daughter of their good friend Ernst Benedikt, the editor of the *Neue Freie Presse*, and of Idel's brother, Leopold, who was now in charge of the technical aspects of the Pan-Europa publishing house, the team set to work to organize the first Pan-Europa Congress.

They persuaded the Ministry of the Interior to waive Austrian visas for foreigners on presentation of their Congress invitation card, arranged special rates at various hotels, and secured a 25 per cent reduction on Austrian railways for all participants. Just a few weeks before the event, RCK held a well-attended international press conference in Vienna's Hotel Imperial to update journalists on progress to date. The resulting coverage gave the Congress extra favourable publicity, announcing to the world that over two thousand participants from twenty-four states would attend, and over one hundred media representatives would also be present. RCK and Idel, heading a small non-governmental organization with barely three years experience behind it, had succeeded in making their Congress a major European political event.

THE PAN-EUROPA CONGRESS opened to the strains of the *Ode to Joy* from Beethoven's Ninth Symphony – the first use of this music as a symbol of European unity – in the largest and most beautiful hall in Vienna, the Konzerthaus. Idel had draped the hall with larger-than-life-size portraits of an eclectic selection of historic thinkers who had contributed to the idea of European unity – Jan Comenius, Abbé St Pierre, Immanuel Kant, Napoleon Bonaparte, Giuseppe Mazzini, Victor Hugo, and Friedrich Nietzsche. An enormous Pan-Europa flag, designed by RCK himself, dwarfed it all: the golden sun symbolizing Apollo and the classical roots of European culture, enclosing a red cross representing Europe's Christian origins, all on a blue background. The Congress programme listed sixty-eight prominent European figures from politics, business, and the arts as sponsors. Many attended in person, some sent letters of support in their absence; just fifteen of them were Austrian, fifty-three were from other countries. The Congress that opened on 3 October was quintessentially

European, and RCK wrote with pride, 'For three days, Vienna was the capital of Europe'.

Despite RCK announcing that the programme of the Congress was not solely political, many of the speakers there were in fact politicians, a few in government, but mostly either recently in office or soon to be in office again. Germany's former chancellor, Joseph Wirth, was high on the list, as was Yvon Delbos, a future French foreign minister. Alexander Lednik from Poland, Marshal Pilsudski's right-hand man, made a speech, as well as Anton Korosec, future prime minister of Yugoslavia. Kaarel Pusta, former foreign minister of Estonia, also took to the podium to support Pan-Europa.

Ranking figures from states not expected to be members of the prospective European organization also spoke, including Alexander Kerensky, the last democratic prime minister of Russia; Leo Amery, colonial secretary in the UK government; and Frederick Allen, representing Pan-Europa's American committee. They stressed the supportive role that their governments could offer for continental integration, even if their own countries would stand outside any resulting political federation.

The mayor of Vienna offered a reception in the Rathaus, and the French, German, and Czechoslovak ambassadors vied with each other in offering hospitality. The Austrian government sponsored one night at the Opera and another at the Burgtheater, where Idel played the leading role in Rostand's *L'Aiglon* (The Young Eagle), the tragic story of Napoleon's son.

After three days of political, economic, and cultural discussions, RCK was unanimously acclaimed as president of the Pan-Europa Union. Knowing of RCK's admiration for Napoleon, a leading supporter from Berlin, Dr Bruno Birnbaum from Humboldt University, presented him with a small marble bust of the emperor, which became one of his treasured possessions, and which he kept on his writing desk wherever he happened to be.[2] The whole event culminated in a gala evening for all participants in the former imperial palace of Schönbrunn, opened for the first time since the end of the Great War and the departure of the Emperor Karl. With his first Pan-Europa Congress, RCK had convincingly upstaged all possible competition, outdistancing Rohan's Kulturbund and Heile's Verband both in numbers and in quality.

Ever since the publication of *Pan-Europa* three years earlier, German-language media in particular had followed developments relating to RCK and the Pan-Europa Union, but after the 1926 Congress there was considerably more media coverage internationally. Newspapers, magazines, and more specialist political-affairs journals across Europe now wrote about the man and the movement, the charismatic young count and his goal of a

United States of Europe. His Jewish wife also received considerable media attention, in particular her professional role as a leading stage actress.

As for RCK himself, many journalists were fascinated by his exceptional origins, his mixed-race family, his handsome figure and urbane demeanour. Some were confused about his nationality. Was he really Czech, or could he be Austrian, as even Chancellor Seipel once (wrongly) assumed, or Hungarian, as Leo Amery (also wrongly) thought? There were a dozen different ways of spelling his complicated name, and should one or should one not use the aristocratic title? Was he really, as the French *Grande Revue* put it, 'the cosmopolitan incarnation of Europeanism'?

As for his character, unsurprisingly his admirers praised some aspects while his detractors criticized others. For a German sympathizer in the *Vossische Zeitung*, he was 'a man of precise thought', whose optimism was both 'far removed from the world' and at the same time such as 'to overturn a reader's view of the world'. Other commentators noted his 'simple, almost childlike power of belief' and his 'youthful, spiritually limpid character'. Another praised his 'quiet and intelligent manner of speech', his 'persuasive voice', and 'his ability to leave the magic of words, time and space to play themselves out, so that even hard-nosed realists were charmed or surprised.' Even detractors conceded that 'his demeanour and speech made a pleasant and sympathetic impression' and that this was part of his 'power over people', his charisma. Some of it, they conjectured, might possibly derive from his Japanese mother, as his ancestry lent him the fascination of all things oriental. Few would have known – though some might have guessed – that Idel had also successfully coached him early in their relationship in order to improve his public-speaking skills.

Even permanently hostile outlets, the Berlin-based right-wing nationalist *Politische Wochenschrift* among them, allowed that there was 'no doubting his personal integrity, the almost fanatical honesty of his convictions, and his heroic or even saintly preparedness to make sacrifices for his ideas.' Slightly more mischievously, the same journal then described RCK as 'Narcissus leaning over the European pool and observing his reflection. The fact that he can remain there motionless, without being aware of the most urgent intrusions of political reality, totally disarms us.' It was this 'psychological naivety' that led some critics to describe him as a 'political and ethical dilettante'. Others criticized him for being so obsessed with his one big idea that he could not see political realities beyond it. The extremes of opinion are illustrated by the views expressed in a note sent by an observer to the Foreign Office in London, praising RCK's 'great energy' and his 'uprightness of character', to which the permanent secretary in

London appended a comment, saying that he knew him personally, and he was a 'frightfully impractical theorist'.

RCK may have liked much of what he read, but he cannot always have appreciated what this wider coverage now exposed. German media, particularly those from the conservative and nationalist end of the spectrum, were more critical than most of the international press. They attacked his lack of any strong national identity, his mixed race, his lukewarm approach to religion, and even Pan-Europa's long-term goals of peace and harmony in international relations, which some saw as 'socialism by another name'. Hitler's assessment of RCK as a 'cosmopolitan bastard' was as yet unpublished, but another critic condemned his Masonic associations, also a bogey of the far right: 'What Coudenhove writes could have been written by any Freemason.'

This stung RCK more than he cared to admit, and he took the rare step of asking his Lodge for *Deckung*, literally 'cover', which meant a withdrawal from formal membership. It was not a question of denouncing his Masonic links, but it meant that he withdrew formally from his Lodge. In the letter explaining his decision, he indicated that he was obliged to take this step 'for political reasons'. Henceforth, he could deny publicly that he was a Mason and that Pan-Europa was in any way controlled by Freemasonry. In fact, it gave RCK the best of all worlds, since he did not lose the personal network that his membership had opened to him, but he could deny in all honesty that Pan-Europa was a Masonic front.[3]

In many respects, style reveals the man, and RCK's literary style revealed very clearly his manner of thinking. He liked to present ideas in terms of opposites, and he used this dialectic frequently to clarify issues and sharpen contrasts. But sometimes it also hid weaknesses in his argument. Behind this use of a stylistic device sometimes lay an assumption that substantive issues could be left to be sorted out later, so long as the propagandistic thrust of the argument was strong enough. This characteristic marred for some critics the whole Pan-Europa Congress in Vienna. RCK had convened it not to *debate* but to *endorse* the goal of a united Europe, and this approach carried many with him. But it also lost RCK some friends and supporters who had higher intellectual expectations for the event, and were, in consequence, disappointed.

Among them was Rudolf Pannwitz, one of RCK's closest early correspondents, who particularly criticized what he considered the intellectually superficial nature of the event, the glitz and glamour rather than the hard thinking needed to elaborate a meaningful and practical political programme that he would have preferred. He wrote to ask formally that his name should no longer be associated with Pan-Europa. His criticism was not welcome to RCK, and as a consequence, their friendship rapidly cooled. Karl Kraus, the editor of the influential Viennese journal *Die Fackel*, also criticized the event for similar reasons, and relations between him and RCK were subsequently more distant.

Two other Austrian writers of the time, however, wrote character profiles of RCK which give an idea of his charismatic personality and the strongly positive impression he made on those he met in the early days of establishing Pan-Europa. The writer and theatre critic, Ernst Lothar, welcomed his positive, creative, factual, patient, exact, clear thinking, noting those sparkling aspects of RCK's character, and adding that 'He is a leader who modestly, rather like a pied-piper, seduces the world into an adventure with an idea, combining evidence with imagination, fact with fantasy, precision with dreaming.' Another writer, Felix Salten, characterized him as

> a delicate, narrow-shouldered youth, modest, distinguished in his bearing, aristocratic through and through in his whole being. What enthusiasm that aroused in those days of proletarian expectations! This young man was coiled like a clenched fist, concentrated like a ball of energy, held back like an elemental power that intends to be used, but not wasted. He is as quiet as an angel, as clever as ever a genius can be, as well mannered as a count and as beautiful as a pageboy.[4]

But behind the eulogies there was also a note of caution, even dissent. Hermann Bahr, a renowned theatre critic and essayist, welcomed what he felt were the 'modest, open, likeable' characteristics of 'young Coudenhove' but added that, as an older man, he knew human nature and human behaviour too well to trust this youthful, utopian project. Thomas Mann wrote an insightful letter of thanks to RCK, congratulating him and Idel on the success of their first congress, but noting that it was only the start of a longer journey that would require RCK's total commitment to bring to a successful conclusion. He knew the strength of nationalist thinking that would hinder progress towards joint action by European countries, and the obstinacy with which existing interests would try to prevent any new dispensation which might harm them. He did not so much preach caution as realism, and realism suggested a long process, and not immediate, perhaps only superficial, success. The project, in his view, was potentially inter-generational and required strong foundations as well as time to mature.

The publicity that RCK and Idel achieved with their first Pan-Europa Congress was so far in excess of what rival organizations could achieve that the opposition took fright. Heile was first to move, and in March 1927, he persuaded the president of the French Republic, Gaston Doumergue, to lend his authority to a new umbrella organization to be called La Fédération pour l'Entente européenne (The Federation for European Understanding). It was an attempt to absorb RCK's Pan-Europa Union along with Heile's Verband and give them a French focus. When that did not work because of German opposition to a high-level French initiative, he and Rohan then appealed to Paul Loebe, the president of the Reichstag, pressing him to create an umbrella organization that would present a common front in Germany for European co-operation. Loebe may well have appreciated that a measure of co-operation would create a valid, single interlocutor for the German government, but from Heile's and Rohan's points of view it was a chance to blunt the competition that Pan-Europa now obviously offered their less-prestigious initiatives.

THERE WERE NOW at least four different organizations operating in Germany, all with an interest in furthering European understanding and each asking for Paul Loebe's support: RCK and the PUD, Heile and his Verband, Rohan and the Kulturbund, and Stern-Rubarth with a plan for a European Customs Union – Der Europäische Zollverein.[5] Personality clashes apart, it was embarrassing for the German government to have so many competing private actors involved in quasi-diplomatic activities – and the publicity associated with them. It made the German government appear disorganized in foreign eyes, particularly the French, and the muddled situation needed to be tidied up.

Late in 1927, Loebe suggested the four German organizations should form a Kartell für europäische Annäherung (Cartel for European Conciliation), which would help to simplify the situation. In essence it would be a non-aggression pact between the four signatories, putting an end to competitive timetabling of events, public criticism of each other, and multiple demands for financial and moral support from industrial and governmental circles. Heile, himself a Liberal, saw a further advantage if Loebe, a leading Social Democrat, chaired such a Kartell, as it might well come more under the influence of mainstream politicians and weaken the influence of RCK, who operated out of Vienna rather than Berlin and lacked any party allegiance.

RCK never looked on the Kartell with any benevolence. He went along with it to please Loebe, whose support he needed, but not to please the others, and after only a few months he formally pulled the PUD – the German chapter of the Pan-Europa Union – out of it and denounced the Kartell as unworkable. He had evidence, he wrote to Loebe in March 1928, that Heile had broken the Kartell's rules by criticizing Pan-Europa to businessmen both in Germany and France and intentionally misleading mutual French contacts about Pan-Europa's intentions. It was impossible to work with him.

Maintaining their independence *and* leading the field was not without its challenges, but RCK and Idel were determined to do just that. They managed it by channelling the support of Pan-Europa towards the extremely experienced statesman who had impressed them on their return from America – Aristide Briand. He had been prime minister of France ten times already and was at that critical moment serving yet again as foreign minister. He would adopt their cause, raise it above these petty quarrels of minor groups, and promote the idea of European integration among political leaders.

11

TRIUMPH IN FRANCE

AS FRENCH FOREIGN MINISTER, Aristide Briand had been informed about Pan-Europa's Vienna Congress in detail by the French ambassador, Maurice de Beaumarchais. RCK wanted to press the French government to take the next steps to make his Pan-European dream a political reality, and he quickly followed up with a visit to Paris, and at the highest political level there he now reaped dividends. He offered Briand the honorary presidency of the Pan-Europa Union, which the minister was happy to accept in principle. But he added that he would still hesitate to back RCK's ideas publicly until there was more widespread sympathy for them in the French media and a groundswell of popular and business support to which he felt he could respond.

Briand directed RCK to his good friend Louis Loucheur, already a member of RCK's French support group, whom he suggested as chairman of an economic committee that would help Pan-Europa achieve its goals in the business community. Loucheur's specific remit would be to explore how German and French businesses might more profitably co-operate rather than compete. If such transnational business interest was manifest, Briand would then lend it political support.

A long-standing fear of competition from the more efficiently organized industries of Germany led French business circles to lobby their government for protection rather than free trade. A mixture of high national tariffs, combined with subsidies for specific sectors, in particular agriculture and food processing, were central to French economic and trade policy. Low tariffs and a larger market through the promotion of exports were the traditional goals of German industry. These policies could not be easily reconciled in a single market, for fear of German domination.

Loucheur, however, considered he could square this circle by encouraging European cartels, arrangements struck among producers, industry by industry, where market shares were guaranteed and costs controlled by agreements on prices and wages between firms from different countries. This would offer protection at an international level against competition from the United States and from Great Britain, and deliver a unified domestic market for participating firms across the continent – albeit at some cost to consumers in higher prices and to workers in lower wages as a result of anti-competitive co-operation between employers.

RCK was impressed by Loucheur's businesslike approach. He was surprised and impressed by this vigorous man's powerful aura of efficiency. He described him as 'half bulldog, half Chinese', a description which, coming from RCK, himself half-Japanese, was a somewhat ambiguous compliment. 'There was something dictatorial about him, but his aggressiveness was tempered by French courtesy and *esprit*,' he wrote. Loucheur considered RCK's national committee of political and intellectual leaders quite useless when it came to achieving anything practical. He counted on business to deliver, he said, and that is what he then did.[1]

Loucheur quickly assembled a committee of leading French industrialists, bringing together representatives from the steel, coal, chemicals, aluminium, silk, wool, and textiles sectors. It took RCK a little longer to bring together a comparable committee from Germany but, with the help of Robert Bosch, he gathered representatives from the German coal and steel, chemical, electricity, machine tool, automobile, textile, linoleum, and finance industries to meet together with their French colleagues a few months later. They then attracted other employers, among them Emile Mayrisch from Luxembourg, who had recently set up an iron and steel cartel, the International Steel Understanding (EIA), and Dannie Heineman, an American engineer of German-Jewish extraction, who had organized leading electrical companies into the 'Sofina', a European trust based in Brussels.[2]

Despite the engagement of industrialists in this Franco-German rapprochement, such was the widespread German animosity towards France that RCK found it well nigh impossible to escape the accusation that Pan-Europa was not neutral, but in effect favoured French domination in continental Europe. Some nationalist commentators in the German press suggested that France's call for economic reassurance was simply a feint, and the French government's real objective was to strengthen its military, political, and financial hegemony over the whole continent. Without either Russia or Great Britain in the European equation, a defeated Germany

was fearful of an alliance with France alone, which could simply perpetuate the inequalities of Versailles. It smacked of a revival of French leadership such as Napoleon had dreamed of – a spectre that RCK occasionally
conjured up inadvertently in his enthusiasm for the long-dead emperor as
one of the founders of a united Europe.

RCK had been criticized by Heile when they first quarrelled in 1926 for
having a 'lust for power like Napoleon', and he certainly was not averse to
riding roughshod over opposition and making sure he got his way with
committees. During the first internal crisis with the Berlin group of the
Pan-Europa Union, in a packed meeting of over two hundred and fifty
Pan-Europa members chaired by Loebe in the Reichstag, Heile appeared
to have won a majority on a crucial vote. RCK, however, surprised everyone by producing over four hundred previously unannounced proxy votes
from absent members that he had gathered as president of the Pan-Europa
Union prior to the meeting. Heile was furious, and even Loebe thought
that the president 'had not acted in a democratic spirit'. But RCK had
his high-handed way, and the Minutes recorded the vote in his favour.
A new committee was duly elected, excluding Heile and including
RCK's nominees. To rub salt into the wound, he then forced through the
meeting's approval to invite other of his personal nominees to become
co-opted members – including Albert Einstein, Gerhard Hauptmann,
Heinrich and Thomas Mann, and Richard Strauss – names that very clearly
were well beyond the reach of Heile and his colleagues. RCK, the well-
connected Austrian aristocrat, was showing these Prussians just what he
could deliver – and they could not.

Three years later, in April 1929, when RCK was in the midst of restructuring the organization yet again, and pressing for new statutes to be
adopted, one of his key supporters, Gerhard Meyer, accepted that what was
needed was 'full trust in the new Leader and his Programme'. Members
did not need to have any rights in the running of the Pan-Europa Union,
he argued in the committee considering the changes, and RCK did not
disagree. Dr von Gwinner, who was responsible for the new statutes, conceded that during the drafting 'the Count frequently deleted any proposals
which tended towards democracy.' Finally, RCK intervened, 'Anyone who
wants to work in a purely democratic organization should join Heile's
Verband für europäischer Verständigung.' As for membership of the Pan-
Europa Union, he declared that he did not care how many members there
were. The number was irrelevant. What mattered was their quality. The
new statutes were approved and RCK, as leader, was free to lead entirely
as he wished.

EVEN WHEN HE HAD SETTLED internal differences within his movement, RCK found it difficult to walk the tightrope between French and German interests. Nationalist newspapers, in particular in Germany, found much to criticize in reconciliation and the prospect of co-operation between the two arch enemies. The more rabid right-wing press in Germany even accused RCK of siding with Jewish capitalism by fattening up Germany economically so that it could more easily meet the continuing French demand for reparations. 'The time will come when the work of Coudenhove will be shown for what it is: preparation for establishing Franco-Jewish dominance in Europe,' wrote the National Socialist newspaper, *Völkischer Beobachter*. Even more moderate newspapers claimed he was simply working for the long-term global dominance of Jewish-American capital.

The left-wing press both in Germany and in France was considerably more positive towards Pan-Europa. *La Vie Socialiste*, for instance, echoed the line taken by RCK, calling on France to pull back from occupying the Rhineland, just as Germany should abandon its policy of seeking revenge for Versailles. And in another left-wing newspaper, *Populaire*, the Socialist leader Léon Blum asserted that, subject to settling the issue of reparations, the only thing that stood in the way of creating the United States of Europe was an honourable and heartfelt reconciliation between France and Germany.

But right-wing papers in France were equally forthcoming with an alternative and extreme view, denying that there was any parallel between Franco-German reconciliation and creating Pan-Europa: 'this illusion of European unity, pursued in an atmosphere of Germanic mysticism at the cost of unilateral sacrifices by France and its Allies'. Versailles was justified revenge for Waterloo, they argued – by which French commentators had the Prussian Field Marshal Blücher more in mind than Wellington. Even if the Germans now seemed more pacifist and Europe-minded since their defeat, it was just a deception, as Germany's longer-term policy, they suspected, was to build up power gradually and challenge France again later.

Unsurprisingly, the target of much of this anti-German suspicion was more often Stresemann as German foreign minister than RCK as president of Pan-Europa. The French ambassador in Berlin reported to Paris that behind Stresemann, 'the good European', there lurked 'the disciple of Bismarck', and while Coudenhove might speak of integration, Bismarck had meant annexation. *Le Figaro*, a conservative newspaper, suggested that lowering customs barriers would simply lead to German economic expansion, and, with that, German political hegemony in Europe.

This same fear was also expressed inside the French Foreign Office, which was by no means united in supporting Briand's Pan-European initiative and remained somewhat reserved towards RCK. Jacques Seydoux, a senior diplomat at the Quai d'Orsay, agreed with Belgian prime minister Theunis that 'even with a blocked nose, RCK smells like a German'. His colleague, Philippe Berthelot, thought likewise, and even Alexis Léger, RCK's closest confidant and supporter in the French Foreign Office, noted that Pan-Europa was in essence a Franco-German alliance without British participation, quite contrary to the official line of the French government at the time. The pacifist newspaper *Monde Nouveau* underlined this concern, describing 'this fearful tête-à-tête' between Paris and Berlin. A Foreign Office official in Paris noted Pan-Europa's weakness in relying solely on a continental entente, writing that '"the real United States of Europe, that is an entente between France, England, and Germany, will be the cornerstone on which all other stones can then be laid.'

DESPITE THESE HESITATIONS AND ALTERNATIVES, Aristide Briand did seriously try to build an entente that included all European states willing to respond to his invitation. Inspired by RCK and Pan-Europa, but also with far-sighted French interests in mind, he sounded out both the German and British governments in March 1929 on the practical idea of a European economic union, suggesting they might build closer co-operation between the three countries on a joint institutional basis. In June, he spoke privately with Stresemann and other foreign ministers in the margins of the Council of the League of Nations, then meeting in Madrid, at the same time as France and Germany were agreeing on the timetable for withdrawal of French forces from the Rhineland. In July, at a press conference in Paris, Briand announced publicly that he would launch a proposal to establish a European union at the next meeting of the League of Nations in Geneva in two months' time.

RCK recalled in his memoirs the enthusiastic press coverage that greeted this news. He felt that all men and women of goodwill across the continent – everyone except communists and nationalists – welcomed with sighs of relief the perspective of peace and prosperity that it opened for them, the prospect that Europe could become 'peaceful like Switzerland and prosperous like the United States of America'.

Continental governments all expressed some degree of diplomatic support for the French foreign minister's suggestion, but not the United

Kingdom, Europe's off-shore island. Prime Minister Ramsay MacDonald, in an interview in the *Daily Telegraph*, stated that the idea of a United States of Europe was premature: 'At best one might speak about it in ten years' time' – an unfortunately prophetic time to choose, as in 1939 the issue of European unity would be posed in considerably less-acceptable terms by an aggressive Nazi Germany.

In a French government reshuffle in summer 1929, Briand himself became prime minister again – for the eleventh time – and also retained the portfolio of foreign affairs. In his inaugural speech to the Chamber of Deputies, he declared, 'For four years the ambitious programme suggested by the phrase "United States of Europe" has been in my thoughts without my being able to commit myself to the gigantic task. However, after a painstaking examination of the whole question I have come to the conclusion that Europe will never be pacified as long as certain problems remain unsolved, certain suspicions are not laid to rest, and as long as the nations of Europe do not try to find ways and means of collaboration.'

This time the German government could not overlook the initiative from Paris. Speaking a few days later at a conference he was attending in The Hague, Gustav Stresemann congratulated Briand on his new European policy and declared that his goals were 'an economic necessity'.

On 4 September 1929, RCK and Idel were in the diplomatic gallery at the League of Nations Assembly in Geneva when Briand put his case. 'I am convinced,' he said,

> that some kind of union is necessary for nations which represent a geographic unit. Such nations should at least be able to associate in order to discuss their common interests, make common decisions, and prove their solidarity. True, the union which we plan to bring about will have to deal with urgent economic problems. I am sure that it will produce results in this field. However, the union should prove advantageous also from a political and social point of view, and should do so without endangering any nation's sovereign rights.

Four days later, Gustav Stresemann went to the rostrum in Geneva to deliver his response. RCK noted that his face was drawn and white and his delivery dull. But the content of his speech was clear and methodical. He dismissed objections that the idea was utopian, and outlined the economic distress of European states more and more driven into political isolation and economic autarchy. The absurdities of customs controls at every border had to be cleared away, he argued, and more common functions executed together.

Aristide Briand for France and Gustav Stresemann for Germany at the League of Nations in 1929.

He also stressed the symbolic value of joint action. 'Where in Europe,' he asked, 'is the European coin and the European stamp?' Germany would happily co-operate with a Europe that was more reasonably and rationally organized. RCK was delighted with such a response. Had he not already suggested there should be a European passport and a European anthem, which would help to build a European identity, as well as a customs union and a single currency, which citizens would appreciate in their wallets?

The Czechoslovak and Italian representatives then spoke, partly in support of Briand's proposal, partly expressing their hesitations. Finally, all eyes turned to the British delegate, Arthur Henderson, now Ramsay MacDonald's foreign secretary, but Henderson declined to take the rostrum and remained silent in his seat.

Briand invited the leading representatives of the European powers to continue the discussion informally over lunch in the lakeside Hôtel des Bergues. Even there, Henderson remained non-committal, but this first informal 'European Council' did agree to mandate Briand to draft a memorandum explaining his proposal in more detail and to submit it to the other European states for their comments. In the light of these, Briand was requested to present the issue again at the annual Assembly of the League of Nations the following year.

On the face of it, and despite British hesitations, all seemed set fair for Pan-Europa. France had taken the lead, and the key idea of structured political and economic integration among the states of Europe had been presented to the League. Even if Briand abstained from mentioning Pan-Europa by name, the essence of Pan-Europa's programme had been endorsed by a major European state. RCK could claim that he had won over France to support his vision.

ON THEIR WAY BACK TO VIENNA, RCK and Idel broke their journey in the Bernese Oberland near Gstaad. They were extremely happy, and in their optimistic frame of mind, light-heartedly made a momentous decision: they bought a farmhouse. It became their country retreat for years to come, the only home that they ever owned rather than rented.[3]

It was quite by chance that Idel and RCK found their farmhouse at Gruben, a small village close to Gstaad, when they were staying at a much larger house on a nearby hillside, overlooking the villages of Sannemöser and Schönried. Idel let it be known that she was a keen collector of folk art, something she did whenever she was travelling in Europe. Word quickly spread in the vicinity, and a local farmer, Franz Bauer, invited them to come to see a pair of antique carved door panels that he was prepared to sell. When they protested that cutting the carved door panels out of their frames would ruin the effect they made where they currently were in the room, the farmer suggested RCK and Idel make him an offer for the whole house instead. They looked around, sized up its unique and striking location, and offered him twenty-five thousand Swiss francs for the property (the equivalent of roughly fifty thousand pounds sterling today). Franz Bauer was delighted as, unbeknown to RCK and Idel, he had bought the property only a few months previously for twenty thousand Swiss francs and appreciated making a quick profit.

Idel and RCK outside and inside their converted farmhouse in Gruben, near Gstaad.

The farmhouse was in an idyllic position, overlooking the valley of the river Sarine, where it flows across the linguistic boundary between German-speaking Canton Bern and the French-speaking Canton Valais. Switzerland was a miniature of the world that RCK hoped Pan-Europa would create, one harmonious country, where people peacefully co-operated, despite linguistic, religious, and political differences. Why should not the whole of Europe share what Idel and RCK experienced every day they spent in Gruben in the heart of the best-governed confederation of modern times?

Over the next few years, Idel immersed herself in renovations. She dismantled and moved a barn further away from the house, and removed one wall of the house itself in order to replace it with the carved façade of another old farmhouse that was being dismantled nearby, in Château d'Oex, a village just across the linguistic frontier. At the end of this reconstruction, their enlarged house had a German inscription carved into the façade on one side and a French inscription on the other, symbolically uniting two cultures and two languages in one home. She filled the house with her collection of European folk art, which she had collected on her travels, and extended the garden, buying half a dozen small parcels of land from neighbouring farmers, including the rolling meadow that fell away to a small stream to the south. Idel and RCK were so taken by this house and its location that they decided to mark off a plot with a short line of trees at the end of the meadow and reserve it as their last resting place.

The hamlet of Gruben, a little higher than Gstaad, was just a small railway halt on the recently opened Bernese Oberland line that linked Montreux on Lake Geneva with Bern, the Swiss capital. In one direction, via Montreux, RCK could easily reach Geneva, home of the League of Nations. In the other direction, he could reach Bern and the main lines that led via Zürich to Austria, via Basel to Germany and France, and via Interlaken to Italy. The small country station was less than a five-minute walk from their house, and RCK noted the times of the trains in his diary each year, so that he could arrange his travels as conveniently as possible.

BUT THEIR SWISS IDYLL had barely started when it was shattered by two thunderbolts that broke out of the clear sky that very October and destroyed whatever hope of European unification RCK had sensed after the meeting of the League the previous month. On 29 October 1929, Reuters reported the Wall Street Crash. The following day Gustav Stresemann suffered a fatal stroke. RCK had noted Stresemann's poor state of health when he replied to Briand's proposal in Geneva in September, but he was shocked to hear of his death, at the age of only fifty-one. He had been, in RCK's view, the only pragmatic statesman in Germany who was intelligent and flexible enough to be a partner for Briand in this great endeavour. The whole weight of this initiative, he now noted, had to be carried on one pair of shoulders, and that might well not be enough for the project to survive.

RCK wanted to ensure that other states were kept under pressure to follow up Briand's initiative positively, and with some urgency. Italy was not enthusiastic about the plan, and Great Britain was potentially hostile. Even if he could do little to encourage those two, he could try to ensure that Germany and the states of central Europe did not turn their backs on this chance. He invited Edouard Herriot, former prime minister of France, to speak with him at public rallies in Vienna, Prague, and Berlin in support of Briand's plan for a United States of Europe. In each of the three capitals, the travelling duo of RCK and Herriot spoke to large crowds at Pan-Europa rallies alongside leading local politicians. In Prague it was a well attended, multilingual event, where the long-serving foreign minister, Beneš, spoke in Czech, Herriot in French, and RCK in German, all without interpretation, as it could be assumed that their listeners, the politically informed elite of the country, could understand all three languages. In Berlin, Herriot and RCK also paid their respects at Stresemann's grave, among the first visiting foreign dignitaries to do so. In Vienna, the evening speeches by Herriot and RCK, together with Austrian Chancellor Seipel, were equally imposing.

The Vienna event was also attended by a young German aristocrat still in his twenties, acting as a torch-bearer for Pan-Europa. He had been recruited by RCK when they met a few months previously in Paris. RCK and Idel had invited him to their hotel for a meal, ostensibly to introduce him to Erika, Idel's grown-up daughter, as he was a friend of RCK's sister, Elsa. It may even have been an attempt – but an unsuccessful one – at matchmaking. Looking back sixty years later, Graf Artur von Strachwitz wrote in his memoirs, 'I found exactly what I was looking for in Dicky's Pan-European thinking, a confirmation of my anti-nationalistic inclinations, and an atmosphere of intelligent Jewish thought created by his wife.' Subsequently, von Strachwitz joined the Pan-Europa Union and volunteered in the organization's offices in the Hofburg while finishing his studies in Vienna.[4]

At the same time, a student in Leipzig, Rolf Italiaander, was motivated by reading Pan-Europa to set up a university student association to discuss and promote RCK's ideas. He invited a number of well-known speakers to discuss the prospects for a United States of Europe with students in Leipzig, and wrote to RCK in person to invite him as the founder of the Pan-Europa Union. Unfortunately, his small association could not meet the travel and lodging costs for both himself and Idel that RCK requested. Despite dedicating Pan-Europa to 'the youth of Europe', that sort of student meeting was not at the level that RCK had now grown used to addressing. By declining to make his visit pro bono, RCK missed an opportunity that might have promised more. Nonetheless, Rolf Italiaander remained devoted to the cause, going on to interview RCK and write the first biography of him in German, which appeared in 1969, just a few years before his hero's death.[5]

Enthusiasm in just a few individuals at grassroots level, however, was not enough to save the day for RCK's grand idea when major economic and political currents were turning against him. He had encouraged Briand to the point where Pan-Europa's core message was launched before all the states of Europe at the League of Nations, and it was now open for diplomatic discussion. But major events – the Wall Street Crash and the death of Stresemann – changed the economic and political context. If the tide was turning and Germany would not respond positively to Briand's invitation, then RCK might have to come to terms with the prospect of losing Germany. That would be critical for Pan-Europa's future.

12

DEFEAT IN GERMANY

THE WALL STREET CRASH on Black Tuesday at the end of October 1929 ushered in the Great Depression. In the space of a few months, its disastrous effects spread from America across all of Europe. Credit collapsed, international trade dried up, investors were ruined, savers impoverished, and workers thrown out of work. Governments turned in on themselves and sought national solutions. Public opinion shifted to the extremes of the political spectrum.

In Berlin, the grand coalition of democratic parties that had denied the extremists of left and right a majority collapsed. In March 1930, President Hindenberg tried to keep the peace by appointing Heinrich Brüning, leader of the Catholic Centre Party, as chancellor, even though he did not have a majority supporting him in the Reichstag. Brüning introduced austerity measures to cope with the rising national debt but, without a majority, he was forced to rely on presidential decrees to put his policies into law. Political clashes between the parties in the impotent Reichstag spread to the streets, where running battles between armed gangs of the Communist Rotfront and the Nazi Sturmabteilung terrorized moderate voices.

In Vienna, too, clashes between left- and right-wing parties polarized politics. The Christian Social Party held the centre ground, but with shifting coalitions holding small majorities in parliament, and chancellors only briefly in office. Living in Vienna and travelling often to Berlin, RCK was well aware how precarious democratic government had become in both countries, and it spurred him on to marshal support for Briand's efforts in favour of European integration in the hope that the prospect of union between neighbouring states, as envisaged by the French prime minister, might serve as a means of stabilizing individual countries.

The second Pan-Europa Congress opened in Berlin in May 1930, the month Brüning was appointed chancellor, just as the economic downturn was gathering pace. It was a sombre background against which to call for economic co-operation between the states of the continent, but it coincided with the date of the release of the text of the French government's draft of its Memorandum on European Union. In it, the main thrust of Briand's challenge had been maintained: European states were invited to establish regular meetings and discuss European issues among themselves, within the context of the League of Nations but without non-European states. RCK decided to make this French offer the centrepiece of his Berlin Congress, and, on the first day, the French Foreign Ministry sent fifty copies of the Briand Memorandum to Berlin by diplomatic bag to be distributed to leading participants. It was 17 May, the date that RCK consequently suggested should be celebrated annually as Europe Day.

RCK was determined to make as big an impression with his second Pan-Europa Congress in Berlin as he had with his first in Vienna four years earlier. But in this ambition the showman and publicist overruled the more sober side of his personality. A close reading of the Briand Memorandum clearly showed RCK that it was only a pale shadow of the vision for Europe that he had once discussed with the French prime minister. The Memorandum was the result of internal compromises, initially within the French government, and then between the French and other European governments, who one by one had all watered down the original text to make it what RCK described as 'a long and detailed document, couched in vague and over-careful terms'. Its main thrust – to establish regular meetings of European leaders to discuss common issues – had been maintained, but it was in no way adequate to reverse, or even halt, the deteriorating political and economic situation, let alone to inspire a younger generation to create the United States of Europe.[1]

Nonetheless, RCK's second Pan-Europa Congress was hardly less theatrical than the first, taking place in the resplendent conference hall of the Choral Academy in Berlin, and opening – as in Vienna four years previously – with Beethoven's *Ode to Joy*, relayed on German radio. That was followed by Idel reciting to rapturous applause the famous, rousing speech Victor Hugo originally delivered to the 1849 World Peace Conference in Paris.

A day will come when your arms will fall from your hands! A day will come when war will seem as absurd and impossible between Paris and London, between Petersburg and Berlin, between Vienna and Turin, as it would be impossible and would seem absurd today between Rouen and Amiens, between Boston and Philadelphia. A day will come when you France, you Russia, you Italy, you England, you Germany, you all, nations of the continent, without losing your distinct qualities and your glorious individuality, will be merged closely within a superior unit and you will form the European brotherhood, just as Normandy, Brittany, Burgundy, Lorraine, Alsace, all our provinces are merged together in France.

Victor Hugo's ideas were remarkably prescient, especially as the speech moved on to shift the resolution of conflict from the military to the political arena.

A day will come when the only fields of battle will be markets opening up to trade and minds opening up to ideas. A day will come when bullets and bombs will be replaced by votes, by the universal suffrage of the peoples, by the venerable arbitration of a great sovereign senate which will be to Europe what the parliament is to England, what the diet is to Germany, what the legislative assembly is to France. A day will come when we will display cannon in museums just as we display instruments of torture today, and are amazed that such things could ever have been possible.

Idel was herself completely convinced of the moral value of the cause of Pan-Europa and, like Victor Hugo, envisaged peace as an act of will that simply required the commitment of each individual to the principle. The devilish politics of trying to reconcile competing economic and security interests was quite a secondary matter. RCK also recognized the imperative of peace as the key pre-condition for the future prosperity of Europe, and he promoted the Berlin Congress essentially as a political act, confirming the launch of the Briand Memorandum as a practical response to contemporary tensions between the major states of the continent, a contemporary – if more bureaucratic – echo of Victor Hugo's enthusiastic political exhortation.

The French government obliged with a positive practical gesture the very same day, declaring that France would pull its troops out of the Rhineland at the end of the following month, five years earlier than scheduled, since Germany had just agreed to a new repayment schedule for wartime reparations. RCK, never reluctant to overstate his case when an opportunity occurred, did indeed claim, by linking all these events to Pan-Europa, that the participants at the second Pan-Europa Congress were 'celebrating this

day a turning point in European history'. RCK was bold enough to claim
that events were conspiring to help his cause, or at least the general cause
of international understanding, as Victor Hugo had conceived it several
generations earlier. Hugo had gone on to note

> a decline in international animosity, the disappearance of frontiers
> from maps and of prejudices from hearts, a movement towards unity, a
> softening of manners, an increase in the level of education and a drop
> in the level of penalties, the dominance of the most literary, that is to
> say the most humane, languages; everything is moving at once, politi-
> cal economy, science, industry, philosophy, legislation, and is converg-
> ing upon the same end, the creation of well-being and benevolence.

Hugo had added that this was the goal to which he would always strive,
'the extinction of misery inside and of war outside'.

As Idel acknowledged the applause of the assembled delegates, RCK of
course agreed with every one of Victor Hugo's sentiments that she had so
dramatically declaimed, but he knew in his heart that, with the Briand
Memorandum, the mountain had brought forth little more than a mouse.
There was still a very long way to go to realize his ultimate goal.

DISCUSSION OF THE MEMORANDUM at the Berlin Congress was detailed, but
the conclusions essentially endorsed its aims and proposals. The form of
union or federal link between states that Briand called for should respect
national sovereignty and the role of the League of Nations, instituting
regular meetings among European states, with a rotating chairmanship
and an executive committee or steering group of larger states, organized
by its own secretariat, which should be separate from that of the League.
It would express a political engagement with essentially an economic aim
of rapprochement, spelled out in separate programmes relating to various
aspects of economic and trade policy, including tariff reductions. In particular it stressed a common approach to third countries as far as development and foreign policy were concerned. Modest enough goals it might
seem with hindsight, but in the political scene of the times extremely
contentious and ever more difficult to realize as the Great Depression
took hold and country after country turned in on itself. Economic self-
sufficiency was the order of the day. International trade, let alone any higher
level of international understanding, was a very much lower priority.

Attendance at the second Pan-Europa Congress was also reduced, both in quantity and in quality. Some high-ranking stalwarts were there – Thomas Mann, for instance, Louis Loucheur, and Leo Amery – but to RCK's regret, several governments declined to be formally represented at the Berlin Congress, Austria and Italy among them, and he had to make do with less-prominent speakers than in Vienna four years before. Daniel Serruys, a senior French civil servant and economist, and Franz Aereboe, a German member of the Reichstag specializing in agricultural affairs, were among the main speakers, but the Berlin Congress reflected in some respects the second tier rather than, as four years previously, the Pan-Europa Congress in Vienna.

Leo Amery, now an opposition backbencher and no longer secretary of state for the Colonies, expounded Great Britain's hesitations about its relationship to the Pan-Europa project, which he knew the MacDonald government shared. Peace and prosperity on the continent were in Britain's interest, he declared, and Britain should further European union by backing Briand's crusade to the full. But Britain could never join a European federation itself, because its future was linked to its overseas dominions. Continental peace was a prerequisite for Britain to enjoy her world-wide possessions, but her wider interests would never be given up for those of the continent. Hence Britain, Amery argued, would sympathize and support efforts to realize Briand's vision, but would not be part of it. He could see that the ideal of European patriotism, even the prospect of European citizenship, was a motivating factor for the continentals, and he compared that to common citizenship under the Crown offered by Great Britain to her subjects in the dominions. Each could provide a sense of identity with a larger Motherland without necessarily creating a political structure as binding as a confederation, let alone a federation.

Amery noted in his diary that both Daniel Serruys and Louis Loucheur argued strongly against the United Kingdom's abstention from Pan-Europa, but judging by British newspaper reports the following day, including those in *The Times*, he could congratulate himself for being much more in tune with media opinion, at least in London. He wrote in his diary that 'My chief part was to make quite clear both our sympathy and our inability to take part in any Pan-European union ... Mentally we are much too far from Europe ever to enter wholeheartedly into its policies.'[2]

Churchill, a close friend of Amery and also out of office at that time, had already put a similar view in a long article in the US *Saturday Evening Post* in February the same year.

We are bound to further every honest and practical step which the nations of Europe may make to reduce barriers which divide them and to nourish their common interests and their common welfare. We rejoice at every diminution of the internal tariffs and the martial armaments of Europe. We see nothing but good and hope in a richer, freer, more contented European commonality. But we have our own dream and our own task. We are with Europe, but not of it. We are linked, but not comprised. We are interested and associated, but not absorbed.[3]

Events would later bring Churchill to a considerably more engaged position vis-à-vis continental union, but at this time his view – like Leo Amery's and much British opinion – was firmly rooted in the imperial perspective that was central to British interwar identity.

Continuing his diary entry on the Pan-Europa Congress, Amery mischievously added, 'A German professor and novelist Thomas Mann read out a fearsome abstruse essay beginning with the olive and fig in the Garden of Eden, the one the male intellectual, the other the female and sensuous principle, but I was too sleepy ever to discover how it linked up with Pan-Europa.'

Speakers from other countries at the Berlin Congress were considerably more supportive than Amery, but Loucheur and RCK both realized that, without the active support of Great Britain, Briand's initiative would have little chance of success. In a spirit of optimism, the Congress voted unanimously in favour of the Memorandum, and the media generally judged the event to be an impressive display of European solidarity. In reality, however, RCK was aware that it was a brave attempt to paper over serious misgivings about the prospects for progress when the League of Nations would discuss the Briand Memorandum later that year.

When, in September 1930, the foreign ministers of the member states assembled in Geneva, everyone had kind words to say about the intention of securing peace in Europe through economic co-operation, but everyone had objections to some part of the project. The best that the League could agree upon was to set up a Study Group, composed only of European states, to consider specifically European, as opposed to global, issues. But it was not to be serviced by a separate secretariat, and it was chaired – at British insistence – by Sir Eric Drummond, the secretary-general of the League, the very man who had told RCK six years earlier not to hurry with his proposals for Pan-Europa. RCK realized immediately that this was a way for those who opposed Briand's vision to deny it any independent existence, to sideline the issue.

While the League was in session in Geneva, news reached the delegates of the surprising results of the German elections. Chancellor Brüning had misjudged the domestic situation in Germany. Hoping to strengthen the parliamentary position of the moderate parties, he had called an early election, but it was the extremists, in particular the Nazis, who benefited. Six million Germans – nearly one voter in five – voted for the National Socialists, making them the second-largest party, with one hundred and two deputies in the Reichstag, not far behind the Social Democrats with one hundred and forty-seven seats. RCK wrote that, at that moment, 'for the first time the prospect of Hitler becoming chancellor dawned over the horizon. It was enough to destroy the embryonic understanding between Germany and France, and to make impossible the prospect of building up Pan-Europa for some time.'

Despite this set-back, RCK submitted a draft for a European Pact, or Treaty, to the first session of the Study Group set up by the League, the first article of which called for an 'eternal alliance with a view to assuring peace in Europe forever'. He also proposed more intense political, economic and research co-operation among European states, but the Study Group failed to reach any decision on this. He further suggested, early in 1931, that it should call an urgent conference specifically on European security, allowing the European states in the Study Group to draw up a common position in advance of the major conference on world disarmament that the League was planning to hold a few months later. But again, national delegates declined to commit themselves to a European initiative in this sector.

Briand's project had now become an intergovernmental project, and there was no agreement among the European states on how – or even if – to take the initial French proposal forward, let alone to support any new suggestions from the president of the Pan-Europa Union. In their eyes, he was simply another voice from civil society, just another non-governmental organization. RCK encouraged members of his Pan-Europa Union, the readers of his *Pan-Europa Journal*, to lobby their respective governments to go further, but conditions were far from favourable. After three years of intermittent meetings, the Study Group suspended its work without any substantive progress.[4] The Briand initiative had run into the sand.

AS THE POLITICAL SITUATION in Germany grew more desperate, RCK redoubled his propaganda efforts. He brought out two short political books: *Stalin & Co.* in 1931, a fiercely anti-Communist tract pointing to the danger from the east, and the following year *Das Paneuropa ABC*, an easy guide to Pan-Europa's policies for the general reader. He also published two more philosophic or historical essays – *Los vom Materialismus* (*Beyond Materialism*) and *Revolution durch Technik* (*Revolution through Technology*). The first set out his anti-materialistic philosophy, suggesting that the desire for perfection rather than happiness was the foundation of ethical behaviour, an elaboration of the initial statement in his university thesis, still marked by his admiration for Nietzsche. The second underlined his faith in technological progress, through which the material needs of humanity would be solved. Such progress demanded a reassessment of international relations, because time and space were increasingly being shrunk by modern developments, and national isolation, even independence, was no longer a practical policy for any European state. Technological advances demanded international co-operation now, and eventually integration.

RCK was much in demand as a public speaker, not only at local groups of his supporters in various German cities – Hamburg, Stuttgart, Karlsruhe, Frankfurt, Kassel, Breslau, Gürlitz, Berlin – but also at universities where students were coming together to form groups interested in Pan-European issues. He also often broadcast on radio, particularly in Germany, Austria, and Switzerland, and corresponded with listeners who wanted to know more about his organization and its political programme. It was not only his programme which was appealing, but also the manner in which he presented it. One listener who wrote to him even admitted that she had not retained much of what he had said, but she was captivated by his voice and wanted to know more.

In June 1931, he was invited to London to present his views on Europe at a meeting in Chatham House. Introducing him, Leo Amery praised RCK as the 'prophet of an idea – the idea of European patriotism'. In light of that patriotism, Amery hoped that national patriotisms, 'in as far as they are sources of friction and war, would be sterilised for mischief while continuing their existence for good.'

RCK's speech was entitled 'The Pan-European Outlook', and he did not mince his words for his British audience. 'Between the national period of humanity and the period, that will come one day, of the organisation of the whole world as a single federation of states, we must pass through a continental period, a time when narrow national patriotism changes into patriotism for large parts of the world. One illustration of this is the movement for British Empire patriotism, another is the movement for Pan Europe.'[5]

He went on to list three reasons why Pan-Europa was necessary: first, to prevent war; second, to avoid economic ruin; and third, to defend Europe from the Bolshevik danger. He stressed the need to inform public opinion about both the high ideals of Pan-European co-operation and also the advantages it offered to further common economic interests. He argued that Pan-Europa was working to make boundaries in Europe invisible, 'as invisible as the border between England and Scotland'. Borders would become 'invisible from the military point of view because of European federation; from the economic point of view by European free trade or a European customs union; and from the national point of view by a real protection of minorities and real equality between the nations of Europe.'

He repeated his basic criticism of the League of Nations, which 'ought to be,' he said, 'not a federation of states, as it actually is, but a federation of federations.' Pan-Europa would be one such federation, and the British Empire another, along with the American states, the Soviet Union, and what he vaguely called the 'Conference of China and Japan'. In this world organization, he pleaded for close co-operation between the British Empire and Pan-Europa, along with the states of North and South America, as the bastion of Western values against Bolshevism on the one hand and the Orient on the other.

RCK was as impressive at giving formal speeches, such as this Chatham House presentation, as he was in private conversation. He made his points clearly and answered questions in a straightforward and serious manner. A member of the audience asked, for example, 'Why is it necessary to exclude Britain from Pan-Europa on account of her Dominions when France has her African possessions, Belgium has the Congo, and nearly every other European state has interests outside Europe?' RCK replied that it was a matter for the British Empire to decide. 'Nobody in Europe would say anything against the entry of the British Empire into the European Federation; it would bring with it great possibilities of emigration and many other advantages for Europe.' But he did not think it was likely that the Dominions would agree to it. 'If they had to choose between a European Federation,' he said, 'or an Anglo-Saxon Federation, which could be crystallised around the United States, they are more likely to choose the latter.'

During another of his visits to London in the early 1930s, his pessimistic view of British engagement in Europe was confirmed by a private debate that Leo Amery set up for him to try to persuade two leading politicians of the strength of his arguments in favour of Pan-Europa. Amery asked Geoffrey Dawson, the editor of *The Times*, to chair the private discussion at his flat, and asked Austen Chamberlain and Arthur Henderson, both former British foreign secretaries, the one Conservative and the other Labour, to debate with RCK and him whether Britain should adopt a more positive policy towards European integration. Henderson and Chamberlain were both determined to put forward every available counter-argument, and in the end Chamberlain summed up the discussion by saying: 'Though my friend Henderson and I hold conflicting views on a great many matters, we seem to agree fully on the fact that the unification of Europe is not in the interests of Britain.' Henderson endorsed this statement, and Amery and RCK clearly had to give in. It was one of the very few recorded moments when RCK was obliged to take 'No' for an answer.

IN THE EARLY 1930S, RCK feared that Great Britain was not drawing any nearer to Pan-Europa, while Germany, he sensed, was rapidly turning away. In the *Pan-Europa Journal* he described the struggle between Brüning and Hitler as the 'battle for the soul of Germany', and went so far as to suggest concessions by other states to a Germany led by Brüning, in order to strengthen his position and prevent his rival coming to power. RCK even reversed his earlier policy of defending the Versailles settlement in its entirety by appealing to other governments to nullify the clause that attributed war guilt to Germany. That, he argued, would be a psychological coup that would cost nothing, and at the same time would help to strengthen Brüning's political position internally, cutting the ground from under Hitler, as it would nullify one of the main themes of his nationalist propaganda.

In March 1931, RCK proposed another revision to the Versailles settlement. It concerned the Polish Corridor, the tangle of rights and obligations affecting Poland's access to the Baltic, as well as Germany's access by land to East Prussia. On behalf of Pan-Europa, he commissioned a technical study from two Swiss engineers. They suggested enhancing rail and road links between Germany and East Prussia with a series of tunnels. This would avoid German transport being dependent on Polish permits and controls to cross the corridor. The engineering support gave the plan a degree of technical credibility, but it also hid a redefinition of political responsibility for the two states, a confusion between sovereignty and practical administrative issues. In RCK's view, a rational, practical, and technical settlement such as this with Poland in the east would be reassurance enough to allow the German government then to give concessions to France in the west. These twin moves would help to integrate Brüning's Germany into a more secure, and hence more peaceful, Europe.

Full of hope, RCK sent his proposal to Chancellor Brüning with a copy to the German Foreign Office. But an internal Foreign Office note objected to what it considered RCK's 'meddling', and Julius Curtius, the foreign minister, turned the proposal down as 'unwelcome', noting that such 'small palliative measures did not suffice to solve the particularly gross state of affairs on the Eastern border.' RCK's proposal found no favour in Poland either, where he was booed by students at Warsaw University while explaining it. He had misjudged the strength of national feeling, the passion which could blind actors – politicians, civil servants, the media, and the populace – to what appeared to a dispassionate observer, such as he liked to consider himself, as rational and practical solutions to a contentious European problem.

RCK's concerned efforts to bolster Brüning as the last and best alternative to Hitler also led him to welcome the announcement of a customs union between Germany and Austria. On Brüning's instruction, Curtius had secretly negotiated the arrangement with his Austrian counterpart, Johannes Schober, and their agreement was made public in March 1931. France immediately rejected this customs union as a breach of the Versailles and St Germain treaties, which required Austria to remain independent from Germany. Italy and Czechoslovakia also objected to the agreement, fearing it would give German industry privileged access to the Austrian market on terms that neither of them enjoyed. Together, they brought the issue to the League of Nations for adjudication. The Court of Justice in The Hague condemned the plan, though by a narrow majority of judges (eight to seven), and the German and Austrian governments were forced to withdraw it. RCK had again surprisingly misjudged what he took to be a technical measure, while others interpreted it much more politically.

In 1931, RCK's American benefactor, Nicholas Murray Butler, was awarded the Nobel Peace Prize for his efforts to strengthen international law and the International Court at The Hague. The citation stressed his belief in peace being brought about by co-operation between elites, and in his wake the following year RCK was nominated for the Nobel Prize for the first time. He was proposed by Erich Koch-Weser, chairman of the liberal German Democratic Party and previously minister of the interior, vice-chancellor, and minister of justice. This attempt was not successful – indeed, no award at all was made in 1932 – but it put RCK clearly in the frame for subsequent nominations and indeed shortlisting – and there were many, both before and after the Second World War.

About this time, Carl von Ossietzky, a pacifist and one of the most highly regarded German social critics, wrote a perceptive-but-damaging commentary on RCK and Pan-Europa in the July edition of the influential German journal *Die Weltbühne*. He argued that Pan-Europa was in danger of becoming a 'movement of intellectuals without any popular base', adding that RCK was prepared to look for and accept 'the titular support of prominent politicians, gladly given to a youthful, elegant aristocrat, as the equivalent of real deeds. He is not selective and simply gathers them, falling back into the bad habits of the early founders of the Peace Movement, like Bertha von Suttner, sending friendly invitations to powerful figures in the imperialistic states and getting nothing in return but a few kindly granted handshakes.'

Gerhard Meyer, one of RCK's stalwart supporters in the Pan-Europa Union branch in Bremen, wrote to von Ossietzky in RCK's defence and received a gracious editorial reply, admitting that perhaps the criticism had been too superficial and that more might be happening behind the scenes, but that the kernel of the article was true: the Pan-Europa Union worked outside of state structures and was not in a position to deliver what it promised. RCK might be a good European, but he had the 'sweet, child-like belief of an Austrian' in the power of influential people, of important names, of connections. Von Ossietzky criticized RCK for having ruined the essentially good idea of Pan-Europa by ignoring the masses and for circulating 'only in grand hotels and exclusive concert halls'.

AS THE SITUATION in Germany deteriorated, RCK lost any sense of perspective in his repeated efforts to support Brüning as chancellor. He continued to champion the idea of a customs union, despite Germany and Austria having abandoned it in the light of the International Court's ruling. It might have been simply a first step, he suggested, that could subsequently have led to economic and even political union across the whole continent, the long-term goal that Pan-Europa was asking for. This was a strange interpretation of the facts, since additional strength drawn from the customs union would have *increased* German, as opposed to French, influence along the Danube, and encouraged steps towards making Germany the dominant state on the continent, a development totally contrary to Pan-Europa's declared aims.

In the worsening economic situation, the collapse of three small French banks in May 1931 triggered the much-more-devastating collapse of Austria's largest bank, Creditanstalt. It brought the financial implications of the Great Depression home to everyone across Central Europe. What little credit there was dried up completely. Two years after the Wall Street Crash, industrial production in Germany had fallen to half what it had been in 1929, and in September 1931 even the mighty pound sterling was forced to leave the gold standard. As investment stalled, unemployment across Europe soared. In Germany it passed six million, and in Austria six hundred and fifty thousand, more than half of them with no alternative source of income at all in their family. The general populace lost hope, and politics became ever more extreme. RCK recognized that this increasingly dire economic situation was opening the door wider and wider for Hitler and the Nazis to pass through and take power.

As long as there was a hope of Franco-German reconciliation, however, whether politically by a security pact or economically through the creation of European cartels, RCK pursued it. Franco-German understanding had to be achieved urgently by identifying common interests in order to stave off war in Europe. In the *Pan-Europa Journal* he even called for a grand international conference to consider revisions to the Versailles Treaty, taking into account all aspects: political and economic, as well as security. But this initiative led him into increasingly deeper contradictions with earlier Pan-European positions, sawing off the branch on which he sat. It lost him support in several countries across central and eastern Europe, whose very existence as new states relied on maintaining the Versailles settlement in its entirety. For RCK, strengthening Brüning's position and preventing a Nazi takeover in Germany had crowded out all other considerations.

He drafted yet another memorandum, entitled 'Versailles and Wilson', and confidently sent it to Brüning. It reviewed and updated President Wilson's Fourteen Point Peace Plan with a view to making it respond better to contemporary needs. Brüning asked the German Foreign Office for their assessment, and an internal note summarized RCK's conclusions: '1. Clarification of the war guilt issue; 2. Solving the problem of reparations; 3. Resolving the problem of the (Polish) Corridor in the sense of his (earlier) plan; 4. Solving the disarmament problem by creating an army for the League of Nations.' The German Foreign Office note continued, 'Here he is obviously trying to go some way to meet French demands.' It concluded with the final point. '5. The return of colonies to Germany.'

This internal note went on to explain RCK's reasoning, and in doing so revealed his remarkably prescient analysis of the geopolitical consequences of failure. RCK prophesied that, if discussions about such a revision did not take place soon, Germany would run the risk of Hitler seizing power as a dictator. Subsequently, Germany would join with the Soviet Union and

Italy in a pact that would drag the states of central and eastern Europe into their ideological thrall. Then Western Europe would fall under American influence, and Europe, as RCK conceived it, would no longer exist.

In April 1932, elections in Germany returned Hindenberg as president with nineteen million votes. Hitler came second with thirteen million, far ahead of Ernst Thälmann, the Communist candidate, with just over three million. As a result of political intrigues in Berlin, President Hindenberg, now eighty-four years old and in ill health, dismissed Brüning from office and replaced him with Franz von Papen. This was unwelcome as well as unexpected news to RCK. He had met von Papen and knew that he was a schemer, a shallow politician with no principles. The old leaders in France, Germany, and Austria who had helped Pan-Europa and fostered the ideas of reconciliation and co-operation were passing from the scene. Stresemann had died in 1929, Briand and Seipel both died in 1932. In RCK's eyes they were giants; their successors were not up to the task by comparison.

As he viewed the world – and Europe in particular – from his office in the Hofburg or his study in the former prior's apartment in Heiligenkreuzerhof, RCK grew ever more concerned and ever more depressed by the political situation. Yet, despite the attrition of the years and the falling away of friends – Louis Loucheur had also died in November 1931 – RCK's efforts to influence people and policies remained unceasing. He was increasingly aware, however, that his preferred methods of winning over influential leaders and the political elite in each country through private diplomacy, such as personal meetings with political leaders, supplemented with public relations (well-argued articles in the press, informed interviews on radio, lectures at international conferences) were no longer the only or the best instruments to achieve his goals.

He needed now to galvanize millions of voters, not just the elite. In the changed circumstances of the day, Pan-Europa's propaganda needed to shout louder and ignore finesse, to compete with the challenge of mass rallies and populist demonstrations in the street, to sway public opinion in its favour, and drown out any opposition. The Nazis had made serious gains in the German elections, and they had to be stopped.

IT WAS AT THIS POINT that RCK decided to transform the Pan-Europa Union from an elite association of peace-minded intellectuals, small in numbers if high in quality, into a mass movement. That way, he hoped, he could save Germany for Pan-Europa, and save Europe from an aggressively nationalist Germany. The Nazis had the wrong policies, but they were past masters at propaganda, and had shown the practical, organizational route that Pan-Europa must now follow.

The next Pan-Europa Congress was scheduled for October 1932 in Basel, and there RCK announced his plan to transform the Pan-Europa Union into the European Party. It would organize in every country of the continent, starting in Germany. Its goal was 'to create the United States of Europe, founded on internal and external peace, economic and social progress, and personal and national freedom.' Its manifesto demanded 'a confederation guaranteeing the sovereignty and security of all states, a revision of the peace treaties to create justice between European states, a European Federal Court for the obligatory resolution of all conflicts, and a European military alliance with a united general staff and a common air force to ensure peace and balanced disarmament.'

The European Party programme, which RCK had drawn up personally, was comprehensive, modern, and forward-looking. Its wide-ranging manifesto covered foreign policy, the creation of a customs union, a progressive social policy, personal and religious freedom, the recognition of private property, democratic reforms to encourage stable government, equality for women, and an education policy to encourage excellence in all fields. It went on to demand respect for national and regional cultures, the protection of minorities, a ban on hate speech, and 'renewed European idealism'. It concluded with an appeal to struggle against 'war policy and the arms race, national repression and international denigration, poverty and unemployment, plutocracy and communism, corruption and demagogy' and – in a final, idealistic flourish – 'the materialism of the nineteenth century'.

The Basel Congress was the first occasion for RCK also to present Pan-Europa's youth wing. Teenagers in blue uniforms modelled on Baden Powell's Scouting movement – a peaceful alternative to the Hitler Youth – acted as marshals at the Congress. The Basel programme claimed a role for the European Party in each and every state, with its common flag designed by RCK and its anthem written by Beethoven, its noble aims and its clearly articulated manifesto. The Congress immediately approved the legal statutes that he had drawn up for the European Party in Germany.

But RCK had misjudged both the moment and the political mood. The numbers attending this Basel Congress were not up to the level of previous ones in Vienna and Berlin. Quarrels with leading figures in the German, French, and Swiss sections – largely due to RCK's insistence on personal dominance in the movement – dissuaded some of them from attending, and he had not consulted widely with patrons or even with other speakers at the Congress about this shift of emphasis in Pan-Europa's work. Max Warburg declined to attend, and Robert Bosch, whose firm had long been a key financial supporter of Pan-Europa in Germany, judged the idea of creating a new political party to be a serious mistake. Better by far, he argued in correspondence with RCK, to rely on other parties and to persuade them to adopt Pan-Europa's policies. Pan-Europa should remain a ginger group, not try to become a mass movement, still less a political party.

There were few consolations for RCK at the Basel Congress to compensate for his fundamental misjudgement about the creation of the European Party, but characteristically he made the most of these. He claimed that the Marquis Quartara, an Italian Freemason and author of *The United States of Europe and the World*, was officially representing Italy, since Mussolini had allowed him to travel to be there.[6] He also used Leo Amery's speech on trading issues as a cue for a copy-cat proposal for Pan-Europa, opportunistically imitating the Imperial tariff arrangements recently agreed for the British Empire.[7] Winding up the Congress, RCK identified his own past narrative with his future vision of Europe, delivering an up-beat speech stressing five key dates in Pan-Europa's short history.

The first date was in 1923, he declared, the day when *Pan-Europa* was published and with Idel he had founded the Pan-Europa Union. Then a political vision was born. After that came October 1926, when Austrian Chancellor Seipel opened the first Pan-Europa Congress in Vienna, greeting the Pan-Europa flag in the name of Europeans of all nations. On that day, RCK now claimed, Pan-Europa became a spiritual and an intellectual force to be reckoned with. Then, in May 1930, when French prime minister Briand, the honorary president of the Pan-Europa Union, sent his European Memorandum for a United States of Europe to all national governments and to the second Pan-Europa Congress in Berlin. On that day Pan-Europa became a political force. The fourth key date was this Pan-Europa Congress in Basel, the launch of the European Party, which his audience had just witnessed that very day. And, he concluded dramatically, the fifth great date would be that moment in the near future when Pan-Europa would usher in the United States of Europe.

But this third Congress in Basel was in reality a damp squib. The European Party was stillborn. It did not put forward candidates in the forthcoming German elections, still less contest the streets of Germany with the Nazis. The July 1932 elections made the Nazis the largest party in the Reichstag, with a third of the popular vote. Although they lost a few seats in the November elections that same year, they were still major contenders for power. Less than three months later, after intense wrangling among the various party leaders, President Hindenberg finally entrusted Hitler with the chancellorship on 30 January 1933.

THAT VERY EVENING Hitler's cabinet met informally, in anticipation, in the Kaiserhof Hotel on the Wilhelmplatz next to the Reich Chancellery in Berlin. Quite coincidentally RCK was due to speak in another part of the hotel to a meeting of the prestigious SiSeSo Society, an elite dining club, named after Walter Simons, Hans von Seeckt, and Wilhelm Solf, three leading German political figures, all acquainted with RCK since his initial visit in 1924. Those coming to listen to him were asked by the management to use the side door to avoid trouble with the Nazi stormtroopers at the main entrance and in the foyer.

The title of his talk was 'Germany's European Vocation', which might have seemed politically aligned to the Nazi Party, but in RCK's hands it was the very opposite – and subversive. He laid out clearly the peaceful alternative that Pan-Europa proposed: Europe united not by force but on the basis of reconciliation, equality, and mutual interest. It was a goal that in the present circumstances there was no hope of realizing, and in retrospect RCK described his speech that evening as the 'swan song of the Movement'. When his audience dispersed, they ran the gauntlet of the torch-lit Nazi demonstration that filled the streets of central Berlin.

With Hitler's assumption of power, RCK knew that Germany was lost to him. The PUD now found itself in a desperate situation. Within a matter of weeks, it became clear that the Nazis were intent on total political dominance within Germany. They would make no exception, least of all for a potential European competitor to their national-socialist philosophy. The *Pan-Europa Journal* was banned, and RCK's books were among those burned in Berlin on 10 May.[8] The bank accounts of the Pan-Europa Union were frozen and later liquidated in favour of the Nazi Winterhilfe charity. In July, the 754 remaining members of the Pan-Europa Union in Germany were forced to agree to dissolve the organization, the decision justified with the specious (and possibly ironic) argument that 'private organizations were no longer needed to pursue activities that lie in the field of government policy.'

'As long as National-Socialism ruled Germany, Pan-Europa was completely impossible,' RCK commented sadly. Many members of his far-flung Pan-Europa Union in other countries were equally dispirited and were disinclined to continue their support. They particularly objected to the prospect of one day, when all this Nazi business was over, having to embrace as co-citizens of a united Europe the very Germans who had brought Hitler to power in Germany. Hitler's assumption of power, RCK wrote, had reduced Pan-Europa to 'a pile of rubble'.

In the period between the Nazi party's first large electoral gains in September 1930 and the night that Hitler came to power in January 1933, the political world that RCK had known had fallen apart. In that period, he had spoken at innumerable meetings, published many books, and written more than seventy articles in the *Pan-Europa Journal* commenting on contemporary politics and international affairs. He had even tried to launch a European political party to oppose the Nazis in Germany itself. In retrospect, his almost-frenetic activity seems not unlike that of the boy holding his finger in the dike, hoping against hope that the waters would not break through and engulf him and all he held dear. But there was a tide of nationalism running against RCK's Pan-European project. When the dike burst in 1933, the waters swept away Pan-Europa in Germany and completely destroyed his political organization there. With Germany lost to him, RCK had to fall back on Vienna, and he needed to completely revise his goal of a peacefully united Europe. He had to reinvent Pan-Europa and adapt it to the changed geopolitical situation.

13

LAST STAND ON THE OLD CONTINENT

FOR RCK THERE WAS NO CONSOLATION PRIZE for losing in Germany. For a while he was in an uncharacteristically depressed state of mind. He and Idel even considered moving Pan-Europa's headquarters from Austria to Switzerland for greater personal security. But when Chancellor Dollfuss eventually agreed to become honorary president of the Austrian Pan-Europa Union, they decided to stay in Vienna.[1]

The post had been vacant since the death of Chancellor Seipel in August 1932, and RCK had first offered it to Dollfuss during the League of Nations meeting in September that year. The new chancellor had not rushed to accept. In a reminder letter that RCK sent to him in November, he tactfully made mention of three leading politicians who were honorary presidents of the French, Czechoslovak, and Romanian committees (Joseph Caillaux, Edvard Beneš, and Nicolae Titulescu), three countries with which Dollfuss specifically wished to improve relations. As a result, Dollfuss asked RCK to come to see him and discuss the terms on which he might accept the role.

Dollfuss had only one year's experience in the cabinet of a previous government before a political crisis had catapulted him into the office of chancellor. He needed all the help and support he could find both from his own political supporters, the Christian Social Party, and from wherever else it might be available. On reflection, Dolfuss recognised that RCK's offer of support could be a godsend for his administration, and together they conceived a plan of action that closely followed Austria's foreign-policy priorities in key areas. Pan-Europa would endorse the independence of the country (no Anschluss with Germany); help to develop defensive alliances with neighbouring states (in particular Italy and Hungary); encourage political co-operation with the Little Entente of Romania,

Czechoslovakia, and Yugoslavia; and strengthen economic relations with all new states of the Danube basin.

For Dollfuss, Pan-Europa was a useful agency that would increase Austrian influence in its neighbourhood. For RCK, Dollfuss was a necessary support to keep Pan-Europa alive. Dollfuss's priorities were largely congruent with Pan-Europa's broader aims of international co-operation in Europe, and both of them saw Germany as the immediate threat and France as a long-term ally. It was not European unity, but local or regional unity against the particular force – Germany – that wanted European domination.

RCK and Dollfuss shared the view that Austria held a key position in the region and hoped that, by playing its cards well, the country could thwart the ambitions of Hitler in central and eastern Europe. RCK noted that 'Austria would probably be the main battleground of Europe for the years to come. Vienna was Europe's first trench line against the Nazi tide.' Together they needed to hold that line as long as possible. Hitler, persuaded by his early experience of Vienna and by Haushofer's geopolitical analysis, thought along the same lines. He knew that whoever ruled the 'heartland' of central Europe would control the whole continent.

In the polarized situation where fascism dominated the right, communism dominated the left, and liberalism and social democracy were more and more squeezed on the middle ground, RCK had a difficult choice to make. He consistently wrote and preached against communism as a political creed. For him it was beyond the pale, based on Asiatic principles and completely antithetical to the Greco-Christian basis of Western civilization. He had witnessed the Communist-inspired General Strike in Vienna in 1927, the burning of the Palace of Justice by left-wing agitators, and fighting in the streets between government troops and the workers. RCK rightly saw the hand of Stalin and the Comintern in every Communist party across the region, and his hostility to the Soviet Union made him no friends in that quarter.

He had his doubts about social democrats and liberals as well, since their embrace of democracy failed his test of 'quality' by sacrificing power to the lowest common denominator in the state, the highest number of voters, which led in contemporary conditions to rule by a plutocratic elite, business interests with the deepest purse. The universal franchise was by definition *too* democratic, opening the door to rule by the masses or rule by money, by an ignorant mob or the pretention of plutocrats who knew the price of everything and the value of nothing. Plutocracy was as suspect in his eyes as Communism.

RCK was already sympathetic to the strong leadership that Mussolini and his fascist movement offered Italy, and consequently had little hesitation in aligning with the authoritarian government imposed by Dollfuss in Austria. Both Mussolini and Dolfuss might lead right-wing governments, but they were not simply the political mouthpieces of plutocracy. They rested on a sense of nationhood, but distinguished themselves from Nazism in RCK's eyes by not being based on theories of racial superiority.

For him fascism had the virtue of mitigating the weaknesses of democracy by organizing the apparatus of government around a strong leader, engaged in constant consultation with professional and other groups with specific expertise, all welded together into a national movement that did away with conflicting political parties and divisive popular choice. For him, that allowed more consideration of quality, intelligence, and expertise in politics, even if at the cost of popular representation. He had no qualms when Dollfuss assumed emergency powers in Austria in March 1933 and governed without reference to parliament. He raised no objection when, over the following months, Dollfuss went on to ban the extremist political parties both of the left and the right, the Austrian Communist Party and the Austrian Nazi Party.[2]

About this time, RCK also achieved his long-standing ambition of meeting Mussolini in person and discussing with him the idea of Pan-Europa. The meeting was arranged through the good offices of the Italian foreign minister, Dino Grandi, whom RCK contacted at the League of Nations in Geneva in March 1933. RCK records how two months later he was welcomed at the Palazzo Venezia in Rome and shown through a series of imposing iron gates and along narrow corridors before being ushered into Il Duce's vast study. The dictator remained seated at his enormous desk in the opposite corner of the room while RCK silently made his way across the room and stood there a moment, waiting for his attention. Then Mussolini rose to his full height, all five feet six inches of him – only slightly more than Dollfuss – and offered RCK a seat. Their conversation began, as RCK noted, in a serious and coolly reserved manner.

He found Il Duce much changed from the man he had first seen in the Senate seven years before. Short he might be, but he was a powerful, stocky man.

His black hair had begun to turn grey. He had become older and stouter. But this also made him look more massive and robust than ever. His movements were no longer as nervous and jumpy as he seemed in the Senate; he now seemed calm and controlled. He had evidently become much more familiar with the part of Caesar for which he had cast himself. There was not a trace now of the temperamental journalist whom I had observed in the Senate; instead I now sat face to face with a wealthy and powerful business leader of unpretentious peasant origin. Whereas formerly I thought of him as resembling a leopard, he now seemed much more like a heavy bull.

They spoke in French and their first topic of conversation was Nietzsche, his views on human nature and on leadership. RCK had come prepared with some of his own publications, and handed Il Duce a copy of the *Pan-Europa Journal*, in which quotations from all Nietzsche's writings regarding European unity had been collected.[3] They also discussed racial theories, and Mussolini scoffed at the idea of Aryan superiority, commenting that it was barbarians from the north who had tried time and again to wipe out the more cultured and creative Mediterranean races. Anti-Semitism, he commented, was 'absurd'. In foreign policy, he favoured a Latin Union between Italy and France, he said, as a kind of protective barrier against the Third Reich, and RCK thought Mussolini even seemed sympathetic to his idea of Pan-Europa. The man changed before his eyes from dictator to intellectual, engaged in intelligent conversation. At the end of the interview, Mussolini even asked if RCK would be staying long in Rome, as he would like to continue their talk on another occasion.

RCK did, however, meet Asvero Gravelli, editor of *Anti-Europa*, who had been instrumental in organizing Mussolini's first fascist conference on Europe in Volta the previous November, to which RCK had pointedly not been invited. It was convened just a month after the Pan-Europa Congress in Basel, and as Gravelli himself commented, was 'more theoretical and philosophical' than the overtly political Pan-Europa event. Gravelli's expressed opinion of the fascist conference was somewhat banal: everyone there was persuaded of the need for European unity, but at the same time shared the view that it was unlikely to come about soon in practice. RCK believed Gravelli's comment that his Italian journal would shortly be transformed from *Anti-Europa* to *Ante-Europa*, thus allowing it to openly show the support for RCK's movement that he personally felt. RCK claimed that this visit represented progress for Pan-Europa, but with the benefit of hindsight, it appears more to have been a publicity exercise by the Italian regime to lull any concerns RCK may have had about its antagonism to Pan-Europa.

But RCK did find some compensation in a meeting, with Cardinal Pacelli, the future Pope Pius XII, whom he described as having 'the brilliant, lucid countenance of a truly good man and a smile which lit up his severe, ascetic features'. Cardinal Pacelli also made no secret of his sympathy for Pan-Europa, which went some way to compensate for the ambiguity of Gravelli and the failure of Mussolini to make a second appointment.

BACK IN AUSTRIA, political tensions were becoming much more threatening. Despite the earlier ban on the two most extreme parties, violent incidents broke out between the paramilitary wings of the Social Democrats (the Defence League, or Schutzbund), and the Christian Social Party (the Home Guard, or Heimwehr). A particularly serious incident in Linz in February 1934 quickly escalated into armed conflict in several other cities, and Dollfuss called on the army to restore order. RCK and Idel were fortunate that the ensuing four days of fighting in Vienna largely spared the more affluent areas of the city, including the Hofburg, where Pan-Europa had its offices, and the Hieligenkreuzerhof, where they had their apartment. But the army shelled working-class districts and there was house-to-house fighting, causing several hundred deaths. The experience of this brief-but-bloody civil war polarized Austrian society for a generation. RCK sided entirely with the chancellor and the need to restore order, even at such a cost.

In the wake of the violence, Dollfuss banned the Social Democratic Party and promulgated a new fascist constitution for Austria, creating corporatist institutions to replace representative parliamentary democracy. His own party, the Social Christian Party, morphed into the Vaterländischer Front, or Fatherland Front, which subsumed all the political forces of the centre and the right in support of the new fascist state.

RCK accepted the changes and continued to work with Dollfuss. In practice, he had indeed little choice, and justified his position by pointing to the larger vision of external peace rather than the detail of internal Austrian politics. Seen in this wider perspective, he felt the form of government in Austria was secondary to the fact that it pursued pro-European policies. In addition to that, Pan-Europa's offices in the Hofburg were adjacent to the chancellor's suite, and RCK had privileged access to the man in power, an advantage that in his eyes certainly outweighed the absence of parliamentary representation. In co-operation with the Austrian government, RCK trusted that he could frustrate the Nazis, who had robbed him of the chance of bringing his vision of Pan-Europa to fruition. Even if he could no longer hope to create a Europe-wide alliance that would ensure a peaceful future for the whole continent, he could that way at least frustrate Hitler's plans for European domination.

But his support for Dollfuss earned him and Idel heightened abuse and character assassination from supporters of the banned political parties, in particular from Austrian Nazis. Nazi sympathizers were intolerant of his mixed-race background as well as her Jewish origins, and even former Social Democrats now looked on Pan-Europa with increased suspicion because of its close association with Dollfuss, Austro-fascism, and the suppression of the workers during the brief Austrian civil war.

Seen from the Pan-Europa standpoint in the Hofburg, there could be only partial European unity without Germany, and partial unity without Germany meant, in practice, building alliances to counter Hitler's growing power. Only large nations could realistically offer any balance of power to neutralize Nazi ambitions, and in the European arena that meant the Soviet Union, Great Britain, France, and Italy. RCK would not contemplate any solution which involved the Soviet Union, and with some regret he realized that the British Empire would hold itself aloof from continental Pan-European initiatives. So, he definitely needed to weave both France and Italy into an Austrian alliance, an incomplete Pan-European tapestry, but perhaps one that might neutralize Germany until, as he hoped, the Nazi mania became history. That was also Dollfuss's view.

JUST HOW HITLER WOULD PURSUE his expansionist policies was also a matter of growing concern in Great Britain. Leo Amery was one of very few British MPs to pay sustained attention to political and economic events in central Europe even before Hitler's assumption of power. Like RCK, he hoped that partial groupings of just a few states – Czechoslovakia, Romania, and Yugoslavia in 1933, for instance, or the Balkan Pact between Romania, Yugoslavia, Greece, and Turkey in 1934, or closer Italian, Austrian, and Hungarian economic co-operation in the same year – might lead to a broader agreement to help balance the increasing might of Hitler's Germany. Any unity in the Danube basin would strengthen French or British opposition to the Nazis.

Time and again in his articles and in his books, RCK wrote of the centrality of Germany in any concept of a united Europe. 'Pan-Europa will either be created with Germany in it, or it will simply never be created,' he asserted in the *Pan-Europa Journal*. That also coincided with Leo

Amery's assessment of the situation. Neither Amery nor RCK wanted the fascist camp to grow to a point where it could seriously challenge the democratic camp militarily, and both of them were generous to a fault in sparing Mussolini from criticism as the price for keeping him away from an alliance with Hitler.[4] For RCK, maintaining an Austrian alliance with Mussolini became a prime, if ultimately a misguided, aim of Pan-Europa's policy. The Austrian Foreign Ministry suffered from the same delusion. Even the French government thought along similar lines. It also feared that Rome might come to an agreement with Berlin, and was willing to make concessions to Italy to keep the country out of such an alliance.

Mussolini demanded colonies in Africa as his price for co-operation, claiming Libya as the 'fourth shore' of the Kingdom of Italy. Aggressive colonization reached a peak in the 1930s and was popular with his supporters at home. Its success whetted Mussolini's appetite for more overseas territory. The Rome agreement with France in 1935 ensured respect for each other's rights in North Africa, and so freed Il Duce's hand for the invasion of Abyssinia in October the same year. Only after the event did France regret the failure of its policy and join with Great Britain in supporting the sanctions of the League of Nations against Italy to mark their disapproval. But Britain and France did not press their sanctions policy too far, lest they push Mussolini into Hitler's arms. They never extended sanctions to oil, for instance, or went so far as to close the Suez Canal to Italian shipping, which would have effectively halted Italy's aggression. They slapped Il Duce's wrist, but did not put a pistol to his head.

RCK'S APPROACH TO ECONOMIC PROBLEMS was very much broad-brush, treating continental Europe as if it were a single country. He appreciated how essential it was to have a well-argued economic framework to parallel his political ambitions for the continent as a whole, but it was not until he fell back on Vienna in 1933 that he was successful in formulating it.

Earlier attempts at setting up a Pan-European Economic Bureau in Brussels had not been realized, nor had his attempt to cap the first World Economic Summit of the League of Nations in Geneva in summer 1927 with a Pan-European economic conference planned for October the same year. Regional co-operation in Europe, he argued, would be much more meaningful than the League's global efforts. But his attempts at coordinating a co-operative approach got no further than the planning stage. He hoped to create a Pan-European Research Institute for Economic and

Legal Issues, designed to encourage co-operation with the League of Nations, the International Chamber of Commerce, and the International Law Association, but the administrative complexities and the financial burden proved too much. A further attempt, in early 1931, to put together a conference with German, French, Belgian, and Luxembourg industrialists to discuss the European follow-up to the second World Economic Conference also failed to materialize.

After 1933, RCK had to concentrate on a more specific, regional target, encouraging economic co-operation among the nations of southern and eastern Europe, and here he was much more successful.[5]

He organized a series of Pan-Europa Economic Conferences in Vienna, the first opened in December 1933 by Chancellor Dollfuss himself. 'With this Economic Conference begins Pan-Europa's economic offensive,' wrote RCK boldly in the *Pan-Europa Journal*. Leading economists and businessmen from Austria, Norway, Hungary, Czechoslovakia, Romania, Greece, and Switzerland – but notably not from Nazi Germany – discussed and made recommendations on monetary issues, customs and trade policy, transport, and employment, including far-reaching proposals concerning the regulation of the working week, minimum pay, public works and public procurement, and even monetary union for their part of Europe. Chancellor Dollfuss took this first Pan-Europa Economic Conference very seriously indeed and attended every session, as did several other members of the Austrian government.

With the help of Ludwig von Mises, a liberal economic adviser to Dollfuss, and Otto Deutsch, economics editor of the *Neue Freie Presse*, RCK organized a poll of opinion leaders across the continent in April 1934, similar to the poll he had undertaken in 1926 on the desirability of a United States of Europe. This time he wrote to economists and leaders of finance and industry asking: a) 'Do you think that creating a single economic space across the whole continent west of the Soviet Union is desirable from your country's point of view?' and b) 'What is the quickest way to create the economic integration of Europe?'

This questionnaire brought considerably less-encouraging answers than his previous political poll. He published only eighteen of them in the *Pan-Europa Journal*, all somewhat sceptical, often with qualifications. Some argued that Pan-Europa should be less ambitious in this field, would do better to concentrate on one sector at a time, or warned that it would take many years before the project could be completed. But the following month he opened the second Pan-Europa Economic Conference in Vienna, attended by over two hundred high-level participants from governments as well as notable independent economists. RCK argued that this conference brought the idea of a single economic space for Europe back into discussion as a solution to the current crisis. Referring to the example of the Ottawa agreement, which had recently formalized imperial preference as the trading policy of the British Empire, he even argued that Britain had applied to the British Empire what he called the 'economic ideology of Pan-Europa'.

PAN-EUROPA FILLED RCK's and Idel's working lives in Vienna. Their only relaxation was taking time away together in Switzerland in the spring or summer, something Idel in particular appreciated, as she had a passion for wildflowers. Dressed in traditional Swiss costume, she would on occasion walk with her dogs in the neighbourhood of their house in Gruben and return with armfuls of mountain flowers with which to decorate their country home. Or if their chauffeur took them on longer outings – never fast and whenever possible with the car windows down – she would ask him to stop at the best meadows and spend time picking flowers to give to neighbours or to leave in the restaurants where they might call *en route*.

They were in their Swiss rural retreat in summer 1934 when dramatic events in Vienna intruded directly into their lives. On 25 July, ten Nazi sympathizers, disguised in Austrian police uniforms, forced their way into the Hofburg, passed Pan-Europa's offices, and occupied the chancellor's suite in an attempted *coup d'état*. When Dollfuss refused to sign their political demand – a broadcast declaration in favour of Anschluss – they shot and badly wounded him. They subsequently barricaded themselves in his office, refused to let anyone in to give him medical assistance, and left him to die an agonizing death.

RCK and Idel were working quietly in separate rooms in their house in Gruben that afternoon when RCK heard a noise that sounded like a groan. He went to check if Idel was all right. She replied that she was fine and had heard nothing. Together they went to find her brother, Arthur, a painter, who was staying with them. He too had heard nothing, and they forgot the incident until that evening on radio they were shocked to learn the news of Dollfuss's assassination. RCK later wrote that, without knowing just what it was, he was sure that some sixth sense had let him know of the disaster as it happened. He had heard Dollfuss's dying groans, he claimed, despite being hundreds of miles distant.

Austrian chancellors Dollfuss and Schuschnigg provided Pan-Europa with offices next to their own in the Hofburg.

Dollfuss's widow, Alwine, and her two children happened to be staying with Mussolini on vacation in Italy at the time of her husband's assassination, and he broke the sad news to them personally. He also immediately ordered Italian troops to the Austrian border, as he had no interest in seeing a pro-Nazi coup succeed in Austria. That would unite the country with Germany, and at that time Mussolini still regarded Austria as a useful ally and a buffer against Hitler. The Austrian Nazis staged an uprising following the assassination, expecting Hitler to invade immediately, but the German army was not yet ready to fight both in Austria and against the Italians, and Hitler backed down in the face of Mussolini's speedy action.

With some Italian help, the revolt in Austria was quickly suppressed by forces loyal to Dollfuss. Several hundred were killed and injured on both sides, four thousand pro-Nazi fighters fled to Germany, and a further four thousand were imprisoned, with thirteen subsequently executed. The number of casualties indicates the scale of the uprising. For a few days Ernst-Rüdiger Starhemberg, the deputy chancellor, took command. Later Kurt Schuschnigg, the former minister of education, was sworn in as Dollfuss's successor.

RCK, who was also on friendly terms with both Starhemberg and Schuschnigg, hurried back to Vienna, where he made an impassioned speech at the chancellor's funeral, claiming with oratorical fervour that Dollfuss had 'died for the cause of Europe'.[6] A grateful Chancellor Schuschnigg continued the arrangement whereby Pan-Europa used offices in the Hofburg in exchange for promoting Austrian foreign policy.

But Schuschnigg too was the target of Nazi assassination attempts. On one occasion he was dining with RCK and Idel in their flat in the Heiligenkreuzerhof, and the three of them narrowly escaped assassination there. A courier from the Austrian Nazi party had delivered a package containing a bomb to RCK's butler, who was also a secret Nazi sympathizer. It was to be detonated beneath the chancellor's armchair in the drawing room when the guests retired after dinner. But the butler's nerve failed him at the last minute and, fearing collateral damage to the rest of the household, he threw the package into the nearby Danube canal.

During Schuschnigg's years as chancellor, Pan-Europa organized several 'Danube Conferences' in Vienna. The first was in January 1935, calling on the six states along the river – Austria, Czechoslovakia, Hungary, Yugoslavia, Bulgaria, and Romania – to co-operate further in trade, monetary affairs, and transport. RCK later announced the opening of the Pan-Europa Economic Centre, housed within the Pan-Europa Union offices in the Hofburg. Its main task was to provide a forum for co-operation between employer and labour organizations from various European countries, and to act as the clearing house for information from a network of national economic offices. The central office in Vienna would produce notes on economic issues and key developments and collect reliable statistics from across the region, acting like a Pan-European statistical office and think-tank in one.

In the light of continued German hostility to the core political concept of Pan-Europa, RCK's priorities had necessarily shifted from political to economic. It was no longer a question of trying to establish a federation or confederation to defend Europe's place in the world, he commented sadly, no longer 'a case of continent against continent, but of European against European'. Pan-Europa's priority was now to encourage states and economic actors – even without Germany – to specialize and to trade together more rationally in order to be strong enough to resist German competition and domination. That, he conceded, would better preserve peace and security, or at least the balance of power, than any amount of constitutional change.

On just one occasion RCK, the idealist, gave the smallest of indications that he might be prepared to accept the reality of the German situation. In a letter in 1935 to the industrialist Eugen Diesel in Stuttgart, he inquired if there was any way in which the Pan-Europa Union might be reactivated in Germany 'in the appropriate form', in order to draw 'the power that lies at the centre of Europe into co-operation with the rest of the continent.' It was a feeler, a tentative move, to see what might be possible, because 'the German nation is an exceptional and essential part of the European community of peoples, and the organisation of Europe is impossible without Germany.' Pan-Europa, he argued, could help this reorganization, because its headquarters were in Vienna, the capital of 'a country that is both essentially Germanic and also truly European'. But when Germany returned to Europe, he added, as opposed to trying to dominate it, its policies would have to be more oriented towards Austrian and Western values and could no longer be imperialist or *völkisch* – specifically German and populist. Not surprisingly, nothing came of this private initiative.

In one of RCK's few personal contributions to the *Pan-Europa Journal* on an economic topic, he wrote in 1934 of the 'Gold bloc' of France, Italy, Belgium, the Netherlands, Luxembourg, Switzerland, and Austria. This group of nations, trading more intensively because of their stable exchange rates, with each currency attached at that stage to gold as the ultimate reserve, could form the basis of a common customs union in Europe, he suggested, with mutual preferences reinvigorating trade even further, and with a stable common currency based on gold.

This currency – as Otto Deutsch had previously suggested in the *Pan-Europa Journal* – could circulate in parallel to the local currencies in each state until the stronger one displaced the others, essentially by the mechanism of consumer choice. It would allow for a more gradual adaptation of economies of different strengths, rather than imposing a single currency for all countries and all uses, retail as well as wholesale, at the same time. It was an idea well ahead of its time, but one which would resurface in the 1980s when various modalities by which a common currency could be introduced in the European Union were under discussion in Brussels. The UK Treasury suggested such a two-tier approach to the single currency, but failed to persuade a majority of other states to support it.[7]

Once he had the economic bit between his teeth, RCK did not let go. In the *Pan-Europa Journal* he also proposed common institutions for managing monetary policy, including an embryonic central bank for Europe. In addition, he outlined a Pan-European colonial policy that foresaw joint exploitation of overseas territories and their inclusion in a common tariff zone. He called for a more rational transport system across the region, including common road signs and common driving licences. And finally, he suggested a policy of legal approximation, aiming to give producers and consumers equivalent rights in all countries. The eclectic palette of measures that RCK suggested then would also be discussed and agreed in Brussels as the European Union consolidated its position in the 1980s and 1990s in policies ranging from external trade with former colonies to consumer rights, from transport to monetary policy.

THE FOURTH PAN-EUROPA CONGRESS was held in Vienna in May 1935 in the same glittering hall as the first Pan-Europa Congress nearly a decade previously. Since Prinz Rohan had recently gone over to the Nazis and discredited the Kulturbund in the eyes of all Austrian nationalists, liberals, and democrats, RCK opportunistically advertised the Pan-Europa Congress as being concerned with 'Europe's Cultural Community'.

As ever, Idel played an important role in managing the technical and practical aspects of this Congress, as well as the many other conferences in these years, even though she was now under contract with the Burgtheater. The theatre director was persuaded by repeated requests – initially from Dollfuss and later from Schuschnigg – to invite her to play Shakespearean roles, and in her mid-fifties she starred as Cleopatra in 1935 and Lady Macbeth in 1936. These roles were the climax of her acting career, and both broke records at the box office. Henceforth, she devoted all her energies to helping RCK to promote Pan-Europa, receiving visitors at their apartment – the embassy of Pan-Europa – and helping to organize the seemingly endless stream of conferences with the devoted team that manned the offices in the Hofburg, as well as keeping an eye on the Pan-Europa publishing house nearby.

This fourth Pan-Europa Congress in fact endorsed far-sighted economic proposals, including tariff reductions to further intra-European trade, economic co-operation, common elements of an agricultural policy, co-operation on transport and tourism, on technological innovation, and on monetary and debt issues, legal approximation and employment. The conference report, published in the *Pan-Europa Journal*, revealed a wealth of economic suggestions, many of which also became reality in the development of Western European integration after the Second World War.

Standardization of electrical norms, easing of passport controls and currency transfers, comparable telephone tariffs, common laws for insolvency and for issuing shares, a common body of European law for trade and transport issues, and the gradual introduction of the forty-hour week may not have been as headline-grabbing in the media as the high politics of previous Pan-Europa Congresses, but in reflecting real concerns of the business community, they confirmed the growing importance of shared economic interests leading to a Europe without frontiers. RCK also proposed a European charter of human rights, a gesture well ahead of its time. It became reality only when the Council of Europe was established in 1949.[8]

RCK worked tirelessly in proposing and arranging many conferences: on mass media, on raw materials, on employment, on transport and tourism. In addition, he convened annual meetings of the Pan-Europa's Economic Network and the annual meeting of the Pan-Europa Union's Central Committee, all in Vienna. At the same time, he continued to write prolifically. In addition to frequent lectures and broadcasts, he kept up a steady stream of articles in the *Pan-Europa Journal*. Among his other publications during these Vienna years were several whose titles repeat the central message of Pan-Europa: *Europa Erwache!* (*Europe, Awake!*), *Europa kämpft für Friede* (*Pan-Europa Fights for Peace*), *Zusammenschluss oder Zusammenbruch!* (*Stand Together or Fall Together*). In addition there was a collection of some recent short essays entitled *Europa ohne Elend* (*Europe without Misery*), which included brief eulogies for three figures of central historical importance for Pan-Europa as a movement and for RCK personally: Briand, Dollfuss, and Masaryk. The book was his personal homage to the political leaders who had helped him in the past, but were now no longer on the scene.

It was a contemporary leader, Mussolini, however, who loomed larger than life in both Schuschnigg's and RCK's calculations. He had saved the day by helping to crush the attempted Nazi coup that followed Dollfuss's assassination, and both the chancellor and the president of Pan-Europa hoped he would continue to play an anti-German role that would preserve Austrian independence. RCK visited Il Duce again in May 1936, discussing the importance of stronger ties between France and Italy to keep the menace of Nazi Germany at bay. It appears he even acted as a go-between for Mussolini, visiting Léon Blum, the newly elected prime minister of France, the following month, in the hope of establishing good relations between the Popular Front government in Paris and the fascist regime in Rome, but clearly without success. When he came back to Rome to report to Mussolini again in July that year, the die was already cast. Mussolini and Hitler had agreed on the Berlin-Rome axis and plans were in hand for a state visit by Mussolini to Germany the following year. Perhaps RCK had been sent to Paris as a diversionary tactic, with Mussolini knowing that anything he may have said could be quietly disavowed by Rome. In any case, for RCK it was a wild goose chase. The power lines across the map of Europe were now being redrawn to run from Berlin to Rome, reducing the options that Vienna could take to preserve its independence.

In autumn 1936, the Pan-Europa Agrarian Conference was scheduled to take place in Vienna in association with the Austrian International Trade Fair. The government needed to reinforce the image of Austria in response to Germany's success of the Olympic Games in Berlin earlier that year, and wanted their autumn events to be an equal success in terms of publicity. RCK wanted government support for his conference, and naturally the cabinet discussed his request. Ernst-Rüdiger Starhemberg, the leader of the right-wing Fatherland Front, whom RCK thought was a friend and supporter, is quoted in the minutes of the cabinet meeting, however, as asking in his naturally blunt manner, 'Why should this Japanese bastard stick his oar in European affairs?' adding that the whole business stank of 'business pressure, Jews and Freemasons'. Trade Minister Stockinger was quoted as saying to his colleagues that, if RCK should come asking for subsidies, 'I suggest you throw him out.'

Perhaps these were just off-the-cuff remarks reflecting some of the envy that RCK – not a politician as the others were – incurred because of the close relationship he enjoyed with the chancellor, but fortunately Schuschnigg and calmer heads carried the day. The Trade Fair and the Agrarian Conference took place as planned, heavily subsidized by the Austrian state. Both were judged successful events by the media, with the conference in particular hosting large delegations from democratic Czechoslovakia and from fascist Italy. The latter, as RCK expressly noted, 'subordinated their national interests to the joint enterprise in a common Pan-European spirit.'

The following year, Pan-Europa organized the first and only Pan-Europa Education Conference, dealing in particular with the teaching of geography and history in the secondary curriculum in various European states. In preparation for this, RCK sent out a questionnaire to several hundred figures prominent in the education scene in nearly thirty countries, and received over two hundred replies. Despite, or perhaps because of, the political tension of the time, participants from nineteen countries: Belgium, Denmark, Sweden, Estonia, Lithuania, Bulgaria, Italy, Hungary, France, Finland, Poland, Luxembourg, Czechoslovakia, Switzerland, the Netherlands, Serbia, and Liechtenstein, as well as Austria and even Germany attended the conference.

RCK insisted on the importance of modern languages for international understanding, and the conclusions of the conference demanded that the teaching of geography and history should have a European as well as a national content, and an awareness of European culture and identity should be developed in all secondary schools. RCK was asked by the conference to write to all European governments, drawing their attention to these conclusions, but in this, as so often, he was far ahead of his time. In the 1930s, nationalism in education was everywhere the order of the day and the conclusions of the experts at the conference were doubtless simply filed away in ministries across the continent, regrettably – perhaps – marked 'Not for Action'.

At the Nazi Party rally in Nuremburg in 1935, two racial laws were promulgated: the Reich Citizenship Law and the Law to Protect German Blood and Honour. In response RCK decided to republish his father Heinrich's earlier work *Das Wesen des Antisemitismus* (*The Essence of Anti-Semitism*), first published at the start of the century. He added an extended essay of his own, 'Judenhass von Heute (Contemporary Hatred of the Jews)', to make a single volume of over three hundred pages.

His father's book, which is twice as long as RCK's essay, offered a comprehensive, historical survey of anti-Semitism in ancient times, as well as in the mediaeval and modern-Christian era. It surveyed relations between Muslims and Jews, and the fate of Jews in Persia, India, and China, concluding with a survey of the evidence about traditional accusations against Jews (usury, avarice, ritual child murder), and compared this with the known facts. Finally, it considered Jewish emancipation and the issue of Zionism.

In his own essay, RCK considered the migration of European Jews after the Great War, the poverty of Eastern Europe, how Bolshevism addressed the issue of anti-Semitism, and how nationalist philosophies dealt with the phenomenon. He analysed what he called the 'myth of race', and at some length took apart the popular forgery, the *Protocols of the Elders of Zion*, which had given rise to conspiracy theories about Jewish aims for world supremacy. He concluded by reviewing the status and role of Jews as a minority, the issue of Zionism, and the question of assimilation – arguing that Christianity demanded it, while the new racial heathenism of the Nazis rejected its very possibility. This joint volume sold over twenty thousand copies in the year it was published, reflecting widespread public concern to understand better the issues which were then receiving so much populist distortion in popular debate and Nazi policy.

With hindsight, much of this intellectual and organizational activity appears to have had little immediate political impact, as RCK relied solely on the power of persuasion by rational argument, while Hitler and now Mussolini were contemplating using force to achieve their political goals. However, his lecturing, broadcasting, and publishing certainly raised the level of information and debate among the elite – civil servants, diplomats, academics, journalists, politicians – and even among the wider public who were looking for peaceful solutions to difficult contemporary economic and social problems. And this work put down innumerable markers that would become points of reference in the 1950s for the post-war effort to build a more integrated Western Europe.

BY THE MID-1930S, however, it was clear that Hitler was ultimately prepared to use force to change the balance of power in Europe, and his first goal was to incorporate Austria into Nazi Germany. Austria, his homeland, should be brought back into the German realm: 'Heim ins Reich'. He instinctively grasped the weakness of Schuschnigg's position, both his personal weakness of character and the geopolitical weakness of Austria, now no longer supported by Italy. From year to year, from month to month, Hitler played cat and mouse with the Austrian chancellor, seeing how far he could go without serious international opposition in moving towards his goal of annexation.

Undermining the confidence of the Austrian leadership had been Hitler's first step in subjugating his neighbour, and the assassination of Dollfuss in 1934 inculcated fear of the reach of the Nazis across the ruling Austrian elite. Economic threats then followed. In 1936 Schuschnigg was forced to relax controls on Nazi activity within Austria as the price for Hitler rolling back an arbitrarily imposed travel tax of one thousand Reichsmark for any German visiting the country. That same year he established the Berlin-Rome axis to prevent Mussolini interfering in Austrian affairs as he had done when Dollfuss was asssassiniated. Austrian society was then subverted from within by a fifth column of Nazi sympathizers working for Anschluss by systematically disturbing public order. Finally, positioning German troops near the border made the external threat of force a reality. Anschluss became no longer a question of 'if' but of 'when' and 'how'. RCK and Idel watched these developments from their privileged apartment in the Heiligenkreuzerhof with mounting anxiety.

Leo Amery had attended the 1926 Pan-Europa Congress in Vienna, the 1930 Congress in Berlin, the 1932 Congress in Basel, and the 1935 Congress in Vienna, and RCK always visited him whenever he travelled to London. In April 1936, after RCK delivered another lecture at Chatham House about the situation in central Europe, Amery noted in his diary: 'C to dinner, very anxious lest Hitler should jump Austria at any moment while the Abyssinian affair is still giving trouble.' They understood each other well and both felt they had the ability to see further into the political future than most.

Just at the moment when he needed all the support he could muster for Pan-Europa, RCK's position on the issue of sanctions to punish Italy for its aggression in Abyssinia seriously weakened his organization in Austria and in Czechoslovakia. A public debate in Austria between RCK and a leading Austrian business supporter, Julius Meinl, on the morality of the Italian invasion forced RCK into the invidious position of trying to justify Mussolini's aggression. Rather than take the moral high ground and condemn Italian aggression, RCK pointed out how this would simply push Italy into alliance with Germany, creating the very Rome-Berlin axis that he feared would supplant the Rome-Paris alliance that he had been working for. For him as president of Pan-Europa there was no problem with Italy acquiring a colonial empire at the cost of war with Abyssinia – the last independent state in Africa – so long as that preserved peace in Europe. It was only if peace was lost in Europe, he asserted, that the idea of Pan-Europa would be lost.

RCK also clashed with the secretary-general of the Czechoslovak Pan-Europa Committee, Vaclav Schuster, on the same issue, another instance that illustrated RCK's authoritarian leadership style. He refused the constituent national committees of Pan-Europa any right to constrain him as president. He would be free to express his personal opinions on contemporary political events, even when they were contrary to the views of the local membership. After all, had he not been confirmed by acclamation as president-for-life of the Pan-Europa Union at the first Congress in 1926? That status gave him the necessary legitimacy, he argued, to speak out on contemporary political and economic issues. It was characteristic of his leadership style, and on occasion it cost him dearly. Meinl withdrew his financial support, and Schuster resigned.

In March 1937 Amery was in Vienna again and recorded a meeting with RCK. They enjoyed political discussion together, and each held the other in high regard, but they both overestimated Mussolini's capacity to remain independent of Hitler's influence. Amery noted their conversation:

> I think I convinced Coudenhove that this country, while it may be helpful, cannot really take the lead continuously in the movement for European unity. I suggested that Mussolini, desiring to make friends with us and cover up his retreat from an untenable position [the invasion of Abyssinia], might well be inclined to take up a movement in

which he might figure greatly and which would ensure Germany's being kept away from the Brenner.

RCK had been convinced of this for some time, and would continue to hope that Mussolini would not only support a Franco-British alliance against Hitler, but might also still be persuaded to lead Pan-Europa. In mid-February 1938, RCK was in London again, and Amery again noted in his diary that he had enjoyed a 'talk with Coudenhove who is not too pessimistic and thinks Schuschnigg may be able to save a certain amount and at any rate to gain time.' A week later, after lunch with him at Brown's Hotel, he recorded RCK's report of Hitler's threat to Schuschnigg in their recent negotiations: 'If you refuse, Salzburg will be a heap of ruins within ten minutes.' Optimistically, he went on to note: 'RCK is much encouraged by our change of policy over Italy and thinks it may yet save Austria. He is writing a couple of articles for the *Daily Telegraph* and for the *News Chronicle* leading off from my remarks to that effect in my speech last Monday.'

On that occasion RCK also met Churchill, to whom he had written earlier in the year, asking for a meeting when next he was in London. Churchill invited him to his country house at Chartwell in Kent after lunch one day at the very end of February, and the two men got on well together. Churchill showed off his success at bricklaying and painting, and RCK expanded on the horrors of the Nazi regime and the prospect of German expansion in central Europe. RCK admired the 'genial aristocrat of tremendous intellectual grasp'. He also noted his own assessment of current thinking in Britain: 'A strong reaction was setting in against the policy of appeasement and there grew up a kind of British resistance movement whose political attitude towards the Third Reich did not differ greatly from the programme of the Pan-European movement on the Continent.'

Churchill was captivated enough to ask RCK to stay on to dinner, inducting him into his routine of a bath and a brief nap before the meal. He also presented RCK with a signed copy of his latest book, *Great Contemporaries*. RCK found Churchill 'far ahead of his countrymen in his appreciation of the need for European understanding', yet at the same time 'a leading advocate of Anglo-American cooperation'. He noted too that Churchill had 'remained faithful to the ideal of Pan-Europe, though for years he had ceased to write and speak about it.'

Meanwhile, rapidly accelerating events were making redundant the views of those who, even when close to power, like Amery and even Churchill, were not taking political decisions that had practical effect.

Churchill in his country residence, Chartwell, in Kent.

Hitler's next move was to force Schuschnigg to appoint a leading Austrian Nazi sympathizer, Seyss-Inquart, as minister of the interior, and at the same time to encourage Austrian Nazis to challenge law and order through demonstrations and street violence. Trusting that a majority of Austrians would favour national independence over being absorbed by Nazi Germany, Schuschnigg announced a referendum for early March; he would ask Austrians if they wanted to remain independent or not. Hitler was furious, for fear that a popular vote *against* Anschluss would frustrate his maturing plans. He demanded the cancellation of the referendum, and meanwhile massed troops at the border.

When they left London, RCK and Idel travelled through France and Switzerland, planning to arrive in Vienna on Tuesday, 8 March. Erika was travelling with them, and in view of the serious situation, they left

her in Zürich with instructions to go on to their country house in Gruben.
On Friday, 11 March, RCK and Idel were hosting a dinner party in their
apartment in Vienna when Chancellor Schuschnigg announced Hitler's
ultimatum, the cancellation of the referendum, and his own resignation.
As he ended his broadcast, Schuschnigg's breaking voice prayed 'God save
Austria'. An anonymous phone call interrupted the dinner, advising RCK
to leave the country immediately, as he was high on the Gestapo hit list.

14

ESCAPE FROM EUROPE

THEIR DINNER PARTY broke up immediately. RCK and Idel quickly packed small travelling cases, scooped up their white Pekinese, Pai-Chuan, and took a taxi to the Czech legation. They carried Czech diplomatic passports and were relying on an embassy car taking them to Prague and safety. At the last moment, RCK pocketed his revolver, just in case.

Pro-Nazi crowds were on the streets of the capital, cheering the news of Schuschnigg's resignation and the nomination of the Nazi minister of the interior, Seyss-Inquart, as the new chancellor. He immediately appealed to Hitler to help maintain law and order, inviting Germany to send in troops and annex the country. The route to the Czech embassy was blocked by jubilant crowds, so RCK redirected the taxi to the nearby Swiss embassy instead. There they learned that German troops had already crossed the Austrian border at Kufstein, Mittenwald, and Salzburg, and had met with no organized resistance. A plane had also set off from Berlin to bring an advance unit of the SS directly to Vienna.

The Swiss ambassador, Max Jaeger, suggested they change their plans and leave the country across the nearest border.[1] He offered them his chauffeur to drive their car, since neither RCK nor Idel could drive, and their own chauffeur, a suspected Nazi sympathizer, was not to be found or trusted. The Swiss embassy chauffeur was sent to their apartment in the Heilgenkreuzerhof to pick up their car, and also to collect their large Russian sheepdog, Sasha. Meanwhile Idel phoned friends in Pressburg (now Bratislava) to tell them they would need help at the border. Once the chauffeur returned, they set off to drive out of Vienna with a Swiss pennant fixed to RCK's Bentley. The chauffeur insisted, however, that he must collect his passport from his flat on their way. He parked in a *cul-de-sac* in an obscure quarter of the city and disappeared into his apartment block to pick it up.

At that moment, a group of local young Nazis wearing swastika arm-bands and carrying iron rods surrounded the car. RCK and Idel feared they were trapped. But the young militants, seeing the pennant and assuming the couple in the car were from the Swiss legation, simply wanted news from the city centre. They petted the dogs and inquired if RCK thought their younthful unit was likely to be needed in the 'revolution'. Eventually the chauffeur reappeared, the militants stood aside, and the car sped off towards Pressburg and the Czechoslovak border.

They arrived shortly after midnight to find that the border had already been closed to all Austrians. The Swiss embassy chauffeur, who was Austrian, was not allowed to pass, but their friends came across from the Czechoslovak side to help by taking over their car and driving for them. Just as they were about to leave, Alvine Dollfuss called to them from a nearby car flying a French pennant. The French ambassador had given her and her two children his car, and along with their governess and chauffeur they too were escaping from the Nazis. Despite having Austrian passports, their status, sweet talk, and a phone call to the foreign ministry in Prague allowed them all to pass, and the two cars drove on into Pressburg to the Carlton Hotel, which was crowded with refugees from the cosmopolitan Austrian elite. There they sat up all night, discussing the desperate situation. Next morning, they heard on the radio Hitler's exultant speech before an enthusiastic crowd in his home town of Linz, proclaiming Austria's annexation by the German Fatherland. There was now no turning back.

Little did RCK and Idel know, but the Gestapo had been on their trail, sending a car in pursuit when they learned that they – as well as Dollfuss's widow – had set off for Pressburg. However, the car never caught up with them, and RCK later learned that it had broken down *en route*.

The next day RCK and his little group drove on to Budapest, where he informed the Italian embassy that he planned to cross the border the following day at Postumia (now Postojna in Slovenia), the nearest crossing to Ljubljana, with Alwine Dollfuss and her family, and wished to travel safely across Italy to Switzerland. But first they drove to Zagreb, where friends of Pan-Europa offered them hospitality for the night. When they arrived at Postumia, they found that Mussolini had not only offered them safe passage, but had also ordered a personal guard of honour to escort them to the Swiss frontier. An Italian officer and four young Blackshirt outriders accompanied RCK and Idel, along with Alvine Dollfuss and her family. The cortège travelled through Trieste to Sirmione on Lake Garda, and then on to the Swiss border at Chiasso.

Meanwhile, in Vienna, Hitler's forces and their Austrian sympathizers rounded up Jews, Liberals, Social Democrats, Communists, and other political opponents. Many were herded into a disused railway station, which was converted into a makeshift concentration camp. Within a matter of days over seventy thousand people were arrested, detained, deported, or murdered.

Under the Nuremberg racial laws, marriage between Jews and non-Jews was forbidden in the Reich. That now applied in Austria as well, and the process of Aryanization began immediately. Jews were driven out of public life, paraded with their partners through the streets of Vienna, and publicly humiliated. Their homes, shops, and businesses were seized. Some were forced to scrub away pro-independence slogans painted on the cobbled streets of the city in support of Schuschnigg's aborted plebiscite. Jewish actresses from the Theater in der Josefstadt, where Idel had often performed, were forced to clean the latrines of the storm-troopers barracked there, the least of the indignities they suffered. RCK and Idel had escaped just in time.

The following morning, the Gestapo forced their way into the Pan-Europa offices in the Hofburg and seized the archives. These were immediately taken back to Berlin to be filleted for information about supporters of Pan-Europa that might prove useful for the Nazis, both in Austria, Germany, and other countries where Pan-Europa had offices and members. Seyss-Inquart commandeered the offices of Pan-Europa to use as his personal quarters in the Hofburg, since they were adjacent to the offices that he now took over as the new chancellor.

The Gestapo also raided RCK's first-floor flat in Heiligenkreuzerhof, Pan-Europa's 'embassy'. Their initial search of the flat was quite perfunctory, much less thorough than the search of Pan-Europa's Hofburg offices, but they scooped up letters and papers on RCK's desk, including the copy of *Great Contemporaries* that Churchill had signed and given to him barely three weeks earlier. As the Gestapo left, they sealed the doors and windows, and thought they had done a good job. But they had overlooked the dumb waiter, the food lift that connected the two floors, and RCK and Idel's devoted servants, who lodged on the ground floor, devised a way to get into the apartment above and rescue some personal items. The diminutive valet, husband of the cook, climbed into the dumb waiter and was hoisted up to the first floor. There he rescued personal ornaments and mementos that the Gestapo had missed, among them the statuette of Napoleon, which was eventually restored to RCK after the end of the war.

AFTER THEIR PRECIPITOUS ESCAPE from Austria to the house in Gruben, now to be their home in exile in Switzerland, RCK and Idel set about re-organizing their lives. He had already had the foresight to shift much of his and Pan-Europa's finances to Zürich, but despite feeling physically safer, RCK soon realized that he could not effectively continue the struggle against Hitler from their rural retreat. Together with Erika, the couple soon moved to Bern, setting up an office for Pan-Europa Union at 6 Bundesgasse, close to the federal parliament and the seat of government. From here RCK travelled a great deal on his Czechoslovak diplomatic passport, often with Idel, notably to Paris and London, to rally leading politicians to the cause of resisting further German demands.

In April, barely three weeks after escaping from Vienna, RCK was in London, giving a lecture at Chatham House. He spoke on the theme 'A Central European View of the European Situation', and was chaired by Professor Seton-Watson, a prominent political commentator and historian who had devoted his life to studying Eastern Europe. When introducing RCK he stressed, 'Great Britain can, if she wants, find a huge Dominion in Eastern Europe, a Dominion of one hundred and twenty million people, very gifted people, who will one day be the most important element of Europe. They are ready to follow Great Britain. The day she wants to take the leadership she shall have it.' This was music to RCK's ears, especially as the discussion after his talk clarified that there was no question of British domination or hegemony, but simply of moral leadership.

In June he was in London again, once more lecturing at Chatham House to the British elite with an interest in international affairs. This time he spoke on the Sudeten crisis, and he met Churchill afterwards for the second time, at a luncheon arranged by Leo Amery. The meeting confirmed their mutual personal admiration and their essential agreement on the need to confront the common enemy, Hitler.

Anschluss had redrawn the map of Europe and changed the geopolitical balance on the continent. Hitler's swift annexation of Austria meant that Czechoslovakia was now bordered on three sides – north, west, and south – by a more-powerful Nazi Germany. Germany's population had been swelled by the addition of five million Austrians, its army strengthened by one hundred thousand additional troops, its iron and steel production increased, and its foreign-exchange reserves enlarged. German influence in southeast Europe and the Balkans became dominant, and the fate of Czechoslovakia was sealed.

Hitler exploited this position of strength to put pressure on the Czechoslovak government for territorial concessions. He demanded that German-speaking areas in the west and north of the country – the Sudetenland – should be ceded to Germany; otherwise he would simply seize them by force. France, Great Britain, and Italy, all allies of Czechoslovakia, attempted to arbitrate between President Beneš and Hitler, but in September finally accepted German demands at the fateful meeting in Munich. On 30 September, Chamberlain flew back to Britain to declare 'Peace for our time', and the next day German troops marched into the disputed areas of Czechoslovakia. That included Ronsperg, RCK's childhood home, where his elder brother, Hansi, now lord of the manor, was playing a prominent role in the local pro-German movement led by Konrad Henlein. It was an additional cause of conflict between the brothers.

When he was back in Switzerland again, RCK reflected on his visit to London and decided to set about writing another book, this one to explain to a new audience in England both the history and the purpose of the Pan-Europa Union. Given the dire political situation at the time, he chose as his title a provocative question – *Kommen die Vereinigten Staaten von Europa?* (*Are the United States of Europe Underway?*) – and to his rhetorical question he gave a clear and optimistic answer. From the ashes of the coming European war – which Hitler would lose – there would arise a realization that all European states needed to federate for their own safety, both internally and externally. The United States of Europe as foreseen by Pan-Europa would then be the obvious and the only solution.

AFTER FIVE MONTHS' SILENCE, during which he had not mailed any propaganda material to his supporters, he now sent them a copy of this new book, the first publication from Glarus, a small, tax-friendly, rural canton between Zürich and St Gallen, where he set up the new publishing arm of Pan-Europa. He dated the preface 1 September 1938, and dedicated the book to the memory of Aristide Briand, the great European who, nine years ago that very month, had taken the initiative at the League of Nations of proposing a federal link between European states. 'After the sorry collapse of the peace system set up by the Versailles Treaty and the universal project of the League of Nations,' wrote RCK,

the fateful question for Europe now is whether in the thirty-four states of this corner of the world brute force, threats, blackmail and plotting will be the order of the day – or whether these states will join together in a European Confederation. Not in a carbon copy of the United States of America, but in a union of independent and equal national states with a common foreign policy, common defence and a single economic policy.

During the several months when his subscribers had received no copies of the *Pan-Europa Journal*, RCK had been piecing Pan-Europa's mailing list together again, checking with all those Pan-Europa committees still outside Nazi control to determine just who was still an active member, and making his printing arrangements in Glarus. In the letter to subscribers that accompanied his new book – dated early October, just a few days after the annexation of the Sudetenland – he promised his readers a slimmed down but trilingual version of the *Pan-Europa Journal*, re-titled *European Letter*, to appear in English, French, and German twice a month from November.

The events of the past few weeks have shown with frightening intensity that our whole culture, and above all the independence of small states, will be lost unless the Pan-European idea can be realised even now at the eleventh hour ... Only through tireless propaganda, enlightenment and active promotion will we finally succeed in overcoming the stupidity, laziness, evil and weakness of contemporary politics and be able to base the future of our people on peace, equality and prosperity.

He invited his readers, now reduced to less than half the number of supporters he had before the loss of Germany, Austria, and parts of Czechoslovakia, 'to fight with us for a free and united Europe.'

In November 1938, as the political stakes in Europe rose ever higher, RCK published an English edition of his trenchant philosophical defence of individual freedom in the face of the tyranny of the state, *Totaler Staat – Totaler Mensch*, under the title *The Totalitarian State against Man*. Wickham Steed wrote a preface to the English edition, translated by Sir Andrew McFadyean. McFadyean had earlier been involved in the Versailles negotiations and later was in the UK Treasury's team dealing with German reparations. He was an MP, now on the council of Chatham House and was also chairman of The New Trading Company, the forerunner of S.G.Warburg, the merchant bank set up by another British supporter, Max Warburg's nephew, Sigi Warburg. Sigi bore the costs of this translation and publication, and to RCK's delight, the first printing of five thousand copies sold out very quickly, and a reprint appeared as early as January the following year.

In this book, RCK attacked the Nazi deification of the state and stressed the virtues of individualism. The chapter headings tell the story – Man and the State, Right and Might, the History of Freedom, Democracy, the Parliamentary System, and the Scale of State Totalitarianism. In them he expounded his argument that all social organization must start with the individual, exerting his or her own free will. Local structures of government should build by degrees upwards and outwards in a pluralist and federal fashion to ever wider and higher circles of responsibility, ultimately reaching world citizenship. His view was the antithesis of the centralized Nazi state with the god-like figure of the Führer imposing ultimate authority and total control on everyone from above.

It was also a decisive step away from the support of Austro-fascism that had marked his recent years in Vienna, and from the way that he personally had run the Pan-Europa Union.

Wickham Steed wrote in his introduction that RCK was

a philosopher and an artist, no less than a man of action. There is no question of the depth or of the luminous quality of the reasoning with which he combats the deification of the State and demolishes the Hegelian conception of the State as 'an end in itself'. The State, Hegel declared, is 'the ultimate end which has the highest right against the individual, whose highest duty is to be a member of the State'. This doctrine Coudenhove-Kalergi shows to be the root of political evil.

RCK himself wrote in his preface,

I have had occasion to discuss fundamental questions of modern politics, culture and economics with men of all people and classes; with Europeans, Asiatics and Americans; with kings and presidents, dictators and democratic statesmen; with leaders of industry and finance, workmen and peasants; with clerical, military and academic dignitaries; with philosophers and artists, inventors and teachers, journalists and writers; with Liberals and Fascists, Conservatives and Communists.

He hoped his book would 'indicate to all men of goodwill a way into a better and a clearer future out of the labyrinth of unsolved problems which vex our age.' The book was intended for 'all men and peoples who are seeking an answer to the riddle of our destiny.'

Duff Cooper, ally of
Churchill, helped RCK
in London.

RCK's answer to the exploitation of man by man was not Marxism but
the rational application of technology. Rather than the brutality of Social
Darwinism, of wage slavery and capitalist greed, of class warfare, envy,
and survival of the strongest, he looked to a future where all human needs
would be satisfied by mass production and the intelligent use of what he
termed 'technical knowledge'. In that age, he declared, men would co-
operate more and compete less. At a philosophical level, he argued for the
completion of the ideals of the French Revolution of Liberty, Equality,
and Fraternity. Liberalism and Social Democracy had made a reality of
the first two principles, he argued, but the third, which he described as
a more caring and feminine characteristic, had still to be made a reality.
Then 'the growing influence of women in politics and in the spiritual life
of our age will be decisive in bringing about a revision of masculine values
and a triumph of the fraternal revolution.'

In December 1938, Alfred Duff Cooper, who had recently resigned as
First Lord of the Admiralty in protest at Neville Chamberlain's policy
of appeasement, reviewed RCK's book sympathetically in the *Evening
Standard*. He described the book's message as 'one which the world is

longing for, because it contains the logical foundations of that faith in which most men instinctively if subconsciously believe, and which emphatically condemns the error of Communism and of Fascism.'

RCK's powers of persuasion – both his appealing arguments and his charismatic personality – conquered hearts and minds easily and everywhere. Leo Amery's son Julian, still an undergraduate at Oxford but passing some weeks with family friends in early summer 1937 in Vienna, made his acquaintance there and wrote to his father: 'I have become a tremendous Pan-European; I was completely fascinated by him ... I have at last found a political ideal in a despairingly cynical world.' Julian had the opportunity to meet RCK again in London early in 1939, when his father invited both Winston Churchill and RCK for political discussions over lunch at his London flat in Eaton Square. Churchill was expanding on his growing friendship with the ubiquitous Soviet ambassador, Ivan Maisky, when RCK interrupted to ask whether he was aware that the Soviet Union would shortly conclude a non-aggression pact with Nazi Germany. Churchill was amazed, as Maisky had given him no indication of this, and he asked RCK what source he had for this information. 'A source in the Vatican,' answered RCK. After an extended silence – and young Julian noted that Churchill was seldom silenced – he commented, 'The Vatican? Then it must be true.'[2]

But events were moving fast, and the long, slow process of gathering information and educating public opinion was being overtaken by new developments on the ground. In March 1939, realizing that neither France nor Great Britain would come to the aid of Czechoslovakia, Hitler pounced. He annexed the rest of the Czech lands, established the Protectorate of Bohemia and Moravia centred on Prague, and created a separate, puppet state in Slovakia, centred on Pressburg. Not only had RCK now lost his nationality, but all his efforts to create Pan-Europa, first with Germany at its core, and later in opposition to Nazi Germany, seemed to have come to naught. Nazi Germany was making the running, and Hitler appeared to be winning game, set, and – soon perhaps – match.

In May 1939, RCK organized what would turn out to be the last major Pan-Europa event in France before the outbreak of war. He chose as the venue the elegant and imposing Marigny theatre on the Champs Elysées. To a packed house, Ernest Mercier, a leading industrialist and successor to Louis Loucheur as chairman of the French Pan-Europa Union, spoke about European economic union. He was followed by Duff Cooper, who came from London to speak on the political situation in Europe. RCK also spoke on the prospects for a politically united Europe after the Nazi tide had ebbed away. The event was a great success, concluding with all present enthusiastically singing *God Save the King* and *La Marseillaise*. It promoted Pan-Europa's profile, received positive press coverage, and also raised the prospect of an ever-closer alliance of France and Great Britain.

On 15 June, RCK was back again in Chatham House, this time at a meeting chaired by Duff Cooper, to speak on the theme of 'Europe Tomorrow'. Duff Cooper underlined the most important development of the past year, the fact that Great Britain had woken up to the relevance of what was happening in Europe, that it had become 'a European state'. RCK spoke optimistically, claiming that, through the horror of a second world war, there would arise 'the union of the European race'. 'To a certain extent,' he argued, 'Europe must be considered as the "Lebensraum" of England', and involvement with the continent would be welcome because, with Great Britain, 'the European federation would be even looser than the Swiss federation.' 'If Great Britain has the European vision and the courage to fight for it,' he added, 'our generation will see the United States of Europe.'

Although RCK concentrated on London and Paris as the capitals of the two European states large enough to oppose Hitler with any prospect of success, he still persisted in thinking that Rome might be persuaded, even at this late hour, to join an anti-Nazi front. Despite ample evidence suggesting it was pointless, he addressed a public appeal to Mussolini to 'save European culture' by intervening to stop Hitler's march to war. RCK had again over-estimated Mussolini, believing that at the eleventh hour he could and would join the Allies and oppose Hitler. He was wrong.[3] Late in 1938, Italy had resurrected historic claims to Nice and Corsica that showed which way the wind was blowing. Mussolini also wanted his share of plunder.

When Czechoslovakia fell to the Nazis, RCK, Idel, and Erika all applied for French citizenship. On 30 August 1939, they finally received their passports from the French embassy in Bern, collecting them as they returned from yet another visit to Paris to further the cause of Pan-Europa. Two days later, Germany invaded Poland, and that weekend France and Great Britain, in fulfilment of their defence agreements with Warsaw, both declared war on Germany.

RCK WAS IN NO WAY SURPRISED, but he was deeply distressed that there was now no alternative to determining the future of the continent than recourse to arms. His sense of depression was compounded when, barely three months later, the Soviet Union invaded Finland and the Winter War began. In an issue of *European Letter* sent to his supporters, he fulminated against 'the brown and the red dictatorships', and watched with growing apprehension as the German war machine consolidated its conquests in the east and prepared for war in the west.

In the previous year, he had published *Kommen die Vereinigten Staaten von Europa?* which set out his message in the clearest possible terms. Now Sigi Warburg financed an English version under the title *Europe Must Unite*, also translated by Sir Andrew McFadyean. RCK quoted from Napoleon's *Memoirs* on the title page: 'The nations of Europe have every reason to put an end to their wars and to federate. Europe is a province of the world, and war between Europeans is a civil war.'

He signed the preface on 1 October 1939, and, ever the optimist, claimed that 'The European War, started by Hitler's attack on Poland, will mark in history either the breakdown of Europe – or its resurrection. Which it is to mark will depend on the organization of Europe after this war.' In his introduction, Leo Amery pinpointed the key element in RCK's political analysis of the state of anarchy in European affairs: the inability of Europeans to think of themselves as Europeans. 'Once Europeans can think of themselves, as Chinese or Indians can think of themselves, as members of an individual culture and tradition, in spite of local diversities of language or gradations of racial origin, then political and economic cooperation will follow and, in their turn, serve to strengthen the sense of common unity.'

When he was not in London, RCK was in Paris. With Idel he took a room in the Hôtel Raphael for five weeks, from mid-November until just before Christmas 1939. That offered them a ringside seat to assess the political turmoil in the French government led by Edouard Daladier. After spending Christmas in Switzerland, they were back at the end of January with Erika, staying in the Raphael until the first week of May. This was the time of the phoney war in the west, while Germany consolidated its victory against Poland in the east, and pursued the distant war in Norway, where reports of German success soured the initial confidence of government and public opinion in France as in Britain. In March, Daladier's government fell, and he was replaced by Paul Reynaud. By the time the Germans launched their main assault, RCK and his family were again on the way back to Switzerland.

On 10 May 1940, German forces attacked France and the Low Countries, and on that same day Churchill replaced Chamberlain as prime minister in London. Four days later the Netherlands surrendered. But surprisingly, RCK returned to Paris just four days after that, lodging again in the Hôtel

Raphael, and stayed for ten more days. What can he have been doing? He must have been aware of the danger he was running, as he left Idel and Erika in the relative safety of Switzerland. Even there, he could not be sure of his or their safety. Before May, he had expressed his fear that neutral Switzerland might soon be surrounded by Axis forces and would then be the next country to fall to the Nazis. Journeys to Paris – particularly this last one – seem highly risky, though surely not unmotivated, as the precarious situation was clear to everyone.

In Paris he heard the news that German forces had reached the Channel coast on 20 May, that the evacuation of British troops from Dunkirk had begun on 26 May, and that two days later Belgium had sued for peace. The French army was now left to face the German onslaught alone.

He claimed in his memoirs that he could have stayed in Switzerland for the duration of the war, even though his political activity would have been severely curtailed, but in fact he had been making preparations to leave for some weeks, arranging with banks in Zürich and Paris to forward money to a bank in Lisbon if he should reach Portugal, and noting exchange rates in his diary. But making banking arrangements cannot have kept him in Paris at that time and for so long. The hotel record simply registers that he left on 28 May for Switzerland.

GERMANY LAUNCHED a second major attack at the start of June, and within a few days General Gunderian's panzers crossed the Somme, fanning out towards the south. On 10 June, RCK and Idel learned of the fall of Norway. On 12 June, General Weygand, the head of the army, informed Paul Reynaud, the new French prime minister, that the battle for France was lost. A day later the French government left Paris for Bordeaux, and Italy declared war on France and Great Britain.

In those desperate days in June, the British government, now led by Churchill, made an historic offer to the French government: that the two states should merge into one united country to continue the war – one government, one nationality, one cause. Jean Monnet, then a senior French civil servant, was in London and helped draft the document with the chief diplomatic adviser, Sir Robert Vansittart. General de Gaulle, then a junior defence minister, was also in London, and backed the plan, but the French government in Bordeaux was divided between those bent on a negotiated peace with Germany and those who wanted to fight on. In the French cabinet, Prime Minister Paul Reynaud was outvoted and resigned. Marshal

Pétain, backed by the majority of the cabinet, took over the premiership, and on 16 June sued for peace.

RCK was not close to political developments in London in these crucial days, as Nazi aggression forced him to prepare to flee again to ensure his own and his family's safety. Just a few days after his return from Paris at the end of May, he left Gruben with Idel and Erika for Geneva. From there he posted his final issue of *European Letter* to his supporters on 15 June, and just two days after that the family received their visas for Spain and Portugal from the respective consulates. That same afternoon, Erika drove her parents in their Bentley, crammed full of their luggage and two dogs, across the border into France. There they picked up an extra driver, an anonymous Frenchman, for additional protection during the journey to the Spanish frontier, hoping to reach Barcelona and subsequently cross Spain to Portugal. Their goal was Lisbon, from where they hoped to travel on to either Britain or to America.[4]

In France, the main roads were crowded with civilians pressing south, like them, to escape the advancing German army. Erika and the French driver took turns steering the Bentley onto minor roads wherever they could, through Annecy, Aix-les-Bains, and Grenoble, not stopping until, in the middle of the night, they reached Valence. There they all slept briefly on park benches as the hotels were full, staying close to their car, which was guarded by their dogs – one large Russian sheepdog and one small Pekinese. They reached Port Bou and the Spanish border late the next day, 18 June, where they paid off their French chauffeur generously. He made his own way home, while Erika drove them over the border into Spain.

That same day, the BBC broadcast Charles de Gaulle's appeal to all French men and women to fight on. Hearing this rallying call for French resistance, RCK took note for the first time of the former tank commander, who had only recently become a junior minister in the French government, little knowing what a major role this French soldier and statesman would play in his later life.[5]

A few days later, Marshal Pétain signed an armistice with Nazi Germany in Compiègne, in the same railway carriage where representatives of Imperial Germany had signed the Armistice that ended the First World War. In Barcelona, RCK heard a subsequent speech by de Gaulle, also broadcast by the BBC, in which he enlarged upon his earlier appeal. 'This armistice will not only be a capitulation,' he said in sonorous tones, 'but it will also reduce the country to slavery. A great many Frenchmen refuse to accept either capitulation or slavery, for good reasons called honour, common sense, and the higher interests of the country. If the powers of freedom ultimately triumph over those of servitude, what will be the fate of a France which has submitted to the enemy?' he asked, repeating his call for all free French citizens, wherever they might be, to continue the fight.

De Gaulle's global and ethical frame of reference, his emphasis on the role of the French and British overseas empires and the importance of technological superiority and military production in America, all struck a sympathetic chord with RCK. He was sure that Great Britain and its Empire, now led by Churchill, would fight to the last and, if America could be persuaded to join in a cause that RCK knew was right and true, together the future allies would bring such military might to bear that the war was certain to end in victory. Metropolitan France might surrender, but the struggle would become global, not just European. It would be three years before he would make the first move to contact de Gaulle, but the name and the man had now registered with him.

RCK's immediate priority, however, was his own and his family's safety. They had been fortunate to get through France and reach Barcelona without serious problems. Many other refugees had been turned back at the Spanish frontier; some were interned, others committed suicide there in desperation. Now the immediate issue was getting across Spain to Portugal and obtaining visas to let himself and his family travel out of Europe – to Britain or to America – away from the reach of the Nazis.

Once in Barcelona, he made contact with an affable and exuberant Catalan, Gabriel Vidal, who owned a large transport company. He was a supporter of Pan-Europa and, given his professional contacts in the world of transport, managed to reserve three seats for them on a flight to Madrid leaving the next day. The plane had already taken off before they realized it was an Italian flight, scheduled to touch down at Madrid and then go on to Rome. It dawned on them that, since Italy and France were now at war, and all three of them had French passports, they were at risk of arrest. After a short while in the air, the captain informed passengers that he had been directed back to Barcelona, with the ostensible reason that bad weather had closed Madrid airport. The weather had been fine so far on the flight, and RCK was suspicious that this might not be the real reason. Had the airline discovered just who their passengers were? Once they got off the plane in Barcelona, they refused to board it again, but contacted Gabriel Vidal. He quickly arranged for them to travel by rail to Madrid that same evening, and from there they took another train the next day to Lisbon. Their luggage was crated up in Barcelona and sent on after them. Their Bentley was left with Vidal.

Portugal might be neutral, but Lisbon was not safe. The city was filling up fast with refugees seeking to escape the Nazis, and among them was Archduke Otto von Hapsburg, the eldest son of the Emperor Karl, along with the rest of the former Austrian imperial family. But the city was equally open to agents of Nazi Germany. There were kidnappings and killings of prominent anti-Nazi refugees, and RCK always carried his revolver. Prices were also extortionately high in the overcrowded city, even for the modest lodgings they could find in Cintra, half an hour or more to the north. RCK's diary reflects his repetitive rounds of appointments and interviews as he applied for visas.

With the fall of France, whose nationality he now held, he told the British ambassador, Sir Walford Selby, that he 'looked to King George for protection'. Selby knew RCK well, as he had been ambassador in Vienna from 1933 to 1937, and he and his wife invited the three refugees to dinner. RCK suggested in his autobiography that Selby argued he could make a much more valuable contribution to the struggle against Germany from the United States than from Great Britain, but the record does show that the ambassador also sent on RCK's application for a visa to London, to be dealt with through the normal channels.

Understandably impatient, RCK wired friends in Churchill's government, Duff Cooper and Leo Amery among them, asking them to speed up a positive decision. But MI5 objected on 'unspecified' security grounds. Notes by civil servants in the margins of his application show the slow passage of RCK's case up the official hierarchy in London through the month of July.[6] Indecision implied delay, and delay was dangerous. On 17 July, Amery wrote to Duff Cooper, who was now in the Ministry of Information, and he intervened personally. As a result, a day or so later the dossier was unblocked. The final message back from the Foreign Office to the British embassy in Lisbon with agreement to issue visas laconically added that this was 'probably now too late'.

RCK had not been sitting around, just waiting. Trading on his mother's original nationality, he had also approached the Japanese embassy, hoping to obtain transit visas to Tokyo, from where he expected to travel on later to the United States. The Japanese embassy advised him that there would be no delay in giving him visas, but RCK had second thoughts about going to a country which, while still technically neutral, had good relations with Nazi Germany and might not offer any assurance of his actually getting to America later.

At the same time, he appealed to the head of the Canadian legation to France, Georges-Philéas Vanier, who had himself taken refuge in Lisbon

In 1940, the *Yankee Clipper* flew RCK, Idel, and Erika from Lisbon to an unknown future in America.

but was still issuing visas to Canada for refugees from France. RCK suggested he might enter Canada on a visitor's visa to give a lecture tour, but the Canadians deferred any decision until the results of his British application were known.

He also went to the American embassy and spoke with the ambassador, Herbert Clairborne Pell. Leaving nothing to chance, RCK cabled his American contacts at the same time, calling for support from his good friend Murray Butler, the president of the Carnegie Endoment and also president of Columbia University, who had helped him during his first visit to the United States in 1925. Murray Butler personally contacted Cordell Hull, the secretary of state, and instructions were sent from his office to the American embassy in Lisbon in the third week of July to issue visas for RCK, Idel, and Erika.[7]

Armed with American visas, RCK now needed money for the government bond required of all immigrants, and to secure berths on the Clipper seaplane that operated a daily service between La Guardia airport beside the Hudson and the seaplane port on the Tagus River. RCK's financial planning had been as thorough as possible, but the sums required were more than he had been able to put aside. The bonds were one thousand five hundred dollars each, the equivalent of twenty-five thousand dollars today. The fares to New York were a further four thousand dollars each, which brought the total bill for the three migrants to over a quarter of a million dollars in today's money. In addition, the Clipper was booked for months in advance. RCK's friends in America intervened to provide or guarantee the necessary funds, or waive the charges, and with Clairborne Pell's help, RCK and his family jumped the queue of Clipper reservations. Finally, after nearly six weeks spent in Lisbon clearing all these hurdles, RCK, Idel, and Erika boarded the *Yankee Clipper* on 3 August. They left war-torn Europe, heading – in some style – for an uncertain future life in the United States.[8]

15

BRINGING AMERICA ONSIDE

RCK'S WARTIME EXILE IN AMERICA starts with a mystery and ends with a triumph. The mystery lies in pages missing from his 1940 diary, and the triumph in his 1948 meeting with President Truman. Between the two, there lay eight years of political lobbying and social networking, combined with academic research, teaching, and writing, all in the cause of rebuilding a more united Europe after the war was won. This activity played out against a background of RCK's personal concern for his financial position and his public image in the new country that he, Idel, and Erika had made their home in exile. It also unrolled against the vast canvas of world affairs, as President Roosevelt led the United States from neutrality to engagement in the war, and President Truman led it on to victory.

RCK kept meticulous diaries for appointments and meetings over the years, noting telephone numbers and addresses, often entered in pencil in his neat, sloping writing. Sometimes they included financial calculations and exchange rates, and sometimes impressive contact lists of the great and the good. In America his new diaries were given to him each year as presents by his stepdaughter, Erika, affectionately inscribed to her father with love and best wishes for success in his endeavours.

In only one of these many diaries were any pages removed. Four pages were torn out from RCK's 1940 diary, running from Thursday, 1 August, to Sunday, 4 August, the two days before he boarded the *Yankee Clipper* with Idel and Erika, the day they took off, and the day they arrived in the United States. The previous entries on Wednesday, 31 July, note the telephone number for the Clipper office, a reference to a possible meeting with the UK ambassador on 4 August (a meeting which never took place), and the cost of three small purchases. There is also a mention of 'Pension Belge', perhaps the small hotel in Lisbon where the family stayed for the final night before boarding the Clipper. Those four pages are the only ones missing from all RCK's surviving diaries.

What could he have noted there that he did not want anyone else to see? A brief confession, his political testament, or personal will? Notes of a conversation, perhaps, or instructions, or comments on the past, pointers for the future? Did those four pages perhaps have contact details which RCK later realized were sensitive, and hence tore out and destroyed? And when did he actually remove them? Before or after he arrived in America? Unresolved but intriguing questions, leading to some speculation.

The flight from Lisbon to New York took just over twenty-four hours, with the *Yankee Clipper* touching down in the Azores and in Bermuda, giving the three refugees plenty of opportunity to talk to other passengers and to the crew *en route*. The United States was then at the very beginning of setting up its own secret services, and passengers on flights to and from Lisbon in 1940 would obviously have been of interest. Service in the Pan-Am crew was later used as cover for members of the Office of Special Services (oss), which was directly attached to the president's office. But what specific interest might the oss, or its informal predecessor, have had in contacting RCK on that flight?

He had already met and corresponded with a number of American ambassadors in Europe. He counted William Bullitt, the volatile American ambassador in Paris, among his friends.[1] His American contacts – probably Murray Butler and the Carnegie Endowment – had found the large sums required for the family's financial bonds and the Clipper fares, and an approach on board this flight to discuss what he might do for the United States in return seems an unnecessarily clumsy move. In any case, the secretary of state had himself agreed that visas should be issued to the family, so why should the oss pay any further attention, at least until they were safely in America?

The *Yankee Clipper* landed in the Hudson at La Guardia on the very day that Charles Lindbergh, the first man to fly solo across the Atlantic, made a major speech in Chicago in support of American neutrality in the war in Europe. After they cleared customs and immigration formalities, the family was driven to the Edgehill Inn in Riverdale, a northern suburb, where they lodged for a few weeks. It was a pleasant, detached, colonial-style hotel in extensive grounds, modest rather than grand, comfortable rather than luxurious.

It would still be some months before the oss was officially formed, but William Donovan, its prospective director, was in touch with members of the New York 'Century Group' of leading East Coast grandees who

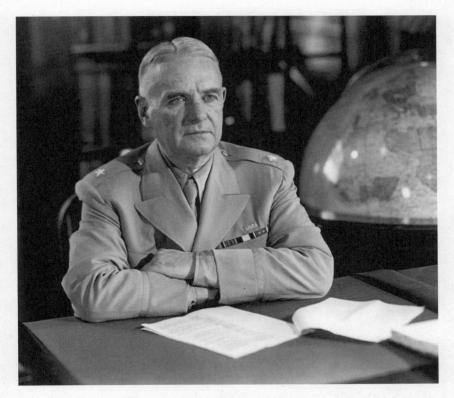

William (Bill) Donovan, Roosevelt's co-ordinator of secret information, initially backed RCK in America.

sympathized with Britain and were consistently anti-Nazi. Some of them, as well as Murray Butler, may well have visited RCK to discuss his analysis of the political situation back in Europe.

AFTER THIS INITIAL PERIOD, the three refugees moved to a spacious apartment at 2501 Palisade Avenue, north of the woods of Westchester County and upstream from the Washington Bridge, with magnificent views over the Hudson. It was in a very respectable suburb of the city, in a speculative development of several large houses and apartments with views across the river to the Palisades, the cliffs on the far side. It was not cheap, and RCK noted with exceptional candour on money matters that they moved in despite 'the financial straits in which we found ourselves'.[2]

As far as he could, RCK had planned the family's emigration carefully, even though, when they left Geneva in June, he had no idea whether it would be in Britain or America that they would eventually settle, or indeed if they would arrive anywhere that was safe. He had made financial arrangements with his bank in Zürich, and also took as much cash in pesetas, escudos, pounds, and dollars as he safely could. Now it was a question of securing a steady income, enough to service a high rent (if indeed the rent was not paid by one or more of his supporters) as well as to maintain his wife and daughter, and to continue his independent life as a political commentator and writer.

It remains unknown whether the growing activities of William Stephenson, the Canadian-businessman-turned-British-spymaster in New York, included RCK as an agent of influence. RCK offered just what Stephenson was looking for: an avid anti-Nazi with good contacts in American society and with a reputation that carried some weight based on his previous work in Europe. And the message that he preached – eventual British victory and the need, indeed the inevitability, of American support for Britain – was just what Bill Stephenson wanted, since his main task was to counter the work of Charles Lindbergh and the America First movement. But RCK had difficult personal characteristics that made recruiting him in any obvious way a problem. His declared desire to remain independent, his claim to lead and to speak his own mind, to run his own show, and the sense of entitlement and even arrogance that went with it, may well have ruled him out. But it is tempting to think – without evidence to prove or disprove it – that he may nonetheless have fitted into the larger plan with which Churchill had charged Stephenson when he sent him to New York to set up the British Information Service (BIS) just a month or so before RCK arrived. RCK certainly needed the money.

For RCK's family, daily life in New York was very different from Vienna. It is hard to imagine that he could support himself financially in this new situation without help from Masonic sources, from the Carnegie Foundation, from individuals from the Century Group, or even directly from the OSS or from the BIS. The family's apartment was several miles north of Manhattan, and there was no Bentley in the New York garage. Since neither RCK nor Idel drove, they had to rely on taxis – it is most unlikely they ever used public transport – for the thirty-minute journey downtown. Their domestic arrangements had to be cut back from what they had been used to in Vienna, but Idel had some domestic help in running their new home, though probably not more than one live-in housekeeper.

They could not afford – nor could the apartment accommodate – the four staff they had employed in Vienna.

But at least RCK and Idel had been to America before, and Erika spoke English well. She soon found a job with the New York Parks and Gardens Authority, which not only gave her a sense of independence, but also brought in a small, steady income of her own over the next few years while she acquired some horticultural qualifications. RCK reports that Idel, however, declined an invitation to Hollywood for fear that her command of English would not be adequate for starring roles. It would also have meant living on the West Coast, where RCK could not easily have pursued his political work. She made a decision, he later wrote, not to pursue her acting career in America at all (she would be sixty the following year) but to devote her energies, as she had in the last few years in Europe, to supporting RCK's political activities.

Years later a neighbour from New York recalls often seeing the couple walking in the nearby Henry Hudson Memorial Park in Spuyton Duyvil:

a tall man of about fifty, patrician in appearance but not proud, in the company of a vivacious elderly woman – the two of them as different as the rock at the head of a waterfall and the water that flows round it, but evidently just as integral to one another ... I see these two people still, and the dignity and intimacy of their bearing, their total unawareness of anyone else in the park as they talked together, absorbed in an ideal which they had first realized in private life. It was as if their vision turned into reality for me as I crossed their orbit, although I did not know until years later what that vision was.[3]

RCK had found generous support to bring him and his family to the United States, but he needed to find regular salaried employment and also financial backers to continue his Pan-Europa political activities and realize his vision in the New World. With his habitual charm, well-placed contacts, and concentrated dedication to his task, he set about achieving his objectives – and met with remarkable success. Not every European exile landed on their feet so well.

RCK MANAGED IT thanks in particular to people he had stayed in contact with since his first visit to America fifteen years earlier, among them the Warburg brothers and Murray Butler, all of them also Freemasons. RCK's formal resignation from the brotherhood in Vienna certainly appears not to have distanced him from the Masonic network in America. Barely two months after his arrival, Otto Tolischus, another Mason and a well-known foreign correspondent, who had been expelled from Berlin in March that year and was now back in America in an editorial position covering European affairs for the *New York Times*, reported to readers that RCK had arrived in town and would soon lecture at the Council for Foreign Relations (CFR), New York's most influential think-tank. Stephen P. Duggan, the chairman of the American support committee that RCK had set up at the end of his first visit in 1926, was now the director of the CFR, and organized a dinner for RCK, with invited guests, on 22 October 1940.

With his usual clarity RCK spoke after dinner about the nature of the war in Europe, how the geopolitical scene would look after the defeat of Germany, and just what options the United States now had. The Nazi-Soviet Non-Aggression Pact had given Germany a free hand to invade Western Europe, but RCK homed in on what he saw as the inevitable future conflict that would break out between Nazi Germany and Soviet Russia, uneasy bedfellows who would soon become deadly enemies.[4] Stephen Duggan took notes and, according to his summary, RCK declared: 'In the present war there are not two fronts but three: Western Civilization, Nazism and Bolshevism. All three are different, and all hate one another. One of them will make the new Europe. Irrespective of whoever wins, Europe will be unified.' Because of its incompatibility with the two other options, he added, the United States will be forced to ally with Britain as the representative of Western Civilization: 'Only if Britain wins can the United States affect the future of Europe.'

RCK predicted that, after the war, Britain's relationship with the continent would also be changed. 'Aviation has made isolation impossible for Britain. If she wins the war, she will have to rule Europe; if she doesn't, Germany or Russia will. The conclusion is unavoidable that Britain must rule Europe and she can only rule by making a European federation of free states. No other form is possible. In advising her on federation, no country is better qualified to render assistance than the United States.' His advice to his audience of East Coast Americans interested in international affairs was clear: 'You not only *should* help Britain, you *must* do so if your voice is to amount to anything in the world.'

RCK correctly foresaw that by the end of 1940 Germany would occupy every country on the continent up to the Russian border. Germany, he declared, would have command of the land, but Britain would have command of the sea. Whoever commanded the skies, however, would win the war. The survival of Western Civilization in Europe depended on Britain winning. If Stalin won, he would convert liberal, Christian Europe into an Asiatic Civilization based on the philosophy of Marx and the dictatorship of the proletariat. If Hitler won, he would remodel it on the basis of the philosophy of Nietzsche and German national dominance. Only if Britain won, he concluded his address, would Western – and hence American – values also survive and flourish in Europe.

RCK's lecture was delivered long before the breakdown of the Nazi-Soviet Non-Aggression Pact and more than a year before America entered the war, but already he was convinced that Germany would lose. 'But who,' he asked, 'will win? Russia or Britain?' If it was a long war, it would be Stalin, he argued, because universal misery and poverty would win friends for Russia among the working classes. If Britain was going to win, he argued, she must win quickly, and 'whether she can win quickly depends largely on the United States.' Britain and Germany could bomb each others' factories, he argued, but 'Britain alone can import planes from the United States.'

The extent of US support for Great Britain was a politically sensitive issue in 1940. The America First Committee was set up that autumn nominally to ensure US neutrality, but the effect of keeping the United States out of the war was to lend support for Nazi Germany.[5] Public-opinion polls suggested that the potential involvement of the United States in the war against Germany was extremely unpopular, with barely 10 per cent in favour. But RCK argued that the United States had to take sides, and should come down clearly on the side of Great Britain. 'The United States,' he argued, 'can give material help to Britain and moral help to Europe. The vision of a *United* States should be made plain to the peoples of Europe. At the present time, the lower classes place their hopes in Stalin as the only one who can help them. The United States must give them an alternative.' His American listeners, he argued, must become 'the champion of European liberty just as Russia is the champion of European equality.'

With as much prescience as pessimism, RCK outlined the ideological struggle that would follow the end of the current conflict: 'Although federation will mean peace in Europe,' he said, 'I envisage very little peace between the federated bloc and Russia. Between these two, there will be religious wars comparable to those between Christianity and Islam in the Middle Ages. There will be alternate periods of war and peace, but in general it will be a period of war.' In the longer term, he expected the world to be divided into four great groups – the Americas, Europe, Russia, and the Far East. Before the war he had foreseen five, but now the British Empire was for him no longer an independent power centre. Britain's fate was, in his view, embedded with Europe. Ideologically and culturally, that was also true for America, even though she was geographically more distant. Since the Americas 'have nothing in common with Russia and the Far East, you can only unite with Europe.'

To prepare for the post-war situation, he argued that practical studies should now be going on to organize the future peace of Europe. 'Britain is too busy to undertake the task; the United States is the natural and logical centre for these studies. For a federated Europe will require considerable forethought and planning. It must be done before the cessation of hostilities. There will not be time enough after.'

Questioned at the end of his presentation about the likely bitterness of other nations towards Germany when the war was over, he replied that, based on his experience of the 1920s, he expected any sense of bitterness to disappear quickly. Building the political and economic federation was what mattered most, and he listed the key steps.

> The first step is to unify all aviation under the control of Britain. Then there must be a customs union. Civil rights must be essentially the same all over Europe. All [European] countries must have parallel rights in Africa. Last, there must be some kind of political council of the unified Europe. It will not be like the old League of Nations – which resembled your articles of Confederation – but a new League with strong powers of the type your second constitution gave the central government.

Not everyone was sympathetic to the views that RCK expressed, but Murray Butler and the Warburg brothers, who did sympathize with his position, ensured that he was also invited to give a speech to a larger gathering at the prestigious International House in New York. On 3 November, he went to the rostrum to speak to the New World about the Old. The imposing auditorium was draped with the flags of all the democratic, and now occupied, nations of Europe, alongside the Stars and Stripes and the Union Jack. Forthright opinions and a far-sighted view such as he expressed at the earlier dinner were just a foretaste of what RCK had to say. Stephen Duggan was again in the chair, and RCK's presentation was this time entitled 'The Defence of Western Civilization'. In it he fleshed out his geopolitical vision of the powers now shaping world history.

It was an awkward moment to launch his vision of Pan-Europa to the United States foreign-policy establishment. The United States was still neutral in the war, and RCK was arguing that the threat to the values of the West came not only from National Socialism but also from Bolshevism. He was convinced that Nazism would die with the defeat of Germany, but Bolshevism would spread from Russia across the globe to become a universal challenge to the civilization that the West had inherited from Greece and Rome and from Christianity. RCK questioned whether Russia, not yet a belligerent, could still be regarded as a part of Europe. Should it not rather be seen now as a Eurasian power in its own right?

His audience were fully aware that Hitler and Stalin were still linked in their non-aggression pact, and one of the official aims of American foreign policy was to ensure that this did not lead to any closer alignment of the Soviet Union with Nazi Germany. That meant weaning Moscow away from its close ties with Berlin – being kind to Russia, not critical, not opposing or frustrating the Kremlin.

Planning for a post-war Europe that was united against Soviet Russia was not on the American agenda. As Arnold Zürcher, professor of political science at New York University and himself a member of the Council for Foreign Relations, commented afterwards: 'During 1940 a number of Americans found it hard to make a distinction between the theoretical notion of a united Europe and the practical reality of Europe already unified by Hitler by force of arms. A unified Europe, without Hitler, seemed a utopian idea totally removed from the realities of practical politics.' RCK set about disabusing his audience, firmly anchoring the notion of a united Europe in the context of post-war reconstruction that would follow an Allied victory in the war, and necessarily in opposition to the Soviet Union.

Many in his mainly East Coast audience were close to the traditional American isolationist position, preferring neutrality and letting the Europeans sort themselves out. Others could agree that the United States should support Great Britain against Nazi Germany. But very few were prepared to take the next step, to realize that America's long-term struggle would be against Bolshevik ideology and a potential Russian adversary. For many in his audience, to see the future as RCK presented it – a three-way geopolitical struggle for dominance between the West (the United States and Europe together), the Soviet Union, and the rising powers of Asia – was a step too far.

But one principle they all could share was that peace needed to be ensured through military might, and the most modern form of military power was overwhelming air superiority. The United States had a technological advantage in this area and should exploit it massively, argued RCK. That would empower the United States to dictate the terms of peace to the rest of the world, and incidentally, he indicated, would be good for business, employment, and profits. But RCK's call for an American rearmament programme of two hundred thousand warplanes per year, with the aim of imposing global hegemony with a Western air force of a million machines, sounded excessive even to the military hawks. After all, the total material losses of the Luftwaffe and the RAF in the Battle of Britain, which seemed at the time to be enormous, had been no more than five thousand planes.

On the strength of RCK's lecture, Henry Luce, the editor of *Fortune* magazine, commissioned an article about likely developments in Europe, and RCK entitled it 'Why England Will Win the War'. The Battle of Britain had petered out barely two months earlier, and the immediate fear of invasion over the Channel was receding. The Luftwaffe had been diverted to night-time bombing raids – the Blitz – a war of attrition on the civilian population rather than directly challenging RAF fighter command for daytime control of the skies over Britain. And there was no end in sight for the war at sea. U-boats were attempting to starve Britain into surrender, and in North Africa the Axis powers planned to capture the Suez Canal and sever Britain's lifeline to the Empire. Britain, though defiant, was financially and economically overstretched, nearly bankrupt, underfed, and close to exhaustion.

When Henry Luce saw RCK's draft, he felt it was too positive about the chances of Britain's survival at that stage, and declined to publish it. President Roosevelt had already gone out on a limb by agreeing to the 'Destroyers for Bases' deal with Winston Churchill in September, but even he did not dare to bring forward the formal proposals for this deal – the Lend-Lease Act – to Congress until December, more than a month after RCK's speech, and it would not be signed into law until March the following year. It was not until August 1941, after the collapse of the Nazi-Soviet Non-Aggression Pact, that Roosevelt was prepared to meet Churchill to agree to the Atlantic Charter, the list of principles that would underpin Anglo-American co-operation during and after the war – a war which, at this point, the United States had still not entered. RCK was far ahead of the curve.

Undeterred by the cool reception to his ideas at the Council for Foreign Relations, and the refusal of *Fortune* magazine to publish his article, RCK requested an appointment with President Roosevelt in December 1940. Murray Butler, in his capacity as president of the Carnegie Endowment for International Peace, wrote to support his request. Following normal practice, the President's Office asked the advice of the State Department

In August 1941, off Newfoundland, Roosevelt and Churchill agreed on the Atlantic Charter.

and – well informed about RCK's extreme position, as outlined in his earlier presentations – they advised against a meeting. Regrettably, RCK never established good personal relations with the long-serving secretary of state, William Cordell Hull, nor with the under-secretary, Sumner Welles, who was the president's point man in the State Department. As far as the State Department was concerned, he might have been a refugee worth rescuing from Lisbon, but his outspoken views were extremely anti-Soviet and not currently welcome. He was rebuffed, and for the first half of 1941 he did not know how to get around the problem.

THE ATLANTIC CHARTER that Roosevelt and Churchill agreed on at their meeting in Newfoundland in August, however, offered RCK an opening. It was essentially a morale-boosting gesture of solidarity that the president made to the prime minister and the British people, but it came at a price. The charter put down a strong marker that Imperial Preference, the trading advantage on which the British Empire rested, would, in time, be dismantled in favour of global free trade. That was what the United States wanted, along with agreement on the principle of national self-determination, and that would be the basis of post-war de-colonization, doing for the rest of the world what Woodrow Wilson had done for the 'captive nationalities' in the old European empires that fell in 1918. Churchill wired his cabinet advising them not to raise objections now, but to appreciate the charter's public relations' value for the war effort. Churchill desperately needed to persuade Roosevelt to join the war against Hitler. Lend-Lease and the Atlantic Charter were the first steps in this direction.

The media in Britain and the United States praised the Atlantic Charter fulsomely. RCK did so as well, and used it as an opportunity to profile himself to both leaders. He wrote to Churchill and to Roosevelt, congratulating them both on establishing the basis for a common effort, and asking each of them for a meeting. Perhaps to make his communication different from the many others that they must have received, he added a reference to an obscure prophecy in the ambiguous wording of Nostradamus that spoke of the alliance of two great princes in the North, of a mighty war with a distant enemy, and of their final victory which would follow. Unsurprisingly, neither of the political leaders responded.

RCK's enthusiasm and imagination got the better of him just as it had got the better of Napoleon, who regarded Nostradamus's prophecies with awe, and of Hitler, equally gullible of prophecy and in awe of soothsayers. Great figures in public life often are superstitious, well aware of the wheel of Fortune. But they seldom welcome being reminded by others that their fate may not entirely be the result of their own will and action, but pre-ordained, written in the stars, or – in the case of Nostradamus – put down on parchment by a physician in the south of France in the sixteenth century.[6]

However, RCK was nothing if not persistent. After the first refusal from President Roosevelt's office and Roosevelt's failure to reply to his congratulations on the Atlantic Charter, he approached him again after the Japanese attack on Pearl Harbor in December 1941. Again, his request for a meeting was refused, based as before on State Department advice. Frustrated at not being able to meet with Roosevelt personally, RCK approached Vice-President Henry Wallace and, early in 1942, he did finally secure an interview to discuss European affairs.

Much had changed in the European theatre since his earlier attempts to be heard at the head of the US Administration. Hitler had unleashed Operation Barbarossa against Russia in June the previous year, and the United States was now doing all it could to strengthen its Soviet ally. But, undiplomatically, RCK still did not disguise his viscerally anti-Bolshevist views, outlining his vision of a post-war world of antagonistic blocs – a transatlantic democratic alliance, Bolshevik Russia, and despotic Asia. This was the very opposite of the Administration's vision of friendly co-operation within a global framework of the United Nations. The interview went so badly that Henry Wallace declined to receive RCK for a second meeting. RCK had now spoilt relations at the highest level, and the US government was not interested in listening to his ideas. Even Murray Butler's letters of recommendation could not batter down those closed doors. Other ideas were in favour in Washington, and RCK did not share them.

In June 1941, a meeting in Washington of representatives from sixteen European, Latin American, and Asian nations had set up the International Free World Association, a liberal-leftist non-governmental organization, strongly anti-fascist, but not anti-communist. Their views fitted the Administration's foreign-policy priorities much better than RCK's Pan-Europa. The association's monthly magazine, *Free World*, published in New York from autumn that year, attracted a government subsidy and could call on many highly placed contributors, including Einstein and Freud, Thomas Mann, Edvard Beneš, Jan Masaryk, Cordell Hull, Dorothy Thompson, and on one occasion President Roosevelt himself. Louis Dolivet, the editor, was – like RCK – a refugee from Europe also living in New York, but he had married into a wealthy East Coast family and enjoyed considerable social status and political access. With minimal resources, he exerted disproportionate influence on elite opinion and on government thinking, promoting views that gave no space to a regional European voice in international affairs. It was unexpected but serious competition for RCK, as it offered an alternative geopolitical vision for the future to rival his. Characteristically, he never mentioned it in his writings, denying his rival the oxygen of publicity as he had also done with Prinz Rohan and the Kulturbund, but it coloured his view of what he felt was excessive communist influence on American foreign policy.[7]

ONCE MORE IT WAS THANKS to Murray Butler that RCK took the next positive step in his relatively speedy establishment in New York, his new home in exile. Murray Butler had contributed the preface to the first American edition of RCK's book *Pan-Europa* in 1926, and had been instrumental in securing his family visas to the United States. Now, as president of Columbia University as well as the Carnegie Endowment, he ensured that his good friend, Harry Woodburn Chase, the chancellor of New York University (NYU) and a fellow Freemason, offered RCK a teaching post financed by the endowment. RCK learnt that he had been appointed to the staff of NYU in April 1941, and uncharacteristically wrote the one word *glückselig* in his diary, an uncharacteristically emotional entry meaning 'ecstatic' or perhaps 'blessed'. He was now forty-seven and was, for the first time in his life, assured of a regular earned income. It was not a professorial chair, but it was an academic perch that gave him some official status and a regular income.

That summer he and Idel decided to spend their vacation in Big Moose in the Adirondack mountains of upstate New York, easily accessible by rail from the city, but remote enough to ensure that they could enjoy the peace and quiet of the mountains, forests, and lakes. In their rented chalet, RCK could prepare material for his teaching and the growing number of articles and speeches that he was called on to make, as well as write his first full-length book of memoirs in English: *Crusade for Europe: The Biography of a Man and a Movement.*

While they were in Big Moose that summer, RCK's mother, Mitsu, died in Vienna. She was buried at the end of August in the Coudenhove mausoleum in Hietzing cemetery, not far from where she had lived when she acquired her flat in Vienna after Heinrich's death. RCK learned about it only some weeks later, through a letter from his sister Olga which was sent from Vienna via the diplomatic bag to Japan and then posted to the United States. RCK recalled well how his mother was pleased and interested when she could read about him and his Pan-Europa project in the newspapers or hear him on radio – but she evidently never understood what he was trying to achieve. She simply bathed in the reflected glow of his celebrity, which irritated and eventually alienated him from her. She had also never welcomed Idel, and he had visited her alone, and then only occasionally during the 1930s, before the Nazis took over Austria. He was blissfully unaware that she had cursed him – along with all her other children except Hansi and Olga – for neglecting her in her old age, the cardinal sin in Japanese tradition, for children were always to revere their parents. On later reflection, he was glad that his mother had died early enough not have learned of Japan's entry into the war with its surprise attack on the US naval base at Pearl Harbor that December, or of America's response of an immediate declaration of war on both Japan and Germany.[8]

Half-Japanese as well as half-Austrian, RCK, remarkably, was not interned in the months following America's entry into the war. Although he also makes no comment on this in his writings, he must have had friends, possibly in the oss, who saw to it that he was not even called in for questioning, but was regarded as a 'good' European in exile. There appears to have been no official concern in America about either his Asiatic or his Austrian roots.

Winston Churchill visited Washington soon after America's entry into the war and addressed a joint session of Congress, stressing how Great Britain and the United States, the two nations that had agreed to the Atlantic Charter nine months previously, would now 'walk together side by side in majesty, in justice and in peace.' It was a solemn moment, a display of unity and resolve, but behind the scenes, both leaders were desperate at the losses their armed forces were suffering, in particular in Asia. By February 1942, Singapore had fallen, Malaya and the Philippines were threatened, and British forces would soon be pressed back to India and to Australia. President Roosevelt and Winston Churchill urgently needed to co-ordinate their efforts, both on the battlefield and in the production of war material, above all aeroplanes. Mastery of the air was vital. RCK asked to see Churchill, but there was no room in the official programme of his visit for an outsider who was not in good standing with the State Department or with the President's Office.

Nor was RCK having much success in sustaining a positive relationship with the British embassy in Washington. He had met and made a good impression on Lord Lothian in London before the war, and Lothian was UK ambassador when he arrived in the United States. But regrettably he was already a sick man, and he died only a few months later. Attempts to develop good relations with his successor, Lord Halifax, were not successful, and the embassy's view reverted to the traditional, mainstream Foreign Office position, which had always been dismissive of RCK. Elizabeth Wiskemann, a long-serving diplomat in the British embassy in Bern, had met him at a party in Vienna in the 1930s given by the *Manchester Guardian*'s correspondent M.W. Fodor, and described him in her memoir, *The Europe That I Saw*, as 'a wildly unrealistic dreamer'. It was a view widely shared by several British diplomats. Equally negative were the unspecified security hesitations of MI5 noted on his original request for a UK visa while he was waiting to get away from Lisbon in 1940. Just as serious was a handwritten note on internal correspondence in the Foreign Office in 1943 noting that RCK was 'more a nuisance than a danger', since 'he has no backing'.[9]

His lack of any national base or of any electoral mandate was indeed a problem for RCK. He was hard to place. What country or what party did he belong to? Half-Japanese, but originally from Austria, and since September 1939 a French citizen, he had in earlier years been travelling on a Czech diplomatic passport and had a home in Switzerland. Where did he belong? The Austria he had known was no more, totally absorbed into Hitler's Reich. The Czechoslovak state, of which he had been a citizen, no longer existed, the Sudetenland also absorbed into the Reich, and the rest of Bohemia linked to Moravia as a German protectorate.

RCK had always regarded his Swiss home as simply a country retreat, a temporary convenience, which had proved useful as a safe haven when he fled from Vienna. He was now a refugee with a French passport in America. Where was his real home? There was no government in exile whose authority he could acknowledge or which he could join. To whom did he owe allegiance? If asked, he would have answered 'Europe', but in the eyes of the Allied governments, he had no locus other than that of an independent author from Central Europe, temporarily employed as a lecturer in New York University. He was a citizen of nowhere.

He had to rely on personal contacts with political leaders and senior figures in public life, because he did not speak for an organized constituency, just for an amorphous body of opinion concerning Europe to which he managed to give a voice in publications and speeches formulated in a striking style. As in Europe before the war, so now in America, he needed some sort of celebrity status, to be newsworthy, to create a public persona and catch the attention of governments. He needed to be more than just another university lecturer in order to penetrate through the defences of the bureaucracies that protected the leaders.

———

FROM HIS MODEST PERCH in New York University, RCK threw himself with his habitual energy into creating a country for himself, a pre-war democratic Austria that *deserved* a government-in-exile like other countries the German Reich had overrun. The Atlantic Charter referred to the Nazi annexation of Austria, and the subsequent Moscow Declaration went even further. RCK planned a joint declaration by notable Austrians in exile, which would condemn the Anschluss and assert the right of patriotic Austrians to represent the interests of their country as the first victim of German aggression. He drafted a memorandum on 'Austria's Independence in the Light of the Atlantic Charter' and sent it to Roosevelt and Churchill. Turning his non-party status to his advantage, he boldly proposed that, being independent of any political party, he was best placed to reconcile the divergent views of all Austrians abroad and would be a suitable candidate to head such a government-in-exile.

In part, his initiative was designed to pre-empt a group of Austrian exiles in New York led by Hans Rott, a former minister in Schuschnigg's last government, who were planning a Free Austrian National Council. RCK considered them far too right wing to possibly be representative of Austrian exile opinion, and claimed he had greater credibility as a bridge between the right- and left-wing groups into which Austrians in exile had divided. However, in the draft declaration that he circulated to all interested Austrians, he claimed that the governments of Dollfuss and Schuschnigg had offered 'heroic resistance' to Nazism. That was clearly too strong an assertion for the left, quite unacceptable for many socialist and social-democratic exiles. The civil war of early 1934, when Dollfuss had ordered the army to shell workers' housing in Vienna, still bitterly divided exile opinion, and they objected to someone with RCK's record of close association with Dollfuss and Schuschnigg taking such an initiative. The wounds from recent political battles had not yet healed.

RCK blamed 'the intransigence of some leaders' among the *émigrés* for this failure to bring together the different parties, but the project was not welcome to the Allies either. RCK had overstated his case. Austria might be considered the first victim of Nazi aggression, rather than a state complicit with Nazi Germany for the war, but there was no prospect of acknowledging a government-in-exile, social-democratic, Austro-fascist, or royalist.[10] It should have been a lesson for RCK that to succeed he needed to take political realities – which included personal histories – into account, not simply assume that his bright ideas would of their own accord be acceptable to all concerned. His blind spot was his self-confidence, thinking that, if he was intellectually correct, as he always assumed he was, he would inevitably be successful.

Subsequently, RCK helped Otto von Hapsburg, the last Austro-Hungarian Crown Prince, who was based in Washington at that time, in his more modest and informal efforts to co-ordinate Austrians in exile. RCK as ever offered plentiful advice, in particular drafting under Otto's signature a memorandum concerning the status of South Tyrol in any future negotiation with the Allies. Their relationship was certainly warm, marked on von Hapsburg's side by genuine gratitude for the intellectual acuity and linguistic fluency of RCK, and on RCK's side with aristocratic deference to royalty, thanking his majesty-in-exile for the kind condescension with which he deigned to write to his loyal correspondent.[11]

While busy in America, RCK was out of the loop as regards discussions in London about the post-war political reconstruction of Europe.

Edvard Beneš, prime minister of the Czech government in exile, Paul-Henri Spaak, foreign minister of the Belgian government in exile, and Wladyslav Sikorski, prime minister of the Polish government in exile, were the moving spirits, co-ordinating their governments to discuss desirable forms – international or supranational – that a new European order might take when victory restored them to their rightful place as national leaders back in their capitals.

They, too, had their difficulties in getting through the defences of the British Foreign Office and making links with Churchill directly, but they were at least in the same city. RCK was obliged to undertake a similar task from the other side of the Atlantic. Not being aware of the internal assessment of him by the Foreign Office, he wrote to Churchill on several occasions through the British embassy in Washington as well as to London directly, congratulating him on military or political successes, offering advice, sending him his publications, and requesting meetings and messages of moral support. Given the difficulties of distance and the obstruction of official channels, he managed it remarkably well, sending at least seventeen messages to Churchill from New York during the course of the war, and receiving responses to many of them.

His first attempts to contact Churchill directly were in 1941, when he asked twice, unsuccessfully, to meet him when he next visited the United States. Churchill responded politely that he regretted he would not have time in his crowded schedules. RCK wrote again in the aftermath of the signing of the Atlantic Charter, offering his congratulations – along with a reference to Nostradamus. The substantive purpose of another message was to urge Churchill to make Austria the same offer of post-war independence that he had just extended to India. RCK argued that such an offer would shorten the war in Europe by a year, since the psychological effect of the gesture would undermine German morale, both in the army and the civilian population, by boosting a separate Austrian identity. There is no record of Churchill's reaction, but RCK felt he had opened a line of communication on a policy issue and hoped he could use it to good effect later.

IN THE WINTER OF 1941, RCK began teaching a seminar at New York University on 'Problems in Post-war European Federation' in conjunction with Professor Arnold Zürcher. They ran this seminar jointly with another on the history of 'European Federalism'. Initially only six postgraduate students signed up for the course, but in the second year they remodelled the content of the two courses, increasing the number and variety of external contributors from the European *émigré* community who were called in to add first-hand experience, and they began systematically to analyse the complex issues that the post-war reorganization of Europe might pose. Student·numbers increased.

RCK very quickly made good use of his new position, not simply to teach but to promote Pan-Europa's ideas more widely. One of the first events that he planned was in March 1942, to celebrate the tenth anniversary of the death of Aristide Briand, the former French prime minister, who had launched his initiative for European unity at the League of Nations in 1929. The event was initially planned for 7 March, but Arnold Zürcher discreetly pointed out to RCK that Americans celebrate birthdays rather than anniversaries of death, so RCK was able to avoid a cultural *faux pas* by quickly moving the date to 29 March, which happened to coincide with the eightieth anniversary of Briand's birth. NYU had granted Briand an honorary degree some years previously and was now more than happy to honour his memory. RCK wrote to Churchill to ask for a message of support to read out at the event, but advice from the Foreign Office to the prime minister suggested that this was simply a publicity stunt, and the request was refused, possibly without ever being brought to Churchill's personal attention.

However, the Briand commemoration event was well attended, well publicized, and was certainly more than just a publicity stunt. Several members of RCK's American Pan-Europa support committee attended, as did Count Sforza, the former foreign minister of Italy, Jan Masaryk, the future foreign minister of Czechoslovakia, and Thomas Mann, the leading exile among German writers and artists. Alexis Léger, who had been a close adviser to Briand at the time of the 1929 initiative, came from Washington and spoke of Briand as 'the apostle of European federal union'. He insisted that this goal was as timely now as when Briand had championed it at the League of Nations. At the express wish of President Roosevelt, Alexis Léger's speech was translated into English and published by the university. Unfortunately, RCK did not have a message from Churchill to read to the assembled guests, but he spoke his mind forcefully about the situation in Europe. Several journalists attended to cover the event in the American press, and its success confirmed RCK's role both within the university and with a wider audience.

In June that same year, Hitler invaded the Soviet Union, and the war in Europe took on an entirely new dimension. In retrospect, Operation Barbarossa is seen as·the Führer's most costly mistake, but at the time it looked likely to consolidate Hitler's gains in eastern Europe and to quickly knock Russia out of the war entirely. News from North Africa was no better for the Allies. The first battle of El Alamein in July was at best a drawn match, causing the British and Allied forces to retreat further and creating near panic known as 'the Flap' at headquarters in Cairo. Diplomats and intelligence officers burned classified files in advance of what was expected to be the Axis conquest of Egypt.

RCK followed the progress of the war closely and was delighted when the Allies turned the tide at the second battle of El Alamein at the end of October that year. He immediately appreciated the importance of this victory and telegrammed Churchill with his congratulations, suggesting that November's Remembrance Sunday might be renamed Victory Sunday in honour of this turning point in the fortunes of the Allies. The Prime Minister's Office kindly thanked him for his suggestion. RCK's line of communication was now well open.

RCK had the comforting habit of concentrating on what he did want to hear and ignoring what he did not want to hear. Sometimes it was a defence mechanism, saving him from having to cope with a difficult situation or bad news, sometimes it was a conscious decision, to deny the alternative version of events any currency, to deprive it of the oxygen of publicity. An example of the first case was perhaps the news of his mother's death, and an example of the second was his and Idel's viewing of *Casablanca*.

Warner Brothers launched the film in New York in Thanksgiving week 1942, but set the story line of the film eighteen months earlier, when America was still neutral. Just a few weeks before the launch, the first combined operation of American and British troops – Operation Torch – successfully opened a second front in North Africa. The Allies quickly took Algeria and Morocco from the Axis forces. Casablanca was in the news. The turning fortunes of the war gave *Casablanca* a propaganda boost that ensured it topical interest. Launched in a blaze of patriotic publicity, the film was an immediate success. RCK and Idel must have known about this cultural event on their very doorstep, but he nowhere mentions it in his memoirs or his correspondence.

One explanation of RCK's silence may be that he concentrated not on the political context of the film but rather on the psychology of the characters. He would have found the character of Victor Laszlo, an admired Resistance hero said to be modelled on RCK, entirely sympathetic. Laszlo is not the central character in the film, but he does take events by the scruff of the neck and command the plot. It is essentially Rick and Ilsa who are at the centre of the moral drama of the story, called on to make

In *Casablanca*, Paul Henreid
(left) played Victor Laszlo,
a character based on RCK.

difficult personal choices that test their emotions and their sense of duty
and propriety. RCK could sympathize with their dilemma but certainly
saw no parallels for Idel there. He might see himself as an actor on the
stage of history, and wanted to be seen as a leader. Perhaps his excuse – if
he needed one – for not mentioning the film would have been that he had
enough of the real world on his plate and could not spend time worrying
about fiction, especially a fiction which did not reflect well, he thought,
upon his wife.[12]

IN THE DAYS JUST BEFORE CHRISTMAS, RCK approached Churchill again,
this time with a copy of a letter he had just published in the *New York
Times* concerning the need for Europe to be constituted as a federation in
the post-war settlement that RCK ever more confidently envisaged. Early
the next year he wrote again, asking for an official British delegate to the

fifth Pan-Europa Congress that he was planning to hold that summer in New York. The Foreign Office politely declined to send anyone to represent the British government, but noted internally that they were aware that RCK had also invited Harold Nicholson, currently a member of the board of governors of the BBC, in his private capacity. The Foreign Office left the decision to Nicholson's discretion, and he also declined.

But RCK's approach had served his purpose, since it meant that Churchill was now informed about the next Pan-Europa Congress in New York. He already knew from Leo Amery of the first Congress in Vienna in 1926, the second in Berlin in 1930, the third in Basel in 1932, and the fourth in Vienna again in 1935, and now he could put this forthcoming New York event into its historical context. Churchill well knew what RCK would be discussing at this forthcoming Congress , since he had been sent the results of RCK's research seminar's work for the previous year, but, again on Foreign Office advice, his office declined to send a supportive message. However, this did not indicate lack of interest. Behind the scenes, the situation was changing fast, and Churchill decided personally to do something much more important.

On 21 March 1943, Churchill broadcast on the BBC his most explicit statement to date about the future of Europe. 'Under a world institution embodying or representing the United Nations, and some day all nations, there should come into being a Council of Europe,' he said, which should be 'a real effective League, with all the strongest forces concerned woven into its texture, with a High Court to adjust disputes, and with forces, armed forces, national or international, or both, held ready to impose these decisions.' As a statement of purpose, it went well beyond the tentative declaration of Aristide Briand before the League of Nations in 1929 when he had asked for 'some kind of federal link' between neighbouring European states, and Churchill knew it. Here he was making a proposal for a post-war European federation.

Churchill certainly had good reason for taking this dramatic step. He was increasingly concerned about an alternative concept for the post-war world order that was supported by the American Administration. Roosevelt was keen on the idea of 'four policemen' – the United States, the USSR, Great Britain, and China – who would enforce world order in their respective spheres of influence. Europe was not one of them, and Churchill feared this would be tantamount to delivering Europe into the hands of Stalin. RCK shared this view. They both realized that what was needed was a stronger Europe, able to resist being drawn into the sphere of influence of the Soviet Union. Europe, RCK had always argued, needed to be present with political and military weight enough of its own to ensure its independence. Under the pressure of developing events, in particular the stalling of the German invasion of the Soviet Union, Churchill's thinking was now moving in the direction that RCK had been preaching since well before the rise of Hitler. Europe should be nobody's sphere of influence, least of all the Soviet Union's. It should instead be an independent federation of nations in its own right.[13]

It is impossible to determine how far it was RCK who influenced Churchill to make such a strong statement of support of a pan-European solution for post-war reconstruction, or how far Churchill was responding to the developing views of Roosevelt on the nature of the post-war world order. Churchill knew the pre-war background of discussions around European federation well, and he was up to speed with RCK's current work. For RCK, however, Churchill's appeal for a Council of Europe with executive power and military capacity could not have come at a better time.

In a couple of weeks, he would open his fifth Pan-Europa Congress in New York and would build on this dramatic public endorsement of his own and Pan-Europa's goals.

16

THE UNITED STATES
OF EUROPE?

THE FIFTH PAN-EUROPA CONGRESS, the first held outside Europe, took place at New York University in April 1943. RCK organized the substantive aspects, while Idel stage-managed the event, including a theatrical opening ceremony in the Judson Memorial Church with a performance of Beethoven's *Ode to Joy,*[1] and a spectacular gala dinner chaired by Ambassador Bullitt in the Waldorf Hotel. It brought together over two hundred Europeans in exile, a cross-party collection of leading figures from the *émigré* world, as well as Americans with both academic and political interests in European affairs. The key purpose was to underline the important role of the university as the main locus, outside government, for thinking about the future of Europe. It fully achieved its purpose.

RCK set up an honorary committee for the event, which included the former prime minister of Belgium, Paul Van Zeeland; the former prime minister of the Czechoslovak Republic, Milan Hodza; the Swiss psychoanalyst Raymond de Saussure; the director of the Polish Institute in New York, Oskar Halecki; and Victor Cazalet, a British MP who also operated as liaison officer with the Polish government-in-exile in London and was fortuitously on mission in Washington at the time.[2] American speakers included professorial colleagues of RCK's from NYU, among them Harold Voorhis, Joseph Hendershot Park, and Arnold Zürcher, in addition to a well-regarded German economist in exile, Richard Schüller, and André Istel, de Gaulle's economic adviser.[3]

The main meetings were chaired by Fernando de los Rios, former foreign minister of Spain, Louis Marlio, member of the Institute of France, and RCK himself as president of the Pan-Europa Union. Three committees considered issues of constitutional law, economics, and cultural history, all with a focus on the reconstruction of Europe after the war. The congress culminated in a resolution outlining what it considered should be Allied desiderata for a post-war European settlement, including political union on the continent along federal lines. It also decided to set up a number of committees that would continue detailed work during the following months.

The proceedings of the congress, published by NYU shortly afterwards, was a solid piece of work, a printed report of over a hundred pages, with contributions from thirty-six participants. It included an essay on 'America and United Europe', by Arnold Zürcher, and one by RCK entitled 'Post-war Europe: League or Federation?' Other authors wrote on 'Switzerland as a Model'; 'A European Bill of Rights';. 'Economic Implications'; 'Monetary Reconstruction'; and 'The Atlantic Charter'.

RCK made sure that copies were circulated to all interested parties, including Winston Churchill and President Roosevelt. The economic and legal committees met subsequently and worked on further papers to flesh out the generalities agreed upon by the congress, and, at later stages during the year, RCK dispatched three shorter reports from them to his friends and supporters, including Churchill.

The media echo of the 1943 Pan-Europa Congress was particularly gratifying for RCK. Journalists of the calibre of Anne O'Hare McCormick of the *New York Times*, Helen Ogden Reid of the *Herald Tribune*, and Herbert Elliston, editor of the *Washington Post*, all reported on it at length, and two well-known political commentators, Walter Lippmann and Dorothy Thompson, both wrote opinion pieces. For RCK, it was the tipping point at which he sensed that observers in the New World began to get to grips seriously with the political prospects for the old continent after the war. This high-quality publicity may well also have helped to ensure that NYU upgraded his post to professor later the same year.[4]

Nonetheless, behind the scenes, official government reaction to the fifth Pan-Europa Congress remained persistently negative. When William Bullitt showed President Roosevelt the final resolution of Allied post-war demands from RCK's congress, with its suggestion for 'a federal organization for Europe', Roosevelt dismissed it out of hand. He commented that such federal proposals would ruin good relations between the Soviet Union and the United States. The British embassy in Washington took an equally negative line, referring to the fifth congress in a dispatch to London as 'of little importance' and noting that both Hull and Welles from the State Department had sent 'most prudently formulated messages' for the opening of the event. Throughout his time in the United States, RCK had difficulty persuading the higher levels of the State Department of the importance of his work, but at a slightly lower level, he did have the convinced support of Cavendish Cannon, assistant chief of the Division of Southern European Affairs, who would circulate his reports from NYU internally for information purposes.[5]

The 1943 Pan-Europa Congress represented RCK's most serious attempt so far to consider the legal and constitutional arrangements for a future association of sovereign states in Europe, a vital prerequisite for drafting a clear founding text for a continental union. Earlier efforts while RCK was still in Europe had been essentially exhortatory, more clarion calls than blueprints. Even the plan that emerged from the New York congress 'was not intended to be the basis for practical action,' wrote Zürcher, 'just to get minds thinking about complex problems that needed to be solved when past the stage of easy generalities and faced with harsh realities of constructing a practical plan of action for the sovereign states of Europe.' It cleared away a host of minor ambiguities and problems, and by the time a draft constitution emerged from the legal committee's work in April the following year, RCK was happy not only to put his name to it, but also to circulate it widely.

Working in academia in New York certainly tightened up RCK's thinking about the legal and constitutional mechanisms of any future association of European states. Before taking up his post at NYU, he had indiscriminately used the terms 'federal' and 'confederal', and sometimes 'Pan-Europa' or even the 'United States of Europe', to describe the end goal of the Pan-European project. But the fifth Pan-Europa Congress clarified his view about the nature of a federal solution. Much influenced by Arnold Zürcher, whose preferred model was contemporary Switzerland, he tended to favour a decentralized, confederal solution, at least as a first step, without excluding a more closely united federation as a longer-term goal.

Zürcher commented later that RCK's years in the United States contributed as much to the cause of European unity as the longer period of work in Europe before his exile. Submitting his utopian ideal to the rigour of academic discipline, both in teaching and by research, had a more long-lasting influence, he argued, than RCK's political work in the interwar years. 'You can see he achieved both beyond his own and his most committed supporters' hope. He was perhaps listened to more on the American side of the Atlantic than in Europe itself. In America the role of prophet gave place to the role of the man of action.'

However, after the arrival of Lord Halifax as British ambassador in 1941, RCK had to battle against a consistently negative appraisal of himself and his work by the British embassy in Washington. This had deepened over the years. An internal minute, dated 16 May 1944, well illustrates how dismissive the official attitude had become. Paul Gore Booth, then

First Secretary, made an internal note of a conversation with a prominent banker, Eric Archdeacon. Because of his past experience in Germany as well as Britain, Archdeacon was a regular source used by the embassy for information about business and commercial affairs. He denounced RCK, claiming that he was in touch with Paul Hagen (alias of Karl Frank), a German Socialist who had fallen out of favour with the official representation of the German Social Democratic Party's executive committee in New York because of his more radical ideas, and as a result should be regarded as untrustworthy.

That RCK and Karl Frank were acquainted was hardly surprising, since Frank had studied philosophy at university in Vienna at the same time as RCK, but Archdeacon then also made an extraordinary assertion that quite unjustly blackened RCK's name. He asserted that 'when he [Archdeacon] was working in Germany, the Count received money from the German General Staff.' In his report to the ambassador, Gore Booth commented, 'This need not necessarily indicate that he now has any relation with them, but it makes the need of great caution towards him all the more necessary.' Lord Halifax, however, added a handwritten comment: 'It does not surprise me that Count Coudenhove-Kalergi is in touch with a number of disreputable people. I have met him and wouldn't trust him at all.'⁶

Halifax would indeed have met RCK in the late 1930s on one of RCK's many visits to London – speaking at Chatham House, meeting Churchill, Leo Amery, Duff Cooper, Wickham Steed, and others. Halifax was then Churchill's rival to succeed Chamberlain as prime minister, and was one of the leading voices in favour of appeasement. In these circumstances, he is unlikely to have formed a positive view of RCK, who was virulently anti-Nazi and consistently opposed to any policy of appeasement. RCK met Halifax at the embassy just once after his appointment to Washington, but he evidently did not overcome the initial hostility of the new ambassador then. With such prejudice against him personally at the top of the embassy, the substance of RCK's teaching activities in NYU and his work in publicizing ideas for post-war European organization appear to have been at least down-played, even dismissed, in UK diplomatic circles.

RCK KNEW NOTHING OF THIS DENUNCIATION and the internal diplomatic exchange. For him, the Pan-Europa Congress had been a success, and later that year he was also enjoying positive reviews of his book *Crusade for Pan-Europe: Autobiography of a Man and a Movement*, which was published by Putnams in New York in October. 'We have had lots of books telling us about what happened "inside Europe", but most of them have been written by specialists,' wrote the *New York Times*. 'This book has been written by an insider as a human document, with an intense understanding of the complexity of European culture and the danger to which it is exposed.'

RCK was delighted with the press reception and sent complimentary copies of his book to all his friends and contacts, using it as a visiting card to impress new acquaintances and as a reward or reinforcement for those who knew him already. He sent a signed copy to Winston Churchill, who replied personally, thanking him warmly for it.

Crusade for Pan-Europe revealed a lot about RCK's earlier life in Europe and reflected on his intellectual development during his years in the United States. However, it said little about his and Idel's day-to-day life in America. Reconstructing an outline of his weekly routine around his duties at NYU, which were not particularly onerous, he appears to have had a considerable amount of free time. He held seminar meetings for his students most weeks and worked alongside his colleague, Arnold Zürcher, in his university office during term time, but this still left him time enough for meetings and lectures either in the university or elsewhere, and time to read and write at home on days when he had no academic duties. His timetable was not pressured, and on occasion he would travel to Washington by train, staying overnight when necessary. RCK does not say how often Idel accompanied him on his travels, joined him in his meetings, or shared his office when organizing the 1943 congress, or whether she worked from home.

As for their weekends and evenings, there is also no record to suggest that they were as socially active as they had been in Vienna but, as inveterate networkers, it seems likely that they entertained in their flat in Palisade Avenue and also were invited to dinner or lunch at the homes of colleagues and contacts in return. There were scores of European exiles of note in New York, many of them already acquainted with RCK and Idel from their years in Vienna and their extensive travels around the continent.[7] But RCK's writings simply reveal that they enjoyed the peace and quiet of the countryside during their vacations at Eagle Bay on Big Moose Lake, where Erika could take the train to join them when she had time off from her job, though that was considerably less than the university allowed RCK. He used his time up-state to prepare his lectures and books, as well as to continue his extensive correspondence.

His first autobiography also dwelt on his ideas for Europe after the end of hostilities. His grand vision, he asserted, was as much influenced by his academic work as by his political networking and lobbying. Before the war, he had published a powerful condemnation of the totalitarian demands of extremist political parties – *The Totalitarian State against Man* – and his American experience decisively moved him into the democratic camp. European co-operation remained his priority, but there was now no question of including fascist or merely 'semi-democratic' states in Pan-Europa. His blind spot as regards Mussolini and Italian fascism was no more in evidence. Nor was there any sympathy with Nietzschean criticism of democratic mediocrity. 'The Europe of tomorrow will be a genuine democratic federation,' he wrote, 'like the United States, Switzerland, Canada, South Africa or Australia.'

His earlier vision of regional powers co-operating in a global organization inspired his view of the optimal structure of future world government. What he called 'the commonwealth of the world' could develop out of the proposed United Nations: Its five leading world powers could become the natural nucleus of the future commonwealth of the world: the United States, the British Empire, the Soviet Union, China, and France, 'which must be considered as a power equal in rank to the other four big Nations.' France would act as a trustee for continental Europe, 'just as the United States is the trustee for Pan-America, China for the Far East, Great Britain for its empire and the Soviets for their own federation.'

RCK was critical of the discredited Assembly of the League of Nations, but was happy to keep in existence ancillary agencies, such as the International Court, the International Labour Office, and the Institute for Intellectual Cooperation, as well as the League's permanent secretariat, adapted to the wider membership of the future United Nations. The council of the United Nations would evolve, he suggested, into a 'permanent board of leading representatives of world regions' – similar to the plan he had taken to Sir Eric Drummond more than twenty years previously, an organization of regional federations.

However, this development of his political thinking in no way implied that RCK's admiration for strong leaders had diminished. He held Churchill in extremely high regard, and Roosevelt as well, despite his refusal to give him an audience. General de Gaulle was now on the point of joining this pantheon. In June 1943, André Istel, de Gaulle's economic adviser and a friend of Pan-Europa, carried a letter from RCK to the General in Algiers, where he had assumed the leadership of all Free French Forces.

In it, RCK offered de Gaulle the post of honorary president of the Pan-Europa Union, vacant since the death of Briand. In the pre-war world, Pan-Europa necessarily required Germany at its heart. In the post-war world, a united Europe would need France to be fully engaged for it to become a reality. RCK was already thinking in terms of a post-war French initiative in European policy that would renew Pan-Europa, and he invited de Gaulle to rally around him 'a new and younger generation with a European manifesto', to become 'the champion of a new Europe as you have become the champion of a new France.'[8]

The General too had a vision, as he wrote later in his *Mémoirs de guerre*, and looked in a similar direction. 'We should try to bring all the states which touch the Rhine, the Alps, and the Pyrenees into a political, economic and strategic entity,' the General wrote. 'We should make it into one of the three world powers and, if necessary one day, the arbiter between the Soviet and the Anglo-Saxon camps.'

RCK was disappointed when de Gaulle declined his offer on the grounds that, until victory was assured, it would be premature to aspire to restructure the continent. He agreed with the principle of Pan-Europa, but the timing was currently inappropriate. Despite his disappointment, RCK was pleased that the line of communication was now open, and the tone of the correspondence was warm. He felt there was enough common ground for them to work together. De Gaulle's enormous prestige as a successful political leader would, he felt, give a powerful boost to Pan-Europa after the war was won, and RCK ensured that from the end of 1943 General de Gaulle was as well informed of his activities as Churchill. He wrote to each of them in their own language, sometimes sharing with de Gaulle some of the opinions that Churchill shared with him.

Just before the D-Day landings, RCK wrote to Churchill to suggest that the Allies should agree at that point on a reconstruction plan for a post-war united Europe, and they should publicize that goal as a war aim. This, he argued, would undermine support for Hitler, not only in occupied countries, but also in Germany itself. Many Germans, he argued, would prefer a solution in which their liberated state was quickly recognized and rehabilitated in a wider regional framework, rather than face a future where they had no option but total defeat, occupation, and isolation as a political and ethical pariah. If Churchill declared such an aim now and proposed what RCK suggested, the gesture would shorten the war in Europe.

To support his view, he sent Churchill a copy of his article published in the April 1944 edition of the *American Mercury*, entitled 'Why Not a United States of Europe?' RCK was pleased to be able to tell readers that the idea of a union of states arising from the ashes of war on the European continent was not just the fanciful idea of a private individual in exile, now teaching in New York University, but that it had backing from many different sources, including Allied governments. In particular, Great Britain, he wrote, 'would be favourable to a European Union, if only she were not alone in doing so.' There was a logic behind British support, he argued, and other powers should support her in this, since the choice after the war would be between a federated Europe on the one hand and Anglo-Russian competition on the other, 'which would once again make Germany the arbiter of the fate of the continent.'

RCK thought little more about this article until the editor of the *American Mercury* rang him one day to say that he had received a stinging response from no less a person than Sir Robert Vansittart, until recently chief diplomatic adviser to His Majesty's government. The editor planned to publish this reply in the next edition of the journal. Would RCK care to write a rebuttal?

Vansittart was known for his adamantly anti-German opinions, having recently published a powerful condemnation of Germany entitled *Black Record: Germans Past and Present*, and he must have been shown RCK's article in London. He claimed that RCK as leader of Pan-Europa 'had never had, and never will have, the support of Great Britain'. He went on to write, 'The Count admits that he hopes for a United States of Europe from which Great Britain and Russia will be excluded' and added that selective quotations from Churchill, Atlee, and Eden, such as RCK had used, could not prettify the pro-German position that RCK had taken in his article. 'I do not think,' Vansittart continued with a tone of contempt, 'that any one of these men believes in the views of Count Coudenhove-Kalergi.'

In his measured reply, RCK suggested that Vansittart should read his published work more carefully, since he would find that he shared Vansittart's aversion to the idea of a powerful Germany dominating the continent. As for support from prominent British leaders, he suggested that he might also read more carefully the Hansard record of parliamentary debates for May that same year, in which both Churchill and Eden had spoken in favour of Pan-European ideas. Eden had even said that the British Commonwealth 'must, can, and will be in a position to use its influence to promote the prosperity and the union of Europe.' Vansittart must have been furious to read this polite, but accurate, rebuttal in the public prints, and he did not prolong the debate.

About this time, RCK recorded a radio interview in New York which was subsequently broadcast to Europe, in all probability by the American Forces Network. In it, he criticized Hitler personally for his inept conduct of the war. Little did RCK realize that this personal insult to Hitler would have extraordinary and disproportionate consequences, all triggered by a formal response from the Reich Chancellery itself. An order was issued whereby all close relatives of RCK were punished for his misdeeds under the Nazi system of 'Sippschaft' (kin). This ordered the dismissal of all close relatives of the 'traitor Richard Coudenhove Kalergi' from the armed forces and from government service as a punishment for this insulting broadcast. It cost RCK's younger brother, Rolfi, his job.

Rolfi was then on the army staff of General von Kleist in the eastern Ukraine as an officer/interpreter. His sudden dismissal sent him back to his home in Prague, where he was also excluded from working with the central government in the Reichsprotektorat office, despite having earlier held a junior administrative post there as a press attaché. However, through his former superior, with whom he had maintained good relations, he was found an alternative – and better-paid – post in a semi-private German/Czech organization concerned with export, something he himself described as a sinecure, 'since there was nothing left in Prague to export'. He and his Czech team simply compiled 'meaningless economic reports that nobody read'. Fortunately, in this undemanding role he could also continue his part-time activity at the university as co-director of the Oriental Institute, teaching Japanese, which was his overwhelming academic interest.

His dismissal because of RCK's broadcast may also have saved his life a year or so later when the German occupation came to an end. Czech police released him after a preliminary interrogation, since, as a result of this order, he was no longer in a sensitive central government job. He was not interned, but allowed to rejoin his family and other civilians attached to the last German column heading westward to surrender to the Americans.[9]

The broadcast that caused Hitler such offence also cost RCK himself his degree at the University of Vienna, where officials in the administration responded to the order from Berlin by rescinding the doctorate the university had awarded him at the end of the First World War. By his flight from the Reich and his subsequent behaviour, RCK had shown himself to be 'unworthy to be honoured by a German university'. It was a bureaucratic gesture which in practice was meaningless, since it could not be transmitted to RCK himself, who remained blissfully unaware of his loss of title until it was restored much later during the 1950s. Even then he scorned to use his title of 'Doctor', preferring the title of 'Count,' which opened even more doors than the academic title.

BY SUMMER 1944, as the war in Europe turned decisively in the Allies' favour, RCK could look back on a period of American exile in which he had achieved much. He had found meaningful employment at NYU, which provided financial security for his family. He had organized high-level conferences on European issues, written and published a book in English about his life and work, and made an impact on American public opinion with many lectures, articles, and broadcasts. He had supervised a successful seminar, which prepared a draft constitution for post-war Europe, refining and improving his original concept of Pan-Europa, and he had clarified his own thinking about key aspects of his grand design. He had networked and lobbied for Europe in American political circles. Even if he had not had as much success as he had hoped with Roosevelt's administration, public opinion, as well as opinion in Congress, was now moving in favour of his ideas.

But RCK could see dangers in the approach of peace, since the pressure that had allowed the idea of a united Europe to gain ground during wartime would soon be capped by the victory of the United States. At that point, the American concept of traditional spheres of influence and President Roosevelt's concept of the four policemen – the United States, the Soviet Union, the British Empire, and China – would move centre stage as the victors organized world peace. In the new UN Security Council, the 'four policemen' would arrange the affairs of the world. What chance was there that a united Europe could emerge from under their shadow as the fifth great power?

In April 1945, shortly before the German surrender, President Roosevelt died, and Vice-President Harry Truman was sworn in as the new president of the United States. By May the fighting had finished, but the nature of the peace was still undecided. Truman knew that the Allies needed to clarify quickly what they intended to do with the Europe that they had liberated.[10]

Soon there were unambiguous signs that Moscow wanted a weak Europe of compliant, satellite states in the east, and was not prepared to see a potential union of democratic and capitalist states built up in the west, seeking strength through unity. The United States, on the other hand, pursued an 'Open Door' policy that encouraged as many liberated states as possible to adopt democratic rather than totalitarian systems of government. With democratic politics would flow the trade and aid that the United States, undamaged by bombing or occupation, could offer. Increasingly, America sensed it was facing the Soviet Union not as an old ally, but as a potential enemy, across what would soon be described as the Iron Curtain dividing Europe.

RCK never served in uniform. Apart from his two dramatic escapes from the Nazis – from Vienna in 1938 and across France and Spain in 1940 – his understanding of war was as an intellectual concept, an extension of his study of politics and government. His war was a war of words, but behind the words were the ideas and the sentiments which shaped future politics and international relations. After the Second World War, he had the same vision of a United States of Europe as he had preached after the First. The united Europe he worked to bring about was to be the antithesis of the warring states that had so desperately mishandled relations among themselves in 1914 and had found no solution but war in 1939. It should never happen again. But peace was never assured through weakness. The only way to prevent war was to be able to deter it through superior force.

To ensure peace, RCK always claimed states needed to be able to wage war. That was one of the big lessons of history, and it was what ultimately separated him from the peace movement. In the last resort, respect for the rule of law was ensured through superior force. Intensifying the war now was for the greater purpose of ensuring peace thereafter. Peace could be imposed by force of arms, and future conflict could be deterred through armed strength. That was as true in the Asian as in the European theatre of the war, and when America used the atomic bomb with the intention of shortening the war in Asia, RCK found this justification entirely convincing – despite his Japanese origins.

In October 1945, two months after Hiroshima and Nagasaki, representatives of fifty nations assembled in San Francisco for the final negotiations that would lead to the founding of the United Nations. Idel and RCK were there as observers and lobbyists, hoping to persuade governments to ensure that the statutes of the new organization did not repeat the mistakes of the League of Nations after the First World War. RCK particularly wanted to ensure that the UN would allow for regional groupings of states, the omission of which had caused, he argued, the downfall of the League. It had failed, he wrote, 'because it had vainly tried to unite the world around a disunited Europe.'

Representatives of some regional organizations were indeed interested – the Arab League and the states of South America, for instance – but not enough to sway the large powers. By the time the Charter of the United Nations was signed on 26 June 1945, a clause had been agreed upon (article 52) that *allowed* the creation of regional groupings within the UN, but did not *mandate* membership on that basis. The door was left open, but the old order of nation states remained the norm, with all the inequalities and variations between them, large and small. Nation would speak to nation in the UN, not region to region. There would be a Security Council with the big powers represented there, but not regional groups of states. Europe would not have a seat at the table.

RCK and Idel were not back in New York from the West Coast for long before they set off again, this time on an extensive lecture tour of eight Midwest US states – Texas, Kansas, Iowa, Indiana, Ohio, Kentucky, Michigan, and Illinois. They found a changed political climate, in which the pro-Russian sympathies of the war years were already fast disappearing in the light of Soviet competition, even obstruction, both in Europe and the Far East. Previously RCK had thought – even feared – that there was a pro-Russian bias, perhaps even a conspiracy, in favour of Soviet interests within the Roosevelt Administration. He recalled the Free World Association, and imagined that it was their sympathizers who had prevented him from meeting the American president and persuading him of the virtues of Pan-Europe. Now he found the situation completely changed, with public opinion shifting in favour of the idea of a United States of Europe as a bulwark against communism. 'Just as the "brown peril" of Hitler had helped the movement in 1939 and 1940,' he wrote, 'so the "red menace" of Stalin now enabled it to become topical again.' For RCK, the public reaction that he sensed during this lecture tour marked the beginning of the Cold War that Churchill would dramatically describe in his speech in Fulton, Missouri, a year later.

The more he pondered this, the easier it was for RCK to understand the Red Scare that swept America after the war. 'An era was coming to a close,' he wrote of the years after 1945, when 'the defeat of common enemies, whose aggression had dragged both capitalist America and Soviet Russia out of their isolationism, had also revealed to them the capacity of their strength and the incompatibility of their ambitions.' America and Russia would come face to face in Europe, but as yet it was not clear which European states would be free enough from communist control to join a common Western effort.

Whatever small gestures they could manage at such a distance from the front line, RCK and Idel did. And it was Idel who led in these practical matters. Through her association with the pre-war peace movement, she had links to the American Quakers, and in the latter part of 1944 helped to gather support for American Relief for Austria (ARA), an organization that she established along with Otto von Hapsburg's youngest sister,

Elisabeth. Together they recruited the wives of several leading senators to join their steering committee, and solicited support from various trade unions, receiving support from two of them, notably the garment-makers and the shoe-makers. To help fund-raising, Idel also designed ARA calendars in 1945, 1946, and 1947. This group of high-society women raised money and solicited gifts in kind, so that shipments of shoes, clothing, and food could be sent through the Red Cross for distribution in Austria. Their action had the additional merit at the political level of associating Austria with other states conquered by Germany, positioning the country in the popular mind, as well as in the thinking of the State Department, as the first victim of Nazism, rather than as part of the Third Reich and complicit in the war.

THE YEAR 1945 brought peace first in Europe and then in the Far East, and with it RCK and Idel might have expected a restful winter. But it was not to be. Two events, one on the political front and the other in their family life, marked their routine more profoundly than they could ever have expected.

Just three days before Christmas, the weekend edition of the popular *Collier's* magazine featured a four-page illustrated article written by George Creel, its Washington correspondent, entitled 'The United States of Europe'. It did not take RCK and Idel completely by surprise, since Creel had shown them a draft in November, but it publicized Pan-Europa more successfully than anything previously in America. 'Today Pan-European Union has become again a major concern,' wrote Creel. 'There may not yet be another Aristide Briand to direct the new movement, but with the approach of winter and the sad certainty that millions will be exposed to the freezing weather and to misery, more and more leaders of public opinion in all countries are falling in behind the flag of Pan-Europa, held aloft by Count Coudenhove-Kalergi.'

Creel had also discussed the article with President Truman. Creel had asked him, a long-time friend from the same small town in Missouri, what he really thought about the United States of Europe. 'It's an excellent idea,' replied the president, and gave Creel permission to quote his opinion.

The article in *Collier's* struck a responsive nerve in popular opinion and was subsequently given world-wide distribution by *Reader's Digest*, stimulating comment in numerous other newspapers, both in the United States and in Europe. RCK realized that Creel had achieved for him what he,

RCK, had come to the United States to do, and noted proudly, 'My aim of winning the White House for the cause of Pan-Europa had been attained.'

A few days before Creel made headlines, however, RCK received seriously disturbing family news. He makes no mention of it in his various memoirs, but it must have marred much of the feeling of success that the article by Creel delivered. RCK learned that his eldest brother, Hansi, a Nazi sympathizer and a prominent local German landowner in the Sudetenland, had been arrested by Czech partisans at the family castle in Ronsperg, and his whereabouts were unknown. RCK immediately sent telegrams to Jan Masaryk, now Czechoslovak foreign minister, and to Eduard Beneš, the president, as well as to Zdenek Fierlinger, the prime minister, all of whom he knew personally, asking them to discover where his brother was being held, to intervene, and if possible release him, preferably expelling him over the border into Austria. The next day he followed up the telegrams with a long personal letter to Jan Masaryk, pleading for his understanding and help as a friend.

A little later he learned that his sister Olga, who had sought refuge at Ronsperg in the closing weeks of the war, had likewise been interned. He wrote again, describing her as completely apolitical, and detailing how she had cared for their mother until her death in 1941. Following his interventions, Olga was released from a labour camp, and Hansi's whereabouts were confirmed, but he was not released. RCK learned that he was being held in a camp near Domazlice, a few miles from Ronsperg, and would shortly be transferred to a notoriously harsh jail in Pilsen. He was being kept in custody as charges were prepared against him for collaborating with the Germans both before and during the occupation of Czechoslovakia. If proven before the provisional Czech revolutionary court, these charges could carry the death penalty.[11]

17

PUSHING PARLIAMENTS TOWARDS POWER

RCK AND HIS ELDER BROTHER had never been really close since their pre-school years together. Now, however, he felt he had no option but to help Hansi, however much this private matter cut across his work for the European cause to which he had devoted all his life.

For many years, he had known that Hansi's personality was slightly odd, or at least not as rational as RCK prided himself on being. He recalled how he had prepared a legal brief when Hansi came of age at the end of the First World War, to try to prevent him coming into the main Coudenhove-Kalergi inheritance as eldest son of the family. That had not gone to court, but he had watched as Hansi, Lord of Ronsperg, subsequently indulged his strange architectural whims, adding decorative towers to the castle and to the local inn and painting his large limousine yellow on the left-hand side and red on the right – the colours of the Coudenhove coat of arms – in order to make it stand out as he or his wife, Lilly, drove through the countryside at high speed. Later he had also given himself as a birthday present a large tiled stove in the shape of his own much-distended belly, which was installed in one of the castle's reception rooms, and had commissioned artists to paint bodies and legs to complete the head-and-shoulders portraits of his Coudenhove ancestors that decorated the main hall.

But all these minor eccentricities paled into insignificance when put alongside reports of Hansi's social and political activities in wartime Berlin. He was reported to have curried favour with senior Nazis by throwing lavish parties, at which the women fought for silk underwear and stockings brought from Paris, while the men looked on and laughed. What he had done locally in Bohemia to privilege German-speakers from the Sudetenland and discriminate against Czechs, and whether that justified the charges, RCK could not know, but in the intolerant atmosphere immediately after the end of hostilities, few people – especially few Czechs – were prepared to give a man in Hansi's position the benefit of the doubt. At the very least, in their eyes, he was guilty by association, and probably much more.

Yet there were some extenuating circumstances that might have spoken in his favour, even though RCK could not have known about them at that stage. In an attempt to avoid fighting in Ronsperg itself, Hansi had hoisted a white flag on the castle tower as soon as it was known that American forces were in the vicinity, encouraging others in the village to put out white flags as well. The commander of an SS unit stationed nearby threatened him on pain of death to ensure that all white flags were immediately removed, and Hansi reluctantly complied. But when the SS withdrew from their positions during the night, Hansi hoisted the white flag again and, with the local priest, the schoolmaster, and a French prisoner of war who was working on the estate, rode out in a cart past Stockau towards the Dianahof to meet the Americans, who were advancing cautiously through the forest from the west. He welcomed them into Ronsperg without any blood being shed and, after a short interrogation, was left in peace in the castle while they continued their advance. It was then that Czech partisans arrested him and interned him in the hastily organized Domazlice camp. There he was harshly treated, partly because of his social status as a German-speaking aristocrat, and partly for his evident Nazi sympathies.

The Czech lawyer assigned to Hansi's defence wrote to RCK and suggested that he should ask some of his well-known Allied contacts to intercede for Hansi's pardon and release, suggesting Winston Churchill. Extra costs associated with Hansi's case, he added, would not be more than five hundred dollars, preferably paid in advance. RCK declined, deciding both not to pay, and also not to involve his influential Western friends in his brother's case. But he did write a second appeal to Masaryk, Beneš, and Fierlinger as leading figures in the new Czechoslovak state.

To the lawyer, RCK suggested that Hansi should plead diminished responsibility, even insanity, implying that his brother did not know what he was doing. Surely no sane man who had married a Jewish woman would hold pro-Nazi views. *Ergo*, Hansi must be insane, and therefore could not be responsible for his acts. The correspondence with the lawyer lasted several months, during which time Hansi fell ill and was operated on in the prison hospital, possibly for a burst appendix. He stubbornly declined, however, to plead 'guilty but insane' – almost certainly remembering RCK's earlier ploy to try and deprive him of his inheritance.

What would eventually save Hansi from the death sentence was a change in the jurisdiction of the court. After eighteen months in jail, and just before he was due to appear before the provisional revolutionary tribunal, the court itself was abolished. All outstanding cases were passed to a regular district court, which was not empowered to pass a death sentence. Hansi managed to avoid trial even before this district court, since at that point RCK's intervention with the leading Czech politicians bore fruit. In 1947, he was simply expelled over the border to the American sector of what would become West Germany, without the case ever coming to court.

In his letters, RCK never mentioned the saga of Hansi's arrest, his intervention, or his brother's eventual release and expulsion. But he carefully filed away the correspondence with his Czech political friends and with the lawyer, uncertain how it would all end. Hansi never thanked him, yet more proof of the strained relations between the brothers. There is no record that they ever met again after the end of the war.[1]

AT THE END OF 1945, Erika presented RCK with a well-chosen pocket diary, aptly called 'The Aristocrat's Diary for 1946', adding in her young woman's handwriting 'which is going to be a most memorable year. Good luck to you, Dicky, from Erika'. As the dust of war settled and the first signs of normal life returned to Europe, RCK and Idel avidly devoured all the news they could find, not only of the political situation in Europe but also about their family and friends. RCK also sent numerous letters to former members of the Pan-Europa Union and to political leaders now fast re-establishing national governments in their liberated countries, reminding them of Pan-Europa's role between the wars and its goal of European federation. He remained in correspondence also with Churchill, first commiserating with him on his 1945 election loss and later telling him of his plan to return to Europe.

Europe in 1945 and 1946 was still in social and political turmoil, with millions of refugees (in the contemporary jargon 'DPs', or displaced persons) moving across the continent, desperate to find food and shelter. RCK and Idel wanted to return to find who among their friends had survived, to piece together remaining parts of their scattered families, and also to find a new role for themselves, now that the storm of war had passed and the broken pieces of the continent were being reassembled. They promised their American friends, who saw them off with generous presents – their cabin, he wrote, was 'half flower shop and half pâtisserie' – that they

RCK sailed back to Europe with Idel and Erika (right) on the SS *Oregon* in 1946. Their cabin was 'half flower shop and half patisserie'.

would be away for only a few months, and they set off for Europe with no clear idea of what they would find or who they would meet there.

Idel and RCK sailed from New York on the SS *Oregon*, a modest steamer with only sixty other passengers, mostly French.[2] RCK recalled with some pleasure the chance that he and Idel had to dream, to relax, and to restore their spirits, far removed from newspapers, from post and telephone, during the ten days' crossing of the North Atlantic. But quite unexpectedly a telegram from Winston Churchill came for them while they were on board, greatly enhancing their status among the crew and passengers. Churchill asked how long RCK planned to stay in Paris, as he very much wanted his son-in-law Duncan Sandys to meet him. RCK's reply suggested Duncan Sandys should meet him at his hotel there in a few days' time.

On 18 June they arrived in Le Havre, and RCK, always keen on anniversaries, noted that it was six years to the day since they had crossed the border from France to Spain *en route* for Barcelona, Lisbon, and finally New York. That very day he had heard de Gaulle's broadcast appeal for France to fight on against Nazi Germany. He noted that de Gaulle had spoken to him as he left Europe, and Churchill spoke to him as he returned. Like them, he too sensed the hand of history on his shoulder. He classed himself alongside leaders of the stature of Truman, de Gaulle, and Churchill. Indeed in 1957 he would work out the outline of a new book which he planned to write, called *Revolution von Oben*.

The opening chapters of *Revolution from Above* would be about Churchill, de Gaulle, and Adenauer, followed by three others on America, Japan, and Austria. In it, RCK would in all probability have featured in the Austrian chapter with his bid for leadership of the government-in-exile. He would also have had a supporting role – at least – in the chapter on Churchill. Here, he identified Churchill's journey under five headings. The first one 'No European' might well have referred to RCK's perception of him as a dispassionate observer of Pan-Europa's efforts in 1930. The second, 'The Anglo-French Union', would have focused on the desperate British offer of unification in 1940. The third 'In the War' could well refer to his dramatic 1943 broadcast vision of a Council of Europe with real powers. The fourth, simply entitled 'Zürich', refers to Churchill's speech there, a clarion call for Franco-German understanding at the heart of a united Europe. The final heading is 'Duncan Sandys' – perhaps this would have allowed RCK to express his sense of betrayal at what Duncan Sandys had done to Churchill's greater vision.

Now leader of the Conservative opposition, Churchill did not wish to become immersed in the minutiae of domestic politics after bestriding the world as one of the three major Allied leaders. He wanted a larger stage than that of domestic politics, and he wanted to deliver something that Clement Attlee and the Labour Party could not deliver. In mulling over how best to seize the opportunity to shape the destiny of the continent as an elder statesman, acting above party and even above country, Churchill felt with some justification that he could carve out a role as the leader who could reunite a peaceful Europe. That would also have the beneficial result of strengthening his political position in Britain when national elections came round again. The circle of his closest friends from whom he took advice, or at least with whom he sounded out his ideas, included his long-standing political mentor, Leo Amery, his former parliamentary private secretary from the late 1920s, Bob Boothby, and his ambitious son-in-law Duncan Sandys. It would now be up to RCK to see what role he could play in the plans that Winston Churchill was elaborating.

ON THE TRAIN JOURNEY through northern France from Le Havre to Paris, RCK and Idel discovered a country in ruins, with destruction and poverty everywhere apparent. The overwhelming need for physical reconstruction was obvious. And yet, despite discovering a continent exhausted by war, the optimist in RCK also claimed that there was already a popular desire to learn the lessons of the past and avoid such mistakes in the future. Echoing Murray Butler's belief in his 1914 interview, he wrote later that hatred between peoples had run its course and was no longer the dominant emotion in public opinion. The extremes of nationalism had played themselves out, and Europeans were now looking for a fresh start that could lead, in a spirit of openness between nations, to a form of unity for the continent. The dividing line was now between the collectivist, communist approach on the one hand, he suggested, and the individualistic, free-market approach on the other. He noted that, just as in the seventeenth century the Thirty Years' War had begun as a religious quarrel but mutated into dynastic rivalry, so in the twentieth century this latest conflagration had begun in nationalistic frenzy and ended in ideological competition.

It was an extraordinarily positive interpretation of the spirit of the times, which was marked in every country that had been under German occupation by innumerable acts of revenge and violence towards those who had collaborated, as RCK knew very well in the case of his brother Hansi. But it was what RCK wanted to find and, as often in his life, he projected what he wanted to happen onto the present to encourage it to happen in the future. Pan-Europa represented the wish that relations between nations in the 1920s should be restructured to bring benefits to all, rather than perpetuate the divisive, competitive, and wasteful relations that had stimulated aggressive nationalism before the First World War. What he projected now after the Second World War was the internal healing of European societies – in the democratic west at least – even at the cost of creating an external enemy in the collectivist system of the Soviet Union. Russia, for RCK, had always been outside his vision of united Europe, and it would stay there now as well.

Truman shared RCK's suspicion of Russia. He wanted to encourage European integration after this war, the contemporary equivalent, in his eyes, of the American colonies coming together when fighting the British Crown nearly two hundred years previously. The dilemma, for Truman as for RCK, was which of three solutions would be most acceptable to the European states, as well as to American public opinion. Would it be the minimalist solution of military co-ordination across the North Atlantic, based on individual countries joining a traditional alliance, each acting independently? Or would the Europeans form a coherent group, a nascent federation that could parley with the United States in what would be a bilateral arrangement? Or could there even be a union that embraced the whole of the free world – essentially the United States and Western Europe, but also Canada and the independent British Dominions? All three models had their promoters, and in the turmoil of the uncertain post-war situation, any solution might be realized.

Governments in Europe, RCK felt, were slow to respond to the change in public opinion that he believed he had sensed. He surmised that the fear of communism prevented them from acting boldly, and that gave him an opportunity for a new role. If public opinion was now receptive to the idea of European union in a way that it had not been before the war, he saw his opportunity in organizing elected parliamentarians across Europe to express this view in their parliaments. As an organized voice they would then press their governments to act. But this window of opportunity would not be open for long. All too soon, he feared, individual governments would fall back into the old ways of doing things on a traditional, bilateral basis. The moment for change – the moment for union – would soon pass.

Following Churchill's telegram, the timetables of RCK and Duncan Sandys did not permit a meeting in Paris, so they arranged for Sandys to come to RCK's Swiss retreat near Gstaad a week or two later. That would offer them both the opportunity to talk through their plans together. RCK and Idel took a train from Paris to Gruben, a full day's journey with at least two changes. There they were met by Berta, their housekeeper, who greeted them with tears in her eyes. RCK recorded how she insisted on showing them round every room in the house, so that they could see for themselves how well she had kept it for them all these years. The house was unchanged, just as inviting and cosy, as *gemütlich* as ever. The biggest difference, they noted, was the low hedge that they had planted before the war. It had doubled its height and looked now more like a small forest.

FROM THERE, RCK mulled over how to contact the parliamentarians of Europe and galvanize them into pressuring their governments to favour continental union. From earlier years attending the League of Nations in Geneva, he was acquainted with Léopold Boissier, the Swiss secretary-general of the Inter-Parliamentary Union, or IPU, and discovered that he was still in his post. He took the train to Geneva to meet him, since he would have the best up-to-date contacts with European parliamentarians.

Boissier suggested to RCK that he should contact the IPU delegates from national parliaments as a way of pre-selecting those interested in international relations. To meet a few of them, he invited RCK to the next

IPU meeting, to be held in the Swiss ski resort of St Moritz at the end of August. Technically, this was a meeting of only the executive committee, but, as it was the first meeting since the end of the war, many more than the three members of the committee – Count Carton de Wiert from Belgium, Professor Hartvig Frisch from Denmark, and Senator Alban Barklay from Washington – were expected.

St Moritz in summer was delightful, with clear skies and long hours of sunshine. While there, Léopold Boissier introduced RCK to other IPU delegates, including Georges Bohy, the Belgian socialist leader, and Eduard Ludwig, an Austrian conservative, both of whom immediately and enthusiastically declared their support for his plans. There too he met the Labour MP Kim Mackay, who had been one of Pan-Europa's pre-war British supporters. In his note to Léopold Boissier thanking him for facilitating this meeting, RCK wrote that it allowed him to make the acquaintance of a 'considerable number of very interesting and important men for the cause of the United States of Europe'. Thanks to Boissier, RCK could now build up contacts in all the parliaments of the democratic states of the continent, and he worked on that immediately.

When Duncan Sandys came to visit him in Gruben, he brought along with him Leo Amery's son Julian, now a young man of twenty-six and considering a career in politics. They talked through Churchill's plans for a single organization to bring together all continental pro-European groups, the many activists who wanted to unite Europe. Some had grown from Resistance groups in different countries, some were federalist in intent, some Christian in inspiration, others based on business interests, and others more socialist. And there were the remnants of Pan-Europa itself. In the changed post-war circumstances, RCK did not think that his Pan-Europa Union, the disparate-but-much-reduced band of supporters from across the entire continent, would have the same leading role to play as in the years before the war. He passed on his list of contacts to Duncan Sandys. A few days later he received in return an invitation to come to lunch with Churchill, who was spending a relaxing short holiday not far away in the Château de Choisi at Bursinel on Lake Geneva.

So, early on Saturday, 14 September, RCK caught the first train from Gruben to Bursinel. It wound its way through Gstaad and followed the meandering valley of the river Sarine, crossing the invisible linguistic boundary from German-speaking to French-speaking Switzerland, then climbing slowly up one of the most picturesque hillsides of the Bernese Oberland. Emerging from the tunnel that burrowed under the peak, the train burst out into the sunlight, with the gleaming water of Lake Geneva more than a thousand metres below. RCK changed trains in Montreux and in Lausanne, and barely three hours later, met Churchill in the grounds of the Château, in reality a spacious lakeside villa, where Churchill was totally absorbed in painting a view of trees and the lawns sweeping down to the water.[3] In his notes on the meeting, RCK compared the boldness and vigour of his painting style with the finesse of his tiny handwriting, a reflection of the opposites within Churchill's soul, he observed, the tension between boldness and caution, temerity and hesitation, which for him characterized Churchill's personality.

Lunch brought together the rest of the company, hosted by Churchill's youngest daughter, Mary, as his wife, Clementine, was unwell. Duncan Sandys, his son-in-law, who had married another of Churchill's daughters, Diana, was present, as was one of Churchill's secretaries, Elizabeth Gilliatt, who was travelling with him to help prepare his speeches and keep up with correspondence. Churchill was on good form, wrote RCK afterwards, in no way spoilt by his fame, straightforward and human, and quite open to advice. They spoke of international affairs, of the need to overcome the residual hatred for Germany and Japan, and of the speech on Europe which Churchill had been invited to give at the University of Zürich just a few days later. Over a whisky and cigar, Churchill promised to give RCK explicit credit in his speech for all that he had done for the movement towards European union. Twenty-four-year-old Mary Churchill was so impressed with a copy of RCK's final *European Letter*, which he had sent to his supporters from Geneva as he fled into exile in 1940, and which he had enclosed with his letter of thanks for her hospitality, that she sent him a handwritten note, hoping to see him again at Chartwell when he was next in England.

RCK and Idel were in their farmhouse in Gruben listening to Swiss radio when Churchill's speech was broadcast in full. His sonorous voice emphasized the horror of Europe's latest war, and the simplicity of the solution that lay to hand.

There is a remedy which, if it were generally and spontaneously adopted, would as if by a miracle transform the whole scene, and would in a few years make all Europe, or the greater part of it, as free and as happy as Switzerland is today. What is this sovereign remedy? It is to re-create the European family, or as much of it as we can, and provide it with a structure under which it can dwell in peace, in safety and in freedom. We must build a kind of United States of Europe.

Winston Churchill, quoting RCK, spoke at the University of Zürich in
September 1946.

This was music to RCK's ears, but better still was to follow. Churchill
continued: 'Much work has been done upon this task by the exertions of
the Pan-European Union which owes so much to Count Coudenhove-
Kalergi and which commanded the services of the famous French patriot
and statesman, Aristide Briand.' RCK was delighted at being named
alongside Aristide Briand, whom he had so much admired, by Winston
Churchill, the wartime leader of Great Britain, who was seen by millions
as the saviour of Europe.

Churchill went even further in explaining the steps needed to reach
this goal:

> The first step in the re-creation of the European family must be a
> partnership between France and Germany. In this way only can France
> recover the moral leadership of Europe. There can be no revival of
> Europe without a spiritually great France and a spiritually great
> Germany. The structure of the United States of Europe, if well and
> truly built, will be such as to make the material strength of a single
> state less important. Small nations will count as much as large ones and
> gain their honour by their contribution to the common cause.

He concluded by stressing the urgency of the situation, the small window of opportunity of which RCK himself had spoken over lunch. Churchill concluded, 'If we are to form the United States of Europe, or whatever name or form it may take, we must begin now.' Churchill's speech was relayed by numerous broadcasters around the world. Reuters and other news agencies quoted the full text of the speech. Over the next few days, numerous newspapers would quote from it and leading articles comment on it, both in Europe and America. RCK sent a personal telegram to Churchill with his heartfelt thanks, adding that, with this speech, Churchill had made him 'the happiest man in the world'. Churchill responded by inviting him to Chartwell the following month before RCK returned to the United States, for further talks about their collaboration on European issues.

RCK remembered clearly his first visit to Churchill's country house at Chartwell in 1938 and his pleasant memories of the event, despite the shadow of the impending war hanging over their conversation. This time, in the more creative atmosphere of peace, RCK admired Churchill's framed original of the Atlantic Charter of 1941, and reminded him of the prophecy of Nostradamus.[4] Leo Amery, Duncan Sandys, and Bob Boothby were also present, and their discussions were businesslike.

The British group was concerned that RCK might want the new effort at co-ordination to result in an enhanced Pan-Europa Union, while they were recommending something quite new and different. Stimulated by the welcome given to Churchill's speech, Duncan Sandys had contacted several prominent groups concerned with European unity and they had begun to co-operate as Churchill had asked.

Some of the groups were European in nature, some nationally based. The most important was the European League for Economic Cooperation, which had been founded in 1946 by leading businessmen and industrialists across the continent, together with moderate trade-union representatives and some academic economists. It was led by Paul Van Zeeland, the former prime minister of Belgium, who had worked with RCK in New York, and its key organizer was Josef Retinger, a Polish *émigré* who had spent the war in London and was so well connected that he was reputed to be able to pick up the phone and get through in person to any prime minister in post-war Europe.

Another group, the European Union of Federalists (UEF), under the leadership of Hendrik Brugmans, was strongly supported by Altiero Spinelli, a leading Italian anti-fascist. A Socialist movement for the United States of Europe had also been set up, led initially by a British MP, Bob Edwards, the chairman of the Independent Labour Party and general

Duncan Sandys,
Churchill's son-in-law
and RCK's nemesis.

secretary of the Chemical Workers' Union, and later by Michel Rasquin, president of the Luxembourg Socialist Workers' Party.

In France, a Christian Democrat movement of support for European unification also emerged, les Nouvelles Équipes Internationales, led by Robert Bichet, former head of information services for General de Gaulle. In addition, there was a second French group, the French Council for a United Europe, led by Raoul Dautry, a minister in de Gaulle's first post-war government. RCK knew many of these men, and sympathized with Churchill's aim of bringing these disparate initiatives into one more powerful and united organization. The key question was how.

At Chartwell, Churchill, Sandys, Amery, Boothby, and RCK discussed the future organization of their United Europe Movement, sketching out who would hold which posts. Churchill would be president, with prominent continental Socialist and Catholic politicians as his vice-presidents. RCK certainly got the impression that he would be the secretary-general, and Duncan Sandys his deputy, but Duncan Sandys did not understand it that way. He understood that RCK would have an honorific or non-executive role, while he, Sandys, would actually organize and run the Movement.

They agreed that the first step over the coming winter would be for Churchill to establish a British Committee, including the surviving members of the British Pan-Europa Committee from before the war, contained in the list RCK had given Duncan Sandys when he had visited him in Gruben. In the spring of 1947, this new United Europe Committee should meet with continental pro-Europeans to settle the final structure of their continent-wide collaboration. By the end of the meeting it was clear to RCK that the British contingent was well advanced in planning a British Committee, but it had got nowhere in setting up continental interlocutors. That was his challenge – and also his opportunity.

A few days later, in the elegant Hôtel Meurice opposite the Tuileries Gardens in Paris, RCK met with René Courtin, a professor at the Sorbonne and economics editor of *Le Monde*. André Istel, RCK's old friend from New York and now one of General de Gaulle's key advisers, had suggested Courtin would be the right man to reorganize the Pan-Europa Committee in France. RCK's advice to Courtin was not to rely on the older members, with their memories of pre-war conditions, but to harness the energies of a younger generation into a new pro-European movement. RCK drafted an outline programme for it, based essentially on traditional Pan-European lines, but specifically suggested to Courtin he should drop the word 'Pan-Europa'. His new committee would be the French counterpart to the British Committee that Churchill and Sandys were organizing. Commenting elsewhere on this strategy, he wrote, 'I was reinforced in my conviction that everyone considered the unification of Europe to be the only solution, but that nobody dared speak of it for fear of being called utopian – and also for fear of Russia and the communists, who were extremely strong at that time.'

The strength of these fears was demonstrated by political events early the following year. In March, Churchill delivered his famous speech in Fulton, Missouri, describing the Iron Curtain that had fallen across Europe 'from Stettin in the Baltic to Trieste in the Adriatic'. In April, the Communist Party in the Soviet Zone of Germany absorbed the Social Democrats to form the dominant Social Unity Party, or SED. In May, civil war broke out in Greece between communists and monarchists. The same month, the Communists emerged as the largest party, following elections in Czechoslovakia. In early June, Communists become the second-largest party in the French Assembly, and a referendum in Italy, with Communist support, installed a republic instead of the monarchy. The capitalist and democratic Establishment in every country was concerned, and with reason.

RCK went on from Paris to his house in Gruben to take the first step in consulting parliamentarians around Europe about their views on European unity. Based on lists of names he had managed to obtain from his contacts at the IPU, he sent close to four thousand letters, in English, French, or Italian, to MPs from all West European countries except Germany, since it had as yet no nationally elected members of parliament. Along with each letter he enclosed a reply card, on which he printed a simple but far-reaching question: 'Are you in favour of a European Federation within the framework of the United Nations? Yes or No?' RCK personally signed every letter, and with Idel and Erika posted them from Gstaad, his nearest post office.

That done, he and Idel packed their bags and caught the train to Cherbourg to board the SS *Île de France* on 10 November 1946 for the return journey to New York. They had been in Europe for just five hectic months.[5]

BACK IN AMERICA, RCK was quickly reassured that he had judged the political mood correctly with his initiative for a European Parliamentary Union, the name he gave to the prospective organization that would grow from the democratic parliamentarians he had contacted across the continent. He soon received hundreds of answer cards, sent on from Gruben to their New York address by Erika, who had stayed in Europe to manage this operation. Encouraged by the positive responses, he wrote again to those who had not yet answered, and to another three hundred fresh parliamentary contacts. He and Idel were overjoyed when the final answers could be tallied. In all, he had 1,818 replies, of which 1,766 were affirmative and a mere 52 negative. Most positive were France and Italy, closely followed by Greece; less enthusiastic were England and Scandinavia. Most significantly, no answers were received from any Communist MPs at all. RCK felt vindicated.

He interpreted the strongly positive response from representatives of democratic parties as an indirect plebiscite, calculating that an overwhelming majority of non-communist voters, reflecting the people represented by these pro-European MPs, was in favour of a united Europe, with only a small minority against it. He then invited all those who said 'Yes' to take two further steps. They should form cross-party pro-European committees in their respective parliaments, and their leaders should come to the founding meeting of the European Parliamentary Union at the Palace Hotel above Gstaad in July 1947.

His key task now was to get back to Europe in time to oversee this critical meeting, which would prepare the first full congress of the EPU. The main issue in that meeting, he knew, would be to decide just what everyone meant by the phrase 'United States of Europe'. Between federalists and internationalists, conservatives and socialists, there was a wide spectrum of opinion from which he would have to craft a compromise. How far would the European model follow the template of the United States? How far the Swiss? How far would it be *sui generis* and uniquely European?

RCK was still responsible for a teaching seminar at NYU, however, and Arnold Zürcher had stood in for him during his extended visit to Europe. Now that he was back, living in the city and sharing teaching again, he was able to sense the change of mood in America since he had left. Public opinion had swung even more strongly anti-communist, with both Democrats and Republicans finding common ground in support of the idea of a united Europe, which would involve all states that were outside the sphere of influence of the Soviet Union.

John Foster Dulles, at that time a senior and well-connected diplomat, who would later become President Eisenhower's secretary of state, declared in a speech at the Waldorf Hotel in January that the economic division of Germany reflected the 'debilitating disunity' of Europe, to which the solution should be a speedy move towards political federation. Dorothy Thompson and Walter Lippmann, who had commented on the fifth Pan-Europa Congress in New York, took up this theme in the media, and even planned a weekly magazine devoted solely to European affairs in order to respond to the growing interest within American public opinion. Winston Churchill published an article in *Collier's* magazine the same month, in which he declared, 'The peace and security of the United States of America demands the organization of the United States of Europe.' This article was picked up by *Reader's Digest*, which ensured it a much wider and international readership.

RCK observed: 'Actually the Soviet Union is primarily responsible for the rapid progress made in the West for a United Europe. Russia provided the West European countries with a common danger which convinced them that their main hope for security lay in the formation of a closely knit, federated organisation.' RCK capitalized on this by preparing a public appeal to the citizens of the United States of America in favour of the United States of Europe. He contacted politicians, writers, academics, journalists, religious leaders, and Nobel laureates for their support. When he asked Senator William Fulbright, the newly elected southern Democrat who was making a name for himself in foreign-affairs circles, he replied that, while he did indeed support the sentiment of the appeal, as a senator he preferred to state his political position in the Senate rather than just sign a public appeal. RCK immediately invited him to put forward a draft resolution and, true to his word, Senator Fulbright, together with a Republican colleague, Senator Edward Thomas, put forward a bipartisan motion, winning a large majority for the resolution that 'Congress supports the creation of the United States of Europe in the framework of the United Nations.' Hale Boggs, a Democrat congressman for Louisiana, successfully promoted the same resolution in the House of Representatives.

Their initiative received considerable media coverage, and Harold Ickes, President Roosevelt's long-serving secretary of the interior, commented in the *New York Times* on the exceptionally wide support for the idea of a United States of Europe, wider support than he had ever seen in America for any international issue in his long congressional career.

On drawing up the balance sheet of his seven years in the United States, RCK could be pleased with the results of his work. On the train back to New York after a brief visit to Washington, he noted how American political opinion had changed from the time of his arrival in August 1940. Then America had been keen to avoid getting involved in Europe's quarrels. RCK had preached a message few people wanted to hear, arguing that the war had to be fought on two fronts: first against Nazism and later against Communism. Now the Administration, the State Department, both Houses of Congress, the serious media, and much of public opinion were all backing his idea of uniting Europe as the best way to consolidate the democratic values of the West.

He had become a symbol for a body of opinion about Europe to which politicians on both sides of the Atlantic now needed to pay attention. In a heartfelt expression of emotion, he noted in his autobiography that tears of joy came to his eyes, and he turned to look out of the train window rather than embarrass those travelling with him. Through damp, blinking eyes he admired the Pennsylvania countryside in spring, and thanked God.

Secure in this success in the United States, that spring, RCK and Idel packed up their belongings and left their home in Palisade Avenue for the last time. They were going back to Europe for good, leaving behind them a country they had grown to love and admire, but one which nonetheless for them as European patriots had always been a place of exile. They sailed from New York on the *Queen Elizabeth* on 26 April 1947.[6] Again, Churchill sent a telegram while they were at sea, this time inviting RCK and Idel to lunch at his London residence the very day they arrived in England. A few hours after landing at Southampton, Churchill and Clementine welcomed them into their London flat at 28 Hyde Park Gate.

18

AN OPEN CONSPIRACY

CHURCHILL WAS DELIGHTED with the positive news of American support for European unity reported by RCK. Churchill himself planned the first public meeting of his new United Europe Movement in the Royal Albert Hall for mid-May. His only regret was that mistrust and suspicion between the two main political parties in Westminster was such that very few British Labour MPs were prepared to join his movement. Despite Clement Attlee's publicly expressed view that 'Europe must unite or perish', Churchill had not succeeded in persuading the Labour leadership or the Labour Party as a whole to join with him.

Labour suspected some political conspiracy, whereby the Conservatives, the party of Churchill, would cunningly undermine them with support of political allies from the continent. Attlee, as prime minister, wondered aloud that the new movement for European unity might endanger close relations with the Commonwealth, and Ernest Bevin, the foreign secretary, warned 'Practical collaboration (with European neighbours) should not infringe on national sovereignty.' Those were significant reservations, which would often be repeated in years to come on both sides of the political divide in the United Kingdom in the debate about how closely the country should or should not integrate with its continental neighbours.

Despite these expressed reservations, however, nearly two-thirds of the one hundred and seventy signatures that RCK had garnered from British MPs in reply to his questionnaire were from Labour MPs. RCK seized what he thought was an opportunity. If party politics was the problem, he suggested, why did not Churchill switch from leading his national political party to standing above all parties and leading a continent-wide struggle for European unity on a cross-party basis? Like Aristide Briand before him, he could become the honorary president of the Pan-Europa

Union. In reply, Churchill remarked that, as a foreigner, RCK could not understand British politics. He, Churchill, saw it as his highest duty to deliver his country from the threat of socialism, and in particular from this present Labour government. If ever he were to face the choice between completing that task and working for the unity of Europe, he would choose the former and not say another word about the latter. RCK immediately took the point, and was sensitive enough not to press Churchill further. He could not help but draw the obvious conclusion that for Churchill what really mattered was the future of Great Britain, while for him it was – as always – the future of Europe.

That did not stop them from working together, as their roads, at least while Churchill remained in opposition, obviously ran parallel. Four days later, RCK spoke at a meeting of MPs in the House of Commons, hosted by Kim Mackay, his leading supporter on the British political scene, motivating those who had signed and returned the reply cards he had sent from Gstaad.

A few days later, he was in Paris at a meeting with French deputies who had also replied favourably. He also met with President Auriol, a socialist and a consistent supporter of European unity from the twenties, and with Foreign Minister Bidault, a Republican who also backed his project. Then he went on to meet with René Courtin, who by then had formed a strong committee for European unity, headed by RCK's old friend and former French prime minister Edouard Herriot, a member of the Radical Party. Co-operation across parties in the interests of European integration appeared not to be an issue in France.

It was unfortunate, but understandable, that RCK was absent from the 16 May meeting in the Royal Albert Hall at which Winston Churchill and Duncan Sandys formally set up the United Europe Movement. The Albert Hall meeting took place without RCK able to take the pulse of the meeting, measure its spirit, and assess its concerns. Had he chosen to attend this London meeting, might he perhaps have been able to rally more support from the Labour Party and cement the role that he still thought Churchill had suggested for him as secretary-general of the United Europe Movement? But RCK had not been invited to speak there, and as the president of New York University had asked him to represent NYU at the University of Bordeaux's five-hundred-year anniversary celebrations on the same day, RCK gave priority to the academic ceremony. From Bordeaux, he travelled with Idel on to their house in Gruben to make preparations for his own new project, the first meeting later that summer of the European Parliamentary Union.

RCK and Idel were hardly back in their house in Gruben before a new announcement from America transformed the debate about the future of Europe. George Marshall's speech at Harvard in early June 1947 cannot have come as a surprise to them, since RCK had corresponded with the secretary of state previously on the question of US post-war aid to Europe. In his speech, Marshall set out the basic facts of the current situation: 'The truth of the matter is that Europe's requirements for the next three or four years of foreign food and other essential products – principally from America – are so much greater than her present ability to pay that she must have substantial additional help or face economic, social and political deterioration of a very grave character.' The remedy, he continued, 'lies in breaking the vicious circle and restoring the confidence of the European people in the economic future of their own countries and of Europe as a whole.'[1]

To make optimal use of generous, but not open-ended, American financing, Marshall set out the key condition on which it would be made available. 'It would be neither fitting nor efficacious for this Government to undertake to draw up unilaterally a programme designed to place Europe on its feet economically. This is the business of the Europeans. The initiative, I think, must come from Europe. The programme should be a joint one, agreed to by a number, if not all European nations.'

For RCK the essential element was Marshall's suggestion that recipient states in Europe should co-operate together to create a joint plan for the use of scarce American resources, not simply queue up independently to ask for help. RCK felt some pride that this element was due in part to his correspondence with George Marshall and his staff. That key point, RCK felt, validated his years of effort to persuade American political opinion about the need for European unity. Within less than twelve months, in April 1948, the United States and seventeen European beneficiaries, all of them states outside Moscow's control, set up the Organisation for European Economic Co-operation (OEEC). Marshall Aid began to flow later that same year, nearly thirteen billion dollars over a period of four years, equivalent to over one hundred and thirty billion dollars in today's money.[2] RCK was reassured to learn that there was no risk of a policy of American isolation such as had undermined European stability after the First World War.

Churchill's United Europe Movement set about gathering all the smaller groups working for European integration into a single movement that could also show some civil-society support for the American initiative, but it was not an easy task. The distinctive character and ambitions of some groups were precisely what had given rise to their creation in the first place, and several of them had little wish to merge with others or be corralled into a larger and less-distinctive umbrella organization. To them, what looked like sensible co-ordination in theory could also be interpreted in practice as a power grab by a British-based United Europe Movement at the cost of the specific concerns of the organizations that were to be 'co-ordinated'.

In this situation, RCK held several strong cards in his hand. As president-for-life of Pan-Europa and secretary-general of the European Parliamentary Union, he did not have anything to compare to Churchill's public reputation, of course, but he did have a head start over other organizations with the practical American support he had put together while in exile there during the war. His American friends, led by Ambassador Bullitt, represented a source of financial as well as moral support for his European work, and served as a useful instrument to encourage America's further involvement in the future of Europe. The reputation of Pan-Europa, in as far as it had survived the war, could be built on anew, and the European Parliamentary Union had the potential to build parliamentary majorities in every country to the west of the Iron Curtain. It could push governments in the direction of a European union.

RCK HAD ALWAYS HAD a strained relationship with one of the more important other organizations, the Federalists, just as he had earlier with the Peace Movement. In both cases, so much of what they wanted, he wanted too, but not as an end in itself. The Union of European Federalists (UEF) argued that the critical choices for Europe no longer lay between free enterprise and the planned economy, between capitalism and communism, but between federalism and the old pattern of power politics between nation states. Hendrik Brugmans, the newly appointed secretary-general of the UEF, reinforced the message that power should be exercised now within a federal structure that made the nationalism of Europe's past redundant.

Brugmans argued that, despite the division of the continent into zones of influence at the Yalta Conference in February 1945, Europe's future lay in asserting its unity, even if, thanks to the Marshall Plan, it could only be the western half that did so now. The western half of the continent should unite in a federal union to engage with America, but the eastern half would not be forgotten. For the UEF, the united Europe of the future would always be open to and on friendly terms with both the states of eastern Europe, and even with the Soviet Union. For Brugmans, who was planning a meeting in Montreux for August 1947, a federally united Europe would be a necessary first step along the road to world federation.

For RCK, federalism was always a means to an end, not an end in itself. He wanted a united Europe – and preferably one that was federal. A federal Europe would certainly be a peaceful Europe, and might lead, so he hoped, to international peace across the globe. But he had no practical interest in plans for a world federation. The priority now was to get out of the impoverished mess in which Europe found itself after the war and use what he thought was a window of opportunity to move towards a peaceful future, secure and united enough to prevent a repeat of the European wars of the recent past. That was a practical political aim that he could see was achievable by working through the parliaments of all nations open to the idea, even if that excluded eastern Europe for the moment, and the Soviet Union for ever.

RCK would concentrate on the democratic states of western Europe, and the instrument for achieving this goal would be the European Parliamentary Union. He therefore invited two dozen leading members from ten national parliamentary committees known to be in favour of European integration to a meeting in Gstaad on 4 July 1947. They were to be the organizing committee for the first full meeting of the EPU a few weeks later.

They met under the chairmanship of Léon Maccas, former Greek minister of foreign affairs, and RCK's opening speech set out the purpose of their meeting. 'Our meeting in the heart of Europe is an Open Conspiracy – to use a word of H.G. Wells. The aim of our conspiracy is to organize immediately, throughout Europe, parliamentary majorities strong enough to compel the governments to execute our programme: a United Europe within the framework of the United Nations.' He went on, 'Let us never forget that it is up to the parliaments to constitute and to overthrow governments; and that, consequently, parliamentary majorities and not governments represent in Western Europe the original source of power.' After twenty-five years of preparation and of propaganda since the founding of Pan-Europa, he added, 'The day of action has come; the Union of Europe has ceased to be a distant dream, it has become an immediate political goal.' The time was ripe, he said, to go beyond declarations of intent. This new organization would put pressure on all democratic governments, or so he hoped, to create a constituent assembly for the United States of Europe.

With a dramatic flourish, RCK called the concluding press conference of this preparatory meeting on the top of the Wasserengrat, a mountain overlooking Gstaad, and delegates and journalists went up by ski-lift on the final afternoon. Standing two thousand metres up on the mountain top, with the valleys of Switzerland spread out beneath them and the azure sky of Europe above, they heard RCK proclaim, in brilliant sunshine, that the first assembly of the EPU would be held in Gstaad that September. Within two years, he prophesied, the vision that he had first outlined twenty years earlier in *Pan-Europa* would become reality.

Idel and a small team of assistants immediately set to work organizing the technical aspects, booking travel, hotels, and meeting rooms in Gstaad, while RCK concentrated on inviting elected members of all democratic parliaments to attend the event and ensuring their quality would give it the character of a real European assembly.

HIS TIMING WAS EXTREMELY FORTUITOUS. When close to one hundred and fifty parliamentarians assembled in the elegant Palace Hotel above Gstaad in September 1947, the first meeting of the member states of the OEEC was taking place in Paris. At the same time, Belgium, Luxembourg, and the Netherlands were negotiating improvements to their Benelux customs union, and France and Italy were discussing a potential Latin customs union. All these other meetings involved delegates sent from national governments. Only the EPU was an entirely private initiative. All parliamentarians attending the Gstaad meting had come in their private capacity, not delegated by their governments, a factor which gave them far greater scope to express what they really wanted. The downside, however, was that their governments were in no way obliged to deliver whatever they might ask for.

The EPU parliamentarians assembled in the hotel's resplendent ballroom, each representative speaking for roughly one million inhabitants of their country. The largest national group, forty-three deputies, came from France and included the former prime minister, Paul Reynaud, the former deputy prime minister, Francisque Gay, and three former ministers: René Coty, François de Menthon, and Pierre Pflimlin. Almost as large was the delegation from Italy with forty members, among them the leader of the short-lived, populist Uomo Qualunque Party, Gugliemo Giannini, former prime minister, Ferrucio Parri, and Ludovico Benvenuti, later destined to be first secretary-general of the Council of Europe. The British delegation was smaller, representing a cross-section of the House of Commons, including the flamboyant and far-sighted Conservative Somerset de Chair, and the outspoken Socialist Kim Mackay. Churchill, who had also been

The Gstaad Palace Hotel, deluxe venue for the first congress of the European Parliamentary Union in September 1947.

invited, sent a telegram of support to the Gstaad Congress, recommending Duncan Sandys as his substitute.

Duncan Sandys represented a particularly British view on the issue of European integration. He shared with Churchill a vision of Europe as a group of nation states with a common cultural heritage which would all benefit by co-operating voluntarily with each other on economic and other issues. But Sandys saw no need for a closer political bond between them, certainly not one which would lead to the creation of a common European citizenship and a federal structure of government, since this would inevitably be exclusive and run counter to the interests of Britain and its Commonwealth – a position not so very different from that of the leadership of the Labour Party.

Within his own party, Sandys's position was not dissimilar to that of Leo Amery, the main difference being that Leo Amery had adopted this position in the aftermath of the First World War when Britain still ruled an empire, and Duncan Sandys went no further, despite his experience of the Second World War. In the interim, the United Kingdom had suffered a singular loss of power, though not yet of prestige. Even if its empire was waning, its reputation as the only European nation that had not been defeated, indeed had been a victor in the recent war, allowed it still to punch far above its weight.

Continental parliamentarians had a different appreciation of the destructive nature of the recent war, essentially because of defeat and occupation. Almost all of them had known domination by Nazi Germany, and the deep and lasting wounds caused by the division between collaboration and resistance within their own societies. To ensure it did not happen again, they were prepared to go further in sharing sovereignty than Duncan Sandys and the wide circle of British opinion that he represented.

RCK and Idel, both self-declared European patriots, were clearly more sympathetic to the continental position. Duncan Sandys remained a British patriot, at pains to move British public opinion in a favourable European direction, but not prepared to step beyond that. Churchill had entrusted to him the task of bringing the various competing organizations for European co-operation into his new United Europe Movement on that basis, but had left its internal organization at best ambiguous. In Sandys's view, authority should be vested essentially in the national chapters, minimizing whatever co-ordination might be necessary at the centre. Its structure was to be intergovernmental, not federal. Sandys regarded with suspicion attempts to capture national governments by means of cross-party, potentially pro-federalist, committees of MPs. He was likewise personally uncomfortable with the charismatic RCK in the role of secretary general, guiding the nascent EPU.

In the opening speech to his new organization, RCK ridiculed the dysfunctional political structure of the continent, where the number of states had doubled over the past seventy-five years, while the economy of Europe had grown ever more integrated. He argued that a politically unified Europe should take its seat at the United Nations instead of the individual states, just as the United States represented fifty states from Maine to California. The idea of 'one world federation might be completely premature', he said, but Europe should pursue the 'one region' solution that was now within reach.

During the final evening of the three-day Gstaad Congress, the heads of the parliamentary delegations met to elect the officers who would lead and guide the EPU as it developed. At this point, the head of the British contingent, Lieut-Colonel E.M. King, a Labour MP, asked if Duncan Sandys could attend the session alongside him to interpret. Thereafter, according to RCK, King said not a word, and Sandys did all the talking, his one aim being to eject RCK from the position of secretary-general.

Playing on the fact that RCK was the only person present who had never been elected to public office, he proposed that there should be two general secretaries for the EPU, one an elected member of parliament and one not. Sandys had already obtained the agreement of a French deputy to stand as the candidate for the post of the 'elected' member, and this would have begun the process whereby RCK could be marginalized, and perhaps even brought to the point of resignation. RCK recognized Duncan Sandys's game immediately, and pre-empted the move by saying that he would happily be a full secretary-general, but never just half of one. If he was not elected there and then to this post as the sole candidate, he would resign immediately. René Coty, who had not been informed of Sandys's initiative by his French colleague, intervened to support RCK, and, with his political authority as leader of the largest delegation, won the day. Duncan Sandys had clearly revealed his hand, and he had lost.

The other elections went ahead as foreseen: Georges Bohy, the Belgian socialist senator, was elected president, with Léon Maccas, René Coty, Enzo Giacchero, and Kim Mackay all elected as the steering committee. Coty would later go on to be president of France and Giacchero became the Italian representative on the European Coal and Steel Authority.

The conference concluded its three days of debates with a final resolution, calling on

> all members of parliaments in Europe to use their influence on their respective governments and on the public at large to achieve the three following aims: a) To create a European regional group within the United Nations, in the spirit of article 52 of the Charter; b) To create a community of peoples entitled 'The United States of Europe' which shall comprise all the states which are prepared to cooperate with a view to uniting the whole of Europe; and c) To call together a European constituent assembly in order to draft a federal European constitution.

The conclusions left open the question of how the assembly was to be constituted. Would it be appointed by governments, elected by national parliaments, directly elected by the people of Europe, or selected through some other mechanism? Whatever the system, its aim would be to constitute 'the United States of Europe as an indissoluble federal community, united through its civilisation, its love of liberty and its shared destiny.' The draft constitution that it would agree upon was to be offered to all states for them either to accept or reject.

The final resolution of the EPU's Gstaad meeting was well reported by European media, and that was as important for RCK as the election of officers. He had invited numerous journalists in order to raise public awareness of the idea of a European parliament representing the whole continent, and he was pleased with the results. For one young Italian journalist, Vittorio Pons, the event made such a memorable impression that, twenty years later, when he was a European civil servant in Brussels, he offered his support to RCK and became secretary-general of the revived Pan-Europa Union. In this role he acted as a close confidant of RCK in his later years and, after RCK's death, became his literary executor.

The Gstaad meeting of the EPU had brought together an impressive gathering of MPs from a dozen countries and, as RCK had hoped, the final resolution that they agreed upon had a galvanizing effect on the post-war European political debate. Over the following months, EPU members worked as pressure groups inside national parliaments to bring forward motions in favour of European union. The MPs who met at Gstaad were essentially a voluntary, informal group, present without any mandate from their parties. Hence the relative freedom with which a private individual, a charismatic former Austrian count who had never held any elected or governmental office but had a clear and powerful vision of a united Europe, could manoeuvre them to agree upon such a politically far-reaching final resolution.

RCK could take justifiable pride in this considerable achievement and its immediate consequences. The EPU meeting may have been a private initiative, but pro-European resolutions in parliament after parliament, from Greece to Scandinavia, subsequently gave it the stamp of official authority. Later developments in the story of European unification would refer back to this Gstaad meeting with a sense of wonder at the near-miraculous birth of cross-border parliamentary co-operation in Europe, stimulated by an entirely unofficial initiative.

But national governments also took note of the federalist tenor of the EPU resolution, and some of them started to erect their defences. If the federal future meant less power for individual nation states, few governments wanted to be cast in the role of turkeys voting for Christmas. That was particularly true of the United Kingdom.

WITH MUCH WORK TO DO in Europe following up the Gstaad meeting, it is not entirely clear why RCK and Idel decided to go back to the United States again that winter. RCK's professorship had been converted into a purely honorary post, so any work at the university would not be remunerated. They had already moved out of their Palisade Avenue apartment, so there was no home to return to in New York. What domestic matters remained outstanding – such as disposing of excess furniture left in storage or selling their small collection of art – could well be dealt with at a distance and left to local agents. Even the weather cannot have played a role, as it was as icy cold in New York as it was in Gruben that winter.

The answer may have been simply a need for money. RCK had to organize transatlantic financial backing for the EPU, since he feared national governments in Europe would be reluctant to subsidize a body working to undermine their role by drawing them into a federation. He also wanted to make or renew personal contact with leading political figures in America in order to strengthen transatlantic support for his work. So he and Idel sailed from Cherbourg on New Year's Day 1948 on the *Mauretania*, and were honoured to be invited to the captain's table for dinner the very first evening of the voyage.[3]

That caused them some embarrassment, however, since Idel's love of animals had led her to smuggle on board a small Siamese kitten called Tiên that she had acquired in Gruben, and did not dare to leave unattended in their cabin. During the day, the kitten posed no problem, as she and RCK could take turns to be nearby, but a public occasion such as dinner with the captain would require them both for several hours, and Idel declined. On the first two evenings, RCK offered her excuses – she was indisposed, she had a headache – but on the third occasion, he confessed to the captain that they had a private stowaway. They need not have worried. The captain also loved cats, and he declared that Tiên could be looked after by a member of the crew while they both came to dinner. He also allowed Tiên to stay in their cabin during the day rather than be put in the ship's 'cage' for pets.

When their ship docked in New York, a reporter asked RCK why he had come back to America. Never short of a good turn of phrase, RCK answered that he had come 'to co-ordinate the union of Europe with the Marshall Plan.' That was an up-beat reflection of his and Idel's appreciation of their international role. But in his absence from Europe there was a downside. While he was meeting the great and the grand in America, he was absent from the European scene for a few crucial months. That risked weakening his position in the political jostling for control of the process of European unification, in particular in the organization of the Congress of Europe that Churchill had called for May 1948 in The Hague.

When looked at dispassionately, Churchill had no better right to call such a meeting than RCK himself. Each was chairman or president of an international non-governmental movement – Churchill of the United Europe Movement and RCK of the EPU – but clearly Churchill's name recognition and wartime record gave him the enhanced status to undertake such a task with a much greater chance of success, and RCK clearly recognized this. But he also expected to play a major role in such an event, and certainly did not expect to be squeezed to the margins.

While in New York, RCK and Idel lodged in 4715 Independence Avenue, an impressively large, early-twentieth-century private house in a leafy suburb not far from their previous home on Palisade Avenue.[4] From there they set about gathering friends and contacting their supporters. His most active collaborator at this stage was William Bullitt, the former ambassador to Moscow and Paris, who had subsequently served with the Free French Forces. Bullitt himself had accepted the post of vice-president of the American Committee for a United Europe that RCK set up in April 1947 under the chairmanship of Senator Fulbright. 'The current political situation,' RCK now declared, 'and the incredible explosion of the idea of federation in Europe itself have created the conditions for transforming our group into a permanent organisation.'

The role he set for the committee was twofold: to encourage the idea of European unity in the United States, and to demonstrate to a united Europe that it would be supported by the people of America. 'It will help to give much needed financial support to groups – such as the European Movement – which are working in Europe in favour of unity,' he promised, banking on US government backing. And in America, he expected it to help Americans to understand better what Europe had already undertaken to promote its unification, encouraging students, citizens, and others to study the consequences and the way in which American policy could advance this work. It was 'to demonstrate to individuals and to the American nation what is needed to help Europe unite, and consequently to help the American nation.' As the only European associated with the project, the American Committee awarded RCK the title of honorary member.

Building on his previous correspondence with Secretary of State George Marshall, RCK managed to arrange a brief meeting, and was surprised to find this quiet military strategist 'less American' than he expected, noting that 'he could have been a European academic'. RCK praised him as 'the man whose global war strategy had won the greatest campaign in history', and added that, like all great men, he was 'modest, human and straightforward'. Behind the scenes, however, it had been no easy task to arrange this interview. RCK had needed to deploy all his customary skill to sell his own role successfully to Marshall's office, so that fifteen minutes could be found in his busy schedule. RCK outlined the recent progress of the EPU and heard Marshall's reassuringly positive assessment of the prospects for European nations coming together into a confederation, as had the United States two hundred years before. It was long ago,

RCK met both Secretary of State George Marshall and President Harry Truman in April 1948.

but the analogy was powerful, and something that both Europeans and Americans understood.

On the strength of this meeting, RCK then secured the State Department's support for his request to meet President Truman. Arranging this required some further diplomatic finesse, as Truman was known to be very selective about whom he agreed to meet. RCK, however, stressed his new role as secretary-general of the European Parliamentary Union, and he finally had an appointment at the White House at the end of April 1948. It was a symbolic culmination of his work in the United States, perhaps his greatest personal coup, a face-to-face interview with the president.

The briefing note for Truman from the State Department described RCK simply – but erroneously – as 'born in Austria of an Austrian father and a Japanese mother', adding that he had been 'working for twenty years for a United States of Europe'. Truman's personal secretary added, 'The Count tried about a year ago to see the President and the State Department did not want him to at that time. However, now the Department thought it was all right for the President to see him.' It was a short, relaxed meeting, and for fifteen minutes the farmer from Missouri who had ordered the first use of the atomic bomb and the half-Japanese Austro-Hungarian aristocrat who before the war had organized an alternative European solution to Hitler and the Nazis discussed the future of the world.

RCK afterwards described Truman as remarkably informal, straightforward, and full of common sense. Though ten years older than RCK, he made a youthful impression on his visitor, and they parted with a cordial handshake.

SECURING THIS INTERVIEW had kept RCK in America until the end of April 1948, less than two weeks before the Congress of Europe that Churchill had called for in The Hague in early May. Duncan Sandys was organizing this gathering in the name of the British and French committees of Churchill's United Europe Movement, along with the European Union of Federalists, the European League for Economic Cooperation, and other small continental organizations. RCK noted with some regret that all the movements involved were newly founded since the end of the war, and, as president-for-life of the Pan-Europa Union, the oldest pro-European organization, he felt slighted. Duncan Sandys appeared indeed to be calling the shots, and this looked to RCK like payback for Sandys's earlier defeat in Gstaad.

Letters and cables went to and fro across the Atlantic. Kim Mackay, the senior EPU representative in London, increasingly and testily regretted RCK's absence from Europe at this difficult time and asked him repeatedly for clear guidance about how far the EPU (which was a postwar creation, like the other organizations involved) should go in offering its support. RCK for his part played for time, initially unsure whether to boycott the Congress of Europe or to see what price he could extract for his support and his attendance.

RCK wrote to Churchill to complain about his exclusion, and immediately received a defensive and barely apologetic reply, which arrived at the same time as a belated formal invitation from Duncan Sandys himself. But Sandys also made it clear that, if RCK wanted either Pan-Europa – or more appropriately the EPU – to be among the organizers, he would have to provide some financial contribution to help defray the cost of the event.

RCK knew from Mackay, however, that even at this late hour Churchill could count on only a mixed assortment of fewer than twenty Labour MPs attending the Congress, none of them approaching ministerial status. Among them were Victor Collins, the Treasurer of Federal Union; the Reverend Gordon Lang, the secretary-general of the United Europe

Movement; Hugh Delargy, a Catholic MP with Irish connections; and Kim Mackay himself, who would be there because of his European convictions rather than his formal leadership of the British contingent in the EPU. This was nothing like the resounding cross-party support that Churchill had been hoping for, and the Labour members who did plan to come were hardly the leading figures he felt he needed. Why were so very few senior socialists prepared to defy the party line and go to The Hague?

The Labour Party's general secretary, Morgan Phillips, told journalists in London that there were three reasons the Labour Party did not wish to be associated with what was being planned for The Hague. First, the project was being led by Churchill, to whose party Labour was diametrically opposed; second, there were socialist organizations that were working for rapprochement already, not just in Europe but internationally; and third, governments needed 'a common understanding of the economic underpinnings of society' before anything of practical value could be agreed by a collection of non-governmental associations. The French ambassador in London, René Massigli, reported confidentially to Georges Bidault, then French prime minister, that 'the Labour Party, in response to the anti-Soviet stance taken by the (former) Prime Minister, has felt it necessary to advise its members against joining or remaining on the Committee for the United States of Europe.'

Churchill did not want to relinquish what he saw as the moral high ground of presenting European unity as an issue that was above party politics, something as much in the British national interest as of benefit to the Conservative Party. Given the refusal of the Labour leadership to co-operate with Churchill and permit British Labour delegates to attend the Congress, however, RCK knew he could play on Churchill's need for a strong continental socialist presence to compensate. Georges Bohy, the Belgian socialist leader, was president of the EPU, and the EPU could attract senior socialist members from other countries. RCK held the key.

At the last moment, barely two weeks before the Congress was due to start, RCK agreed to join the sponsors, but on three strict conditions: that *all* EPU members should be invited; that the main congress hall, the ceremonial Ridderzaal, or Knights' Hall, in the Binnenhof at The Hague, should be hung with Pan-Europa flags; and that he, RCK, should be the next speaker immediately after Churchill at the opening ceremony.

Assuming all was now well, RCK and Idel sailed from New York on 29 April 1948 on the *Queen Elizabeth*, their second voyage on this ship. As ever, the isolation of the ship at sea was a welcome relief from the hectic work of the previous weeks, and this time it was not disturbed by any telegram from Churchill. They disembarked in Cherbourg on 4 May and travelled on by train. Two days later they arrived in The Hague and went to the Binnenhof, the meeting place for the Congress, only to discover in the Knights' Hall the full extent of Sandys's duplicity.

19

BEHIND CHURCHILL

THE FIRST THING THAT RCK AND IDEL SAW on entering the Knights' Hall in The Hague was not the highly symbolic Pan-Europa flag – the golden cross of Christendom within the red sun of Apollo against a deep blue background – but a new and undistinguished flag of the United Europe Movement, a large, red capital E on a white background. Five metres long and draped across the centre of the long wall of the mediaeval throne room, it dominated the scene, just as RCK's Pan-Europa flag had dominated the pre-war congresses in Vienna, Berlin, and Basel. It was a body blow to RCK. Pan-Europa's flag was well known in European circles before the war, and RCK had used it in New York for his wartime congress as well. He had ordered several boxes of them to be sent to Sandys to dress the meeting rooms of the Congress of Europe. Where were they?

Sandys's first excuse was that the Pan-Europa flags had never arrived, a line he modified later to say they had been subsequently mislaid. However, in correspondence that RCK had not seen, Sandys had commented that he thought the old Pan-Europa flag was both nondescript and meaningless. His new United Europe Movement needed a new flag, up-to-date and eye-catching, he maintained, and he would design one. And the congress would be badged by him, not by RCK. He made sure that his new flag, the large red capital E on a white background, which later became known to supporters and opponents alike as 'Sandys's pants', not only dominated the Knights' Hall, but was flown prominently around the town as well.[1]

Sandys had won on the issue of the flags, and RCK also very nearly had not secured the prestigious slot of second speaker. In the middle of April, Josef Retinger, now secretary of the International Committee of the Movements for European Unity, the joint body preparing the event, wrote to Kim Mackay to tell him that, despite his best efforts to give RCK 'an

Churchill addressing the Congress of Europe in May 1948. RCK is seated in the row directly behind him.

opportunity to make a speech in a plenary session, so that he may receive the acclamation of the Congress which is his due for his long years of pioneer work in the wilderness,' he had 'come up against strong opposition on personal grounds'. Who could that opposition have come from if not Sandys? Mackay insisted and made sure that RCK did not lose that slot, but it was a close-run thing, and RCK never knew.

Although belated, RCK's agreement to associate the EPU with the Congress of Europe did ensure a strong attendance by MPs of other European states. He insisted that all EPU members were invited, not just the socialists, whom Sandys and Churchill needed. Over two hundred continental MPs accepted, making up just over a quarter of the seven hundred and forty participants at The Hague. In addition, he added several names to the list of over a hundred international journalists, to help ensure that the event received extensive and positive media coverage.[2]

When it opened on Friday, 7 May 1948, the Congress in The Hague brought together leaders of society from all the free countries of Europe, statesmen of all political democratic parties, leading figures from the churches, eminent writers, lawyers, leaders of industry, and the professions, as well as prominent trade unionists. They were there not as representatives of governments or parties or professions, associations or organizations, but each in his or her own individual capacity.

It was an eclectic gathering. Within the 145-strong British contingent was a press baron, Lord Layton, former editor of *The Economist*, and now chairman of the *News Chronicle*; an international civil servant, Sir Harold Butler, former head of the International Labour Office; literary critic and Oxford historian Professor Gilbert Murray; Lord Moran, president of the Royal College of Physicians; Sir Adrian Boult, chief conductor of the BBC orchestra; the philosopher Bertrand Russell; Charles Morgan, a successful and well-connected author, who later became chairman of PEN International; and Churchill's literary agent, Emery Reves. Despite the informal nature of the selection process, Churchill said as he opened the proceedings, 'This Congress, and any conclusions it may reach, may fairly claim to be the voice of Europe.' He was well aware of Destiny standing at his shoulder.

Arthur Salter, a former British civil servant who had worked at the League of Nations before the war, wrote in the *Manchester Guardian* a week later in glowing terms.

> There has perhaps never been a conference equal to this one in the range and personal eminence of its delegates. There were some twenty ex-Prime Ministers, a greater number of ex-Foreign Ministers and Finance Ministers, and others of corresponding eminence in literature, the arts, science, religion, economics, industry, commerce and workers' organisations. Their presence, and obvious agreement in main purpose, was a profoundly impressive demonstration.

Harold Macmillan, then an MP and later prime minister, noted that it was 'a landmark for future historians ... more important, perhaps, than any other event in the second half of this century'. Emery Reves commented that the Congress brought together 'more European statesmen of the first order than the League of Nations, even in its best years'. For RCK, it was reminiscent of the first Pan-Europa Congress in Vienna in 1926, which had equally attracted the support of the great and the good from across the continent. That had been all his own work, while this Congress was essentially the creation of Duncan Sandys, at the behest of Churchill, topped up and balanced better with RCK's support.

De Rougemont, the rapporteur of the Cultural Committee at The Hague, who had himself worked with RCK in Vienna in the early 1920s, somewhat caustically recorded the scene. In his reminiscences, published twenty years later, he wrote,

I was sitting on the platform, behind two rows of fascinating backs and necks which extended above the backs of the chairs. A white, puffy neck rising out of the collar of a Victorian frock coat, that was Winston Churchill. To left and right of me were several friends in profile; that young man was a former Dutch Socialist Minister, another young man was a former British Conservative Minister, the slit eyes of Coudenhove, Lord Layton's Voltaire-like smile, a man in black wearing a long chain round his neck. Very near to me, Churchill was talking into a microphone, and his voice came back to me from the hall: 'The task before us, at this Congress, is not only to raise the voice of Europe as a united home. We must here and now resolve that a European Assembly shall be constituted.' Yes, it was a dream which had come true.

In his opening address, Churchill stressed that this Congress of Europe represented not a movement of parties, but a movement of peoples. With an eye clearly on the Labour Party back home, he declared,

There is no room for jealousies. If there is rivalry of parties, let it be to see which one will distinguish itself the most for the common cause. No one can suppose that Europe can be united on any party or sectional basis, any more than any one nation can assert an overweening predominance. It must be all for all. Europe can only be united by the heart-felt wish and vehement expression of the great majority of all the peoples in all the parties in all the freedom-loving countries, no matter where they dwell or how they vote.

All were welcome, he claimed, if they came from countries 'where the people own the government and not the government the people'.

'It is,' he said, 'impossible to separate economics and defence from the general political structure. Mutual aid in the economic field and joint military defence must inevitably be accompanied step by step with a parallel policy of closer political unity.'

Then RCK rose to speak, and the microphone failed. RCK was so committed to the speech that he had prepared that he carried on regardless.

But much of the audience could not hear the opening sentences, in which he praised the name of Churchill, 'which yesterday meant victory over Hitler's tyranny, and today means victory for a United States of Europe.' RCK reminded those in the audience close enough to hear him that this date was also the twenty-fifth anniversary of the founding of Pan-Europa, and paid tribute to the many who had struggled for the cause of peace and freedom in Europe before the Second World War.

Was it just a brief technical fault, an accident for which nobody was responsible? Or was there a hidden hand that wanted to upstage RCK? It lasted barely a minute, and when the microphone came back to life, RCK was urging the audience to work not only for European unity but also for European reconciliation.

> Let us not forget that the unification of Europe is only a means, and not an end in itself. Hitler wanted to unify Europe, and Stalin today pursues a similar goal. What distinguishes us from them is that we want to build a free and humane Europe, not a Europe in the service of one race or one class, but a Europe for the wellbeing of all men, women and children. We want to unite Europe in order to ensure lasting peace between the peoples of Europe and to banish forever the spectre of total destruction through war. We want to unite Europe in order to raise the standard of living of millions of Europeans through a free market with a stable currency continent-wide, to save them from the indescribable misery under which they are now suffering. Finally, the goal of the movement for European unity is to ensure that every European is safe from the threat of murder, kidnap and torture by secret police, and that they will never again be interned in concentration camps.

He concluded his speech with a reminder of moral duty which so marked his approach to politics, and echoed the voice of his father, Heinrich: 'If we should ever be uncertain in our journey, let us think rather of the people than of governments, rather of the powerless than the powerful, rather of the poor than the rich, rather of those who are less fortunate than of those who are happy. Let us remember that we are not here on earth to conquer empires and to seize fortunes, but to help one another to bear the sometimes-heavy burden of existence.'

After he had finished his own oration, RCK then read out a message from Senator Fulbright, the chairman of his American support committee, encouraging 'in every possible way the political unification of Europe.

The European peoples must themselves voluntarily bring about their unification in their own way and in a manner consistent with their history
and culture.'

RCK's own words and his message from America were well received.
While Churchill was the great and victorious wartime leader, RCK,
though much younger, was for many in the audience the grand old man
of pre-war Pan-Europa. He was the embodiment of the movement on the
continent that had stood as an alternative pole to the Nazis in both ideological and political terms in the 1920s and 1930s. Despite his still-youthful
appearance at little over fifty years of age, he personified a positive strand
of continental politics that stretched back to an earlier age.

After the opening plenary session, the congress split into three large
committees, dealing with political, economic, and cultural affairs. RCK
and Idel flitted between the three of them, greeting old friends and receiving the respect due to the 'elder statesman' of Pan-Europa, the current
secretary-general of the EPU.

The committees were chaired by old acquaintances of RCK from pre-
war days: Paul Ramadier of France, Paul van Zealand of Belgium, and
Salvador di Madariaga, originally from Spain but, since the victory of
Franco, now in exile as a senior academic at Oxford University.

The work of the congress had been well prepared, with initial draft
reports laid before each committee and various resolutions drawn up for
comment and amendment. The proceedings, however, sometimes appeared
anything but organized. There was an air of enthusiasm about many of the
speeches, with verbal rather than written proposals added for debate and
voting. Anyone using a language other than French or English was asked
to distribute a summary of what they had said, translated into those languages for participants to read themselves. Rooms for committee work
were not all arranged theatre-style for a formal presentation; some were
in cabaret-style with small tables with chairs grouped around them. This
encouraged conversation rather than attentive listening, and chairmen had
on occasion to shout to obtain quiet for speakers to be heard. *The Times*
commented that during the three days of intense debates conditions were
on occasion 'chaotic'.

Every day was punctuated by lunches in the best restaurants of The
Hague and dinner each evening in the Kurhuis in the nearby coastal suburb of Scheveningen and, to add drama to the proceedings, there were
several unscheduled late-night sessions. Twice the economic committee sat past midnight, and the political committee excelled itself, sitting
from ten one evening until nearly seven the next morning. For many

participants it meant inconvenient travel late at night or early in the morning to distant lodgings on the edge of town. The British delegation was more fortunate, since Duncan Sandys had efficiently housed them in two centrally located hotels, which he had block-booked in advance.

A number of RCK's friends helped to draft the final committee reports, including René Courtin, his main contact in Paris; Daniel Serruys, who had spoken at the 1930 Pan-Europa Congress in Berlin; Lord Layton, former editor of *The Economist*; Alexandre Marc, a leading French federalist; and Denis de Rougemont, a well-known Swiss cultural historian who had overseen translations into French for RCK's Pan-Europa publishing house back in the 1920s.

RCK was happy to endorse the conclusions reached by the three committees, all of which tended in the direction he favoured: politically in favour of setting up a constituent assembly for Europe, economically in favour of close co-operation between European states, and culturally endorsing a notion of a common identity for all Europeans, something in which everyone could take pride alongside their particular nationality.

TO EVERYONE IT WAS CLEAR that the Congress of Europe was an exceptional event, called in exceptional times. Chairing one of the sessions, Senator Kerstens from The Netherlands compared it with the Paris Peace Conference after 1918, which he had attended as a young man. Then, despite the horrors of the First World War, everyone had insisted on self-determination and ever more nationalism, he claimed. After the experience of the recent war, he trusted that participants would now be prepared to share sovereignty.

That was precisely where the divide lay in the political committee. Federalists, who were prepared to merge sovereignty in a larger political entity, argued with nationalists, who would not. The economic committee divided essentially along the left-right split apparent in most parliaments and societies, between those who thought in socialist terms of common ownership and the planned economy, and those who insisted on free markets and capitalism. Within the cultural committee, debate swirled around the secular or religious nature of European heritage, and whether there should or should not be an explicit role for the churches as representatives of organized religion within society.

In conjunction with Josef Retinger, Denis de Rougemont had drafted a stirring 'Message to Europeans', which endorsed a number of strong federalist demands. It was printed at the top of a long roll of parchment, and together the two men planned that, at the end of the closing session, de Rougemont would solemnly read the text, and all the delegates, headed by Churchill, would then sign it. With such a well-publicized launch, the federalist message of the final declaration would be sure to gather millions of signatures as it circulated in each country, becoming a powerful instrument in a campaign for a united Europe. But this initiative was foiled by the well-organized opposition of a group of British delegates who thought this was a step too far.

De Rougemont later recalled what happened with great clarity.

While I was doing a radio interview in a corridor, ten minutes before the time fixed for the closing session, someone was sent to get me: Duncan Sandys urgently wanted to see me in the Knights' Hall where the plenary sitting of the economic section was drawing to a close. I saw Churchill standing at the microphone, his hands grasping the lapels of his frock coat. Every now and then, all the lights dimmed and, for a few seconds, were extinguished, by a violent storm which was raging outside. At the back of the hall, near the main entrance, I saw Duncan and his brother-in-law, Randolph Churchill, who said to me: 'I believe you want a unanimous vote of the Congress on the text of a commitment at the end of your message. Now, I know at least 30 delegates who will oppose it, because of the sentence: "We want a common defence system."' Sandys added: 'That sentence wasn't debated by the Congress. I am sorry, but we must forget about the Message.'

De Rougemont replied angrily, 'At the next European Congress, Stalin, who is stronger than you, will be sending fifty delegates! And there won't be any united Europe at all!' Van Zeeland, however, who was to chair the closing session of the Congress, helped to craft a compromise which allowed de Rougemont to read the Message, but left out the sentence to which the thirty British delegates objected. That seemed at the time a reasonable way of proceeding, but what it meant in practice was that nobody could now *sign* the Message, as it was already printed on the parchment roll with the offending sentence concerning European defence still in it. Hence the Message was never circulated and the public campaign that de Rougemont wanted, in order to publicize the agreed-upon conclusions of the congress, came to nothing.

To add insult to injury, de Rougemont was just getting to the final points in his presentation in French in the plenary session when Sandys gave an imperious sign to the effect that no one in the hall was to stand up to applaud. 'I had a paltry revenge,' de Rougemont wrote afterwards. 'While Senator Kerstens was reading the Message in English, I was back in my seat on the platform, just behind Churchill, who was rocking backwards and forwards on his chair, and I heard him say out loud: "We should stand up at that! We should all stand up!"'

Commenting on the discipline of the British delegation by comparison with all the others, in particular the French, René Courtin, RCK's key man in Paris, wrote in *Le Monde* that the British had deployed their efforts

in support of a very cautious policy, much supported by the Nordic participants, and which is easily explained: the plans for European coordination are still regarded with great suspicion by a large section of British public opinion, and those who had come to The Hague felt they could only take prudent steps for fear of cutting themselves off from the majority of the nation and the Parliament. Like it or not, all the other delegations had to align themselves with this position in order to avoid a possible split.

This hesitation is also apparent in Duncan Sandys's own assessment of the follow-up to the Congress. A month or so later, he wrote a memo to circulate at Westminster, possibly with RCK and his supporters in mind, noting an 'apparent cleavage of approach' between the British and a vocal section of the continental representatives 'on the idea that one should forthwith set up a Constituent Assembly, an Economic Council, and a Cultural Centre, and all would be well.' There was also, he found, some confusion about what was expected of governments, the difficulty of informing public opinion, and even in how best to ensure that the organizations involved would continue along this co-operative path. He recognized 'the real advance made at the Congress', but wanted to indicate some things that he felt needed careful watching, 'lest we create in some quarters a great unease of mind and a disappointment of hope.'

Apart from speaking immediately after Churchill and forwarding the good wishes of Senator Fulbright, RCK also had the opportunity to make personal contact with numerous friends and acquaintances at the Congress, in particular with Konrad Adenauer, an active and early supporter of Pan-Europa in the 1920s, now Christian Democrat mayor of Cologne. But in his eyes the duplicity of Duncan Sandys marred his view of the events over those three days, and RCK was not one to forgive and forget. Sandys's growing impatience with RCK was matched by the Count's increasing truculence towards him.

Later that year, RCK sent a letter to Churchill in which he complained about his son-in-law's attitude and the actions which he considered hostile to him personally and to the EPU. Churchill's emollient reply suggested that Sandys was only doing what he had been tasked with, namely ensuring the unity of the disparate pro-European movements. In a handwritten footnote to his reply, Churchill added that he personally always gave RCK credit for his pioneering contribution to the movement towards European unity – a gentle reminder of Churchill's explicit support in his Zürich speech two years earlier.

It was probably during the following months that RCK gave up, at least temporarily, on the idea of formal British involvement in the future integration of Europe. It confirmed his initial impression that Great Britain was absorbed with its empire and would not, or could not yet, wholeheartedly engage in a closer European community of nations. Correspondence between them right up until the end of 1949 shows Churchill maintaining that initiatives on the continent should not go ahead without the United Kingdom's involvement, while RCK casts doubt over the full commitment of the UK to the process of European unification.

As RCK saw the position, the British empire might be fast falling away – India had already been granted independence – but the British attitude remained semi-detached as far as the continent of Europe was concerned, not so very different from where it had been after the First World War. The experience of the Second World War seemed not to have yet taught the British ruling class any further geopolitical lessons in that regard. As a result, RCK looked about for another statesman who might better embody his ideas on the future of Europe.

20

BRINGING GERMANY
IN FROM THE COLD

RCK HAD KEPT CHARLES DE GAULLE INFORMED of his European activities from 1943, and in some detail from the time of the Gstaad meeting of the European Parliamentary Union in 1947, so it comes as no surprise to find him complaining to de Gaulle late in 1948 about the 'British grip' on the European Movement. In his view, the British government was trying to strengthen its continental position by posing as the protector of Germany in an effort to create a Germanic *entente*, including Scandinavia and the Netherlands, which would be opposed to a Franco-Italian bloc. In his view, Britain might even wish to incorporate a unified Europe into its Commonwealth. Only a close rapprochement between France and Germany could stop such a development, he suggested to de Gaulle, and the time was right for France to take such an initiative. Much better a functioning Franco-German axis than 'trying to get consensus from negotiations with eighteen European states under British protection'.

De Gaulle must have been intrigued to read RCK's opinion, indeed to receive any information such as this at all. His reply was supportive, but also enigmatic. 'Between England which needs its Commonwealth and Germany which has still not found its new identity, I have always thought that France was destined, even by geography itself, to promote European union. For that reason I cannot but rejoice at what you do personally to facilitate the achievement of this union.'

Meanwhile, following the public-relations success of the Congress of Europe at The Hague, the UK government under Clement Attlee looked afresh at its European policy. The Labour Party had played its cards badly by leaving Churchill to lead the United Europe Movement uncontested. It now pushed hard for an intergovernmental agreement that would outflank this non-governmental initiative, an agreement for which Labour could take credit, even if it meant borrowing some of the ideas promoted by Churchill's congress.

The British government was not alone in needing to show that it was not lagging behind the curve. In July, the French government also ran before the wind in favour of greater European unity and floated a proposal to set up a Council of Europe. This formal initiative built on RCK's earlier proposal, amplified by Churchill in his radio broadcast in 1943, and which had now been reinforced by the conclusions of the recent Congress of Europe at The Hague. The proposed Council of Europe would have a Parliamentary Assembly, the first official European parliament. The idea immediately gained the support of the Benelux countries (Belgium, Netherlands, Luxembourg) and – in principle – the support of London as well.

The United Kingdom used the intergovernmental structure already established by the Brussels Treaty on Western European Union and invited its ten members to negotiate this new treaty, the Treaty of London. The Council of Europe might be the brainchild of Churchill and a foreign aristocrat rather than of Attlee or Ernest Bevin, and it might be proposed by a Frenchman and supported by continentals, but Labour in government would hold the whip hand and negotiate just what such a Council of Europe could or could not do, just how federal it might or might not be, just how much it might or might not act in Britain's interest.

RCK's thinking had already gone beyond these first steps. It was hard not to overlook the fact that the proposed Council of Europe would not include Germany, for the very good reason that it was not yet an independent state. Stalin would not relax his grip on the Soviet Occupied Zone, but at some stage the three occupying powers in the west would realize that an independent West Germany aligned with them was better than a potentially neutral Germany that included the eastern zone and could not or would not be allowed to align with its western neighbours. Germany – or as much of Germany as could be kept out of the grip of the Soviet Union – must certainly not be left outside the Council of Europe. In RCK's eyes, there was no reasonable alternative to accepting West Germany back into the family of democratic nations, primarily for reasons of European political integration, and secondarily as additional military security in facing up to the Soviet Union.

Reconciling Germany and France was therefore a major practical step towards a united Europe. But how should that united Europe be organized politically? Should it or should it not be a federal union? That federal question was to form the agenda of the second EPU Conference, planned for Interlaken later that year.[1]

FROM GRUBEN TO INTERLAKEN was under two hours by train for RCK. There he welcomed nearly two hundred MPs from thirteen countries to the event in the Grand Casino Hotel. It was a larger number of delegates than had attended the inaugural meeting of the EPU in Gstaad a year previously. Two distinguished visitors also came from America, Ambassador Bullitt and Congressman Hale Boggs, both of whom had strongly supported RCK during and after the war years in New York. RCK also welcomed his old friend Konrad Adenauer, then president of the provisional West German Parliamentary Council and soon to be the first chancellor of West Germany, a man who knew well the weaknesses of the old order of pre-war Europe and had been a supporter of Pan-Europa from the 1920s.

Participants at Interlaken debated at length the issue of federation or confederation for Europe, concluding unanimously with a plan for a European Confederation as the first stage that could – and for some should – lead to an eventual federation. The road plan that they agreed on called first for a constituent assembly and then for a Europe-wide plebiscite to endorse its conclusions. The Interlaken Declaration was subsequently signed by over five hundred sympathetic European parliamentarians back in the various capitals, helping the EPU to set the pace in the wider public debate on Europe. The MPs also took this proposal back into their parliaments, where it was debated and voted on country by country. The EPU agreed to meet again in September the following year in Venice, this time under the chairmanship of Kim Mackay, to discuss the next steps.

However, the British government, which like other governments had carefully noted what happened in Interlaken, had no intention of losing control of the process of European unification to a private initiative of MPs. The supranational parliamentary assembly the EPU envisaged for the Council of Europe might well turn itself into a constituent assembly for a European federation. For the government in London, this was not an issue for parliaments to decide, but governments.

When the negotiating parties met, Foreign Secretary Ernest Bevin insisted that, as the price of British support for the French and Benelux plan, the decision-making power in the Council of Europe would remain firmly in the hands of the member states' governments. They would be represented in the new Council of Europe in a committee of ministers that would retain decision-making powers. There could be a parliamentary assembly as well, but it would have power solely to make recommendations, not to pass laws. It would not be in control of its own agenda, let alone have the power to transform itself into a constituent assembly.

The British foreign secretary had declared himself in favour of 'a consolidation of Western Europe', but he wanted to remain secure in the knowledge that decision-making power lay with governments, not with parliaments. Ministers would run the show and individual countries would enjoy a *de facto* veto. He pointedly noted in an internal memo that Britain could agree to the assembly on these conditions, since in its emasculated form it would be little more than a 'talking shop'.

The intergovernmental negotiations for the new treaty in London were held, as was usual, behind closed doors, but enough information leaked out to indicate that an agreement would soon be reached. RCK and Idel decided to change their travel plans and stay in Switzerland through the winter of 1948–49. They cancelled their steamer passages back to New York, which had originally been booked for 25 January, and experienced for the first time winter snow and sunshine in the Bernese Oberland. RCK wrote that he saw in the blue sky and the snow-covered ground a reflection of the national colours of Bavaria. Idel decided she loved the sunshine and the blue skies, but loathed the snow, which for her looked like a winding sheet of white over the cold corpse of the dead land.

RCK and Idel heard the news of the final breakthrough in negotiations for the Treaty of London on Swiss radio in late January 1949. He was now engaged in regular correspondence with de Gaulle – at this stage exchanging up to a dozen letters a year – and welcomed the treaty. It was signed in May, and its main conclusion represented a major success for RCK personally, as it realized one of Pan-Europa's prime demands from twenty-five years before and the keystone of the EPU's more-recent campaign. Irrespective of whatever powers it might actually enjoy, there would now soon be, for the very first time, a democratic assembly at a European level, drawn from MPs of all member states. It was a major step in the direction of a united Europe.

As he and Idel reflected on this success, it seemed to them that it had all come about remarkably quickly after their return from America. It was barely three years since RCK had taken his Gstaad initiative to write to European MPs and ask if they were in favour of a United States of Europe. Just two years ago, he had stood on the mountaintop near Gstaad and declared to the press that he would succeed within precisely that time span. Less than a year later, the governments of Western Europe had started to negotiate seriously, and by August 1949, the Council of Europe with its Parliamentary Assembly was a reality. RCK felt convinced that a permanent body of MPs from all democratic states, called to deliberate on European issues, could yet create for itself the power to put forward a constitution for a united Europe. It should, could, and would become a constituent assembly.

He recalled a prophecy, which had been made some years before the war by a Swiss psychic or fortune teller, Fridolin Kordon-Veri. One day RCK had asked Kordon-Veri on the spur of the moment when he thought Pan-Europa would actually become reality and not just a dream. The clairvoyant had answered without hesitation, 'In 1949.' RCK found his belief in prophecy amply confirmed by political events that year. For him, the creation of the Council of Europe was the first concrete realization of the aims of Pan-Europa, aims which had now become agreed-upon policy carried forward by European governments. Who knew where that might end?[2]

With national MPs delegated to Strasbourg for the Parliamentary Assembly of the Council of Europe (PACE), governments, national parliaments, and public opinion in all European democratic states now had a political stake in a new and highly visible European institution. In his enthusiasm for the newly founded Council of Europe, RCK sounded out de Gaulle to ask for his support in nominating him (as a French citizen) on his party list as a member of the French delegation to PACE. De Gaulle's enigmatic reply was not a blunt refusal, but was certainly not encouraging: 'Can one really hope that Europe will emerge from the work of this Consultative Assembly such as it is conceived of now?' He clearly shared Bevin's low opinion of the value of this 'talking shop' rather than RCK's enthusiasm.

Although RCK did not know it, a close adviser of Churchill's, Bob Boothby – whom he had met at Chartwell a few months previously – had similar ambitions, and begged Churchill – in vain – to add his name to the British list of parliamentary delegates for PACE. Boothby was not nominated from the United Kingdom, and RCK did not press the point with de Gaulle. Had he been nominated for the French delegation, it might have been a transforming moment for him, gaining a formal political role, even at the price of sacrificing his independent status. Who knows if his story would have been different had he publicly been identified with a political party, a group, or even seen simply as de Gaulle's man in the assembly.

IN ANTICIPATION of the first Council of Europe session in August 1949, RCK arranged for the EPU's central committee to gather in the Strasbourg town hall that July in order to prepare a message of welcome, together with a list of demands to be sent to the Committee of Ministers and to the Parliamentary Assembly. For the first time German delegates from the provisional West German Assembly attended the EPU, and passions ran high in French public opinion, especially in Strasbourg, as Alsace had a turbulent history, torn between France and Germany in their struggle to control the territory. To protest against the presence of this first quasi-official German delegation in the city since the end of the war, the French Communist Party organized a noisy demonstration outside the town hall. RCK, in his memoirs, noted with pride the strength of French police protection needed to ensure that this international meeting could formulate its message of welcome to the new council, undisturbed by 'nationalists' demonstrating beneath the windows of the town hall.

As there were no premises specifically built for the new council at that stage, the venue for the opening meeting of the Council of Europe was the main lecture hall of the University of Strasbourg. That event brought together leading European politicians, both in opposition and in government, across the ten founding states, and RCK and Idel had places of honour in an improvised diplomatic gallery. Even Duncan Sandys was moved to send RCK a generous letter of congratulations. 'Those of us who joined your crusade in its later phase congratulate you as initiator and leader,' he kindly wrote. 'Europe owes you sincere thanks for all your faith and enthusiasm in the past – and I am convinced that Europe in the future will need more than ever your creativity and leadership.'

The first meeting of the Council of Europe took the opportunity to invite three more states – Greece, Turkey, and Iceland – to join the initial ten members. But RCK's reflections on the occasion were tinged with regret for missed opportunities in the past, for the failure of European states to unite when he had first set up Pan-Europa in the 1920s or when Briand had proposed a 'federal link' between states in 1929. 'If Europe had united then,' he wrote, 'Hitler would never have come to power and the human race would have been spared the Second World War.'

Barely a month after the opening session of the Council of Europe, the European Parliamentary Union held its third session, this time in Venice. Kim Mackay was in the chair, and the final resolution naturally welcomed the establishment of the Council of Europe. But it went further, stressing that the new European Assembly's powers were still incomplete, since it needed to hold legislative power rather than just the power of recommendation. The EPU urged its members to press for this both in the Council of Europe itself and also in their respective national parliaments, so that eventually the committee of ministers of the Council of Europe would be obliged to accept all resolutions agreed by the parliamentary assembly.

To those in national governments who felt that creating a Council of Europe with a national veto was already a major step in the direction of unifying Europe, this seemed quite extreme. Such opposition came to a head in a meeting of the central committee of the EPU in Paris the following January, when it was discussing its future policy vis-à-vis the Council of Europe. There Duncan Sandys attempted another coup. This time Kim Mackay, now head of the British delegation, was his chosen instrument. The volatile Mackay, possibly under pressure from his party whips back in London, proposed without any prior notice that either the EPU should immediately decide to move its headquarters from Gstaad to London and join the new European Movement of which Duncan Sandys was now secretary-general, or else he and all his British MPs would withdraw from the organization.

Such a step would have emasculated RCK, and he only just managed to win a wafer-thin majority in the central committee, thanks to quick intervention organized, as earlier in Gstaad, by René Coty. As a result, Mackay and most of the British members walked out. Subsequently Duncan Sandys formed a Parliamentary Committee of the European Movement in London, led by Mackay, which attracted support from Scandinavian and Dutch parliamentarians. A few French and Italian members cannily joined both organizations, but RCK could see that British opposition to his own role and the role of the EPU was not going to end quietly.

Faced with this opposition from London, it is hardly surprising that RCK concentrated much of his efforts on Franco-German relations. In his Zürich speech, Churchill himself had stressed how important a 'spiritually great France' and a 'spiritually great Germany' would both be in the reconstruction of Europe. With an eye to future developments, RCK could see the obvious value of bringing French and German politicians closer together on an informal basis. Something was needed that would establish good personal relations between them and ease the eventual entry of West Germany into the Council of Europe. He discussed his plan for a bilateral meeting of parliamentarians from both countries with his old friend and supporter Konrad Adenauer. They were both aware that such a meeting of parliamentarians could not easily take place in either France or Germany without attracting opposition, so RCK chose Basel, the Swiss city bordering them both. To the first informal post-war Franco-German parliamentary conference in January 1950 he invited forty French deputies, led by René Coty, to meet with thirty German MPs, led by Foreign Minister Clemens von Brentano. They all accepted.

It was a private initiative of significant political importance. For the first time since the war, elected delegates from both countries discussed together ways of improving relations between their two countries. RCK was so pleased with the political meeting of minds that he travelled to Paris as soon as the conference finished in order to brief de Gaulle in person.

Just six months later, he called an equally successful second Franco-German conference in Rheinfelden, a short distance up the Rhine from Basel, to confirm the centrality of Franco-German reconciliation as the bedrock of a united Europe. These networking meetings helped prepare the formal entry of West Germany into the Council of Europe in July that same year, and earned RCK lasting respect in government circles both in Bonn and Paris.

BETWEEN THESE TWO Franco-German parliamentary meetings RCK and Idel revived their travel plans and sailed to New York from Cherbourg on 2 February 1950. Facilitated by Ambassador Bullitt, RCK held talks in Washington with Paul Hoffmann, the administrative head of the Marshall Plan. 'The realization of the objective you seek, a united Europe,' wrote Hoffmann in a letter to RCK after their meeting, 'is essential to the economic health and security of the free world, indeed to its very survival. The aims of the Marshall Plan run parallel to yours on this vital issue. The sweep of world events has caught up with your inspired vision and now more than ever free men everywhere recognize the urgent and inescapable necessity of working together and fighting together in building one world of freedom.'

Elsewhere, however, RCK was discovering that all was not going well as far as possible financial support from American sources for his initiatives was concerned. Since he and Idel had last been in the country, Churchill had sent Duncan Sandys and Josef Retinger, the secretary-general of the International European Movement, accompanied by Edward Beddington-Behrens, a well-connected businessman and strong supporter of the European Movement, to Washington and New York. As a result, the nature of American support for uniting Europe had undergone a distinct shift of emphasis. The American Committee for a Free and United Europe that RCK and Bullitt had set up back in April 1948 had been reconstituted under the guidance of 'Wild Bill' Donovan, the head of the Office of Strategic Services. At the end of March 1950, Donovan wrote a diplomatic, but essentially negative, letter to RCK. On the one hand he wanted to associate himself with the kind words of appreciation for RCK's work for Europe, spoken by Alan Dulles at a lunch they had both recently attended at the Waldorf Astoria, but on the other hand he felt obliged to tell RCK that it would be best if the American Committee co-operated in future with the International European Movement rather than the EPU.[3]

Despite Donovan's kind words of appreciation, RCK could see what this meant in practice. Duncan Sandys and Josef Retinger had dislodged him from favour in the eyes of the American Administration. Donovan was in charge, not only of the committee, but more importantly also of the Office of Strategic Services, and any subsidies that the OSS might set aside for the political dimension of European reconstruction would now be channelled to Churchill's European Movement, not to RCK's EPU. He tried to repair bridges while he was still in America, hoping for at least a share of the support the United States was prepared to devote to this aspect of European unity, but it looked very much as if the die was cast.

There were nonetheless some surprising compensations. That same month, RCK was delighted to receive an unexpected letter from the mayor of Aachen, Dr Maas, informing him that his city had decided to award RCK the Charlemagne Prize for his outstanding contribution to European unity. He would be the first recipient of this new prize, which the city of Aachen would like to present to him at a ceremony on Ascension Day, 18 May 1950.

RCK was still in his mid-fifties, and the award of this prestigious honour publicly crowned his career. He and Idel saw it as an acknowledgement of their life-long struggle to make Europeans aware of their continental identity and heritage, their shared values, as well as their shared interests. The publicity attached to the award and the ceremony would help to bring Pan-Europa's political message to millions across the continent who might not have been aware of it before. It demonstrated the primacy of politics over economics, of identity over interests, a distinction that marked his approach out from those of others – such as Jean Monnet or Duncan Sandys – active though they were too, in their different ways, in promoting co-operation between European states.

RCK and Idel were barely back in Europe before they heard the news of the Schuman Declaration of 9 May 1950. It came as a surprise to many political observers, since Jean Monnet, now an adviser to Robert Schuman, the French foreign minister, had discussed the initiative – the Schuman Plan – in advance with only a small circle of French civil servants. Pooling continental coal and steel – the sinews of war – was a dramatic bid to share resources among European states in a politically sensitive industrial sector, a major step towards shared security, preventing one country arming against another. On the day that the Treaty of Paris came into force, establishing the European Coal and Steel Community (ECSC), Jean Monnet would declare that all coal and steel that originated from France, Germany, Italy, Belgium, the Netherlands, or Luxembourg was now no longer national but European. In future, none of those states would be in a position to produce armaments independently of the others. War between them was now over for good.

Observers were in no doubt at that time about the major political step this represented. The goal of the ECSC was political, and it aimed to reach that goal through economic means. Proponents of the 'community method' of co-operation that Jean Monnet elaborated stressed the common economic interests of the parties involved. The preamble to the Treaty of Paris stated the method in outline: 'Europe will not be made all at once, or according to a single plan. It will be built through concrete achievements which first create a de facto solidarity.'

Merging these vital sectors was an example of European integration that RCK had long advocated, but this specific initiative had come about without his involvement. He was not operating inside the governmental apparatus that had proposed and would negotiate the agreement, and the lines along which it would progress did not represent how he had envisaged European union. Here were governments taking an initiative to harmonize economic interests with their immediate neighbours in just one sector. How many more sectors would need to be united before this looked like the political union he favoured? The stated goal of the ECSC might be political union, but in practice that was so far distant that, if such a method was to be followed, European union, he felt, would take generations before it achieved its goals.

When Robert Schuman came to London immediately after announcing the Schuman Plan to invite Britain to participate in the scheme, British ministers had very little room to manoeuvre. Just three months before, the British Labour government had called an election which it nearly lost. Its majority was slashed to just five, and it could not afford any splits on policy for fear of losing a vote of confidence in parliament. The Labour government was not prepared to take a decision which might antagonize any section of its supporters. Herbert Morrison, the deputy prime minister, who was dining at the fashionable Ivy restaurant the evening when the proposal was brought to him, rejected the offer with the memorable phrase: 'The Durham miners won't wear it.' Ernest Bevin, still British foreign secretary, would later conclude that, because of its links with the United States and the Commonwealth, Britain was 'different in character from other European nations and fundamentally incapable of wholehearted integration with them.' At the time, however, party considerations appeared to loom much larger in the United Kingdom's decision. Supranational regulation of as sensitive a sector as coal and steel entailed too great a sacrifice of national sovereignty for Britain, a victor in the last war, to accept, and certainly too much for an insecure Labour government.

THE NEWS OF THE SCHUMAN PLAN was still fresh when RCK arrived in Aachen to be awarded the Charlemagne Prize. He might have been absent from the birth of the Schuman initiative, and never close to Jean Monnet, but this was his opportunity to make his mark again on the course of events through the publicity attached to this prestigious award. The ceremony was redolent with history and symbolism, beginning with a high mass in the ancient cathedral where the Emperor Charlemagne had been buried over a thousand years before. To the accompaniment of an angelic boys' choir, the cardinal blessed RCK's life and his work, Pan-Europa. The assembled company then processed to the Kaiserpfalz, Charlemagne's medieval palace, for the formal part of the ceremony. Branches of spruce and fir still masked shell-pocked walls and windows, but even in its damaged state the ancient palace stood as a symbol of a united Europe, with echoes of imperial glory from the days of the Holy Roman Empire.

After the mayor had placed the deep-blue ribbon with its heavy gold medal around his neck, RCK in his speech of thanks called for a revival of the empire of Charlemagne in the spirit of the twentieth century, a clear reference to a future *political* goal of federation for the states of the European Coal and Steel Community, whose borders roughly coincided with that ancient empire. Once the ceremony concluded, the group moved back to the town hall and RCK made another speech, this time to the large crowd assembled outside in the square. With Idel at his side, and to enthusiastic applause from the audience, he stressed the spirit of Europe, of European identity, and of European patriotism, all conjured from the ruins of war to inspire and give life to a sense of European unity. That spirit, he declared, was what would ensure peace in the future among the peoples of Europe, even more importantly than their shared economic interests.

The award spoke of RCK's 'lifework for the establishment of a United States of Europe' and considered 'no one more worthy to be awarded for the first time with this, the highest distinction of the City of Aachen.' He was particularly proud to receive this honour, and above all to be the first to receive it. It allowed him to attend award ceremonies of later

RCK was the first recipient of the Charlemagne Prize, May 1950 in Aachen.

laureates, all considered major contributors in the service of European unity – Hendrik Brugmans, Alcide de Gaspari, Jean Monnet, Konrad Adenauer, Winston Churchill, George Marshall, Paul-Henri Spaak, Robert Schuman, Edward Heath, and Roy Jenkins among them.

After the ceremonies, RCK and Idel motored from Aachen to Bonn, where they dined privately with German chancellor Konrad Adenauer, and subsequently went south by easy stages up the valley of the Rhine to Switzerland, 'through the ruins of war and the blossoms of May' as RCK poetically describes it in his memoirs. But over this scene the bad news from America hung like a large black cloud. Donovan's committee would not fund the EPU, financing the European Movement instead.

In July that year RCK spelt out his objections to Donovan in an angry letter. 'Under the influence of Duncan Sandys and Josef Retinger, the two real leaders of the European Movement,' he wrote,

> you have broken off your original cordial relations to the EPU and become the American Agency of the European Movement, providing it with funds and publicity in the USA. As you knew, the European Movement has from the very start been most hostile to the EPU because the latter is promoting a genuine United States of Europe, while the EM has been set up under British leadership with the very purpose of preventing such a European Federation by organising Europe as an association of sovereign states. Of course, many members of the 'European Movement' are convinced federalists, but its leadership is definitely hostile to the idea of a European Constitution and a European Government.

He went on to regret that Donovan had become a victim of this unfair propaganda directed against the organization of which RCK was president. But he went even further in asserting that 'the great majority of Americans share our federal views concerning Europe, views that are upheld by most people of the European continent. Therefore,' he threatened in conclusion, 'we shall carry on our friendly contacts with American opinion, regardless of the attitude taken by the American Committee for a United Europe.'

It is hard to disentangle just what role in this imbroglio may have been played behind the scenes by Sir William Stephenson, the MI6 representative in New York, to whom Bill Donovan was much indebted for professional advice in setting up the OSS, and who had recently been awarded a knighthood in the 1945 New Year's Honours. Churchill certainly had much respect for Stephenson, and Retinger knew him as well.[4]

President Truman favoured European federation in principle, but in practice it came down to the influence of personalities. In American eyes, Churchill was a bigger player than any other European, certainly more influential than RCK. The European Movement was Churchill's movement, set up by his people, and Donovan had sided with him. RCK had lost. With his uncompromising reply he had permanently lost the funding as, after this exchange, not a dollar came to RCK or to the EPU from the American government.[5]

RCK had suffered reverses on two important fronts: in America, where he forfeited official government support, and in regard to the Schuman

Plan, where he had no hand in the new initiative. He redoubled his efforts to ensure the relevance of the EPU to contemporary political developments by pushing for it to stay ahead of the curve and to debate major European options before events determined the course of action.

In June 1950, barely two weeks after RCK and Idel arrived home in Gruben from the Aachen ceremony, the Korean War broke out. America and Britain found themselves deeply engaged in war again in the Far East, the first ever fought under the auspices of the United Nations. When the EPU Congress met in September in Konstanz, still more than six months before the European Coal and Steel Treaty was officially signed, it debated the need for a united West European military response to the Korean crisis. Should there be a European army, he wondered, and, if so, could it subsume German forces and so avoid creating a new national German army? Would German participation be better contained within a federation of the six states that were intending to join the European Coal and Steel Community, or in the larger structure of the Council of Europe?

The EPU decided in favour of the former, and a few weeks later Prime Minister René Pleven of France proposed a European Defence Community, based on the six member states of the Coal and Steel Community. His plan foresaw three stages in a journey towards political union: first the Coal and Steel Community, then a European army, and finally political union itself. Already the Council of Europe was losing its gloss, and the tighter-but-smaller ECSC – without Britain – promised more. Britain was invited to join in discussions about the European defence initiative but, while agreeing in principle on the need for co-ordination, the Labour government refused to take part unless the supranational elements that reflected the ECSC structure were changed. 'The Six' were in no mind to sacrifice what they had just so laboriously negotiated among themselves, so they went ahead without the United Kingdom and formally drew up the European Defence Treaty.[6]

SINCE THE KONSTANZ CONGRESS IDEL, who had as usual organized the event down to the last detail, had complained of heart problems. RCK is nowhere more specific, but in later writings noted that, from November 1950, she was lacking her habitual energy and was unable to keep up her usual busy schedule of activities. She had never enjoyed the winter, always regretted the passing of autumn, and looked forward to the arrival of spring.

So, in mid-February the following year, leaving Erika in Gruben, their chauffeur drove her with RCK by easy stages through Annecy, Valence, and Avignon to a quiet spot that they knew on the Riviera, at Le Rayol, between Hyères and St Raphaël, a region full of mimosa trees. There they spent three weeks resting, without even having post sent on to them. In mid-March they set off again, travelling slowly back to Geneva in stages, through Theoul, Cap d'Antibes, and St Paul. Easter was early that year, and as their house in Gruben was still snowbound, they decided to spend the weekend beside Lake Geneva near Nyon, at the Clos de Sanex, an old country house converted into a hotel. Idel enjoyed a lakeside walk on Good Friday and fed the swans that were nesting nearby. Erika came from Gruben by train to meet them on Saturday, and they spent a happy day together, enjoying the crocuses, the primroses, and the first violets that were flowering in the sheltered garden.[7]

On Easter Sunday, Idel suffered a severe heart attack. RCK summoned a specialist from Geneva. He could relieve her pain with morphine, but was unable to save her. Idel lost consciousness and died on the Tuesday after Easter. Ever an enthusiastic supporter of the peace movement, she had devoted all her energy to turning RCK's utopian vision of a united, peaceful Europe into reality. From this apolitical artist, he wrote, had grown a European patriot: 'With her death the curtain has fallen on the second act of my life, which began thirty-seven years earlier when I first met her. I lost with her my dearest friend and closest colleague.'

RCK was overwhelmed with messages of condolence from their extensive network of friends and acquaintances in political and artistic circles across the continent, including a telegram from the pope himself. Idel was buried in a private grave at the end of the meadow in front of their house in Gruben, dressed in her dramatic white burnous, the full-length, hooded, white cloak she had brought back from her first holiday with RCK in Morocco, shortly after the end of the Great War. The Pan-Europa flag was draped over her coffin. The simple inscription on her tombstone read *Ida Roland, Countess Coudenhove-Kalergi, 18 February 1881–27 March 1951.*

RCK was grief-stricken and bereft. Over her tomb he erected a sturdy wooden mausoleum, decorated in a traditional Swiss style and large enough to house his grave beside hers when his time should come. He wrote a heartfelt book in her memory, simply entitled *Ida Roland: In Memoriam.* It was illustrated with twenty-four large black-and-white photographs of Idel in her many stage roles, along with five more intimate and domestic portraits of their life together with Erika. RCK wrote of her as a woman and his wife, of her professional role as an actress as well as her work for

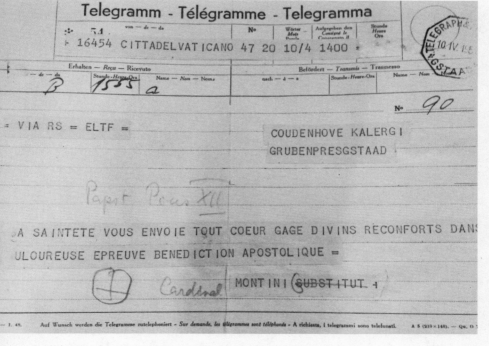

Telegram of condolence from Pope Pius XII on the death of Idel.

peace, of her love of travel as well as her pleasure in being a home-maker in Vienna, Gruben, and New York, and also of her efforts in America for Austrian post-war relief. Published in a limited edition by Phaidon, a fine-art publishing house in London, and printed in Italy, the book was given by RCK to friends and family as his heartfelt and lasting gesture of remembrance.

21

MONEY MATTERS

THE LIST OF THOSE who sent condolences to RCK in Gruben on the death of Idel was written out in a neat hand by Countess Alix Tiele-Bally, a widowed countess hovering close to the widowed count. Alix was a competent and not-unattractive woman in her late fifties who knew how to command and how to get things done. She was well educated and spoke French, German, and English fluently. She had been married to Wilhelm von Redern, Count Tiele-Winckler, an extremely rich German landowner with considerable property holdings in Silesia. She separated from him in the early 1930s, a few years before his death in 1938.

The countess's first husband had made her an allowance for life when they parted. But the fortunes of war had stopped that at the end of 1944. If this could in some way be recovered or continued, or if some share of his inheritance could be secured for her now, even so many years later, then RCK's financial concerns would be resolved. RCK and Alix may well have each thought the other to be richer than they actually were, and as time passed, each had to come to terms with the fact that, in this respect at least, they had deceived themselves.[1]

Alix came from a well-established Swiss family, the Ballys from Bad Ragatz, and had spent some years during the Second World War with the Swiss army, successfully organizing refugee reception in the Jura on the border with France. She had already visited RCK and Idel in Gruben on a number of occasions, though what the initial reason for contact was remains obscure, and so was acquainted with RCK's all-consuming passion for the United States of Europe. She had not been an enthusiast for his ideas on Europe from the very start, as Idel had been, but RCK appreciated that she found the concept of Pan-Europa self-evident, an obvious solution to the problems of interstate relations in Europe, not something that required discussion and argument. For her, it was simply a desirable as well as an inevitable development for Europe – like Switzerland, but on a larger scale. Countess Alix quickly enlarged her role as the widowed RCK's first port of call for solving numerous practical problems.

Money was always a concern for RCK. Over his lifetime there were periods of feast and periods of famine. He had a small sufficiency from his family inheritance, there was a steady stream of royalties from his publications, and Idel's considerable earnings had boosted their income in the 1920s and the 1930s. When he published *Pan-Europa*, he received generous backing for his political movement from Max Warburg, and the only condition imposed was that it should not be dominated by left-wing politicians. But that seed money lasted only three years, and from 1928 he had found it necessary to levy fees for membership of the Pan-Europa Union and to search for other funding.

About that time, Robert Bosch stepped into the breach and organized several German firms to contribute to a Swiss foundation set up to further Pan-Europa's aims. After the Nazis came to power, however, these funds also dried up. By then, the Austrian government was on hand to provide a grant, and the Czechoslovak and Romanian governments also donated funds that enabled RCK and Pan-Europa to work through the 1930s until Anschluss. However, after 1938, RCK's position had become precarious. He had relied on various undisclosed sources while he organized his activities in the months before and after the outbreak of war, and when he fled in 1940, despite having bank accounts in Paris and Zürich, he can have had little idea of where he would find subsequent funding for his work – and indeed for his and his family's livelihood. Because of the war he found it impossible to release funds from either Paris or Zürich, and American sources must have subsidized the cost of crossing the Atlantic and paying guarantees for him and his family as refugees in New York, as well as covering his living costs at least until he secured his teaching post at NYU.

His financial situation was equally uncertain in the troubled years immediately after the war when he returned to Europe. Only in the 1960s would he establish firm enough relations with the French government to receive a regular remittance, and to be able to ask them to subsidize the major conferences that he organized for Pan-Europa. For instance, the French Foreign Office is known to have paid three hundred thousand French francs to RCK for organizing two Pan-Europa congresses, one in Nice in 1960 and the other in Vienna in 1966.

In practical terms, RCK had always ensured that the finances of the Pan-Europa Union covered his and his family's current living expenses.

Donations to the Swiss foundation were tax exempt, and he lived on the foundation's moneys. Exceptionally, the property in Gruben was bought solely in Idel's name and with her own money. Following her death, RCK inherited the house jointly with Erika, and thereafter issues of money – both capital and income – would become inextricably entwined with relations between them and with Countess Alix, who increasingly took Idel's place in RCK's life, but without her predecessor's capital or earning power.

Perhaps it was inevitable that RCK would formalize his relationship with Alix by offering to marry her, but it came so soon after the death of Idel that it contributed in no small way to his estrangement from Erika. On 2 April 1952, barely a year after her mother's death, the couple were married in St Pierre de Chaillot, a modern church built just before the Second World War in the fashionable district of Paris 16ème. They chose it specifically because the architect, Émile Wood, had evidently been sympathetic to the cause of Pan-Europa. A red Christian cross surrounded by a golden circle – ironically Apollo's sun disc – the symbol of Pan-Europa, had been incorporated as a repeated motif in the marble floor of the nave.

In two letters at around this time, RCK wrote in quite different tones about his feelings for his second wife. In one he states somewhat matter-of-factly, 'Cooperation between Countess Alix and myself was set from the very beginning under a good sign. From sympathy and trust grew friendship, from friendship grew love, founded on the similarity of our temperaments and a similar attitude to life.' In another he wrote more lyrically that 'the miracle of this late love transformed the autumn of my life into a new spring.'

A few weeks after his second marriage, RCK legally adopted the countess's son, Alexander, a young man on the cusp of adult life. Alex, he thought, might support his mother in her new role with the Pan-Europa Union by taking on some of the organizational tasks of the future conferences they were planning. The two of them together would in this respect replace his first wife, making 'our work together as harmonious as our life together'.

With his somewhat distant, aristocratic manner, RCK always made out that money was a sordid topic that he would rather not deal with, but his correspondence shows that it was actually a major and continuing concern for him. When there was plenty, then it posed no problem; he could spend lavishly and be generous. But when it was short, he was required to fund-raise actively, even for relatively minor projects, and he found that burdensome. He had to ask among his circle of personal friends and well-disposed corporations to cover the expenses of the planned conference in Paris in the early 1950s, and to keep his secretarial team afloat. Later in life, one of his former secretaries recalled that, to avoid having to pay hotel bills himself, he would give the name of a sponsor, asking that the bill be sent on to their office, but he would generously tip staff gathered at the door when he left with whatever small change he had on him. Gone were the pre-war days in Vienna when there had been no money worries, with thousands of members of the Pan-Europa Union paying their subscriptions, and with the governments of Austria, France, Czechoslovakia, and Romania all generously backing the organization financially.

Pan-Europa maintained several offices, often located in elegant and expensive quarters of the various cities he frequented. When his project of a joint congress in Paris collapsed, RCK moved the office of Pan-Europa back to Switzerland, first briefly to Lausanne, at number 13 in the rue Centrale, then to Geneva, then to Bern, and later still to Zürich in the Rotes Haus, a prestigious modern office development in the Beethoven Strasse. The organization always had a small office in Basel in the Leopoldsgraben, centrally located in an up-market block of private apartments not far from the university. It was the legally registered address for the Pan-Europa Union, and there RCK as president met the treasurer and the secretary for the formality of Pan-Europa Union's annual general meeting. There was also an outpost in the Dreifaltigkeitsgasse in Salzburg, which RCK used as a networking location most years when attending the Salzburg Festival. The office was little more than a room with a secretary on stand-by duties when he was there, but it housed copies of correspondence and was difficult to close, as the rent for the room bolstered the secretary's personal income, and RCK did not have the heart to drop her from Pan-Europa's payroll, however modest the salary. All these offices involved ongoing costs that were not always readily covered.

From 1933 until Anschluss, RCK had been much helped in Vienna by Lilith Friedman, his private secretary, referred to by contemporary observers as his 'alter ego'. She was a safe pair of hands as far as managing the outflow of money was concerned, but when RCK and Idel escaped in 1938 to Switzerland, she fled to England. Although she lived on until 1998, she does not appear to have had any further involvement with RCK's affairs.

The finances of RCK's years in America remain opaque. His academic salary certainly provided a steady income, but not one large enough to maintain the lifestyle he and Idel led, and certainly not to cover the annual voyages to Europe of the first post-war years. When Idel died in 1951, RCK had to pay much more attention to financial matters, and he was not good at managing his money.

His first serious step was to remortgage the house in Gruben. The bank offered him sixty thousand Swiss francs, which was more than double what Idel had paid for the property originally, but nothing like its market value, and the interest rate was 6 per cent. Erika was a co-owner, but was persuaded not to object to this arrangement, as RCK settled a small regular monthly allowance for her, to be paid from the sum raised. The capital went, either as a loan or a tax-deductible donation, to the Pan-Europa Union. This account then covered his own and his new wife's living expenses, the allowance for Erika, and another for Alex.

In 1956, he took out an insurance policy against both his and Alix's lives, to ensure that whoever survived the other would have an income in their declining years. It cost him the princely sum of 14,757 Swiss francs per year. That must have been a drain on his finances, because when Alix died in 1967, he cashed it in and received a capital sum of 43,174 Swiss francs from the insurance company. By that time, he was courting his third wife, and that extra capital sum must have seemed most welcome.

Personal and professional finances had always been closely associated, and now they were inextricably muddled. Alix had prospects of compensation for wartime losses to property owned by her former husband, both in Silesia and in Nairobi, where he had also invested. But they proved to be frustrated prospects, since the Polish authorities would not countenance them, and the British authorities, who had seized the premises in Nairobi during the war as enemy property, were equally reluctant to recognize any claim. In any case, over the years the sum involved had been whittled down by inflation to an insignificant figure. The prospect of a share of some money from a smaller inheritance already received by Alix's brother-in-law, who lived near Hamburg, also came to nothing.

Following up all these possibilities took a great deal of RCK's time, and over several years he scribbled down numerous calculations of the historic value of the assets and their potential return over the intervening period. He filed these calculations away in hope, among his private papers, and incurred considerable expense with Swiss lawyers, particularly a Maître Arx in Zürich, only to reach unsatisfactory conclusions. He must have felt frustrated and considerably disappointed with the lack of results.

Relations between Erika and Countess Alix, little more than ten years older than her stepdaughter, quickly deteriorated after RCK's second marriage, as the two women clearly disliked each other. Erika was not happy with her new stepmother or with RCK's admiration for her new half-brother, Alex, who – at least initially – was enthusiastic in helping his mother promote the European cause.

Countess Alix was in any case happier away from the house in Gruben, which she so closely associated with RCK's first wife, and she and RCK increasingly spent their time together either in her flat in Zürich or travelling from hotel to hotel. During this time, he decided to rent out the now-mortgaged Gruben property. But RCK was no businessman, and letting the property was not a success. Prospective tenants demanded an expensive upgrading, which made the whole project uneconomic, and in 1954 RCK put the Gruben house up for sale.

The first sale fell through, but RCK was fortunate to find another buyer fairly quickly, an American businessman by the name of Wagner, who thought highly both of RCK and of Pan-Europa. He did not quibble about the asking price for the property, which was over two hundred and fifty thousand Swiss francs, five times the price Idel had paid for it twenty-five years earlier.

RCK's relations with Erika fell to their lowest point when they quarrelled over the sale of the house in Gruben. The trigger for their quarrel was the minor issue of who should meet what proportion of the estate agent's costs, but with little sense of self-awareness he accused his stepdaughter – just as his Japanese mother had accused him many years before – of a lack of obedience to parental wishes. Erika was in her late forties, and RCK was then sixty, and yet he could not accept that she would behave to her father (in point of fact, her adopted father) in such a way. His pressing need to sell the house, and have access to money, clouded his personal relations with her.

Sadly, the quarrel with Erika continued even after the sale of the house, this time focusing on how they should divide items of furniture and Idel's collection of folk art. Eventually, after each choosing a few items which they particularly wanted – and which could be seen to be of approximately equal value – they donated the remainder to a local folk museum. The rift between RCK and Erika was deep, and only healed a dozen years later, after the death of Alix.

The proceeds of the sale of the house initially seemed a large capital sum, but RCK's continuing outgoings soon drained it away. As regards food and drink, RCK was personally abstemious, but he travelled ceaselessly, Alix always with him, and they lodged in the best hotels. He dressed well in a classic style, and his clothes lasted, but he shopped only at establishments of the highest reputation, and the price was commensurate. His lifestyle did not come cheap. And now he needed more income to cover not only his household expenses, but also the costs of his political work as president of his renewed Pan-Europa Union. The mid-1950s were lean years for the Count.[2]

DESPITE THE FRUSTRATING PURSUIT of distant rewards, which must have been a major distraction for RCK personally, he continued to write diligently about both political and philosophical issues. Perhaps in an effort to maximize his royalties, he published three books in 1953 alone, with three different publishers in three different countries: *Die europäische Nation* (*The European Nation*), published in Germany; *Mutterland Europa* (*Europe, Our Motherland*), published in Switzerland; and *An Idea Conquers the World*, written in English and published by Hutchinson, a publisher with offices around the world, in London, New York, Toronto, Melbourne, Sydney, and Cape Town. RCK dedicated this last book to the memory of Ida Roland, Countess Coudenhove Kalergi, and it brought his earlier autobiographical *Crusade for Pan-Europe* up to date.

RCK concluded *An Idea Conquers the World* with the image of the mountaineer, turning to look down the long and steep path that lies below and behind him.

This book is the story of the long way that led Pan-Europe from the dream to a book, from a book to a movement, from a movement to a political achievement. It is the story of an idea which captured the imagination first of hundreds, then of thousands, then of millions – until it became a reality; like a rivulet in the mountains swelling to a river, to merge with the broad stream of human history.

RCK also made good use of this retelling of the story of his life by presenting a signed copy to Crown Prince Akihito when he met him at the Japanese embassy in Bern in 1953. The prince was much impressed, and remembered the event when he invited RCK on an official visit to Japan later in the 1960s, during which RCK and the Countess Alix would be received by his father, the Emperor Hirohito.

The year after RCK first met the crown prince, the European cause suffered a severe setback. In August 1954, a vote in the French Senate rejected the European Defence Treaty. This was the first formal setback for the cause of European integration since the Treaty of London had created the Council of Europe. RCK was both concerned and saddened, but noted the strength of national feeling in France, along with the decisive opinion of de Gaulle, whose party was strongly against the treaty. Indeed, following a letter from RCK, the General wrote in reply in June that year, diplomatically pointing out that: 'There is in effect still much to do to construct Europe and establish peace, and it seems that what governments have done to date has not been done with enough awareness of the reality of national positions.' The General's political fortunes were of great concern to RCK, who hoped that he might one day be of use to de Gaulle as president of France, hoping for support then from the French Foreign Office. That might be in the not too distant future, since the General was still active in French politics. It was certainly more likely – as turned out to be the case later, and we shall see when discussing RCK's relations with President de Gaulle – than there ever being any prospect of financial assistance for Pan-Europa from British sources.

22

THE BRITISH DILEMMA

PRE-WAR PAN-EUROPA had left open the issue of whether Britain would join with the continent or not, but with the establishment of the Council of Europe in 1949, the question of Britain's role within Europe appeared to have been resolved: Britain was 'in'. Indeed, it had been a moving force in negotiating and putting its stamp on the Treaty of London. That, however, was something of an illusion, since the Council of Europe promoted only a loose method of collaboration, proposing Conventions, a form of legal agreement that member states could sign up to in whole or in part, as they pleased. Despite the grand European rhetoric that accompanied the creation of this first European Assembly, any more-binding structure had – at British insistence – been avoided.

But Churchill, in Opposition, was uncomfortable with this British position. In a letter he wrote to RCK, dated 22 December 1949, he tellingly revealed his support for Britain in Europe: 'British participation is essential to the success of a European Union.' Churchill argued that they should try to strengthen the Council of Europe as a first step. RCK was already doubtful that the Council of Europe, while it included Great Britain, would lead to this desired goal.

The following year the Schuman Plan put the British question on the table again, and more insistently. Would Britain become a member of the European Coal and Steel Community (ECSC), and if it did, what role would it play in that clearly supranational organization? The Labour government's refusal to join effectively postponed any substantive answer to the question and left the country to face the dilemma again at a later stage.

Conservative success in the UK general election of October 1951 meant that Churchill, now prime minister again, would have a major voice in formulating an answer.[1] RCK wrote to congratulate Churchill on his victory,

28, HYDE PARK GATE,

LONDON, S.W. 7.

22 December, 1949.

My dear Count Coudenhove-Kalergi,

Thank you for your letter of November 2 and enclosures.

I do not agree that the solution to our problem is to create a Europe excluding Britain. As M. Schuman said in the French Chamber recently, and M. Spaak strongly reiterated in a public meeting which he addressed in London, British participation is essential to the success of a European Union. It is impossible to say at the moment what form this union will ultimately take, but I am sure that the next immediate step is to develop and strengthen by every means in our power the new Council of Europe.

With good wishes for Christmas & the New Year,

yours sincerely,

Winston S. Churchill

Count R. Coudenhove-Kalergi.

Churchill's December 1949 letter, asserting a European union without Britain would not be a success.

and noted that Duncan Sandys had been given a ministerial post in the new government. As a result of entering the government, Sandys stepped down from his role as secretary-general of the International Committee of the European Movement and was succeeded shortly afterwards by Paul-Henri Spaak, a good friend of RCK's. Spaak himself would soon resign from the chairmanship of the Council of Europe's Parliamentary Committee in disgust at the member states' failure to allow PACE to share power and become a constituent assembly, so he knew all about the British dilemma.

The combination of European political developments and RCK's personal circumstances in late 1951 persuaded him that this was a good moment to complete the work that Churchill had spearheaded with the 1948 Congress of Europe in The Hague in trying to bring together some of the disparate organizations that were promoting closer European ties. This was business that Churchill (and Sandys) had left unfinished as a result of the Conservatives' electoral success. Churchill's return to power in London encouraged RCK to propose a joint meeting of his Pan-Europa Union with Paul-Henri Spaak's European Movement, and the Union of European Federalists (UEF), led by Henrik Brugmans, to be held in Paris in early 1952. He hoped that all three organizations might press now for a continental federation, the original plan of Pan-Europa in its pre-war heyday.

RCK hoped that, if these three organizations could create a common front as a single non-governmental organization representing pro-Europeans in civil society, he might well play a prominent role in it, no longer undermined by Duncan Sandys, who, acting with the authority of Churchill, had put a brake on the early federalist ambitions of the immediate postwar years. It might also mean that RCK would have access to some of the American largesse that Donovan and the OSS were steering towards the European Movement. RCK was so sure that this was a feasible plan that he even moved the headquarters of Pan-Europa from Gstaad to Paris and installed Countess Alix in a suite of rooms in the Hôtel Raphael to make the necessary practical arrangements for the meeting while he travelled to Italy and Germany to gather support for his plan there.

But his optimistic assessment of the position of the UEF was misplaced. Hendrik Brugmans, in 1951 the second recipient of the Charlemagne Prize, was now rector of the College of Europe in Bruges, and had a self-esteem to equal RCK's. Neither he nor other members of the UEF wanted their federal vision diluted by the prospect of close collaboration and possible merger with organizations that did not unequivocally share the same commitment. Indeed, it was only a matter of months since the

UEF had distanced itself from the European Movement precisely because that organization – then still under Duncan Sandys's leadership – had shown itself unenthusiastic about the prospect of a federal Europe.

RCK's efforts for a joint meeting came to naught, and he pointedly attributed his failure to jealousy among the leadership of the federalists, who 'feared Pan-Europa as a rival rather than welcoming it as an ally'. Whatever the real reason, with optimistic over-confidence, he had misjudged the potential for common action. RCK dropped his idea at this stage, but kept good relations with Spaak, which would serve him very well a few years later.

RCK then had a problem on his hands with financing the European Parliamentary Union. Without American support, it was not bringing in enough money to cover its costs. In addition, his role as secretary-general did not give him free rein to express his own political opinions on current events as openly as he wished. He was, at least officially, obliged to consult the members of the Presidium before making public statements. So RCK decided to cut his costs by winding up the EPU and concentrated his attention on a restructured Pan-Europa Union which would give him freedom to range over the European scene at will and make whatever interventions he considered appropriate concerning political issues of the day.

It was widely recognized in political circles that the Council of Europe's Parliamentary Assembly had come about in large measure as a result of RCK's personal pre-war efforts and the pressure exerted more recently by his EPU. RCK was rightly proud of being the 'spiritual father' of the Council of Europe. The Gstaad meeting of the EPU in 1947 had demanded a constituent assembly that would shape the future of Europe. The Interlaken Conference in 1948 had pressed for a federal solution to the constitutional issue of a united Europe. The Venice Conference in 1949 had called on the Parliamentary Assembly of the Council of Europe to act as the voice of public opinion on key issues of European integration. That could all be put on the credit side of his account, but what the EPU could now do for him, or for Europe in the future, was not at all clear.

GOOD PERSONAL RELATIONS with Paul-Henri Spaak soon offered a way to solve the problem. The European Movement already had a parliamentary committee, formed by the breakaway group of former EPU parliamentarians led by Kim Mackay. He, however, had lost his parliamentary seat in the 1951 election and was no longer leading the 'rebels'. With Sandys now in government, RCK's offer to merge the EPU with the parliamentary wing of Spaak's European Movement in exchange for an enhanced status for himself inside the movement could not be seen, he felt, as a personal capitulation. On the contrary, it was a constructive gesture that strengthened the parliamentary wing of the European Movement.

The change of status came about in June the following year at a meeting in Luxembourg called by two of RCK's old friends, de Gaspari, the former Italian Christian Democrat prime minister, and Georges Bohy, the Belgian socialist leader. Bohy became chairman of a new Parliamentary Council of the European Movement, which incorporated the EPU, and RCK was compensated for losing the role of secretary-general of the EPU by being elected an honorary president of the European Movement. In that role, he took his place alongside Churchill, Adenauer, Schuman, and Spaak, as well as de Gaspari himself.

Justifiably, RCK looked on this as a singular honour. He was still in his mid-fifties and was the only honorary president who was not a professional politician, a fact he proudly reported to de Gaulle. He could never have hoped for such an honour while Duncan Sandys was in charge of the European Movement. He had now wound up the EPU through this successful merger, shed the increasingly onerous task of being its secretary general, saved money, and gained a formal status alongside some of his greatest political contemporaries. He was now free to restructure the Pan-Europa Union to ensure that he could continue to play a public role in European politics, maintaining his independence and commenting as he saw fit in the cause of uniting Europe.

Pan-Europa indeed needed to be restructured, because it was still – in legal, financial, and administrative terms – the same organization that he had set up in the 1920s. To make it fit now to be a pressure group in the mid-1950s, it needed a new structure and a new programme. He called two congresses in quick succession, one towards the end of 1954 and the other in March the following year, both in the Kurhotel in Baden-Baden. The first was to deal with the organization's structure and the second with its programme.

To achieve his aims, he brought together just a few key supporters to form his central committee. They did not need to be such major political figures in their own countries as he had called on before the war, and they did not need to represent a complete cross-section of political forces. It was enough that they came from different countries and all shared his vision of the potential for a united Europe. Changed circumstances demanded a changed structure to achieve his consistent goal, and he successfully drove those changes through the first Baden-Baden conference.

The new Central Committee for Pan-Europa consisted of just twenty-two members, one or two from each country, and with four representatives of the 'enslaved' east (from Estonia, Czechoslovakia, Hungary, and Poland), all well known to him and now living in the west. This was the small group of hand-picked friends and acquaintances with whom RCK was in direct and regular contact. He left it up to them if they felt the need to set up branches in their respective countries, but only if there were sympathetic volunteers willing to staff and finance them, as would turn out to be the case for France, Germany, Switzerland, and Austria. For RCK, the Central Committee was now the only administrative element that mattered.

This committee duly elected the vice-presidents that RCK proposed: Karl Arnold, André le Troquer, and Paul van Zeeland. Arnold was a well-respected Christian Democrat and former prime minister of North Rhine Westphalia and brought RCK political support in West Germany, where in any case RCK was on good personal terms with Konrad Adenauer. Le Troquer was president of the French National Assembly, and van Zeeland was also a former prime minister and now deputy-governor of the Belgian National Bank. These were high-level, experienced, and very busy figures nationally, and the last two regrettably resigned within a year or so. They were replaced by three equally well-trusted friends: Pierre Billotte, a former defence minister of France and close adviser to de Gaulle; O.M.E. Loupart, a member of the Supervisory Board of Philips at Eindhoven, who brought RCK access to a network of business contacts and financial support in European industrial circles;[2] and Walter Keller-Staub, a leading international lawyer from Switzerland, who acted as treasurer, giving RCK legal as well as accounting assurance.[3]

At the second Baden-Baden congress RCK established the new programme for the Pan-Europa Union, which concentrated the organization's concerns on just three sets of issues. The first was the narrow focus of Franco-German relations, with which RCK already had an outstanding track record. The second was issues relating to the central core of the 'Six', the member states of the ECSC, their possible enlargement to include Great Britain, and the prospect of a Common Market then under negotiation. The third was the wider circle of Europe as a whole, encompassing, in his words, 'the enslaved East and the free West'.

He planned these two congresses well and got from them just what he wanted: a hand-picked membership of committed supporters to assure political legitimacy, and organizational independence for himself as president to speak his mind on international affairs.

RCK's goal remained, as ever, the creation of the United States of Europe. The East-West dimension might prove to be the most challenging and – eventually – the most successful of the areas of Pan-Europa's future work. The second part of the programme, the British issue, was the most politically sensitive, and at that time the special role that Britain seemed to be playing outside the prospective European core was a growing concern.

SEEN FROM LONDON and through Churchill's eyes, the situation seemed quite different. He had achieved his primary goal of defeating the socialist government and was back in power now, and giving the country the alternative policies offered by the Conservatives. He and RCK stayed in touch, exchanging Christmas and New Year greetings, but the future of Europe was no longer a central concern of the prime minister. Their personal relations were still warm enough for RCK in 1953 to invite Churchill to write an introduction to his new book, *An Idea Conquers the World*, and Churchill obliged with a short foreword, in which he speculated in general terms that echoed his 1930 article on the prospects for a united Europe:

> The movement towards European solidarity which has now begun will not stop until it has effected tremendous and possibly decisive changes in the whole life, thought and structure of Europe. It does not follow even that this progress will be gradual. It may leap forward in a huge bound on spontaneous conviction. It may even prove to be the surest means of lifting the mind of European nations out of the ruck of old feuds and ghastly revenges. It may afford a rallying ground where socialists and capitalists, where nationalists and pacifists, where idealists and businessmen may stand together. It may be the surest of all the guarantees against the renewal of great wars.

For RCK, Churchill's endorsement was a considerable coup, as writing a foreword was a favour rarely granted by a busy prime minister. This time Churchill avoided giving any indication about where Britain would stand in the process of European integration. In *Pan-Europa*, the book that started his political movement in 1923, RCK stated clearly that England would not be a member of his continental union. It would be impossible, since England ruled a global empire and had global interests that were manifestly not European. He had added, however, 'It would be a serious and irreparable mistake for the Pan-Europa Union to set itself up in opposition to England or to allow itself to be misused for anti-British purposes.' The mutual advantages that Pan-Europa and Great Britain could both enjoy through peaceful engagement were so great that any alternative was obviously sub-optimal. Britain needed a security agreement that protected it from the continent, and such an agreement should offer each side advantages. RCK listed a few of them – more practical then than they may seem today – including an exchange of colonies in Africa, east and west, between France as a member of Pan-Europa and Great Britain as a closely aligned outsider, and additional European settlers for the British dominions. Good relations between them would ensure regional security and be an exemplary peace project for the rest of the world.

Little more than a year after publishing his book, RCK had visited London, and his conversations there had shown him the reluctance of the British political elite in the 1920s to envisage any choice between Pan-Europa and the British Empire. Both government and the private sector were concerned much more with the future of Empire than with the future of Europe. They avoided thinking about a solution to the British identity by disregarding Europe as an option. For them, the future of Europe and the future of Britain were only indirectly related issues.

After the Second World War, Britain was a victor militarily, but virtually bankrupt economically. It was nominally head of a vast subject empire that was in practice being reconstructed as a commonwealth of independent states. For some political commentators, the role of Britain was to stay as close to America, the western superpower, as possible. For others, its role was likely to be more advantageously determined by drawing closer to its continental neighbours. The division 'for or against Europe' cut across political party lines. In sum, Britain was an unhappy country, failing economically, pulled this way and that, in and out of the closer union to which its continental neighbours, with a very different history, had committed themselves. Europe was now a political question to which Great Britain had to find an answer, and for economic reasons the question was growing more and more pressing.

Pan-Europa meanwhile had morphed from an idealistic programme for European union in the 1920s, through opposition to Nazism through the 1930s, to a pressure group and think-tank in exile during the war, planning the post-war reconstruction of the continent. Now that the Council of Europe, in particular its Parliamentary Assembly, was functioning as a locus for European political debate and, hard on its heels, the ECSC was demonstrating clearly the success of supranational decision-making in contemporary Western Europe, the first practical steps towards European unity had become hard facts. For RCK, one of the most important contemporary tasks now for Pan-Europa was to formulate an answer to the largest outstanding issue: solving the British dilemma.

CHURCHILL HAD ALWAYS AVOIDED answering the British question unequivocally. He sought refuge in an image of three overlapping circles, with the homeland at their centre. One circle was Britain's European commitment, the second was the Commonwealth, and the third was the transatlantic relationship with the United States. He was certainly in favour of European integration, perhaps even unification, but he was not in favour of exclusively privileging any one of Britain's three spheres of influence by making it dominate over the others. Constructive ambiguity was the order of the day. It was a temporizing position that served the Conservative Party well enough, and Churchill retired from active politics in 1955 with the dilemma still unresolved.

He was succeeded by Anthony Eden, and the very next year the already-reduced status of Great Britain was brought home to a wider public by the disastrous Suez affair, a botched and illegal invasion of Egypt in response to the nationalization of the Suez Canal by President Nasser. The invasion was abruptly stopped by the United States with the threat that both the British and French currencies would be weakened, and their international credit blocked, if they did not halt hostilities immediately.

France and Britain responded to this humiliation in different ways. The French response was to intensify economic and financial co-operation with its European partners, while the British response was to align itself ever more closely with Washington, where power demonstrably now lay. From this time dates the cooling of France's participation in NATO, and Britain's increasing reliance on America in defence and security issues.

The Europeans, however, did not give up on Britain, led now by Harold Macmillan following elections in 1957. When the Six began informal talks that would later lead to the Treaty of Rome, the Conservative government was invited to join, but the British government was torn both ways. After some hesitation, it pulled out of the negotiations that led to the creation of the European Common Market (EEC) In the same year, 1958, it signed a defence agreement with the United States and also set up the European Free Trade Association (EFTA), seven states – all the others much smaller than Britain – which planned to compete with the already well-established Six. Europe was literally at Sixes and Sevens, divided between the EEC, with France the dominant power, and the EFTA, centred on the United Kingdom.

To continentals it looked as if Britain – with American support – was returning to the policy of divide and rule, frustrating the creation of any coherent European union. To overcome this, RCK suggested publicly that the two trading blocs should merge. RCK had met Harold Macmillan at the Congress of Europe in The Hague more than ten years previously, and was well aware that he appreciated the nature of the British dilemma as well as any other politician of the day. Faced with this, Macmillan sought to divide his favours between Europe and America. Perhaps the United Kingdom might satisfy America and Europe at the same time, might both have its cake and eat it.

In January 1961, under his leadership, Britain applied to join the EEC. The Benelux countries were all keen that Britain should join them in the EEC, because they saw in her a third power able to balance the developing co-operation between France and Germany. France, now led by General de Gaulle, feared that Britain would upset the balance achieved with Germany and deprive France of its leadership role on the continent. With its continuing transatlantic links, Britain might also act as a Trojan horse for American economic interests.

RCK knew well that the arguments were evenly balanced and interests in Britain divided. Both major parties in Britain were split by internal disagreements on the question of Europe. That autumn, Hugh Gaitskill, leader of the Opposition, explained in his speech to the Labour Party Conference the reasons why he thought Britain should be cautious about too close an association with the developing EEC. 'This is not an open-and-shut issue, this is not a clear-cut thing, not a matter of either going in unconditionally or staying out on any terms. On the contrary the arguments, when you think them through, massive and difficult as they are, are evenly balanced: and whether or not it is worth going in depends on the conditions of our entry.'

But when he came to sum up, Gaitskill was scathing about the Conservative government's ability to say one thing to one audience and another thing to another.

Of course, the Tories have been indulging in their usual double talk. When they go to Brussels they show the greatest enthusiasm for political union. When they speak in the House of Commons they are most anxious to aver that there is no commitment whatever to any political union. We must be clear about this. It does mean, if this is the idea, the end of Britain as an independent European state. I make no apology for repeating it. It means the end of a thousand years of history.[4]

In July 1963, General de Gaulle shocked Europe and London by issuing a veto that prevented Britain joining the EEC. But his 'Non' did not close the debate in Britain, where political and public opinion was growing more polarized. The British dilemma – to join or not to join Europe – featured in the October 1964 elections, which brought to power a Labour government with a very small majority, headed by Harold Wilson. With some difficulty, Wilson persuaded his cabinet to make a formal application to join the EEC.

De Gaulle considered carefully the implications of this second approach. RCK shared his concerns about the supranational nature of the nascent European institutions in Brussels. Would the United Kingdom be a partner in leading the group, joining France, Germany, and maybe Italy to give intergovernmental leadership to this embryonic supranational entity, making it clearly confederal and blocking off the road to a federal state? An informal note to this effect from the French president was passed via the British ambassador to Prime Minister Wilson. This might open a path both to resolving the British dilemma and satisfying at the same time France's demand for political leadership by the larger states. But unfortunately, the note was made public, either intentionally or accidentally still appears unclear, and it caused serious offence to the smaller European member states. To them it seemed that France was inviting Britain to stitch up the future of Europe without consulting them at all.

To regain the moral high ground, de Gaulle very publicly and dramatically rejected the second British application at a news conference at the Elysée Palace in November 1967. At this well-stage-managed event, attended by more than a thousand diplomats, civil servants, ministers and journalists, the president accused Britain of a 'deep-seated hostility' towards European construction. He said London showed a 'lack of interest' in the Common Market and would require a 'radical transformation' before joining the EEC. 'The present Common Market is incompatible with the economy, as it now stands, of Britain,' he said, and went on to list a number of factors – from working practices to agriculture – which, in his view, made Britain unfit and unable to join Europe.

RCK had stayed close to de Gaulle throughout the post-war years, in particular during his years in the presidency. But the General's hold on power in France eventually waned. In 1968 he narrowly survived the widespread student revolt, but resigned the following year when he lost a referendum on regional reforms. Two years later he died, and in the same year Edward Heath, who had included negotiating Britain's membership of the European Communities in the 1970 Conservative manifesto, became prime minister.

Heath had already forged a personal friendship with the General's successor as French president, Georges Pompidou, who soon found a convenient opportunity to lift the French veto. Pompidou had very different ideas about European unity from de Gaulle, having been a member of the Pan-Europa Union in his youth, and he was quite open to the argument that the existing structures of the European Communities would be strengthened by accepting Great Britain as a new member. Prime Minister Heath agreed. When the House of Commons approved the European Communities Bill in 1972 on the basis of the negotiations that Heath had by then successfully concluded, the prime minister could claim, 'Many millions of people right across the world will rejoice that we have taken our rightful place in a truly united Europe.' However, the decision taken in London was won only with support from a breakaway group of Labour MPs who voted with the government, and both the major parties and wider public opinion in Britain continued to be seriously divided on the issue.

RCK lived just long enough to welcome the momentous British decision as the European Communities Act was voted into law. But he could have had no idea of how the issue of Britain's role in Europe would continue to bedevil British politics in years to come, right up to the present day.[5]

23

'MON CHER AMI, MON PRÉSIDENT'

RCK'S RELATIONSHIP with de Gaulle was both professional, personal, and mutually beneficial. It had begun with RCK's 1943 invitation to the General to assume the leadership of post-war Pan-Europa, and it endured to the day de Gaulle died.

RCK's admiration for de Gaulle dated from his famous 1940 radio appeal on the BBC for all French people to continue resistance against the Nazi aggressor. But it was not until de Gaulle became head of the provisional French government in Algiers in 1943 that RCK started to correspond regularly with him. Initially, he wrote to offer him the honorary presidency of the Pan-Europa Union, suggesting he take over where Aristide Briand had left off, and build not only a free France but a united Europe as well. De Gaulle politely declined, arguing that, while the war was still in progress, his socialist and communist compatriots would not understand such a constructive gesture towards their as-yet-unvanquished enemy. But first contact had been made, and RCK continued to write to the general and share with him his ideas on the future of Europe, even though the general was often more cautious in reply than RCK would have liked.[1]

General de Gaulle served briefly as prime minister after the war, but then spent nearly a dozen years in the political wilderness, leading a relatively small group of loyal Gaullist members in the National Assembly until his return to power in May 1958. During those wilderness years, he had not had his hands on the levers of power, and decisions had been taken internationally with which he did not agree. When he came back to power, however, the Treaty of Rome had been ratified by all signatory states, including France, and although he did not like the supranational element in the Coal and Steel Community, the Common Market or Euratom, he simply had to live with it. He realized that any one state, even France, had more to lose than to gain by denouncing or breaking that treaties.

RCK and the General had been in correspondence throughout these wilderness years, and they found much to admire not only in each other's ideas of contemporary politics but also in each other's character. To RCK, the General seemed a 'great and lonely man, whose actions were always guided by the compass of his conscience, and whom many of his contemporaries found strange and uncomfortable.' De Gaulle may well have thought similarly about RCK's actions, respecting what he saw as a strong conscience and a clear awareness of right and wrong. On one occasion, when de Gaulle was approached by Duncan Sandys about the merger of pro-European movements soon after 1945, he asked his advisers, 'Does Coudenhove think it is all right? If he does not, then it stinks.' In a letter to RCK much later, in 1966, he described RCK's personality in 'this great and fine struggle' for European unity as 'convinced, enthusiastic, subtle, and above all with an understanding for human nature'.

From an early stage in their relationship, RCK was certainly prepared to go the extra mile for de Gaulle. In December 1944, RCK shared with him a memorandum on the future of Europe that he had prepared for the US wartime intelligence agency, the OSS, in Washington with a view to influencing State Department policy. In 1946 and 1947 he also shared with him sensitive elements of his correspondence with Churchill. Mutual admiration and practical help at this level, however, did not exclude disagreements about policy.

RCK never fell into the error of thinking that de Gaulle must agree with him on everything, nor that he had to agree with the General on everything either. For him, de Gaulle's genius was to see that Europe could have a global role alongside America and Russia, and that, in order to achieve it, France needed to encourage a more closely integrated Europe. De Gaulle accepted that the key to that was close Franco-German co-operation.

RCK focused on this, and he played an important part in repairing Franco-German relations after the war. It took many years, but French antipathy towards its traditional enemy – les boches – was eventually replaced by an increasingly relaxed approach to a friend and ally across the Rhine.

RCK proposed that de Gaulle, now leader of his own opposition movement in France, the Rassemblement du Peuple Français, or RPF, should visit Aachen and deliver a speech in German that could be broadcast to Germany. Bolstered by the status given him by the recent award of the Charlemagne Prize, RCK assured de Gaulle that he would arrange everything for January 1952. The speech, he added, would have as powerful an effect as Churchill's speech in Zürich five years earlier. The General initially accepted, but a few weeks before the proposed event he called RCK to his offices in Paris where, in the presence of his closest members of staff, he regretfully acknowledged that it was still too soon to reach out over the Rhine. Many of his French supporters would not understand the importance of this gesture towards their former enemy, he said, and he feared they might desert him.

Two years later, de Gaulle's party was still unable to leap over its national shadow. Its opposition to the European Defence Treaty contributed in a major way to the French Senate's refusal to ratify the agreement, frustrating German aspirations to normalize relations with its European neighbours on equal terms.

When de Gaulle assumed power in 1958, RCK's restructured Pan-Europa Union was in the midst of an upheaval of its own. In 1959 it was divided as never before over the newly created European Economic Community's efforts to choose a capital for Europe, or at least where to site its institutions: the European Commission, the Council of Ministers, and the European Parliament. It may well have seemed a secondary and merely symbolic issue to de Gaulle, who had much more substantive political problems to deal with, including an incipient revolt of the army in Algeria. But it was an issue on which RCK's personal enthusiasm badly clouded his political judgment, and he only just avoided a clash with the General.

The location of the EEC's main institutions was seen by RCK as a decision as important for contemporary Europeans as the revolutionary American colonists choosing Washington for their capital two hundred years previously. The institutions themselves had reduced the short list to just three candidates: Milan, Brussels, and Strasbourg, and their final choice would determine the capital of Europe.

The majority of French deputies in the National Assembly and the Senate had indicated their preference for Paris, and RCK, a loyal French citizen by adoption, threw himself enthusiastically into the campaign for Paris in the name of Pan-Europa. But the support of the mayor of Strasbourg, Pierre Pflimlin, had been vital for de Gaulle and the adoption of the new French constitution, and he was now calling in political favours, in particular from the president. The French government refrained from promoting Paris as the political capital of the continent, instead diplomatically supporting Strasbourg against the competition from Belgium and Italy.

There now ensued a complicated dance involving national governments, media opinion, and parliamentarians, all profiling themselves and their choices, declared or preferred. Into that dance stepped RCK and the Pan-Europa Union.

RCK misread the internal politics of his adopted country and rode to the rescue – or so he thought – for what he imagined was de Gaulle's obvious choice. He campaigned for 'a European city in the heart of the Paris region'. In May 1959, his campaign culminated in an open letter to the foreign ministers of the six member states of the European Economic Community, widely published in the European press, appealing for them to choose Paris.

Inside the Pan-Europa Union, the outspoken opinion of RCK as president on the question of the new capital of Europe triggered two important resignations: Pierre Pflimlin himself, and Paul Van Zeeland, a former prime minister of Belgium, the one supporting his own city, Strasbourg, and the other his own capital, Brussels. RCK was reluctantly obliged to accept the resignations of these two old friends of his, but he doubtless noted – at least to himself – that he had made a mistake. He had not even consulted them when he published his open letter, and he had gone against the new French president's preference. His mistake had lost him two political allies and, added to that, he did not win the day, since the European Parliament ultimately chose Strasbourg. An opportunity to repair relations vis-à-vis the General soon presented itself, however, when RCK was able to help him promote one of his other European goals.

DE GAULLE WAS CONCERNED that the large states in the EEC – specifically Italy and Germany – should offer stable government and that no unwanted upheavals there should have negative effects in France.

In Italy, the problem was the size of the Communist Party which, although evolving slowly towards democratic socialist policies, still commanded a third of the popular vote. France wanted a strong Christian Democrat Party to maintain power there, to frustrate the prospects of the French communists. And the General also wanted to strengthen the Christian Democrats in West Germany, where they were led by Konrad Adenauer. The Social Democratic Party had only recently stepped back from a more extreme socialist programme, and de Gaulle feared it might still be open to blandishments from the German Democratic Republic, or GDR, the former Soviet Occupied Zone of East Germany.

The situation in West Germany was even more worrying than in Italy, since the GDR was promoting what it called the 'Deutschland Plan'. This plan, backed by the Soviet Union, offered West Germany the prospect of unification with East Germany, but the price would be to make the entire country neutral. In the geopolitical struggle between east and west, between the Warsaw Pact and NATO, neither France – nor America – could afford to lose West Germany.

RCK concentrated on this issue, knowing that stability in West Germany – and by that both he and de Gaulle meant a continuing dominance of the political scene by Adenauer and the Christian Democrat party – was the *sine qua non* of good Franco-German relations. He sent memoranda about the German question to both Paris and Bonn, outlining the need for grassroots activity to persuade the trade unions and the media that the plan was a trap being laid by Moscow and not in the interests of West Germany at all. Over twelve months he conducted an extensive publicity campaign to halt the Social Democrat Party's drift towards neutrality, and claimed in a letter to the general in April that he had sent up to ten thousand letters to leading Social Democrats and to the media, contributing in a major way to the SDP's reversal of its previous policy. The 'Deutschlandplan', he proudly announced, had been defeated

Just as he had sided with Dollfuss in Austria in 1933, RCK now offered his services to de Gaulle. He attended a formal lunch at the Elysée Palace in March 1961, which was chaired by the president in honour of his finance minister, Wilfrid Baumgartner, previously Governor of the Bank of France. RCK was seated next to Madame de Gaulle and opposite the president, and the decision to grant him a retainer may have been made around that time. From the early 1960s, he received an allowance from French public funds amounting to the equivalent each year of a retired ambassador's pension, perhaps as much as a hundred thousand pounds sterling annually at today's value. It relieved RCK of the major part of his day-to-day financial concerns, even if it may not have actually covered all the expenses of his and Countess Alix's lifestyle.

For political reasons General de Gaulle did not look kindly on the European treaties that his administration had inherited when he came to power, but he was realist enough to see that the treaties formed a basis for close economic integration among the six member nations, which increased national wealth and stimulated job creation and growth, all of which he welcomed. The European unity he was really interested in, however, was not measured solely in economic terms. Indeed, he doubted it could ever grow simply from economic integration. For de Gaulle,

President de Gaulle, the incarnation of France, hosted lunch at the Elysée Palace, with RCK seated opposite, next to Madame de Gaulle.

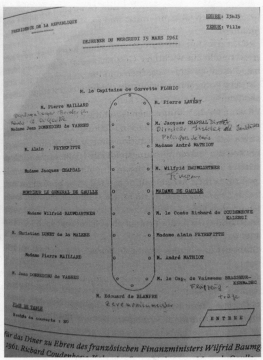

European unity had to be based on the reality of nation states, their lived history and their sense of identity, not on what he considered a lifeless theory of supranationalism. For him, the economic integration of the Six through the European Economic Community was only a small part of the story. RCK completely shared this view.

What was needed was a larger framework that included both political, security, educational, and cultural aspects, something that touched the heart rather than simply appealed to the brain or the bank account. And for de Gaulle as for RCK, it should be established under the authority of the heads of the elected governments involved, not borne on the shoulders of national civil servants delegated to Brussels. He valued in particular a close association between France and Germany as the essential building block of a united Europe that would have a political weight in world affairs vis-à-vis the United States of America and the Soviet Union. That political weight would, however, be expressed as much through its military and security strength as in economic and trading terms, and these former matters were not the concern of Brussels.

By the end of the 1950s, Europe was split into not just two halves – East and West – but Western Europe itself was split between the customs union of the EEC and the free-trade bloc of EFTA. RCK urged a merger of the two associations. They should form, he suggested, 'one European customs union', a goal he had championed since the 1920s. But from the start it was clear that the EEC, with its embryonic single market, was growing faster and would dominate economically. EFTA would have to align itself with the EEC as best it could, not vice versa. Indeed, within eighteen months of setting up EFTA, the United Kingdom itself, the moving force in the organization, along with two other EFTA members, Denmark and Norway, as well as Ireland, applied to join the EEC.[2]

With the economic security of the continent increasingly assured through the EEC, and the prospect of a neutral and united Germany eliminated, conditions seemed ripe for a new French initiative to organize the leadership of Europe. De Gaulle's insisted that leadership of the continent could only emerge from co-operation among the big players – France, West Germany, and Italy. The interests of small states would be looked after by those larger states nearby who were capable of defending their own and their neighbours' long-term security. RCK floated this suggestion in *Le Monde*, describing it as 'the Plan of the President', and in September 1960 de Gaulle himself outlined his ideas at an international press conference in Paris. His subsequent instructions to his prime minister, Michel Debré, underlined his determination: 'The Europe that we want will be achieved through cooperation' and over time it will put the Brussels institutions of the Common Market 'in their place'. This plan, later named the Fouchet Plan after the French ambassador who chaired its steering committee, aimed to ensure that Europe would really be organized by the big states, the ones that really mattered, on an intergovernmental, not a supranational, basis.

THIS APPROACH WAS ANATHEMA to the man responsible more than any other for the successful development of the inclusive and supranational EEC: Jean Monnet. His career had strangely intertwined in its ambition with that of RCK, and his brainchild was the cluster of European institutions in Brussels – in particular the ECSC – along with the 'Community method' of identifying economic interests that all nations shared and attempting to pool their responsible development. The international pressure group that Monnet set up in 1955 after he left public office as president of the European Coal and Steel Community – his Action Committee for the United States of Europe (ACUSE) – went into top gear to lobby against de Gaulle's proposal.

But for RCK the Fouchet Plan held out a good possibility of giving priority to political issues, stressing foreign policy and security, and providing for Europe the strong leadership in the wider world that he had always wanted it to have. For him this was far more important than concentrating on small steps taken together in the general economic interest as the only path to European unity. And equally importantly, it was also a means for clearly distinguishing his approach to European unification from that of Jean Monnet.

The detailed elaboration of the plan was the responsibility of the Fouchet Commission, chaired by the French ambassador to Denmark, Christian Fouchet, and composed of representatives of all six states who were members of the EEC. The Plan foresaw the creation of a European Council of the Heads of Government, meeting regularly to settle the most important issues, with subordinate councils of ministers dealing with foreign affairs, defence, culture, and education, as well as economics and trade. Only these two last topics would be managed within the supranational Brussels structures already established. For the other topics, the framework would be traditionally international, overseen by the heads of government.

For de Gaulle, establishing such an overall structure would lead to a *directoire* – a leadership group – where the larger nation states would automatically carry more weight than the smaller ones. For him this became a prerequisite for any enlargement of the EEC. Leadership should clearly be held by the large states, potentially including the United Kingdom if it eventually joined the Six, and even if it brought some of the smaller EFTA states with it.

Unsurprisingly, the Fouchet Plan was opposed by the smaller states of the EEC, led by Belgium. Paul-Henri Spaak insisted that Great Britain must join the EEC before talks on the Fouchet Plan could proceed further. Only Great Britain, he argued, could balance French predominance in any *directoire*, so it would be better to wait until the British joined the EEC. Negotiations on the Fouchet Plan among the Six were deadlocked for many months, and subsequently abandoned in 1962. But the idea never died, as the two problems – leadership and the supranational nature of European union – remained unresolved.

In the eyes of both de Gaulle and RCK, the close relationship between France and Germany was the bedrock on which the increasing unity of Western Europe would rely. It was also the key to its eventual expansion to include other democratic states. Their vision went beyond the confines of the Six and the Seven to consider how the whole of the continent might one day be brought together, 'from the Atlantic to the Urals', but it was clear that only when the western half of Europe was united and strong could the re-unification of the divided continent become a realistic goal of foreign policy. The General realized that France could not aspire to be come a world power alongside the United States and the Soviet Union unless it could carry the rest of Western Europe with it, but in doing so it should also keep open the door to co-operation with Eastern Europe as well.

In April 1961, army generals in Algeria launched a coup against de Gaulle. RCK immediately wrote to support the president: 'By defending France, you are defending Europe.' A few weeks later, after de Gaulle had faced down the revolt, RCK wrote again to congratulate him specifically on his broadcast to the French people, which, RCK asserted, was the secret weapon that had led to his triumph. Broadcasting across frontiers was the instrument that would allow him to overcome the *impasse* in Europe as well, he suggested.

ECHOING HIS PREVIOUS OFFER for de Gaulle to broadcast a speech to Germany as influential as Churchill's Zürich speech of 1946, RCK suggested that the president broadcast in German to the people of Germany during a forthcoming bilateral meeting with Chancellor Adenauer in Bonn. In that way he would 'win the hearts of millions of supporters for the cause of European confederation and for Franco-German friendship'.

RCK strongly endorsed de Gaulle's strategy of bilateral political co-operation with the German chancellor, and he was personally invited by de Gaulle as '*l'ami du Président*' to the solemn mass in Rheims Cathedral in July 1961 to celebrate Adenauer's state visit to France. A friend of both of them, and exceptionally a member of neither national delegation, RCK sat behind the two leaders in the cathedral, public recognition of his import-ant personal contribution to reconciliation between the two countries.

He enthusiastically welcomed the signature of the Elysée Treaty of friendship in January 1963, which signalled the formal end of a long history of Franco-German rivalry and pledged both countries to prior mutual consultation on all important questions of foreign policy, including

EEC matters. It also put more public funds into strengthened cultural co-operation across the Rhine, with co-ordinated youth policies, enhanced language learning, town twinning, and increased tourism. For RCK, Franco-German understanding was to be the basis for a European awareness that would eventually underpin European patriotism. On the starting point both RCK and the General were in complete agreement, even if the General abstained from contradicting RCK's espousal of the distant goal of European patriotism.

While relations across the Rhine were improving all this time, relations between the superpowers, the United States and the Soviet Union, were in free fall. The Cuban missile crisis in October 1962 turned a spotlight on the United Nations as the locus for global debate, rather than any regional arrangement such as the EEC. This emphasis on the UN stimulated RCK to give de Gaulle some outspoken and undiplomatic advice. He had witnessed the creation of the United Nations in San Francisco nearly twenty years earlier, and at that time had canvassed the idea of a series of regional chapters. His own proposals then echoed the proposal he had put to Sir Eric Drummond in the League of Nations back in the 1920s, but it gained hardly any more traction then than previously. Now he revealed in a letter to de Gaulle his growing hostility to the way that the UN was expanding too quickly in the age of decolonization. It risked marginalizing Europe, and RCK could see in this much more of a threat than an opportunity.

In controversial terms he wrote, 'The UN represents for Europe, indeed for the whole of the white race, the worst danger since the days of Genghis Khan.' Over time, he feared that the nations of a growing Afro-Asian bloc would outnumber the static number of 'white' European and American states, creating a stalemate in the UN and 'making the Soviet block and its supporters the arbiters of the fate of the West'. By taking an initiative now, he suggested, de Gaulle could head off this disaster. If France called Americans, Russians, and Europeans to a peace conference to end the Cold War, it would bring to the same table almost all the representatives of the white race in the whole world, and these states had overwhelming military force at a global level. From a truce between these two blocs would grow a Council for Peaceful Coexistence, which would not only save the world from nuclear disaster but could become the nucleus of a new organization to replace the UN.[3] RCK took a surprising position for someone of mixed race himself, but it was perhaps an indication of how far he identified himself as essentially European.

On another occasion, RCK wrote to recommend to de Gaulle that, as a powerful president, he could bring about the United States of Europe by force of will. Undiplomatically, he pointed to the example of Bismarck, who, surrounded by larger powers beyond the borders of Prussia, had united the variety of small German states in the previous century. All that was needed now was the endorsement of de Gaulle's leadership by a Europe-wide referendum:

> Europe today is in a situation analogous to Germany a hundred years ago ... Only a strong and solid Federation, led by a President with the authority of election by universal suffrage, will be capable of solving this problem. Europe's youth, all those born after 1930, would be ready to march towards the United States of Europe – if only they had a Leader. They would follow you with enthusiasm if you would only place yourself at the head of this glorious revolution.

Two months later, the General undertook an official journey to Germany and, in addition to governmental discussions in Bonn, he visited Cologne, Dusseldorf, Hamburg, Munich, and Frankfurt. Everywhere he was greeted by enthusiastic crowds, many of them young people. In Frankfurt he delivered a perceptive and encouraging speech in German that was also broadcast nationally. In it, he asked young Germans to help build a common understanding between the two nations as the bedrock of a united Europe that would reflect all that was beautiful, just, and good in Western civilization. De Gaulle had translated the original French text into his own fluent German, but the sentiment and even the vocabulary were as if they had come from RCK himself, who may well have had a hand in drafting an early version of the speech.

When RCK was invited to Vienna on the fiftieth anniversary of his year group of Theresianum alumni to address those who had matriculated with him in summer 1914, he took as his theme 'Austria and Europe', and it was an opportunity for him to consider the prospect of eventual reunification of the two halves of the continent. He spoke from the historical perspective of his own and his audience's experience, pointing out that, from the headquarters of the EEC, 'The Iron Curtain looks like the border of Eastern Europe, but in Vienna it feels like a bleeding wound that splits Europe in half.' Healing the division was as much a task of reconciling ideologies and historical animosities as of balancing out the economic interests of member states, he argued, as much a question of hearts and minds as of national accounts.

Austria's role, he suggested, should not be passive neutrality between west and east, but an active policy of bringing the two sides of the divided continent together again. It was a human as well as a political problem. In the long term, the example of Austria, restored to independent nationhood barely ten years earlier by agreement between the wartime Allies, presented the perspective of peaceful union for the whole continent. As ever, RCK was far-sighted. The changes he foresaw came about only some years after his death, when the Helsinki Accords very slowly eased Soviet control over Eastern Europe. But he had identified the problem and suggested both solutions and methods well ahead of others.

ALL HIS LIFE de Gaulle had time for RCK. He appreciated his foresight, the breadth of his vision, and his lateral thinking, even as the president tempered this admiration with his own practical concern for everyday politics. Just before Christmas 1966, RCK sent him a German copy of his newly published autobiography *Ein Leben für Europa* (*A Life for Europe*), and de Gaulle replied with his congratulations, addressing RCK not just as *Monsieur le Président* (of Pan-Europa) but adding for the first time *'Mon cher ami'*. De Gaulle clearly read the book in detail and, in his reply, he wrote that he found in it

> your passionate enthusiasm for an idea, your ceaseless activity pursuing it in the midst of a continent and a world in tatters, the sure and certain progress of both a hope and a plan, despite events which seem to counter them at every turn. And there is also a magisterial description of world politics during the better part of half a century, along with lively and moving portraits of leaders of opinion and of states who had responsibility for public affairs at that time.

RCK's loyalty to de Gaulle was heartfelt and lasting, as shown in 1965 when he felt obliged to resign from his much-cherished role as honorary president of the European Movement. At a meeting in Nice, the European Movement voted in support of François Mitterrand as Socialist candidate in the French presidential elections. This was an overtly anti-Gaullist gesture, and RCK argued that the European Movement should be above party politics. In any case, Europe could never be united without France, he insisted, and France was represented, indeed incarnated, by de Gaulle. Consequently, he resigned his position. Some months later, he took great delight in personally congratulating de Gaulle on defeating Mitterrand in the presidential election.

332 | Hitler's Cosmopolitan Bastard

RCK concentrated on foreign affairs in his correspondence with the General, and essentially on European policy, but he appreciated that there were also domestic priorities that the General needed to respect and which determined some aspects of his European stance. When de Gaulle twice vetoed the entry of Great Britain into the Common Market, RCK agreed with him the first time, but not the second.

The first was in 1963, soon after the common agricultural policy had been adopted in Brussels. This policy would favour French farmers, and de Gaulle wanted to ensure that it was successfully implemented before Britain joined the Common Market and complicated that process. RCK could both understand and, in some measure, sympathize with this.

But RCK had less sympathy with the General's veto in 1967, which he felt was a mistake. By then he considered the issue of the common agricultural policy had been largely resolved, and expected Britain to be an ally of France in bigger issues. RCK could see that the countries thought similarly about institutional issues, much more confederal than federal, and he summed up his position in an article entitled 'Britain, France, and Europe', which he published in February 1966. 'The latest crisis in the EEC has isolated France. France's five partners are for making Europe a federal state and only France is for making it a confederation.' Great Britain was in the process of divesting itself of its colonial empire, and RCK tried to convince de Gaulle that the time was now right to support Britain joining the EEC. 'France's reason to exclude Britain has gone and it now needs Britain. For Britain, like France, is in favour of a European confederation, not a European federal state.'

The two French vetoes were bitter blows to the British governments in power at the time – first the Conservatives led by Harold Macmillan and then Labour led by Harold Wilson – and British commentators in particular were extremely critical of de Gaulle. With good reason, political commentaries identified Gaullist policies as being hostile to the sort of Europe that the institutions of Brussels exemplified. De Gaulle's vision of a union of European nation states – *L'Europe des patries* – was seen by many observers, especially those outside France, as the negation of the ultimate prospect of a federal Europe enshrined in the ambitious preamble to the Treaty of Rome – 'the ever closer union of the peoples of Europe'.

But de Gaulle's national priorities in no way disturbed RCK. He pragmatically accepted that de Gaulle was 'both a patriot and a nationalist by his heritage and upbringing, but a European through his intelligence, the breadth of his imagination and the grounding of his politics in history.'

RCK welcomed the big picture of Europe that informed de Gaulle's foreign policy, and he largely sympathized with it.

This argument came to a point in an exchange of views between RCK and Lord Gladwyn, former UK ambassador to France and a vice-president of the Pan-Europa Union, as well as a member of its Honorary Committee. At the end of July 1965, *Le Monde* published an article by Louis Terrenoire, a former minister of de Gaulle's and chairman of the French Committee of Pan-Europa, expressing strong opposition to majority voting in Brussels and arguing in favour of unanimity in decision-making in the Council of Ministers, a central Gaullist position. The dignity of France required it to maintain the power to veto decisions with which it could not agree, he wrote. It was not a country whose interests could be sacrificed to those of lesser nations.

Lord Gladwyn wrote to RCK to object. For him, the only basis for a Europe which was 'more than a collection of totally independent nations' was the Treaty of Rome. The treaty, he continued, 'contains clear provision for majority voting at a certain date, in other words for a limited, but definite measure of 'supranational power'. France has signed the Treaty and must observe this provision.' The Pan-Europa French Committee should rescind Terrenoire's statement, argued Gladwyn. Otherwise he would feel obliged to resign as vice-president.

RCK replied, 'National groups must be free to express their respective views, whether I share them or not.' That had certainly not been his position in the past, when he had broken with colleagues – Wilhelm Heile in Germany, Julius Meinl in Austria, and Vaclav Schuster in Czechoslovakia – rather than let them express opinions that diverged from his own line as president of Pan-Europa. Had the passage of years begun to mellow him? 'Personally,' he added, 'I am fed up with the quarrel about who is responsible for the present most regrettable crisis. The only thing that interests me is how to go ahead on the stony road leading to a United States of Europe.'

Perhaps his confusion was understandable, caught between the 'rock' of Gladwyn's insistence that Britain would join the common European endeavour only if the prospect of majority voting was maintained, and the Gaullist 'hard place' of insisting on national sovereignty and the veto. 'Must the whole notion of a supra-national European body (which is the only means whereby we could come together) really disappear?' wrote Gladwyn. 'If you yourself no longer favour this last conception, then I must certainly resign from your Comité d'Honneur.' And resign he did.[4]

RCK'S VIEW OF BRITAIN'S ROLE evolved in the late 1950s and during the 1960s. His early quarrel with Duncan Sandys had been in part because Sandys professed a pre-war conception of the United Kingdom's role, a state with an empire separate from, though concerned about, the continent. By the 1960s, RCK had changed his view of Britain, which he now saw as a potential partner in a strong and independent Europe, alongside France, West Germany, and Italy. Particularly in the nuclear age, the military resources of both Britain and France together would help to assert European independence as a world power.

The French concept of a leading *directoire* – a leadership group – could simply be enlarged, he argued, to include the United Kingdom alongside the other three major states. British participation, RCK now argued, was necessary, because Great Britain 'since the end of the Commonwealth' was too small to stay isolated. If she were rejected by Europe, she would become, 'like Canada, Australia and New Zealand, a satellite of the United States'. Only an agreement between France and Great Britain could prevent the hegemony of Germany, which would be inevitable if Europe were merely continental.

RCK therefore sent a note to de Gaulle in April 1967, six months before the General issued his second veto against British membership of the EEC, suggesting a new *Entente Cordiale*. Then, in June, he suggested a bilateral Franco-British pact relating to nuclear issues: 'This political initiative is both more urgent and more important than all the questions concerning Britain's relations with the Common Market,' he added.[5] Just how the United Kingdom should be associated with the EEC – in July that year to be 'merged' with the ECSC and Euratom into a single authority called the European Communities – mattered less to him than pragmatically recognizing the fact that the UK was useful, helpful, possibly even necessary, in the European equation. With his incorrigible optimism, he assured de Gaulle that, if he came to an agreement with Prime Minister Wilson on Franco-British Union, 'Germany, Italy and the small states of Europe will follow. Europe would become in a few months a World Power, the equal of the United States and the Soviet Union.'

De Gaulle noted all these international suggestions from RCK, and he appears to have appreciated the fertile mind and flexible responses of his correspondent. He particularly appreciated the fact that he concentrated on foreign affairs and could envisage a leading role for France that matched the General's ideas of *grandeur*. Above all RCK was not associated with any particular French political party, and so did not have any specifically party-related axe to grind, and never interfered in what caused the General so much grief, the domestic politics of the country he governed. 'How can you govern a country with two hundred and forty-six varieties of cheese?' de Gaulle once complained.

May 1968 was the month of student revolt across Europe, west and east. Protesting students at the barricades in Paris almost forced de Gaulle to call out the army to quell the rioting. In Prague, Warsaw Pact troops suppressed tentative moves towards democracy – or at least 'socialism with a human face'. Typically, RCK saw these phenomena in a wider context. East and west, the student riots were just a symptom of much greater dislocation in world affairs, which RCK felt could create an opportunity to advance Pan-Europa's goals.

Having sent a draft to de Gaulle for his approval ten days earlier, RCK published an 'Open Letter to the President' in the French press on 1 June, claiming that there was a world-wide political upheaval under way that offered Pan-Europa a new opportunity to encourage a united Europe, free from American, as well as Russian, domination. The opportunity 'arises from the reconciliation and entente between Moscow and Washington, putting a stop to the Cold War that under the atomic menace has dominated international world policies ever since the Second World War ended. RCK feared a perpetuation of the division of Europe agreed to at Yalta in 1945.

> Disunited, Europe would be merely an ensemble of satellite States, hostile and weak. United, Europe becomes equal in strength to her two great neighbours, the United States of America and the Soviet Union, and would be their ally and friend – the heart of a more vast Europe, spreading from San Francisco to Vladivostok, the champion of world peace and of the fraternity of mankind ... The first step towards the renaissance of Europe would be England's joining the Continent. Without the British Isles, we will always remain inferior to the United States, of which England, excluded from Europe, would inevitably become a satellite.

De Gaulle, he urged, should call a peace conference in Paris that would settle the fate of the world in the way that the Congress of Vienna had settled the fate of Europe after the end of the Napoleonic wars. In that settlement there would be a place for a united Europe.

His perception may have been accurate, but the timing could not have been worse for the president, who was in no position to attend to the wider international ramifications of the upheaval that was shaking France to its core. His government managed to survive the crisis of 1968, but it was at considerable political cost, and the Warsaw Pact invasion of Czechoslovakia drove off the international agenda any prospect of a new Europe-wide settlement that might lessen the control of the Soviet Union over its satellite states.

Along with his New Year's wishes for 1969, RCK sent de Gaulle an even-more-explicit memorandum outlining the route he recommended for uniting Europe. 'The three hundred and fifty million men and women of the twenty states between the Soviet Union and the Atlantic,' he suggested, have 'all the qualities of a world power except unity.' Since neither the Council of Europe nor the Common Market were capable of bringing about European unity, 'Europe will remain divided unless the four key powers – France, Germany, Great Britain, and Italy – agree to act together in foreign affairs and defence, and introduce a common currency,' he added, warning that 'Associating Great Britain is the only way to avoid German hegemony tomorrow in a continental Europe.' De Gaulle should call a conference of the four powers in Paris to establish this *directoire*. Later the smaller states of Europe could be invited to join them.

Fortune's wheel can turn extremely quickly, especially in politics. Just one month later, at the end of April 1969, de Gaulle lost a referendum on the redistribution of power from Paris to the French regions and resigned. RCK was shattered.

On 10 May, with his secretary-general, Vittorio Pons, he drafted a profoundly sad *cri de coeur*, a two-page letter from the president of the Pan-Europa Union to the erstwhile president of France:

> By rebuilding France, by signing the Elysée Treaty, you placed the keystone of a united Europe. By demanding that a political union of Europe be built on the basis of a popular referendum, you pointed the road to follow. By realizing the need for a permanent agreement between France, Germany, Italy, and Great Britain you pointed to a Europe of realities instead of a Europe of illusions. Must we now leave the domination of the world solely to the United States, Russia, and China? What can, what will Europe do now without you?

A few days later, RCK then wrote to de Gaulle, stating baldly that he did not believe that it was in his nature to retire. He sent him subsequent memos about forthcoming conferences in The Hague and Helsinki, notes which de Gaulle appreciatively acknowledged. But eventually, on

4 December 1969, the General wrote laconically in reply, 'I no longer concern myself with public affairs.'

Less than a year later, RCK's *cher ami* died at home of a heart attack and was buried in the local cemetery of Colombey-les-deux-Eglises. RCK had lost his friend, his financial patron, and his closest political interlocutor.

24

EUROPE'S FATHER, EUROPE'S GRANDFATHER

ANDRÉ FONTAINE, the editor of *Le Monde*, knew both Jean Monnet and RCK well, and once described the pair as 'the father and the grandfather of Europe'. However, he later admitted that it was a surprise to discover that the father, Monnet, was in fact a few years older than the grandfather, RCK. Contrary to what you might expect, the grandfather appeared younger than the father. RCK had worn better than Monnet. He had kept his youthful, handsome looks.

RCK's relationship with Jean Monnet played out alongside his relationship with de Gaulle. The Schuman Plan, announced in May 1950, had come to RCK – as to almost all other political observers – as a surprise. Jean Monnet and RCK had known of each other for many years, but were first in direct contact only eighteen months after this watershed event, when Jean Monnet became president of the European Coal and Steel Community in 1952. That contact became closer after Monnet was awarded the Charlemagne Prize in 1953 and RCK attended the ceremony.

Jean Monnet was born in 1888 in Cognac, eight years before RCK, and it is reasonable to assume that he and RCK knew nothing about each other until after 1918. Monnet was then in his thirties, and RCK in his twenties. The first moment when their professional paths crossed could well have been when the Frenchman was deputy secretary-general of the League of Nations, a post to which he was appointed in 1919. Two years later, RCK brought his proposal for a separate European section to the League in Geneva. Although RCK's memoirs report only his meeting with Sir Eric Drummond, the British secretary-general, it is unimaginable that RCK did not know the name of Jean Monnet as Sir Eric's deputy, even if they did not meet face to face on that occasion. The secretariat of the League was then still very small, and it would also have been standard administrative practice for RCK's initial memorandum, his correspondence, and possibly also a summary of his meeting with Sir Eric to have been shared with his deputy.

Pan-Europa was published in 1923, and it is more than likely that Monnet became aware of the book then. Although he had resigned from his post with the League a few months earlier that year in order to rescue his family's ailing brandy business in Cognac, he certainly kept abreast of international politics and possibly read reviews, or even the book itself, at that time. Although there is no record of correspondence between them in the 1920s, Monnet cannot have been ignorant of the public profile that RCK enjoyed. But he may also have been negatively prejudiced towards him because of an earlier incident of which RCK himself had no knowledge.

From 1925 until his death in 1931, Louis Loucheur was one of the moving figures in the Pan-Europa Union in France, and neither Loucheur nor Monnet thought well of each other. During the First World War, when Loucheur was minister in charge of supplies and recruitment, Monnet was a junior French civil servant on attachment in London to help co-ordinate Allied shipping across the Atlantic. Despite his rank, his responsibilities meant that he reported directly to President Clemenceau, who endorsed Monnet's memoranda and recommendations and sent them on to Loucheur.

Irked by being told how to run his department by some bureaucrat in London, Loucheur made inquiries to find out just who this Monnet was. On discovering that he was still a young, junior official, temporarily exempted from military service, he insisted he should enlist in the army immediately and be replaced by someone from his staff. Only the intervention of President Clemenceau saved Monnet from being sent to the front. For the rest of their lives Monnet and Loucheur were not on speaking terms, and, given Loucheur's links to RCK, this incident may well have prejudiced Monnet against Pan-Europa.[1]

After he left the League of Nations, Monnet put his family's brandy business back on its feet and then spent the late 1920s and 1930s in America and the Far East as an international banker, involved in stabilizing currencies and encouraging foreign trade. He returned to Europe shortly before the Second World War, and was in London in the critical days of June 1940, when he helped Vansittart, the chief diplomatic adviser to the British government and later no friend of RCK, to draft Churchill's offer to France of 'an indissoluble union'. At that time RCK was in full flight from Switzerland, first to Bareclona, then Lisbon, and finally to New York. It is unlikely that Monnet would have heard about RCK and his escape to America while he was still in London, but later the same year he was sent to America by Churchill and joined Roosevelt's staff. Monnet and his wife lived in New York at 1158 Fifth Avenue, and it would be most surprising if they did not know that RCK and Idel were living in the same city.

Given his London experience co-ordinating transatlantic supplies during the First World War, and his role in drafting the offer of joint Franco-British citizenship, Jean Monnet had useful experience that could help the American administration on planning industrial production with wartime priorities in mind. He had worked on Wall Street in the 1920s and had cultivated friendships with influential Americans, some of whom were also now advising the president. Ambassador Bullitt introduced him to Roosevelt, who was starting to think how best to adapt US industrial capacity to armaments production, particularly aircraft, and Monnet soon gained an insider's view of just what industrial changes were required to assure Allied victory. Much more the diplomat than RCK, he also did not air his views on Bolshevism publicly, nor show antagonism to Stalin, who, in President Roosevelt's view, was a necessary ally for the United States at that time.

Neither Jean Monnet nor RCK mentions meeting or corresponding with each other during their time in America, but each was convinced of Allied victory from a very early date, and each must have learned something about the other's activities there, either from public print or from conversations with mutual acquaintances.

It was in America that each of them refined their respective visions of the path to a united Europe. But their different ways of life in America also go some way to throw light on how much Monnet and RCK acted very differently to achieve their aims. The contrast was between the publicist and the civil servant, the man who projected ideas and the man who knew how to turn them into practical reality. It was a question as much about personalities and roles as about policies and politics. Jean Monnet's biographer, François Duchêne, asserts that 'Monnet was chosen to make contact with Roosevelt as much for his anonymity as for his skills.' That was not something that would be said about RCK.

While RCK was dramatically preaching about the need to produce two hundred thousand planes a year to gain global dominance in the air, for instance, Monnet drafted a carefully researched balance sheet of US potential and actual armaments capacity.[2] RCK may have made the issue public and raised awareness of the need in general terms, but it was Monnet who supplied the practical solution, indicating which companies and which plants could be reorganized to produce the necessary aircraft and other war materials. It was Monnet who had the ear of the administration and helped to persuade the president to put the American economy on a war footing well before Pearl Harbor and America's declaration of war against Japan and Germany.

In 1943, while RCK was publishing his first book of memoirs, establishing his research seminar at NYU, and organizing the fifth Pan-Europa Congress in New York, Monnet moved to Algiers to join de Gaulle's National Liberation Committee as commissioner for armaments. By that time, he was also intellectually convinced of the necessity of European post-war federation, and wrote, 'There will be no peace in Europe if the states are reconstituted on the basis of national sovereignty. The countries of Europe are too small to guarantee their peoples the necessary prosperity and social development. The European states must constitute themselves into a federation.'

After the German surrender and the division of that country into zones of occupation, Jean Monnet was once more on the inside track in France as a senior civil servant. He persuaded de Gaulle, who was then prime minister, to ensure economic control of the key German coal-producing areas in the Ruhr, then part of the British Zone, by means of an inter-allied agency through what was called the Monnet Plan. The aim of this plan was to secure a cheap source of coal for French industry at the expense of the defeated enemy. It was similar to the policy pursued after the First World War, but rather than French occupation, the chosen instrument was an international commission to oversee German coal production. This international authority – without German participation – took control of production and sales of Ruhr coal and, at French insistence, directed a considerable portion of output to French concerns at low prices.

This worked satisfactorily as far as France was concerned for a number of years. Not surprisingly, however, once it was formally established as an independent country in 1949, West Germany found this arrangement intolerable. Monnet then conceived a more acceptable alternative: the European Coal and Steel Community. This would offer *joint* control, not only of coal, but also of iron and steel production. This joint control would be exercised by a supranational authority, not simply by an international body, thus reducing the ability of the government of any member state to intervene and steer the new organization.

Robert Schuman's declaration of 9 May 1950, drafted by Jean Monnet, stated: 'Through the consolidation of basic production and the institution of a new High Authority, whose decisions will bind France, Germany, and the other countries that join, this proposal represents the first concrete step towards a European federation, imperative for the preservation

Jean Monnet, who shared with RCK the goal of a united Europe.

of peace.' French domination was to transmute into shared sovereignty as soon as there was a West German state to deal with, and that shared sovereignty also served to dilute the national role of each government in the High Authority. Changed circumstances demanded a changed policy, and Monnet persuaded a sympathetic minister, Robert Schuman, to endorse it. If not direct French control, then co-operation in managing key resources under a supranational authority rather than international competition again. Like RCK, Monnet was clearly able to adapt his position in the light of changing circumstances, and yet still to pursue his main goal.

When Monnet was appointed president of the ECSC in 1952, RCK wrote to congratulate him and received a courteous acknowledgement. When he stood down from the chairmanship of the High Authority two years later, he and RCK also exchanged cordial notes and hoped to meet shortly afterwards to discuss future plans. RCK suggested Paris in February 1954, or perhaps Baden-Baden later that year, where the Pan-Europa Union was planning to hold its next congress. Monnet's carefully drafted reply agreed they should indeed meet, but without mentioning any specific date or place.

It was the start of an epistolary sparring match that would last until RCK's death, Monnet always careful not to endorse RCK's specific activities, while RCK claimed they were always in pursuit of the same central goal.

In addition to the Ruhr there was another European political and economic problem to be solved at that time: the Saar region, rich in coal and iron ore. A small territory between France and Germany, with a population just under one million, the Saar had been constitutionally separated from defeated Germany in 1947 (still then under French occupation) and turned into the Saar Protectorate, a separate political territory still under French control. It was a frozen conflict, a left-over from the war, and it posed territorial as well as economic problems that were a major obstacle to improved Franco-German relations. That was where it stood until a plebiscite at the end of 1955 produced a clear majority in favour of taking the region out of the control of France and returning it to West Germany, now an independent state.

As president of the Pan-Europa Union, RCK wrote to both Bonn and Paris with rational and carefully calculated suggestions about how to solve this potentially explosive clash of sovereignty and interests. Essentially, he proposed the two sides share the spoils, with the Saar passing into German administration as a new Land of the Federal Republic of Germany, but with the quid pro quo of prolonged preferential exploitation of its coal and iron resources by France. In any case, this economic activity was now regulated by the ECSC, and dealing with it at the European level took some of the nationalist sting out of the issue. Such a reasonable compromise was also the solution finally achieved in 1957 after several rounds of diplomatic negotiations.

RCK boldly marked it up as another success for Pan-Europa, although he was never associated with the formal negotiations that achieved that goal. And, in his writings, he never gave credit to the ECSC for the practical role that it undoubtedly played in finding a solution.

IN HIS WORK AT THE ECSC, Jean Monnet had seen at first hand just how reluctant member states were to pool aspects of national sovereignty in pursuit of wider economic and industrial benefits. They only agreed in as far as they could identify specific economic advantages – for instance security of supply, reduced costs through shared overheads, and controlled domestic competition. The only way to keep up momentum towards the less easily defined goal of political union for Europe, and yet not to frighten

the member governments, was to proceed by small steps. It would be necessary, he thought, to prove by these steps that the direction of travel
was beneficial to everyone, while never belabouring the ultimate goal.
He concentrated on a 'community method' that delivered incrementally
useful and practical economic integration while diverting attention away
from what seemed to many long-term and more-contested goals. Monnet
feared that the momentum in favour of greater integration would be lost
if states were asked to commit themselves too quickly to an overarching
goal of a political Europe.

This was not RCK's approach at all. He had a political vision that
appealed to the heart and imagination. Monnet had a method, bringing economic interests together and appealing to the head and rational
calculation. Not that Monnet himself was satisfied with progress on this
front. Indeed, he left his official position at the head of the ECSC to galvanize political opinion better as the independent leader of a ginger group.
The title of his organization spelled out his goal explicitly: the Action
Committee for the United States of Europe, known as ACUSE. Operating
from January 1955, it was a continent-wide group of close to one hundred
leading politicians from the Christian Democrat, Social Democrat, and
Liberal parties, along with representatives of the trade unions and employers' associations from the six member states of the ECSC. Just like RCK's
Pan-Europa Congress in 1926, the Action Committee was not designed
to discuss *whether* closer integration was a good thing, but to determine
how to achieve it.[3]

Robert Schuman had declared at the founding of the ECSC that 'Europe
will not be made all at once, or according to a single plan. It will be built
through concrete achievements which first create a de facto solidarity.'
Monnet and his Action Committee pursued this step-by-step approach
to applying the lessons of the ECSC to other sectors of the economy. This
approach and this method were remarkably quickly crowned with success.

In May 1955, Paul-Henri Spaak chaired a committee of representatives
from the six states of the ECSC – to which the United Kingdom was also
invited to send a delegate – to prepare a treaty that would create a common market across the continent. The Spaak committee suggested that
the treaty should set out a timetable for creating a customs union and set
up special arrangements for agriculture, transport, and energy, including
atomic energy, and – to ensure the support of the trade unions – also contain
provisions on social policy.

These proposals were music to RCK's ears, as he had called for a customs
union in the 1920s and had considered key sectors such as energy, transport,

even social and labour policy in conferences organized in the 1930s in Vienna. His context at that stage had of necessity excluded Nazi Germany and concentrated on the states of southeast Europe. Now Monnet's ACUSE was aiming to bring together the six members of the ECSC – three large states of France, West Germany, and Italy, with three small states of the Benelux – putting pressure on governments to merge economic interests and create what he had first asked for thirty years previously. RCK envied his success, and at this point he must also have realized that Monnet was not simply a co-worker in a common cause, but actually a rival whose methodology was proving more successful than his. Monnet's standing in the eyes of governments was probably also by now overshadowing RCK's own.

Monnet's and Spaak's 's project of the European Economic Community (EEC) came to fruition with the 1957 Treaty of Rome that created the basis for a customs union. Excluded from this by its own decision, the United Kingdom then set about creating a European Free Trade Area (EFTA) that brought seven states together in a looser free trade area, a trading rival to the EEC. Like many other observers, RCK saw the folly of dividing Europe into competing economic areas and pressed for the two organizations to negotiate as much commonality in their trading arrangements as possible, a somewhat pious hope, given the fundamentally divergent economic philosphies behind the two organizations.

But in RCK's view, the specifics of their trading relationship were less important than having the intellectual honesty to accept that they would all have to form a single European confederation, perhaps even a federation, to survive in a hostile world. He argued that it was the bigger picture of geopolitics that was really driving the move to integrate economies, rather than the incremental accumulation of minor advantages that Monnet preached. Once states realized the necessary political and security goal, he argued, then the detailed arrangements that create common economic interests would be obvious, sector by economic sector. He had his doubts about giving priority to economic integration, since, if nation states grew used to making economic concessions only to secure economic benefits, they might never reach the point where they would make the decision which would really count: political federation.

RCK was naturally disappointed that Britain had missed an opportunity to help shape the common market of the EEC while possibilities to influence it were still available. The United Kingdom might have taken the lead. That was the view of the UK's chief negotiator on the Spaak committee, a civil servant from the Department of Trade. Russell Frederick Bretherton wrote that, if Great Britain had been able to commit to the overall principle of European integration, 'We could have had any type of common market that we wanted.' But, as Jean Monnet had foreseen, the long-term goal was also the stumbling block. The Conservative government under Anthony Eden recalled Bretherton from the negotiations, and the Six were left to put together the Treaty of Rome and the Euratom Treaty amongst themselves.[4]

RCK WANTED TO BUILD EUROPE by settling the large issues first and then looking at the details, getting the generalities right politically and leaving the economic particulars to civil servants and businessmen. Jean Monnet, on the other hand, built from the finer detail of shared interests 'to make men work together to show them that, beyond their differences and geographical boundaries, there lies a common interest.'

Unlike RCK, he had worked much of his life inside either French governmental or international business structures, and he had a shrewd idea of what the motives and the limits to governmental action were. He was prepared to start with relatively small steps and see where the pragmatic path led. And, based on his experience, he also knew that timing was always important: 'Men only act out of necessity, and usually only recognize necessity in times of crisis.' The right proposal needed to be made at the right moment to have any chance of success. Politics was a matter of timing as much as of content.

The correspondence between RCK and Monnet, which continued on an intermittent basis until a few months before RCK's death, was characterized by enthusiastic approaches from RCK, assuring Monnet that they were both really working towards the same goals, and initially cautious and increasingly deliberate replies from Monnet, specifying just what the differences between them were.[5] RCK was always keen to enclose Monnet's efforts within the broader sweep of his own geopolitical concerns, the big picture that framed the sometimes tedious details that he felt could later be left to others to negotiate. Monnet also strove to pin down the details, to see what the big statements really implied.

RCK and Monnet did meet on several occasions, often at social events such as the annual dinner for recipients of the Charlemagne Prize, but their correspondence reveals numerous occasions when RCK asked for a meeting, but Monnet found some excuse – illness, travel, another engagement, even late receipt of an invitation – which prevented it happening.

On one occasion Monnet apologized for failing to reply to a telephone call, since he had such a cold that his voice failed him.

RCK's diaries indicate only a few other occasions, one on 20 February 1956, when they may have met for a professional exchange of views. In 1960 RCK invited Monnet to become an honorary member of the committee of patrons of his forthcoming Pan-Europa Congress in Nice, but Monnet declined. He made the formal excuse that, as president of ACUSE, he had a self-imposed rule not to participate in other conferences except in this role, and it required the agreement of all his members for him to do so. Regrettably, he wrote, it would be impossible to consult them all in time. On another occasion, in September 1962, Monnet declined to give a supporting statement to the fortieth anniversary meeting of the Pan-Europa Union in Vienna, with an answer to RCK, signed by his secretary, indicating that he would be away from his office until the end of the month.

RCK certainly took the initiative to inform Monnet of his activities more often than Monnet informed RCK of his, though RCK does appear to have had regular access to the conclusions of the meetings of ACUSE. It is almost always the younger man, the slightly insecure RCK, the 'grandfather' by right of having launched his Pan-Europa Union thirty years before Monnet's ECSC, who seems to be asking – though never explicitly – for confirmation by the older Monnet, the 'father', that what he was doing was right. But that implied request also included an implicit assumption that, if Monnet did not comment, then he could well be assumed to agree with what RCK had done or was planning to do. By taking the initiative in keeping in contact with Monnet, RCK was trying not to lose the moral high ground in the debate about Europe's future, not to be overshadowed by the unchallengeable facts on the ground that Monnet's method was creating.

There were a few more serious clashes of substance that also revealed the psychology of the two men. In September 1958, RCK published a long article in *Le Figaro* entitled 'De Gaulle's Plan for a Confederation', in which he reported on a private meeting with the French president and pointedly regretted the lack of constructive thinking within the European institutions. He endorsed de Gaulle's suggestion that regular meetings of heads of state should oversee the process of European integration, and also suggested that defence, economic affairs, and culture should be part of their agenda, and that these meetings should have an international secretariat quite distinct from the European Commission.

In summary, RCK was promoting the key elements of the Fouchet Plan, to be floated by France more formally in 1961. What mattered for de Gaulle was that France should receive the respect and deference that it had historically felt was its due as the largest state in Western Europe. It was both inconceivable and unacceptable that France's actions should depend on the agreement of, for instance, as small a state as Luxembourg, which with its veto could block France in any question requiring unanimity. And the European answer – that qualified majority voting would be better than the veto when taking decisions – was equally unacceptable, since that gave proportionally more strength to smaller states. What Europe needed was leadership by the larger states. For RCK, as for de Gaulle, it was a fact of life, proved by history, that large states mattered more than small.

That was not the position of Jean Monnet or ACUSE. Those who thought like him wanted to see a model of interstate relations that pooled sovereignty, sharing it in a supranational organization such as the European Commission in Brussels, which was legally required to act in the common interest. That meant not overriding the interests of small states in favour of the large, but of working out compromises that allowed everybody to share in the success of common ventures. In de Gaulle's eyes, it robbed France of its role as leader of the continent. The tensions and misunderstandings between Jean Monnet and RCK were a personal reflection of the tensions between the supranational institutions of the EEC and the adamantly nationalist president of France. Their exchanges were part of a proxy war, reflecting divided opinions between larger players.

A rare telephone discussion between Monnet and RCK on 5 February 1964 illustrated these tensions. The main points that Monnet noted when he put down the receiver must have seemed to him a clear statement of the main differences between their two approaches.

The first issue was RCK's plan for a large Pan-Europa Union meeting in Milan, at which the question of whether Europe should be united or not would be on the agenda. Monnet pointed out that the time had passed for such discussions, and the question now was not *whether*, but *how* the construction of Europe should be moved forward. Since RCK did not contradict this assertion, Monnet assumed that he agreed.

The second issue was RCK's surprising comment that all three of them – General de Gaulle, Monnet, and RCK – were Frenchmen, and therefore of course they were all in favour of a united Europe, but Italians, Germans, and other foreigners might not think in similar terms. Monnet responded that this was precisely the attitude that was holding back the construction of Europe. Europeans needed to revise the notion of who was a 'foreigner' in their own continent. Had RCK been aware of Monnet's reaction, he would have been mortified, since his claim to European patriotism rather than any national vesion of it was central to his own identity and one of the strongest political cards in his hand. By stressing their common French nationality, he was probably trying diplomatically to emphasize some common ground, but did so in an uncharacteristically clumsy manner.

The third issue was RCK's assertion that Europeans should move on from being in favour of a confederation to supporting a federation. Monnet simply noted that this was not the way to frame the debate. Everyone needed to agree that the correct method, the one that actually worked, was when national governments delegated powers to common European institutions. Labelling that process, and in particular the final goal, was not helpful.

RCK had finally argued for a large symbolic event, convening an assembly of two thousand parliamentarians from the six member states to draft a European Constitution. Monnet declined to comment on this exuberant gesture.

In conclusion, Monnet, ever the efficient bureaucrat, recorded that the conversation had been quite confused and did not require any follow up. It had, however, shown the limits of direct discussions between the two men, and clearly strengthened Monnet's resolve to avoid any subsequent invitations to meet face-to-face to discuss Europe. RCK was never invited to be a member of Jean Monnet's ACUSE, nor was Monnet ever a member of the Pan-Europa Union.

The two men did continue to correspond, each assuring the other of their mutual respect and goodwill, even addressing each other as 'cher ami', but that was simply a diplomatic formality. There was never any personal warmth between them. They each accepted that they were working for a united Europe, but they each ultimately also accepted that their approaches to this were not the same. It was always Monnet, however, who pointed out the differences, despite RCK's repeated rhetorical assurances that they were aiming in the same direction. To borrow a British diplomatic phrase, Monnet thought that RCK was simply 'not sound'.

On occasion, he even spelt it out explicitly. In August 1966, for instance, Monnet wrote to RCK, who was in Salzburg at that time, 'I do not want there to be any misunderstanding between us. You know that on important points, we do not agree.' To clarify matters, Monnet exceptionally invited RCK to meet to discuss their differences when he was next in Paris. RCK paid him back in the same coin that he was used to receiving from Monnet. His slightly aloof reply stated that he had looked at ACUSE's latest conclusions and could not see any major points of disagreement. Their ideas on Europe were never antagonistic, he concluded, since only minor questions separated them. Nonetheless, he would be in Paris at the end of the following month, and they should meet. When that date proved inconvenient for Monnet, RCK then suggested that Monnet might phone in the new year to make another arrangement. There is no record that the telephone conversation ever took place.

In July 1967, the three Brussels-based institutions – the European Coal and Steel Community, the European Economic Community, and the European Atomic Agency – merged into a single body, the European Communities, and the 'community' method of working together as outlined by Jean Monnet took on a further lease of life. ACUSE was clearly closer to community thinking than was RCK, and it is hardly surprising that Jean Monnet grew increasingly cool to approaches from him as the years progressed.

Early in 1969, RCK was in London for a meeting of the Central Committee of the Pan-Europa Union and wrote to Monnet on the spur of the moment from the Grand Committee Room of the House of Commons, using its headed notepaper. He started in a complimentary tone by referring to Jean Monnet's 1940 initiative for a political union of Britain and France, and went on to state how he felt they were 'travelling along separate tracks with the same goal'. Out of the blue, he then proposed a new *Entente Cordiale* between London and Paris and invited Jean Monnet – 'one of my closest allies', who, as RCK asserted, was 'lacking vanity and personal ambition' – to endorse the proposal as soon as possible. The letter was a strange mixture of truth, flattery, and self-deception. Monnet did not respond.

In the spring, RCK wrote again to congratulate Monnet on the latest resolutions from ACUSE, but at the same time he could not resist stressing how pleased he was that the French government had adopted what he called Pan-Europa's programme for reaching out to America, Great Britain, and Russia as it reviewed its foreign-policy objectives. This was a small barb to which Monnet also did not reply.

RCK and Jean Monnet maintained formal civility in their letters, here revealing themselves as competitors rather than colleagues. With varying degrees of personal ambition, they both wished to be seen as the founder of European unity. Their methods as well as their personalities were what set them apart, even though their long-term goals were essentially similar. In his 1958 autobiographical book, *Eine Idee erobert Europa* (*An Idea Conquers Europe*), RCK gave Monnet credit for initiating the 1940 proposal of the British government for an immediate union with France, with common citizenship, common government, and a common parliament for the two states. He conceded this might have formed the kernel for a united post-war Europe, had not the French prime minister, Paul Reynaud, failed to push it through his divided cabinet, and power then fallen to Marshal Pétain. He also credited Monnet with preparing the Schuman Declaration, for successfully chairing the ECSC from 1952 to 1955, and for steering ACUSE as it subsequently influenced European policy. But he could not resist undermining his rival's achievements by referring on the same page to his friend, Paul-Henri Spaak, who, he suggested, decisively helped Monnet overcome all obstacles in government circles of the Six, and so should share the credit for creating both the EEC and Euratom.

As far as they go, RCK's comments constitute a modestly generous reference to his rival, but it is limited to just this one page in his book, neutral in tone and largely factual in content, and it is the only reference to Monnet in the whole volume. Monnet paid him back in kind, however, by omitting any mention of RCK in his 1976 *Mémoires*.

25

REAPING REWARDS
IN THE TWILIGHT YEARS

RCK'S PROFESSIONAL LIFE was marked strongly in its last decade by his relations with President de Gaulle and with Jean Monnet, and for much of that period his personal life was affected by his marriage with Countess Alix. She was in good health for the first years of their marriage, but underwent surgery late in 1961, in all probability to remove a cancerous tumour, and her subsequent treatment involved morphine. As recovery and relapse alternated over the ensuing years, she gradually became dependent on stronger and stronger doses of her medication, to the point where she required continuous attention. RCK's diaries in those years illustrate his constant care for an ailing wife, who by the late 1960s was often in a wheelchair. He was obliged to spend much time and effort in travelling from one specialist clinic to another across Europe in a vain search for a cure. In their quest for better health, they rented a fine house, Kreuzhof, on the Heilbronnerallee in Salzburg from 1962 to 1967. Salzburg was a city that Alix loved for its musical associations and RCK appreciated because it attracted European political leaders with whom he could network during its music festival.

When he travelled with Countess Alix, he usually also took his office with him, including a secretary and a driver, as well as the nurse and the carer for his wife. His secretary, Hanne Dézsy, in her portrait of RCK, *Gentleman Europas*, describes with a mixture of shock and amusement the strange appearance of their cortège arriving at up-market hotels in their overloaded Buick, or climbing onto a night sleeper for the next stage of what seemed like unending journeys from grand hotel to grand hotel – Hôtel Meurice in Paris, Beau Rivage in Geneva, the Baur au Lac or the Dolder in Zürich, the Bayerischer Hof in Munich, and the Bristol in Vienna – in search of better treatment and better health for the Countess.[1]

Yet throughout these years, RCK's political activity and his literary output did not slacken. He was in regular correspondence with de Gaulle and was an occasional visitor at Colombey-les-deux-Eglises, and also a guest at both social and official events in Paris, as was the Countess before her health declined. In short succession in 1965 and 1966 he also published two books: a revised and enlarged edition of his pre-war critique of totalitarianism, *Totaler Mensch – Totaler Staat* (*The Totalitarian State against Man*), and an historical overview of Pan-Europa's activities, *PanEuropa, 1922–1966*. He also kept up a demanding schedule of radio and television appearances in France, West Germany, Austria, and Switzerland, as well as correspondence, conferences, and lectures.

Sometimes the audiences at his lectures were smaller than he would have liked, occasionally the events and venues were not quite in the same class as they had been in earlier years, but he remained diligent and in demand. His secretary recalled one occasion in the mid-sixties when he arrived at Frankfurt University to speak on European unity and, seeing crowds assembling in the main hall, assumed that he was speaking there. To his chagrin he learned that the crowds were for an alternative celebrity event, not for his talk. That was scheduled in another lecture theatre nearby, attracting a smaller, but still attentive, audience.

It was during the time of his wife's deteriorating health that RCK received a fortuitous offer from Vittorio Pons, now a European civil servant in the Commission living in Brussels. Twenty years earlier he had covered the Gstaad meeting of the EPU as a correspondent for an Italian socialist newspaper. In 1966 he offered to help organize RCK's work schedule and oversee his administrative affairs, an unexpected and welcome boost for RCK both practically and psychologically. Pons acted as political adviser, intellectual sounding board, and friendly companion, exchanging long telephone calls very early each morning to discuss the main matters of the day. He took on the role as secretary-general of the Pan-Europa Union, and it was largely due to his capable organization of affairs that the aging RCK was able to work so diligently through the late 1960s, despite the increasing demands on him occasioned by Alix's failing health.

During a period of remission in her illness in 1966, RCK and Countess Alix met with Otto von Hapsburg and his wife, Regina, in Salzburg, and collaboration between the two men thereafter grew closer. Otto had been vice-president of the Pan-Europa Union from 1957, and the time had now come for RCK to seriously envisage him as his eventual successor as president. With his imperial pedigree and his wartime experience, like RCK, in exile in America, Otto brought a valuable perspective to Pan-European issues, and RCK arranged for the tenth congress in Vienna that year to profile him in the role of president-elect.[2]

This Vienna Congress opened under the slogan 'Europe and Peace'. RCK had been preparing this event from the moment he had addressed the fiftieth-anniversary meeting of his 1913 Theresianum colleagues three years previously. It was held to mark the fortieth anniversary of the very first Pan-Europa Congress in Vienna in 1926, and his former classmates ensured that the older generation was well represented.

RCK also wanted to rejuvenate support for Pan-Europa by attracting a large number of younger people to this event, particularly from Austria. He was helped in this by Lacy Milkovics, the new young secretary-general of the Austrian branch of Pan-Europa, whose political-discussion evenings, his *jours fixes* in the Bristol Hotel, had already become a popular meeting place for politicians of all generations. Whenever RCK was in Vienna, he would also attend these soirées, and this helped to familiarize a new generation of young Austrian leaders with the ideas of Pan-Europa.

Participants at the 1966 event were just as numerous as at the first Pan-Europa Congress in 1926, with over two thousand assembled in the same grand hall of the art-nouveau Konzerthaus to hear the *Ode to Joy* that opened proceedings. There was an obligatory historical nod in the direction of Bertha von Suttner, the *grande dame* of the Austrian Peace Movement at the start of the century, but the event was far from being a feast of nostalgia. Its agenda was resolutely turned towards the future.

RCK still had pulling power among the political elite and could call on speakers of rank and expertise. Valéry Giscard d'Estaing, the former French minister of finance, for instance, came to this Pan-Europa Congress and revived RCK's pre-war call for a common currency for Europe, proposing the introduction of the *écu*, the forerunner of the euro. The Austrian chancellor, Dr Josef Klaus, also made a speech, which outlined his country's contemporary role as the hinge between the two halves of Europe.

RCK built on the chancellor's speech to challenge the contemporary effects of this division of Europe as decided at Yalta. He stressed the need to build a more positive future for the next generation, where Pan-Europa would encompass the whole of Europe, not just the free and democratic half in the west. He wanted to see a united Europe playing its role on the world stage, and provocatively asked his audience how many world powers there might be in a generation's time. 'Will it be just three – the USA, the Soviet Union, and China? Or will it be four, with the United States of Europe among them?'

RCK challenged his audience to imagine an overarching agreement between east and west, Russia and America, achieving the peaceful union of all countries between San Francisco and Vladivostok. Could the European Communities in the west evolve towards political union at the same time as the eastern half of the continent grew into freedom? Would they ever join together again? Could Pan-Europa prepare the structure that might contain them all? RCK was posing questions that were far ahead of their time, embroiled as the two superpowers then were in the height of the Cold War. RCK held fast to his life-long belief that the solution to this geopolitic opposition was a united Europe that could stand on equal terms alongside both these superpowers, a position conveniently close to that of the French government, which heavily subsidized this event. RCK and Paris were, in this, singing from the same hymn sheet.

DESPITE THE CONTINUING CLAIMS of European politics and his wife's ill health, RCK published another work at the end of the decade which bridged both his political and his philosophical concerns. *Für die Revolution der Brüderlichkeit* (*For a Revolution Based on Brotherly Love*) was a plea for the goals of liberty and equality to be completed by a third revolution, clearly associated in his mind with the eventual triumph of Pan-Europa, which would deliver brotherhood to all the peoples of Europe. Behind the somewhat eccentric title lay the core message of continuing self-improvement that had long been dear to his heart and was central to the tenets of Freemasonry to which RCK was still emotionally and intellectually, if not officially, attached.

It also resonated with his notions about education. In the early 1950s, he had accepted an invitation from Ichiro Hatoyama, a well-known Japanese educator and the translator of RCK's book *The Totalitarian State against Man*, to become honorary chairman of the Yuai Youth Association, of which Hatoyama was president. Its aim was to strengthen bonds of brotherhood or fraternity among young people as a powerful defence against the depersonalizing effects of the modern state. RCK was happy to accept this unexpected invitation then, and it would lead – although he did not know so at that time – to an invitation to visit Japan a few years later, in 1967, from Hatoyama's widow. The theme of the talk and discussions with members of the Japanese association during his visit would also resonate with recent developments in Catholic social teaching, as reflected in the 1967 encyclical of Pope Paul VI, entitled *Progressio Populorum*. This called for the brotherhood of all men in their common striving for human development, and RCK was sure to have been aware of its relevance internationally.

Despite Alix's illness, RCK also responded positively to an invitation from Rotary International in America to address their congress in Atlantic City in 1968. His speech there associated the goals of liberty and capitalism with the American and French revolutions, equality and socialism with the Russian Revolution. There was another goal, he argued, that should be fraternity or brotherly love, an essential virtue that no doubt he identified in Pan-Europa. His words were well received by Rotary, and the shades of William Penn, Immanuel Kant, and Victor Hugo, as well as his father, Heinrich, must all have smiled to hear his pleas for universal harmony.

RCK also devoted a considerable amount of his time during the 1960s to researching an ambitious historical work entitled *Die Amazonen* (*The Amazons*). It was essentially concerned with early matriarchal societies around the Mediterranean and the Black Sea, and involved extensive correspondence with archaeological experts and museum curators in Europe, Russia, America, and the Middle East. His research gave him a solid academic base from which to speculate on the importance of female influence – and female political leadership – over the course of more recent European history. He laboured at this work for nearly ten years, writing and rewriting various versions, and when he died in 1972 it was almost ready for publication.[3]

It was in the early sixties that RCK discovered the Kurhotel Montafon in Schruns in the Vorarlberg, the most westerly region of Austria, to which he subsequently returned every year. The Kurhotel was run as a quiet retreat on the edge of the small town, with plentiful walks, medical facilities, a swimming pool, and a good restaurant, although the latter may not have increased its attraction for RCK, as he appears throughout his life to have been as indifferent to exercise as he was to *haute cuisine*. More importantly, it was frequented by the conservative political elites of nearby Bavaria, as well as of Austria and German-speaking Switzerland, in search of rest and relaxation, recovery or rehabilitation. The medical facilities were overseen by Dr Albrich, a renowned heart specialist, who had invested personally in building the new spa hotel in 1950. His establishment was much admired for its discretion. Franz-Joseph Strauss, leader of the Bavarian Christian Social Union, was a frequent guest.

RCK visited the hotel with Countess Alix for the first time over Easter 1964, when they stayed for more than four weeks. They came back again in late August and early September for ten days, booking two extra rooms for Alix's attendant carers. The following year they came again for two longer visits in spring and autumn, and for a further week just before Christmas. They were there again the following year for ten days just after Easter, and for the last time together in 1967, for two weeks in May.

Later that year, in October 1967, came the invitation to Japan. It was not just a personal invitation to renew links with the Yuai Youth Association, but also to receive the Kajima Foundation's prestigious Peace Prize. RCK saw this as a sign from fate that he was to return to his roots, the land of his birth, in the evening of his life. Morinoshuka Kajima, for many years a diplomat and now a member of the Japanese parliament, had extended the invitation. He had first met RCK in Berlin in 1922 and had been so impressed by the enthusiastic young aristocrat that he translated *PanEuropa* into Japanese. The Yuai Youth Foundation, now under the presidency of Kaoru Hatoyama, the founder's widow and herself a well-known educationalist, associated themselves with the invitation, as did the national broadcaster NHK, giving RCK the opportunity both to broadcast and to speak to young people in English. Alix was in a period of remission and well enough to travel, though in a wheelchair, and RCK invited his niece Pixie, Hansi's grown-up daughter, to accompany them to help care for her.

While in Tokyo, RCK met Crown Prince Akihito again, whose acquaintance he had already made in Switzerland in 1953, and he and the Countess were granted an audience with Emperor Hirohito and Empress Kojun. RCK regaled them with the story that his mother, Mitsu, used to tell her children when they were young, about how she had been received by the empress in the autumn of 1895, before leaving with his father, Heinrich, for Austria. On that occasion, the Empress Haruko had given his mother the ivory fan that she had faithfully guarded all her life as her most prized possession. He recounted that the empress had advised her always to behave as an ambassador for her country, advice she had loyally tried to follow throughout her life.

RCK was awarded an honorary doctorate from Nihon University in Tokyo and was made an honorary citizen of Hiroshima. At his own request, he also met Daisaku Ikeda, the leader of a breakaway Buddhist sect that stressed the value of individual effort in social and political reform. 'A great inner revolution', the guru had written in the main exposition of his moral teaching, 'in just a single individual will help achieve a change in the destiny of a nation and, further, will enable a change in the destiny of all humankind.'[4] It was a message that RCK was personally delighted to hear, as in his own eyes it justified his personal life-long efforts in the cause of European integration. He judged Ikeda to be 'very energetic, life-loving, honourable, friendly, and intelligent', and it appears his interlocutor thought likewise of him. Each recognized the exceptional leadership qualities of the other.

RCK'S CONTRIBUTION TO PUBLIC LIFE was frequently recognized, from the honour of being the first recipient of the Charlemagne Prize in 1951, to the award of the *Légion d'honneur* and the German *Verdienstkreuz* later in the 1950s for his work on Franco-German reconciliation. Further recognition came with the Sonning Prize of the University of Copenhagen in 1965, for his contribution to European culture. It was an award for which he was widely congratulated by many in both the political and artistic world. In high spirits, he travelled to America with the Countess to give a lecture at a minor university immediately afterwards, spending, according to his secretary, the whole of the considerable value of the prize on this single trip.

At Whitsun 1966, he was awarded the Sudeten-German Karlspreis, the citation underlining his services in favour of 'a just settlement of nations and people in Central Europe', and given to 'a man who has fought throughout his life for the unification of Europe'. For similar reasons he was later awarded the highest Luxembourg honour, the Order of Merit of the Grand Duchy, the Grand Silver Medal of Honour of the Austrian Republic, and the Order of the Star of Italy. At the start of the next decade, yet another honour came to him with the award of the prestigious Konrad Adenauer prize. As the inscription on the medal states, it is awarded for 'strengthening peace, preserving freedom and justice', and RCK's work well merited the award.

But the Nobel Peace Prize eluded him, despite numerous recommendations by many well-placed supporters, including Edvard Beneš, Leo Amery, his American friend Arnold Zürcher, and others from almost every country of the continent. From 1932 onwards, RCK was nominated almost annually, occasionally short-listed, but always without ultimate success. 'Better to have deserved it but never been awarded it,' he is said to have remarked, 'than to have been awarded it but not deserved it.'[5]

Some six months after their return from Japan, Countess Alix died in Salzburg in May 1968. She was buried in the private graveyard in Gruben not far from RCK's first wife, Idel. For RCK, her death was a release from an increasingly depressing situation. He had dutifully cared for Alix during the past several years, while her personality fell apart under the pressure of her illness and addiction, continuing his political work through all the alarms

RCK with his second wife, Countess
Alix, in a wheelchair, visiting Japan;
Melanie Benatsky, RCK's third wife.

and relapses of her long illness. General de Gaulle and his wife, Yvonne, sent
their personal condolences, as did many other friends in the political world.

Among the condolences was also a personal letter from Erika, now
undergoing treatment at an institution linked to the Lutheran church in
Zürich for single women recovering from alcohol addiction. Written in
pencil on a scrap of paper, it opened again the relationship with her adopted
father which had been quiescent since their quarrel over the inheritance of
the Gruben house and the arrival of Alix in RCK's life. Occasional letters
and notes followed and, although there is no evidence that they met again,
it healed the wound of their earlier separation. During this time in recovery, Erika may also have converted to a Protestant version of Christianity,
since she would be buried later in the closest church to her old home at
Gruben, the Lutheran church at Saanen.

IN NOVEMBER 1968, when he turned seventy-four, RCK could look back on
a full life, both intellectually and emotionally.[6] He had lost his first wife
while he was still in the prime of life. Now his second wife had also died.

Despite his sadness being alleviated by a sense of relief that was both palpable and immediate, this was the second time that he felt bereaved and alone.

There was always an element in RCK's personality that craved companionship, especially female companionship. As one of his secretaries remarked of him, 'He could not exist without women around him.' He was impeccably well behaved towards them, mirroring in some respects his father's care for Mitsu, but without the evident sexual attraction of that relationship. RCK was clearly heterosexual, and to judge by the impassioned tone of a letter written to Idel at the outbreak of the First World War, they enjoyed a strong sexual relationship. But there is a coolness in RCK's matter-of-fact description of his working relationship with his second wife, Alix, which gives little hint of sexual attraction, particularly in the years after she fell ill.

Indeed, his secretary described an almost comic scene of his lack of interest on one occasion when they were staying in the Kurhotel Montafon. Countess Alix wanted to encourage RCK to take some morning exercise in the hotel's swimming pool, and suggested to his attractive young secretary that she should buy a new bikini and accompany her husband. RCK and the secretary were going down to the pool with their bathrobes over their swimwear on the first morning when the lift stopped at the ground floor just as the postman arrived. RCK immediately insisted that they take the post back upstairs straight away, and they spent the next few hours, still in their bathrobes, opening letters and dictating replies. The swim never happened.[7]

With his third wife, RCK's life blossomed once more. Melanie Benatsky was a long-standing friend of RCK from the time of his first marriage. She was the widow of Ralph Benatsky, the composer of *White Horse Inn*, and several years younger than RCK. He and Idel had known Ralph Benatsky and an earlier wife, Josma Selim, in Vienna in the early 1920s. Josma died in 1929, and Ralph married Melanie Hoffmann the following year. She was a dancer and had performed in several of his operettas. After their marriage, they moved to Thun in the Bernese Oberland, about an hour's drive from where RCK and Idel had their chalet-farmhouse in Gruben. Both couples had escaped to America in 1940, where the Benatskys took American nationality. Both couples lived in New York during the war. RCK's diaries indicate that they may also have met there during those years, and on at least one other occasion he and his second wife, Alix, lunched with Ralph and Melanie in November 1956, probably in their villa beside Lake Thun. They were family friends.[8]

Undeniably, there was a certain mutual convenience in RCK and Melanie coming together. For him, Melanie combined younger, vivacious, and attractive feminine company, which he craved, with financial independence derived from the ample royalties that she had inherited. For Kirschi, as Melanie was known to friends and family, the relationship offered an enviable title and an enhanced social position. She is credited with saying that living alone as a widow in Zürich for ten years had been tantamount to having no social status at all. There, she was a nobody: 'gar nichts'. Being married, and with a title, was a considerable improvement.

After the years of travelling with Alix, RCK may also have felt the need for a fixed abode. Most unusually, in May 1968, he gave the French government a private address in an up-market suburb of Basel – Schlossgasse 11, Binningen – as a destination for post from Paris. It may well have been Kirschi's apartment at that time, or one they rented together, and he appears to have lived there for almost a year, from soon after Alix's death.

Kirschi was quite a different character from Alix. Twelve years younger than RCK, she was healthy, outgoing, happy, and engaging. With her as his companion, RCK was encouraged to restore family relationships and to visit his remaining brothers and sisters again, and they all liked her. Letters in these later years reveal the warmth of feeling that Kirschi generated, both towards herself and towards them as a couple.

Under her guidance, and probably with her help, RCK also supported some of his wider family financially, in particular Olga, his youngest sister, as the income from her pension as a former refugee barely covered subsistence. RCK gave her a monthly allowance, with extra for a medically prescribed spa holiday, or 'Kur', each year. Kirschi also remembered birthdays and sent presents to nieces and nephews and to their children.

RCK's relations with his younger brother Rolfi improved to the point where he would send Rolfi proofs of books and articles for reading before publication. In their letters they would exchange views on current political and social issues, as well as family news. Kirschi also encouraged him to respond to a plea from Erika on behalf of the son of his father's old retainer Babik. Erika had discovered that Babik's son and his wife, now well past working age, were living in Vienna in appalling conditions, and asked if RCK could help rehouse them and give them some financial support. With Kirschi's encouragement he did – without any fuss or fanfare – and told nobody else about it.

On 1 May 1969, RCK and Kirschi were married in a church ceremony in Salzburg. A few weeks later they travelled to New York, doubtless looking up some of their old haunts from the years of exile, and in May arranged for their union to be blessed at another church ceremony there. They circulated the news widely to their friends and acquaintances, omitting only to mention that the marriage was never legally registered. This might be explained by a rumoured stipulation in Ralph Benatsky's will that, if his widow should marry again, then she would no longer enjoy the royalties from his works. In addition to the *White Horse Inn*, Benatsky had composed over twenty operettas, as well as music for a dozen films and over five thousand popular songs. The royalties must have been considerable.

Later in 1969, RCK moved into a new flat in Zürich with Kirschi. The Pan-Europa office also moved again, this time to the Rotes Haus, a prestigious central office location at 7 Beethovenstrasse, a short tram or taxi ride from Kirschi's fashionable modern apartment in 47 Wehrenbachhalde in the suburb of Witikon, located high on a hillside, with magnificent views over the lake. For RCK, Kirschi offered the golden glow of feminine warmth and friendship through his evening years, and relieved him of some of the incessant concern about extra money to make ends meet.

26

A PATRON SAINT
FOR EUROPE

KIRSCHI AND RCK ENJOYED travel together, visiting friends and relations across the continent. RCK happily explained to her the historical and cultural associations of wherever they went. He also explained to her that, just as all countries have a guardian or patron saint – St George for England, St Joan for France, St Boniface for Germany – he had once suggested to the Pope that Europe too should have a patron saint. Some years later, in 1964, at a ceremony in the great Benedictine Abbey of Monte Cassino, Pope Paul VI had declared St Benedict of Nursia as Patron-Protector of Europe. RCK was delighted therefore when in 1970 Pro Europa Una, a Munich-based Catholic cultural organization supporting European integration, invited him to take part in a ceremony of dedication at the original Abbey of St Benedict at Subaico in central Italy.

The invitation was flattering because it brought back to his mind a reflection he had shared with one of his secretaries some years previously. If the road had forked differently at an earlier stage of his life, he mused, he might have become a prince of the Church, guiding souls to God and reconciling his interests and qualities as an academic with his faith. Or indeed the head of some multinational trading company, leading a vast business effort in an ethical direction to produce not only more, but better, and caring equitably for shareholders, employees, and customers. Or a senior civil servant, co-ordinating and directing all the political energies of a great nation without sullying his hands with the less-acceptable aspects of party politics. As it was, he had become a leader in a political sphere that also had a spiritual and intellectual dimension. He had not taken a turning that led him into administration, government, business, or the Church, but remained a private individual with celebrity status in political and intellectual circles that attracted just such an invitation as he had now received. He would play a leading part at the inauguration of the shrine of the patron saint of Europe.

RCK accepted with great pleasure, endorsing the reforming and ecumenical approach of the current pope, Paul VI, and comparing the founding of Pan-Europa to the experience of St Benedict, who founded his order in the early sixth century under the motto of *Ora et labora* (*Pray and work*). Both Kirschi and Vittorio Pons accompanied him on this pilgrimage to the monastery, built over the original sacred grotto in which Benedict had lived as a hermit more than fourteen hundred years earlier. There, on the saint's day – 11 July 1970 – before an international audience of dignitaries drawn from church and state, RCK lit a votive lamp in the name of Pan-Europa, to hang in perpetuity in the grotto of Europe's patron saint, one of the oldest holy shrines in Western Christendom.

Later that same morning, the dignitaries reassembled on Mount Livata, a nearby mountain in the Apennines, for an event at which, in the name of peace and brotherhood, relics of war were ceremoniously buried beside an ancient wayside chapel, and the mountain was renamed the Mountain of Europe. The party included the Italian under-secretary of state for foreign affairs, the primate of the world-wide Benedictine Order, the president of the European Veterans' Association, a former French minister, as well as the abbott of St Benedict's monastery, all entertained on what must have been a memorable first day in office by the newly elected local mayor of Subaico.[1]

Taking a cue from his father, Heinrich, on matters of religion, RCK was nominally a Catholic, but he welcomed all practices and faiths that contributed to his broad concept of what he understood was noble and good. That was made up of all the worthy ideas that had crossed his path over his long life, as well as his memories of good people he had met from the world of Islam, from the Protestant and Orthodox Christian traditions, and more recently from the Buddhist tradition in Japan.

His father, he once claimed, had been 'an observant Catholic, a disciple of Schopenhauer, and an admirer of the Buddha'. He shared his father's views, including a high regard for the Judaic tradition, as well as the Enlightenment ethics of Freemasonry. To that RCK added the Nietzschean aspects of his academic work on truth and beauty as the objective basis of morality. He stood by his father's and his own writings on the nature of anti-Semitism, and his thinking matched his practice: both the first and the last of RCK's wives were Jewish. RCK was respectful of all faiths, eclectic and also tolerant. He successfully persuaded the local Protestant vicar of Saanen to include a small shield with his initials and Pan-Europa's emblematic cross on the sun of Apollo against a background of Marian blue when the vicar was renewing the decorations in his church in the 1960s. He may not have gone out of his way to stress the Greek mythological element in his conversations with the parson, or the Catholic aspects of the blue background, but the shield is still there to be admired.

Increasing age in no way diminished RCK's delight in travel, and when the opportunity to visit Japan again presented itself, he gladly accepted the invitation, especially as he could now travel simply with Kirschi and not, as in 1967, with the medical entourage necessary for his previous wife. They travelled there in October 1970 at the invitation of Soka Gakkai, the sect of Nichiren Buddhism led by Daisaku Ikeda, whom he had met on his previous visit. While there, RCK explored more of this individualist and personalized variant of mainstream Buddhism, holding long discussions with its leader, all of which were recorded and later broadcast in Tokyo. He also visited the campus of the Soka University under construction there and addressed a large student audience.[2]

No sooner had Kirschi and RCK returned to Europe that November than they learned of the death of President de Gaulle. RCK was deeply moved. He wrote as much, in few words, with his condolences to Madame de Gaulle, and in her reply, she noted that her late husband had held RCK 'in high esteem'. She sent him a copy of her husband's *Mémoires*, with a personal inscription that he had added just before his death, but had not been well enough to send: '*en hommage de ma très haute et amicable considération*'. RCK was deeply moved by the General's expression of 'esteemed and friendly' feelings, but he also had a practical concern that the financial support that de Gaulle had given him might not be continued by his successor.

NEITHER FOREIGN TRAVEL nor the loss of friends, however, distracted RCK from the European and international political scene. Above all, he feared the prospect of the United States withdrawing support from Europe, creating a power vacuum that the Soviet Union might well exploit. On 7 December 1970, he sent letters to President Pompidou, Chancellor Brandt, Prime Minister Heath, and Prime Minister Colombo – the leaders of the four major states of Europe – urging the United Kingdom and Italy to join the Franco-German friendship treaty now in order to give Europe the united leadership it needed.

Even with de Gaulle no longer on the scene, RCK held on to the central tenet of the Fouchet Plan, that Europe needed the leadership of the large states, and its concerns should be primarily political, leaving only economic affairs to the European Communities. A truly united Europe would need to take hard decisions that involved geopolitical priorities, defence capacity, and a common foreign policy, issues which, in his view, were well beyond the potential of the short-term rotating chairmanships and weak bureaucratic governance of Brussels.

On 14 April 1971, he followed up this initiative with a long article in *Le Monde* entitled 'Le grand dessein du Général de Gaulle'. He claimed this great plan was in essence what de Gaulle had proposed in February 1969 to Christopher Soames, Churchill's son-in-law and British ambassador in Paris. That confidential proposal had been rejected by Harold Wilson, the British prime minister, in his last few months in power, but RCK revived it because it embodied what he and de Gaulle had broadly agreed on: the need for strong leadership in an enlarging Europe. Neither the United States nor the USSR, he added, should have a dominant role in European affairs. While America would remain a world power for the foreseeable future, Russia would become increasingly unable to compete on the military front and could no longer maintain the same status. That would be hastened if Europe would stand on its own feet. Russia would soon become, RCK predicted, just 'the Eurasian neighbour' of a stronger Europe.

RCK enjoyed excellent relations with de Gaulle's successor, President Georges Pompidou, who had been an early supporter of the Pan-Europa Union since the start of his career in the late 1930s. He became vice-president of the French Committee of Pan-Europa in 1960, and also hosted meetings of its International Finance Committee. In 1971 he elevated RCK to the rank of *Chevalier*, or Commander, of the Légion d'honneur 'for his constant efforts in favour of developing European unification'. It was public recognition at the highest level for this adopted French citizen by the new president of the Republic, an expression of gratitude for all that RCK had promoted for the past decade. RCK was also reassured that the financial arrangements he had come to with the general would be maintained by Pompidou.

Pompidou's views on Europe in the widest sense confirmed what de Gaulle had also wanted, a united continent from the Atlantic to the Russian border. RCK now launched an urgent initiative to force the pace of *détente* and bring the two halves of Europe together. This was triggered by plans that were under discussion between the United States and the USSR to convene a Conference on Security and Co-operation in Europe. If it were left to Washington and Moscow, he feared they would simply make permanent the Yalta Agreement of 1944 that divided Europe into

American and Russian spheres of influence. The four leading nations of Western Europe should press for real *détente* and bring about change that would allow all Europeans to work together, allowing Europe 'to stand on its own feet'.

In a series of Open Letters published in leading European newspapers and addressed to European leaders – Willy Brandt in Germany, Edward Heath in Britain, Jacques Chaban-Delmas in France, and Arnaldo Forlani in Italy – RCK urged that they take a joint European stand in the forthcoming international negotiations. They had to overcome the heritage of Yalta and create a Pan-European grouping of states that would ensure freedom and democracy across the continent. This United Europe would then stand as an equal international power, mediating between America on the one hand and Russia on the other.

In the spring of 1972, Pan-Europa organized a major conference in Vienna, which fortuitously also facilitated an important reconciliation between long-standing rival factions in Austrian politics: the monarchists and the republicans. During the conference, an occasion arose when Archduke Otto von Hapsburg and Chancellor Bruno Kreisky, the one representing the old monarchist tradition of the Hapsburgs and the other the new tradition of the Austrian Republic, were standing side by side in the room. Kreisky offered his hand to von Hapsburg and, after a moment's hesitation, the son and heir of the last Austro-Hungarian emperor took it. That historic handshake buried the animosity that had poisoned political relations among two generations of Austrians, and Pan-Europa had finally been the catalyst that permitted the rival factions to be reconciled to each other. RCK regarded this as one of his finest achievements.

THE KURHOTEL MONTAFON at Schruns had a reputation for discretion. Discretion, Dr Albrich told his staff, was the highest virtue. After Alix's death, RCK came back for two weeks over Christmas and New Year 1968–69, taking just one room. With Kirschi, he booked two rooms in December and July in both the following years, first for a fortnight, and then for a month. In 1972, they arrived on Saturday, 15 July, and looked forward to an enjoyable summer in the Vorarlberg.

RCK's diary shows that on Monday he caught a late-afternoon train to Zürich and then took the sleeper to Paris. On Tuesday, he had appointments in the foreign ministry and the president's office, pursuing political discussions and possibly also confirming that his financial support would indeed continue to be paid. Accession of the United Kingdom to the Common Market, agreed to by the British parliament only shortly before RCK's visit to Paris, had become the trigger for a change of personnel, and possibly also a change of policy, in the French government. President Pompidou had dismissed his prime minister, the reformist Jacques Chaban-Delmas, and appointed the more traditionalist and conservative Pierre Messmer. RCK felt he needed to touch base to confirm that all was well with his continuing activities on behalf of France.[3]

On Tuesday night, he caught the sleeper from Paris back to Zürich. There he had a short wait until the local train set off across the border to Schruns, but he arrived well before lunch, and the taxi took him to the Kurhotel, where he was welcomed by Dr Albrich. Kirschi was not there at that moment, so he went up to his room on the first floor to rest. He lay down on the bed, and it was late in the afternoon when he woke, still fully dressed. He felt unwell and called for attention. Dr Albrich diagnosed stress and over-exertion, and prescribed further rest. He ordered a light supper to be brought to RCK's room.

When the meal had been cleared away, Kirschi wished him goodnight and retired to her room. RCK settled down, but he could not find sleep. His mind raced through all the outstanding business, both political and personal, that he had before him. The coming weekend he planned to walk the three or four kilometres to have tea with Marthe, the carer who had tended Alix in her last years. He treasured the connection because she had a sixth sense, an uncanny ability to see the future, which always fascinated and sometimes reassured him. The following week he had a meeting planned with Lacy Milkovics, the dynamic young head of Pan-Europa's Austrian youth movement. They were to meet in Salzburg and work out a new programme for the youth wing of the Pan-Europa Union.[4]

As a young man, RCK had analysed political events and foreseen the future with great clarity and had proposed solutions to international problems. He had created a political movement that he was convinced could have saved Europe from the horrors of another world war. In exile, he had carved out a niche for himself in public life and helped to change American opinion, encouraging the political class to support his cherished dream of a United States of Europe. In Europe after 1945, he had the ear of leaders, men of the stature of Churchill and de Gaulle, men he could count among his friends and who valued his views on international affairs.

But throughout his life he had also been concerned about his legacy. When Aristide Briand had proposed to the League of Nations, his idea of a federal link between the countries of Europe, RCK had considered buying a ruined castle with a chapel on the heights overlooking Lake Brienz, beyond Interlaken in the Bernese Oberland. He planned to make there a dramatic family mausoleum.[5] Nothing had come of the idea, because Idel, with her more practical mind – and with her own money – had decided to buy their house in Gruben. There they had marked out more modest graves nearby for them both. Strange that he had always expressed the wish to die in Austria, though he had indicated in his will he wished to be buried in Switzerland, in Gruben, alongside Idel. His simple tomb in the wooden mausoleum there might not be a dramatic place of pilgrimage, but he would leave as his lasting legacy not a ruined chapel overlooking a Swiss lake, but the grand idea of a united Europe.

On the morning of Thursday, 27 July, RCK was found unconscious with his hand reaching out to the telephone on the bedside table. He never regained consciousness, and the death certificate gave the time of death as close to midday, the cause of death as heart failure. It was signed the following day, exceptionally not by the owner of the Kurhotel, his friend Dr Albrich, but by the undertaker. He had not been called until late that evening, after dark, so that his presence should not publicize the fact that someone had died at the hotel.[6]

RCK was seventy-seven, but, despite his age, his death was recorded as unexpected. All concerned were indeed surprised, and so unprepared and upset that they had no plan of what to do. Kirschi stated baldly to the undertaker that she wanted to have nothing to do with the dead body, and it was not until Erika arrived the next day, along with Mlle Schmidt, RCK's Zürich secretary, that plans for the funeral were finalized.[7] Kirschi knew that, despite his pension from the French government, RCK was in debt, and she had wisely kept her financial arrangements separate from his. When the Kurhotel bill was presented, she declined to take responsibility for his room and suggested that RCK's part of the bill should be charged to his estate.

Some years later, a former secretary suggested that he may have committed suicide, taking poison held in a large signet ring he always wore. He was, she stressed, from an old Samurai family, and would have seen suicide as a more noble and courageous way to end his life, in particular as he faced the potential shame of being bankrupt. Suicide, however, is a sin in the Catholic faith, not bankruptcy, and even raising this hypothesis caused distress to the family.[8]

The death notice was sent from Kirschi's Zürich address on Wednesday the following week. It was drafted by Vittorio Pons and published in the local newspaper in Gstaad on Friday, announcing that the church service

A Zen garden at Gruben encloses RCK's grave, along with his first two wives'.

on Saturday, 5 August, would be held solely with the close family in attendance (*im engsten Familienkreise*). The burial was to be the same day in the special plot of land, now a private graveyard, close to RCK's former house in Gruben.

The undertaker drove the hearse from Schruns to Gstaad on Friday, having to phone the office of Pan-Europa to report to Mlle Schmidt in Zürich and register his progress several times along the route. He arrived at the church late in the afternoon, and had difficulty finding the sexton to open the building for him, so he had to work late to prepare the catafalque and flowers.

Families are often unpredictable, and funerals do not always show them at their best. Erika, despite her earlier quarrel with RCK over financial matters, seems to have been the most engaged and loving at the end, organizing the funeral arrangements and persuading Countess Kirschi – despite her not wishing to attend – to take her place at the head of the funeral procession. In all, two dozen close friends and family were present, including staunch supporters of Pan-Europa.

At the graveside in Gruben, a short drive away from the church in Gstaad, the situation was also unusual. RCK's grave had been dug next to that of his second wife, Alix, a few paces away from the wooden chalet-like mausoleum which enclosed the tomb of Idel, with whom he had lived much longer and beside whom there was clearly space for a second grave. But the chalet was locked, and the grave-digger had no special instructions to find the key.

Telegrams and letters flooded in from the great and the good of European politics. From Germany alone there were condolences from Willi Brandt, the Bundeskanzler, from Walter Scheel, the foreign minister, and from Gerhard Schroeder. Also from Hermann Abs at the Bundesbank, Otto Friedrich from the Christian Democrats, Richard Jaeger as vice-president of the Bundestag, and Dr Göppel, minister president of Bavaria, who recalled RCK's 'noble simplicity and his unique charm'. Jean Rey, the former president of the European Commission, wrote that RCK would have been pleased to see 'the beginning of the realisation of his European ideas for which he had been fighting since the end of the First World War, and of which he had himself been the originator.' Gaston Thorn, then foreign minister of Luxembourg, and later to be president of the European Commission, valued him as 'a man of high competence who has merited in the highest degree the thanks of the European Community'. Salvador de Madariaga, the philosopher, and his wife, Mimi, sent their heartfelt personal regrets at the loss of a 'great European', as did Guy de Rothschild.

After Idel's death, there had been the helpful Alix nearby and ready to list those who sent condolences and prepare the replies for RCK. Now there was the faithful Vittorio Pons to reply on behalf of the Pan-Europa Union, and, for those kind wishes that came from the wider family, either a reluctant Kirschi or a deeply saddened Erika.

RCK's handwritten will left everything to Kirschi, with the exception of a valuable carpet, which was for Erika, despite their having quarrelled about it years before. But RCK must have known that he was so deeply in debt that he could not bequeath personal effects of any value, since there were so many claims against them.[9] Kirschi refused to accept the will, since it would have implied accepting RCK's debts as well. The absence of a registered marriage certificate supported her case for this financial separation, but in no way did it prevent her from continuing to use the title of Countess which she so much enjoyed.

In a typed codicil to his will, drawn up in August 1970, RCK bequeathed his literary heritage to the Pan-Europa Union, the whole to be managed by Vittorio Pons as secretary-general. As for the Pan-Europa Union itself, he proposed Otto von Hapsburg, whom he had already prepared for the post, as his successor as president. After RCK's death, Otto wrote of him that he 'was always ahead of the age he lived in, and he ceaselessly showed an admirable intuition. If one day Europe is really united, the people of our continent will owe it to Coudenhove in a much greater measure than they are prepared to admit it today.' Under his leadership, RCK must have been aware that his own reputation as the founder and the prophet of European union would be assured.

Julian Amery, the son of his closest English friend, Leo Amery, wrote of RCK, 'Dicky was an inspiration to me since boyhood ... It is given to few to dream great dreams and contribute to their fulfilment. In this, as in his perpetual youth, he was surely happy.' John Biggs-Davison, a supportive Conservative MP, added, 'He never gave in or gave up – not when hopes raised by Briand and Stresemann were dashed (not for the last time) by London; not when on the run from Hitler. As a young man he saw visions. As an old man he dreamed dreams. He lived the future in his devoted life.'

POSTSCRIPT

RICHARD COUNT COUDENHOVE-KALERGI was a passionate European with a dynamic vision of a powerful and united continent. He was born before the end of the nineteenth century, when the fate of the world was decided by the great nations of Europe, and he came of age during the First World War, when they bled each other dry. His response to this disaster was to propose a continent-wide design for peace and unity – the United States of Europe – and he dedicated his life to this all-consuming political idea.

He grew and suffered with his cause, sharing its successes and setbacks, and thanks to his tireless efforts he saw European unity grow in his lifetime from a utopian vision to practical policy. As a young man in the 1920s, he built a continent-wide political movement to promote Pan-Europa. In 1933, the Nazis destroyed that, and he narrowly escaped arrest by the Gestapo in Austria in 1938. He and his wife fled into exile, first to Switzerland, and then to America. During the war, he persuaded the American political elite to promote the idea of the United States of Europe as part of the Marshall Plan for European reconstruction. After the war, he returned to Europe and played a seminal role in the development of Western European integration. He advised Churchill and de Gaulle, and was valued by them both, and he lived long enough to learn that the United Kingdom would join the continental states in an enlarged European Union.

He died when the Cold War was at its height and Europe was divided in two, the chessboard on which the two superpowers from beyond her borders, the United States and the USSR, played out the great game of world domination. Three years after his death, America and Russia, together with all their European satellites, agreed on the Helsinki Accords, the first international agreement signed by all the states of contemporary Europe since the Congress of Vienna. The Helsinki Accords confirmed

Posthumous fame: A road sign
in Paris 16ème and an Austrian
postage stamp.

the post-war territorial settlement on the continent, but also signalled the beginning of a thaw in East-West relations. they were a game-changer that powerfully revived the prospects of RCK's vision of a united Europe.

He was well known throughout the continent in his lifetime and widely honoured after his death. Streets, squares, parks, and avenues in Paris, Vienna, and Berlin have been named after him. His writings became part of the curriculum in schools, and students at university can study his life and work. On the centenary of his birth, the Austrian postal services issued a commemorative stamp and the Council of Europe installed a bust of RCK in the gallery outside its main debating chamber in Strasbourg, alongside other leading statesmen who helped to build the political structure of post-war Europe. Despite his achievements, however, he remains virtually unknown in the English-speaking world today.

Across the European Union the European flag now flies in every city, citizens use the common EU currency, travellers have a European passport, and the European anthem is played at major European events – all ideas first proposed by RCK. In his seminal book *Pan-Europa*, which he published when he was not yet thirty, he challenged the leaders of Europe to fundamentally change the continent by merging their rival states – large and small – into one greater whole, the United States of Europe. As RCK realized a hundred years ago, only a united Europe has the size to count in world affairs. In the new world order, all its individual states are small.

During the last quarter of the twentieth century, Vittorio Pons, RCK's literary executor, and Otto von Hapsburg, his successor as president of the Pan-Europa Union, promoted the legacy of the man who had first set about organizing a united Europe. Vittorio Pons established a foundation in Geneva to promote the spirit of Pan-Europa and keep alive the memory of RCK, arranging several high-level Pan-Europa conferences at Gstaad. Otto von Hapsburg, elected to the European Parliament in 1979, gathered a group of influential MEPs to reach out to dissident groups in the East European satellite states and help spread Western ideas of human rights and the concept of a democratic civil society independent of communist political control.

In June 1989, Pan-Europa instigated the symbolic ceremony at which the foreign ministers of Austria and Hungary first cut the wire mesh of the Iron Curtain. Two months later, Pan-Europa organized another symbolic event, a Pan-European Picnic, a peaceful demonstration that offered hundreds of East German tourists in Hungary the opportunity to cross unhindered into Austria, while border guards looked the other way. Encouraged by the policies of *perestroika* and *glasnost* introduced by Mikhail Gorbachev in the Soviet Union, such symbolic events helped to stimulate a swelling chorus of protest and dissent in the satellite states, culminating in the fall of the Berlin Wall in November that year.

As communist regimes in Eastern Europe fell and democratic states took their place, the prospect of making RCK's vision of Europe a reality improved considerably. For these new states, economic integration was the route, but political union was the destination of a European Union that now extended from the Atlantic to the borders of Russia, as RCK had hoped it would when he wrote *Pan-Europa* more than fifty years before.

The Swiss foundation moved to Vienna and merged there with the European Society Coudenhove-Kalergi around the turn of the millennium. It now awards a bi-annual prize to prominent politicians from east or west who have contributed in a major way to the development of a united Europe. Prize-winners from the West include German chancellors Helmut Kohl and Angela Merkel, the president of the European Council Herman van Rompuy, the president of the European Commission Jean-Claude Juncker, and British chancellor of the Exchequer Kenneth Clarke. Central and Eastern European leaders have also received the prize, including the presidents of Estonia, Latvia, and Romania.

RCK lived and died in the belief that the pre-war archive of the Pan-Europa Union, which had been seized by the Nazis in 1938, had been destroyed in the Second World War. But at the end of the Cold War, it was rediscovered in Moscow and opened to western academics for the first

Vittorio Pons (left) with Otto von Hapsburg (right) present the RCK Prize
to Helmut Kohl in 1991.

time in 1989, allowing Pan-Europa's inter-war efforts to be better appreciated. From the turn of the millennium, studies appeared in both French
and German, some sponsored by the European Society in Vienna, testify-
ing to a continuing interest in the Count and his vision of a united Europe.

Behind RCK's dream of a political role for Europe lay his conviction
that he was a European patriot and that Europeans of other nationalities
could be European patriots as well. He thought in terms of continents
rather than countries, beyond the barriers of different languages, of borders and passports, and he confidently assumed that one day all who lived
in Europe would recognize the force of his arguments and draw strength
from their common identity as Europeans. Over time, Europe would
develop its own political identity, where people in every country would see
themselves as citizens of the whole continent as much as nationals of any
single country. He wrote in *Pan-Europa*, 'A Pan-European sense of community, a sense of European patriotism, must take its place as the crown
and completion of the sense of nationhood.'

Now Europe includes virtually all the nations of RCK's original vision
of Pan-Europa. The moment is propitious. 'Time is pressing,' he wrote
even then, adding, 'Tomorrow it could be too late to solve the European
question.' He sensed the urgency of the task. There are sure to be many
more twists and turns in the European story yet, but RCK must rest content
with having shared his vision and its challenge with his contemporaries
and bequeathed it, even if still incomplete, to successive generations.

The Coudenhove-Kalergi Family

RCK'S GRANDPARENTS

Franz Karl von Coudenhove (1825–1893) was an Austrian diplomat posted to Dresden, the capital of the kingdom of Saxony. In later life he played a political role as a member of the Austrian lower chamber from 1871 and of the Herrnhaus, or upper chamber, from 1881.

In 1857, Franz married **Marie** Kalergi (1840–1877), the daughter of Jan Kalergi and Maria Nesselrode. They married in Paris, lived in Austria, and had six children, establishing the Coudenhove-Kalergi branch of the Coudenhove clan.

Their eldest son, **Heinrich** Johann Marie, was born in 1859. Their five other children were **Friedrich** (born 1861), **Johann** Dominil Maria (born 1863), Maria **Thekla** Walburga Franzisca (born 1865), **Richard** Joseph Franz Maria (born 1867), and **Marietta** Anna Sophie Viktora (born 1874). These were RCK's uncles and aunts.

RCK'S PARENTS

While posted to Tokyo as a diplomat, **Heinrich** married **Mitsuko (Mitsu)** Aoyama (born 1874), daughter of Kihachi and Tsune Aoyama, who died in 1908 and 1910 respectively. Heinrich died in Ronsperg in 1906, and Mitsu died in Mödling, near Vienna, in 1941.

RICHARD COUDENHOVE-KALERGI — 'DICKY' TO FRIENDS AND FAMILY. RCK FOR SHORT.

Richard Nikolaus Eijiro (1894–1972) was Heinrich and Mitsu's second son. He married **Ida** Roland, née Klausner (1881–1951) and adopted her daughter, **Erika**, from her dissolved first marriage to Gerd Bastian, a German-Ukrainian businessman. RCK's second marriage, in 1952, was to Alexandra (**Alix**) Tiele Winckler (d.1968), the widow of a rich Silesian landowner, and he adopted her son, Alexander (**Alex**), from her dissolved first marriage to Count Thiele Winckler. His third marriage, in 1969, was to **Melanie** Hoffmann-Benatsky, known to family as **Kirschi,** the widow of Ralph Benatsky (1884–1957), the composer of *White Horse Inn*. Richard had no offspring.

RCK'S BROTHERS AND SISTERS

Richard's elder brother was **Johannes** Evangelist Virgilio (1893–1968). Known to family as **Hansi**, he married the Hungarian aviatrix Lilly Sternschneider-Wenckheim and they had one daughter, Pixie. They separated during the Second World War, when Lilly and Pixie went into hiding in Italy and Switzerland, and their marriage was dissolved in 1960. Lilly died in 1970 in Geneva. Pixie emigrated, married in America, and died in California in 2000. Hansi remarried in the early 1960s to Ursula Grosch, an actress, and lived in Regensburg until his death in 1968.

Richard's younger brother was **Gerolf** Joseph Benedikt Maria Valentin (1896–1978), known in the family as **Rolfi**. He married Sophie Pállfy and they had four children – Hans Heinrich, Karl-Jakub, Barbara, and Michael. Hans-Heinrich died in London in 2004. Karl-Jakub died in Vienna in 2017. Barbara, a well-known journalist, lives in Vienna at the time of writing, and Michael, an established artist, lives in Tokyo.

Richard's eldest sister was **Elisabeth** Maria Anna (1898–1936). She was a secretary in the office of Chancellor Dollfuss until his assassination in 1934. She died of a brain haemorrhage in Paris two years later. Elisabeth did not marry and had no offspring.

Richard's next sister was **Olga** Marietta Henriette (1900–1976). She cared for her mother, Mitsu, until the latter's death in 1941. She then lived in West Germany, supported by RCK in her later years. Olga did not marry and had no offspring.

Richard's youngest sister was **Ida** Friderike Maria Anna (1901–1971). She married Walter Görres, an engineer from Leipzig, and became well known as a Catholic writer. They had no offspring.

Richard's youngest brother was **Karl** Heinrich Franz Maria (1903–1987). Called **Ery** by family and friends, he married Anita Neuber, a psychotherapist and artist, and lived in Australia, France, and Austria, then in Greece during the Second World War, and subsequently also in Venice, Zürich, and Vienna. They had no offspring.

RCK'S FIRST WIFE AND HER SIBLINGS

Ida Roland was the stage name of Ida Klausner, born in Vienna in 1881, the first child of a Jewish businessman and his Slovak wife. She and RCK married in Munich in 1915. RCK called her **Idel** to distinguish her from his youngest sister, Ida. She had three brothers and three sisters, but little beyond what is mentioned below, is recorded of their lives.

Arthur Klausner was a brother of Ida Roland and was a painter. He was staying with RCK and Idel in their house in Gruben when Dollfuss was assassinated in 1934.

Leopold Klausner was another of Idel's brothers and trained as an engineer, applying his skills to managing the Pan-Europa publishing house in Vienna during the 1920s and 1930s. He died in France during the Second World War, and his body was exhumed at RCK and Idel's request after 1945 to discover the cause of death, with a possible view to compensation if at the hands of the Nazis. He was reburied elsewhere in France.

Theresa Klausner, one of Idel's sisters, trained as an actress and married Walter Rille, a journalist on a Breslau newspaper and editor of *Die Erde*, the political monthly in which RCK's first article appeared. Rille later also pursued an acting career in Vienna and Berlin. He and his wife escaped to London in 1933, as soon as the Nazis came to power. He worked for the BBC during the war, and they later returned to West Germany, where he was a successful novelist.

Idel's other two sisters also trained for the stage, and subsequently lived for some months with RCK and Idel in Pöstlingberg during 1917–18, but no more is recorded about them, nor about their third brother.

RCK'S SECOND WIFE

RCK married **Alix Thiele-Winckler (née Bally)** in Paris in 1952. She was the widow (previously separated) of a rich Silesian landowner, Wilhelm von Redern, Count Thiele-Winckler, who had died in 1938. Richard adopted her son, Alexander, the same year that he married Alix. She died in 1968 after a prolonged illness.

RCK'S THIRD WIFE

RCK married **Melanie Benatsky** known as **Kirschi (née Hoffmann)** in 1969, with religious ceremonies reported both in Salzburg and in New York, but their marriage was never officially registered. She was the widow of Ralph Benatsky (1884–1957), the highly successful composer of songs and operettas, including *Zum Weissen Rössl* (*White Horse Inn*). The couple had known RCK's first wife, Idel, from the 1920s and had also been in exile with them as a couple in New York from 1940 to 1948. RCK's second wife, Alix, was also acquainted with them after 1951.

WHY THIS TITLE?

1 'This Pan-Europa, the way that cosmopolitan bastard Coudenhove conceives it,' wrote Hitler, 'would only be able someday to play vis-à-vis the United States of America or a nationally awakened China the same role that the old Austrian state played vis-à-vis Germany or Russia ... It is the rootless spirit of the old imperial capital, Vienna, that city of half-castes from East and West, that speaks to us in that vision.' Published in 1925 and 1927, the first two volumes of *Mein Kampf* did not sell well enough for Hitler's publisher to bring out the third volume in 1928. The manuscript came to light only after the end of the war and was published in Stuttgart in 1961 as *Hitler's Zweites Buch: ein Dokument aus dem Jahre 1928*.

INTRODUCTION

1 Jonathan Coe satirized the concept in his recent novel, *Middle England* (London: 2018): 'The white races of Europe ... were being slowly bred out of existence, and the whole process was the devilish invention of an Austrian aristocrat from the beginning of the twentieth century called Richard von Coudenhove-Kalergi. "The Kalergi Plan", as some liked to call it, was a plan to create a pan-European state in which, in the words of his book *Praktischer Realismus*, "the man of the future will be of mixed race. The Eurasian-Negroid race of the future, similar in appearance to the ancient Egyptians, will replace the diversity of peoples with a diversity of individuals." And this genocidal pan-European state, of course, was already established, and doing its fiendish work, in the form of the European Union, of which Kalergi was nothing less than the spiritual founder.' Even members of the European Parliament have asked for clarification from the European Commission on the subject. See written question E001516 of June 2019 under parliamentary questions at www.europarl.europa.eu. White-supremacist adherents of this theory usually refer to *Adel* (*Nobility*, 1924), reprinted in *Praktischer Realismus* (1926), in which the Count describes – but does not prescribe – the phenomenon of racial mixing. As Coe comments, 'The way these people twist his ideas is incredible.'

CHAPTER ONE

1 Originally from Crete and later from Venice, the wealthy Kalergis family was allied through marriage with the even-more-wealthy Russian Nesselrode family. Karl Nesselrode led the czar's delegation at the Congress of Vienna in 1815 and was Russian foreign minister for thirty years. Marie's mother, called Maria, was his favourite niece, artistically gifted and a celebrated beauty. Still in her teens, she married Johann Kalergis, and their daughter was born within a year of the marriage. But the personalities of Maria and Johann were entirely incompatible, and the couple split up immediately thereafter. Johann went to live independently in London, while Maria Kalergis led a life of luxury with a brilliant salon in Paris. It was there that her daughter, Marie, first met Franz Coudenhove in 1857.

2 The *cause célèbre* is well described in Hanna Dézsy, *Gentleman Europas: Erinnerungen an Richard Graf Coudenhove-Kalergi* (Vienna: 2001). Hanne Dézsy was RCK's secretary in the mid-1960s. The newspaper that broke the story was the *Das Neue Wiener Tagblatt*, and its editor claimed he acquired the pamphlet from Crown Prince Rudolf, who later committed suicide with his young mistress, Baroness Vetsera, at Mayerling in 1899.

3 The dates of the family's life in Tokyo have been ably researched by Masumi Schmidt-Muraki and presented in anecdotal fashion in her attractively readable biography of Mitsu, entitled *Die Gräfin kam aus Tokyo: Das Leben von Mitsuko Coudenhove-Kalergi* (Strasshof, Austria: 2017).

4 Despite his flair for languages, it is hard to imagine that Heinrich negotiated all the necessary arrangements with Mitsu's father without help from the embassy's official interpreter, Heinrich von Siebold (1852–1908), the second son of one of the earliest European explorers and traders in Japan, Philipp Franz von Siebold (1796–1866). Heinrich von Siebold and his brother learnt Japanese as young boys in Dejima, near Nagasaki, which was the only port permitted to trade with foreigners, and became, like their father, noted collectors of Japanese antiques, many of which were bequeathed to European museums. Heinrich von Siebold was already serving as an interpreter in the Austro-Hungarian legation when Heinrich Coudenhove-Kalergi came to Japan in the 1870s. In the early 1960s, RCK would employ a Frau Siebold in Zürich as his private secretary, in all probability a descendant of the same family.

5 RCK's life-long belief in the power of prophecy and second sight may well stem from this incident, which became part of the family's oral history and which he recalls in several accounts of his early life. Countess Ushida met Mitsu again in 1906–07, when her husband was posted to Vienna as Japanese ambassador, and again in September 1928, when she broke a journey from Tokyo to Paris to see Mitsu in Mödling, the suburb of Vienna where she was then living in retirement.

6 Marriages between a Japanese and a foreign partner were extremely rare, on average less than ten a year over the twenty years since the opening of the country to foreigners. Heinrich and Mitsu's was the 173rd to receive imperial approval, and the exotic nature of such arrangements fascinated European artists and writers, most famously Pierre Loti, a French naval officer who was briefly also stationed in Japan. His short novel of Japanese manners, *Madame Chrystanthème*, appeared in

1887 and served as the inspiration for André Messager's opera of the same name in 1893, as well as for Puccini's *Madama Butterfly* in 1904.

7 Confirmation of these dates can be found in 'Die Grafen Coudenhove: Die japanischen Taufen', by Philip Georg Graf Gudenus, 716–19, *Genealogie: Deutsche Zeitschrift für Familienkunde.* Heft 10, Band XIX, October 1989.

8 In 1933, Mitsu dictated her memoirs to her daughter Olga in the form of selected scenes and incidents from her life: *Memoiren von Gräfin Mitsu Coudenhove-Kalergi, die auf dem Schloss Ronsperg gelebt hat,* published by Verlag Cesky Les (Domazlice: 2014). She dedicated them to Hansi, his wife, Lilly, and their daughter, Pixie, but insisted the manuscript should not be published in her lifetime.

9 Heinrich's younger brother Johannes was briefly also in the Austro-Hungarian diplomatic service, but resigned after the death of his mother, Marie, to live with his widowed father, Franz, until the latter's death. He may have laboured under the false impression that he would inherit the family estates, or at least manage them during Heinrich's absence abroad. When Heinrich decided to settle in Ronsperg, Johannes emigrated to East Africa, where he lived as a recluse for the rest of his life, preferring the company of savages and animals to the 'civilised but duplicitous world of Europe'. In the family he was referred to as the Hermit, but maintained a desultory correspondence later in life with RCK's younger brother, Rolfi. He published his memoirs, *My African Neighbours: People, Birds, and Beasts in Nyassaland* (New York: 1925), in English.

10 Richard Bassett describes a revealing incident from this time in *Last Days in Old Europe* (London: 2019). A member of the Coudenhove family – probably Aunt Marietta – grandly asked the young Japanese woman on her arrival, 'What does it feel like to be marrying into a family of five hundred years of unbroken noble ancestry?' The Japanese girl coolly responded, 'I do not know because my family is more than two thousand years old.' Subsequently the two women got on well together.

11 Now an overgrown ruin in the forest, the hunting lodge was reduced to rubble by Czechoslovak border guards who used it as a target for tank firing practice during the Cold War.

12 The richest picture of Ronsperg is to be found in Franz Bauer's work of edited reminiscences, *Ronsperg: Ein Buch der Erinnerung,* published in West Germany in 1970 by the Heimatkreis Bischofteinitz, the association of refugees from Bischofteinitz in the Sudetenland. It includes this quoted comment by RCK. Even more detail about the estate and the surrounding forest is included in RCK's introduction to *Unser Heimatkreis Bischofteinitz* (by the same publisher: 1967) under the evocative heading *Mein Paradies.*

13 This cannot have been an easy step for a member of the Coudenhove clan. His uncle Maximilian was famous throughout the Empire for having led a heroic cavalry charge to cover the Austrian retreat at the battle of Königgratz in July 1866, little more than a generation earlier.

CHAPTER TWO

1 During the Communist years, neglected graves in the Catholic cemetery were cleared. Although the large sarcophagus for Heinrich remains, Babik's smaller grave has been lost.

2 The schoolmaster was Franz Bauer, editor of *Ronsperg: Ein Buch der Erinnerung* (Heimatkreis Bischofteinitz: 1970).

3 Artur Graf Strachwitz, *Wie es Wirklich War: Erinnerungen eines Achtzigjährigen* (Dülmen: 1991).

4 Ida Görres was best known for her biography of Saint Theresa, published in English as *The Hidden Face* (London: 1959). In her diary, which runs from 1951 to 1959 – published in 1964 as *Broken Lights* – she reflected on her earlier upbringing under Mitsu's domestic regime: 'Take my own case: from nursery days we were taught to believe the worst of people. We were drilled, in principle and emphatically, never to believe anyone, never to trust anyone, all people are liars, people are always hypocrites, especially if they are nice to you, everyone can be bought, etc. Scandal was the sole topic of conversation in Stockau: "Just to show you what the world is really like." I was fiercely determined to have no illusions, to confront even the ugliest reality face to face. I would smuggle *The History of Prostitution* and such-like books out of the library, disclosures of financial scandals I couldn't understand, books on the crimes of colonial government. And what was the result? I believed every word people told me, they could lie and swindle and make up whatever they liked. Could it be that my insatiable and often so incautious hunger for people who are good, pure, beautiful, and holy is in fact the direct result of that early training to despise people?'

5 Ery was never close to his siblings, despite returning to Paris in 1930 and subsequently living in Vienna from 1934. When Austria was annexed to Germany in 1938, he and his wife fled to Greece, where they survived the war. Subsequently they moved to Venice, Switzerland, and finally Vienna again. See Ery Coudenhove-Kalergi, *Da fällt mir meine Geschichte ein: Erinnerungen* (Zürich: 1982).

6 Dr Franz Josef Mayer-Gunthof, president of the Association of Austrian Industry from 1960 to 1972, would later prove to be the moving force among RCK's classmates, organizing support for him and Pan-Europa in the 1950s and 1960s. Information from the author's June 2017 interview in Vienna with Adolf Lacy Milkovics, former secretary-general of the Austrian section of the Pan-Europa Union.

7 For an overview of British writers, including Wickham Steed, who were both interested and informed on European affairs at this period, see John Pinder, 'Pre-war Ideas of European Union: The British Prophets,' in *Eminent Europeans*, edited by Martyn Bond, Julie Smith, and William Wallace, 1–21 (London: 1996).

8 Uta Kroll's unpublished University of Vienna 1970 thesis entitled *Ida Roland* relates Ida's stage history in detail. She trained for the stage at the Otto acting school in Vienna from the age of fifteen, and her three sisters all followed in her footsteps.

9 An historical drama by the Hungarian authors Melchior Lengyel and Lajos Biro, which Eugen Robert's troupe brought to Vienna following a successful run at the Kammerspiele in Munich. Some sources suggest Idel was also briefly married to

Eugen Robert, but there appears to be no evidence for this assertion. Her first marriage, to Theodor Bastien, a German-Ukrainian businessman, was dissolved in 1908.

10 See Caryl Emerson, *Cambridge Introduction to Russian Literature* (Cambridge: 2008).

CHAPTER THREE

1 For detail of Hitler's early years, see William Shirer, *The Rise and Fall of the Third Reich* (London: 1960) and Ian Kershaw, *Hitler: A Biography* (London: 2010). At this stage of their lives, RCK and Hitler were completely unaware of each other's existence. Later Hitler would devote several pages in the unpublished (third) volume of *Mein Kampf* to Pan-Europa and RCK, condemning him as a 'cosmopolitan bastard'.

2 RCK was proud of Professor Walter Geffcken's portrait of Ida as Czarina Catherine II and he reproduced it as an illustration in his first autobiographical book in German, *Der Kampf um Europa: Aus meinem Leben* (Zürich/Vienna: 1949).

3 Houston Stewart Chamberlain's popular theories about the supremacy of the Aryan or European race were expounded in *The Foundations of the Nineteenth Century*, published in German in 1899 and 1900. The book was a best seller, reprinted four times before the First World War. Chamberlain lectured at the University of Vienna until three years before RCK studied there. In the Chamberlain Kreis, a group that met weekly in Vienna to discuss the professor's ideas, RCK's Aunt Marietta, his father's youngest sister, made the acquaintance of both Rudolf Kassner and Count Hermann Keyserling, conservative writers who subsequently influenced RCK's thinking, in particular his notion of an 'intellectual aristocracy'.

4 RCK signed his name in different ways throughout his life, although his handwriting style remained similar from his twenties until his final year. He signed simply Richard or Richard Coudenhove-Kalergi on most occasions, and when he wished to impress the recipient, added his title of Count, or Graf. Over the years he often used just his initials – RCK – but to close friends and members of the family he was known and would always sign himself simply as Dicky.

5 *Der Rosenkavalier* enjoyed immediate success when first performed in Dresden in 1911, and also in Vienna, where it opened in April 1912, a year before RCK met Ida Roland.

6 This quotation is from an untitled, unsigned, and undated single-page typescript in the Lausanne archives. It reads (in the third person) like a police or informer's report on their relationship, but gives no indication of context.

7 Joseph Arthur Gobineau, a reactionary French aristocrat, published *An Essay on the Inequality of Human Races* in the 1850s. He preached white supremacy, opposed racially mixed marriages, even marriage between aristocrats and commoners, and was ferociously anti-Semitic. He exerted a strong intellectual influence on Houston Stewart Chamberlain, Richard Wagner's son-in-law. In 1923, 1929, and 1932, RCK reprinted his own father's study *Das Wesen des Antisemitismus*,

originally published in Prague in 1901, which powerfully rebutted Gobineau and Chamberlain's arguments. RCK added his own short essay on *Antisemitismus nach dem Weltkrieg* to these editions. A new edition in 1936, together with his expanded essay, now entitled *Judenhass von Heute*, quickly sold over twenty thousand copies.

8   RCK's doctoral thesis was an extended and much revised version of the sixth-form essay that had so absorbed and distracted him at school. The professorial panel called on to decide on RCK's doctoral thesis was divided, because some of the professors considered it more a work of popularization than an academic study.

9   These rumours were reported to RCK in a letter from Aunt Thekla, now preserved in the archives in Pilsen.

10 The Treaty of Brest-Litovsk between Bolshevik Russia and the Central Powers (Germany, Austro-Hungary, Bulgaria, and the Ottoman Empire) in March 1918 followed an initial armistice on that front in December 1917. By this treaty, Russia ceded control over Finland, the Baltic States, and Russian Poland and recognized the independence of Ukraine. Peace on the Eastern front released German and Austro-Hungarian troops for redeployment, enabling the German High Command to launch their final, but unsuccessful, assault on the Western front in May 1918.

11 Memoirs by Gerolf (Rolfi) Coudenhove, *Achtzig Jahre: 1896–1976* (unpublished ms) in the Lausanne archives.

12 RCK prepared a legal case in 1916–17 (preserved in the archives in Pilsen) contesting his elder brother Hansi's right, under the will of his grandmother Marie, to inherit the Coudenhove-Kalergi estates when he came of age. He argued that the term 'eldest son' of his father Heinrich should be interpreted as 'surviving sons', thus permitting an equal share to Hansi and to himself, Rolfi, and Ery. In correspondence with a Czech lawyer in 1946 (preserved in the archives in Lausanne), he asserted that he was ready to swear on oath that he had tried to persuade his family in 1916 that Hansi was not of sound mind and should not therefore inherit the Coudenhove-Kalergi estates. The context for this exchange was the prospective trial of Hansi on charges of treason for collaborating with the Nazis before and during the Second World War.

13 Karl Heinrich (Ery) attended the Theresianum in the 1920s, just three years ahead of Paul von Henried, the son of the recently deceased Baron Karl Alphons von Henried and his wife, with whom Mitsu was well acquainted. Paul Henreid (the spelling of his name was changed by the Hollywood studio – just reversing two letters and deleting 'von' – to make it seem less German) went on to play Victor Laszlo in *Casablanca*, a role partly modelled on RCK's early adult life. See Ery Coudenhove-Kalergi, *Da fällt mir meine Geschichte ein. Erinerungen* (Zürich: 1982).

CHAPTER FOUR

1   President Wilson's Fourteen Points can be summarized as follows: 1. No secret agreements between any states; 2. Freedom of navigation on the seas; 3. No economic barriers between nations; 4. General disarmament; 5. Impartial decisions in regard to colonies; 6. The German army to leave Russian territory, and Russia

to determine its own political structure; 7. Belgium to regain independence; 8. France to have Alsace-Lorraine returned; 9. The borders of Italy to expand to include adjacent territory with Italian majorities; 10. National self-determination for the peoples living in Austria-Hungary; 11. National self-determination for the Balkan states; 12. The Turkish government to govern only Turkish people, not any religious (Christian) minorities; 13. The state of Poland to be recreated and have access to the Baltic; 14. The League of Nations to be established to guarantee political and territorial independence of all states.

2 The following brief assessment of the characters of the three main protagonists can be found in *The Collected Writings of John Maynard Keynes*. Vol. 10: *Essays in Biography*, published for the Royal Economic Society in London 1972: 'Clemenceau, aesthetically the noblest; the President, morally the most admirable; Lloyd George, intellectually the subtlest. Out of their disparities and weaknesses the Treaty was born, child of the least worthy attributes of each of its parents, without nobility, without morality, without intellect.'

3 The arrangements were negotiated by Colonel Strutt, the personal emissary sent by King George V to protect the Hapsburg family. King George did not wish to see his Hapsburg relatives summarily executed by revolutionaries, as had happened to the Romanovs only a few months previously at Yekaterinburg. Karl von Hapsburg, the former emperor, initially went into exile in Switzerland in May 1919, accompanied by his wife and children. However, after two abortive attempts in 1921 to restore the monarchy in Hungary, the Allies decided that the family's place of exile should no longer be mainland Europe. Exiled to Madeira, Karl died of pneumonia the following year. RCK would later work closely with Karl's eldest son, Otto von Hapsburg, when both sought refuge in America during the Second World War, and later still on his return to post-war Europe. See Gordon Brook-Shepherd, *Uncrowned Emperor: The Life and Times of Otto von Hapsburg* (London: 2003).

4 Walter Rille, the husband of Idel's sister, Theresa, was born in 1899 and studied in Königsberg, Breslau (now Wroclaw in Poland), and Lausanne. He was features editor of the *Breslauer Neueste Nachrichten* at the time when he was also editing *Die Erde*, in which he published RCK's first article. From 1923 he became a stage and film actor, with some success in Vienna and Berlin. As a Jewish intellectual, he was forced to emigrate in 1933, and subsequently worked with the BBC in London until 1945. After that, Rille returned to West Germany and wrote novels: *Saat der Zeit* (*The Seeds of Time*) an eight-hundred-page panorama of his heroine's life in war-torn contemporary Europe – much admired by Thomas Mann – and *Ohnmacht des Herzens* (*Leucadian Leap*), published in English and German in 1956.

5 Kurt Hiller and RCK shared a mutual admiration for Heinrich Mann, whose essay 'Geist und Tat' ('Thought and Deed') had made him the unofficial leader of a group of socially engaged contemporary young writers. Relating literary criticism closely to the economic and social conditions of the age, Hiller termed its new approach 'literary activism' or 'literature in the cause of political intervention'. For RCK, it offered a bridge between the intellectual world of books and the practical world of politics. Daniel Mänzer's thorough biography, *Kurt Hiller: Der*

Intellektuelle als Aussenseiter (Göttingen: 2015), reveals among other things that, having fled Germany in 1933, Hiller spent many years in England, fifteen or so of them on the payroll of MI5.

6 RCK was in good company. Many of the signatories were progressive writers and thinkers of the time, but their paths diverged dramatically in later years. Walter Benjamin (1892–1940), a German-Jewish philosopher and Marxist cultural critic, committed suicide at Port Bou, while trying to escape from occupied France. Otto Flake (1880–1963) was an extremely popular author during the First World War and the Weimar Republic, signed the declaration of loyalty to Adolf Hitler after 1933, and stayed in Germany during the Second World War. Max Brod (1884–1968), a German-speaking Jewish author, born in Prague, was well known before 1914 for his expressionist novels, and became Kafka's literary executor. He emigrated to Palestine in 1939 and disobeyed Kafka's instructions by publishing his work after his friend died. Heinrich Mann (1871–1950) was the older brother of Thomas Mann and a committed anti-Nazi. He fled to France in 1933 and to America in 1940. His left-wing views led him to accept the presidency of the East German Academy of Arts in 1950. He died while still in America, but his ashes were ceremonially buried in East Berlin.

7 Max Harden was injured by right-wing thugs in Berlin in 1921 and retired to Switzerland to recover. He invited RCK to take over as editor of *Die Zukunft*, but RCK declined. In a letter in 1924, Harden pointed out that they had been preaching the same message of European unity ever since they first corresponded during the First World War. After Harden's death, RCK published a sympathetic obituary in *Pan-Europa Journal* 1 (1927).

8 The first volume of Oswald Spengler's *Der Untergang des Abendlandes* (*The Decline of the West*) sold a hundred thousand copies in the five years before the second volume appeared in 1924. RCK was indebted to him for his analysis of several aspects of contemporary society, in particular the relation of democracy to plutocracy, but rejected his more extreme reactionary and racist views.

9 Five separate treaties were negotiated at the Paris Peace Conference in 1919 and 1920 concerning Germany (Versailles), Austria (Saint Germain), Hungary (Trianon), Bulgaria (Neuilly), and Turkey (Sèvres). Collectively referred to as the Versailles Settlement, they each limited the size of the specific country's armed forces, fixed reparations to be paid to the Allies, and adjusted the borders of the state and its neighbours. In sum, they created as new states Poland, Estonia, Latvia, Lithuania, Czechoslovakia, and the Kingdom of the Serbs and Croats. For a comprehensive analysis of the Paris Peace Conference, see Margaret MacMillan, *The Peacemakers: Six Months that Changed the World* (London: 2001).

10 Although Vienna was the city that he knew best, RCK had little sympathy with the dominant party in Austria, led by Karl Renner, a Social Democrat politician with Marxist leanings. Despite his personal admiration of Count Karolyi, briefly the leader of the new Hungarian state, RCK was opposed to Magyar nationalism. He certainly lacked any respect for the Bolshevik, Belá Kun, who ousted Karolyi in March 1919, let alone the White Terror that followed the communists' fall from power later the same year. Idel was half-Jewish, half-Slovak, and if he had

to have a nationality, then Czechoslovak was the least unacceptable alternative. Also, his family knew Thomas Garrigue Masaryk, the new president. His Uncle Max had handled the peaceful transfer of power from Vienna to the new president in Prague at the dissolution of the old Austro-Hungarian Empire.

11 RCK may not have known of an earlier scheme for European economic co-operation that the Allies had vetoed at the Paris Peace Conference in April 1919 when it was proposed by the French minister of commerce, Etienne Clémentel. Jean Monnet – deputy secretary-general of the League of Nations after the First World War, and the moving force behind the creation of the European Coal and Steel Community after the Second World War – was then an adviser to the minister. Masaryk was referring to an informal initiative that he himself undertook at around the same time, specifically to group together East European states as a *cordon sanitaire* between Russia and Germany.

12 This was confirmed for RCK later when he learned that, just before his death in 1937, Masaryk told a journalist in an interview that, if he were thirty-five again, he would put all his energy into establishing the United States of Europe.

13 The League of Nations solved or prevented the escalation of several small international disputes – the issue of the Aaland Islands between Sweden and Finland, of Memel between Poland and Lithuania, and of Upper Silesia between Germany and Poland. However, it failed to solve other conflicts, for example at Fiume (between Italy and Yugoslavia), at Teschen (between Poland and Czechoslovakia), at Vilna (between Poland and Ukraine), and at Corfu (between Italy and Greece). The League was also powerless to stop the invasion of Manchuria by Japan and of Abyssinia by Italy, or later the intervention by Germany and Italy in the civil war in Spain. See Margaret MacMillan, *The Peacemakers*.

14 Until 1933 the League's Secretariat was headed by a British diplomat, Sir Eric Drummond. For the first three years his deputy was Jean Monnet, and until 1930 the head of the Economic and Finance Section was Arthur Salter, who had worked with Monnet in co-ordinating Allied shipping in London during the Great War. In 1933, Arthur Salter, a critical supporter of RCK's Pan-Europa programme, published a collection of essays about the League, entitled *The United States of Europe*. Drummond was succeeded by Joseph Avenol from France, a fascist sympathizer, who wrote of the need for a 'new soul for a new France' which would 'work in collaboration with Germany and Italy and keep the British out of Europe'. He resigned from his post in August 1940, and was succeeded by Seán Lester, his Irish deputy, whose caretaker function ceased in April 1946, when the League of Nations was wound up and its assets passed to the United Nations.

CHAPTER FIVE

1 The main area of dispute between Austria and Italy was South Tyrol (Alto Adige in Italian). In order to bring Italy into the First World War on the side of the Allies, the region was promised to Italy by Great Britain and France in the Treaty of London in 1915. It was incorporated into the Kingdom of Italy in 1919 as part of the Versailles settlement. Heavy-handed repression of the German-speaking

majority by the Italian regime after 1921 – banning German from public services and censoring the German-speaking press, except for *Die Alpenzeitung*, the fascist newspaper – alienated much local opinion. Austria raised the issue in the League of Nations, but to no avail.

2 Gaius Marius was a Roman general and statesman (157–86 BC). He held the office of consul an unprecedented seven times. Known as the 'third founder of Rome' for his important army reforms – recruiting landless citizens and reorganizing the structure of the legions into separate cohorts – Marius defeated the invading Germanic tribes. The Rokitno Swamps are known in English as the Pripet Marshes, lying across the borders of Poland, Belarus, and Ukraine, the scene of a major German victory against the Russians at Tannenberg in the opening months of the First World War.

3 Hitler may have first come to the embassy's attention when, in his absence from Munich on a visit to Berlin, a small group of opponents tried to oust him from the leadership of the National Socialist German Workers' Party (NSDAP) and merge the party with another right-wing group. He returned to Munich, outmanoeuvred his opponents, forced their resignation, and secured his own full control over the nascent Nazi Party in July 1921.

4 The *Völkischer Beobachter*, as part of the Eher Verlag, was for sale for 115,000 Reichsmarks and the NSDAP did not have this sum available. Army funds – either as a loan or a gift facilitated by officers from Hitler's former regiment – enabled its purchase. By 1923, the newspaper had become a daily with a circulation of twenty-five thousand, with all shares registered in Hitler's name.

5 Two American publications laid the basis for the study of social psychology and political manipulation in the 1920s: Walter Lippmann's ground-breaking analysis, *Public Opinion*, in 1922 and Edward Bernays's *Crystallizing Public Opinion* in 1923. 'As a result of psychological research, coupled with the modern means of communication, the practice of democracy has turned a corner,' wrote Lippmann. Bernays (a nephew of Sigmund Freud) added, 'No serious sociologist any longer believes that the voice of the people expresses any divine or specially wise or lofty idea. The voice of the people expresses the mind of the people, and that mind is made up for it by the group leaders in whom it believes and by those persons who understand the manipulation of public opinion. It is composed of inherited prejudices and symbols and clichés and verbal formulas supplied to them by the leaders.'

CHAPTER SIX

1 The Social Democratic Party's chairman, Otto Bauer, was a fully assimilated Jewish intellectual with a doctorate from the University of Vienna. He served as foreign minister in the first coalition government in 1918–19, and his family was held in high social esteem. His sister was a patient of Freud, and her case is recorded as that of 'Dora' in his writings.

2 Bert Riehle, in *Eine neue Ordnung der Welt* (Göttingen: 2009), lists no fewer than sixty initiatives for restructuring Europe that were launched in the German-

speaking world in the forty years before 1933. Of these, seven were by elected politicians, thirty-five were by academics, and twenty were by independent writers active in the peace movement. RCK may well have read articles or heard speeches by several proponents of reform, among them an acquaintance of his, Harry Graf Kessler, but RCK's Pan-Europa is the only coherent project that created an international membership organization, made a serious political impact, and left a lasting intellectual heritage.

3 Despite the deep impression that Fried's *Pan-Amerika* made on RCK, he claims he first heard of the notion of 'Pan' organizations from Abdullah Al-Mamun Suhrawardy, a visitor to Ronsperg while his father was still alive. Suhrawardy, a brilliant young Bengali Muslim lawyer and academic, founded the Pan-Islamic Society of London and edited its journal, *Pan-Islam*. He was a follower of Sayyid Jamal al-Afghani (died 1897), an early proponent of Pan-Islamism, and visited him in Paris around the time he was staying in Ronsperg. He conversed with RCK's father, Heinrich, in Arabic.

4 This opposition was most clearly articulated within the peace movement at a conference in Berlin in 1924 which brought to a head the schism between supporters of RCK's view and those holding more fundamental and traditional pacifist views.

5 Freemasonry was regarded with suspicion and banned for many years in Austria (but not in Hungary), and Heinrich, RCK's father, wrote a pamphlet defending it against certain Catholic prejudices. It was only formally reinstated in Austria under the new Republic in January 1919. Humanitas was the most prestigious Masonic Lodge in Vienna at the time, and membership marked a personal achievement for RCK, extending his circle of friends among the Austrian elite and helping promote his ideas. Freemasons were to support his Pan-Europa Union financially as well as morally for years to come.

6 Nicholas Murray Butler was then president of Columbia University and a potential Republican candidate as president of the United States. The interview was reprinted in a small brochure and widely ciculated in Europe as well as the United States. Murray Butler later helped to finance RCK's first visit to the United States on a lecture tour in 1925–26 through the Carnegie Endowment for International Peace, of which he was the president. He also supported him financially as well as politically when he arrived as an exile in New York in 1940.

7 Anglophone readers may feel uncomfortable at RCK's admiration for Napoleon, who is usually portrayed in the teaching of British history more as a tyrant than a modernizer and law-giver. A more measured assessment may be found in Peter Geyl, *Napoleon: For and Against* (London 1957).

8 It is to the essay entitled 'Adel (Nobility)' that white supremacists and other far-right extremists with a penchant for conspiracy theories refer when they invoke the 'Plan Coudenhove' or 'Plan Kalergi'. This conspiracy theory, which initially blossomed around the turn of the millennium, claims that RCK aimed to eliminate the white race through racial mixing with immigrants from outside Europe. Their interpretation represents a gross misreading of the text, in which RCK objectively describes what was already occurring and would increasingly occur – racial

mixing – as various factors of globalization became ever more apparent. RCK perhaps rashly, and certainly with no convincing evidence, expressed the opinion that people of mixed race had less independent spirit and were more easily ruled by a more resilient elite, among which he counted the Jews, since they had a less-diluted genetic line. From this incautious observation, white supremacists extrapolate the false argument that European elites in Brussels are now planning genocide for the Aryan race and Jewish domination of the whole world.

9 RCK originally excluded Russia and Great Britain from his vision of Pan-Europa. In defence of these exclusions, he cited both contemporary Pan-America, which excluded Canada, and the Pan-Hellenic movement of the classical era, which excluded Macedonia, each clearly for very different reasons, despite those countries being part of their respective geographic regions.

CHAPTER SEVEN

1 Frau Andy von Zsolnay attracted many artists, writers, and musicians to her country house, Schloss Oberufer, among them Hugo von Hofmannsthal, Gerhart Hauptmann, Arthur Schnitzler, and Bruno Walter, as well as RCK and Idel. One evening, Alma Mahler (the composer's widow, now divorced from her second husband, Walter Gropius) was there with Franz Werfel (whom she later married) and suggested that Paul, Frau Zsolnay's son, might become a publisher, impulsively offering him the manuscript of Franz's recently completed biography of Verdi. It headed the pz Verlag's first list and became a best seller. Paul went on to publish many other leading German authors – among them Heinrich Mann and Max Brod and many contemporary foreign authors in translation, making his pz Verlag the most successful literary publishing house in Austria before the Nazi take-over in 1938.

2 RCK set up his publishing house, the Pan-Europa Verlag, in 1923 in the Gumpendorferstrasse, only a few hundred yards away from his flat in Schmerlingplatz. Until the annexation of Austria in March 1938, it published all his books and also the monthly journal *Pan-Europa*, intentionally using the same title as his own best-selling political book. To differentiate between the two, in this biography the monthly is referred to as the *Pan-Europa Journal*. Ten editions each year were distributed to an international readership of over ten thousand subscribers, RCK always contributing well over half its content.

3 After discussing the geographic, historical, and cultural borders of Europe, RCK defined the limits of Pan-Europa as follows: 'Europe as a political concept includes all democratic states of continental Europe, including Iceland which is linked to Denmark in a personal union.' A footnote to the word 'democratic' adds: 'and semi-democratic', the effect of which was to include Mussolini's Italy within his definition.

CHAPTER EIGHT

1 This volume, commonly known as *Hitler's Second Book*, was intended as volume three of *Mein Kampf*, but it was not published as planned in 1928. It first appeared as *Hitlers Zweites Buch: ein Dokument aus dem Jahr 1928* (Stuttgart: 1961).

2 Geheimrat Dr Fritsch of the Dresdner Bank was trustee for the German half of the Warburg grant, and Vice-President Brosche of the Kreditanstalt for the Austrian half, which also covered activities in other countries. Max Warburg himself is characterized in Ron Chernow, *The Warburgs: A Family Saga* (London: 1993) as 'not a cautious, sober man holding out against the frenzied crowd, but a red-blooded buccaneer'. He was active on twenty-seven boards of directors of German companies, including the giant IG Farben and, exceptionally for a Jew, was on the board of the Reichsbank, chaired by Hjalmar Schacht. He held this post until 1938, when his Hamburg bank was eventually 'Aryanized', and he was finally forced to leave the country for America.

3 Idel enjoyed a stellar career after conquering Vienna as *Die Czarina*. She played numerous daring parts, including trouser roles as the lead in *Hamlet* and as Napoleon's son in Rostand's *L'Aiglon*, as well as the first openly lesbian role on the Viennese stage, Ruth in Kaltneker's *Die Schwester* in the Renaissancebühne in 1923. She joined the Burgtheater Ensemble from 1924 to 1927, and subsequently pursued an independent star career to great critical acclaim. Her final roles, in 1935 and 1936 respectively, were as Cleopatra and Lady Macbeth, both as a visiting star at the Burgtheater.

4 Like RCK, Rohan was an early admirer of Mussolini. Fascism for him was also the most acceptable realization of the conservative revolution. His increasingly anti-democratic views, however, alienated many of his early liberal supporters. In 1932, he dismissed Max Clauss, the progressive editor of his quarterly *Europäische Revue*, and in 1935 Rohan himself joined the Austrian Nazi Party. In 1938, immediately after Anschluss, he declared his support for Hitler and subsequently played a marginal role in the literary world of Nazi Germany. He served in the Intelligence Services (Abwehr) during the war.

5 Hjalmar Schacht was known as the 'Old Wizard' for his financial acumen and maintained his post as president of the Reichsbank under the Nazis, despite never joining the Nazi Party. As minister of economics from 1934 to 1937, he invented a parallel system of private industrial credits (loans from the Metallurgische Forschungsgesellschaft, or Metallurgical Research Foundation: MEFO bills) not reported within Nazi Germany's national accounts, thus secretly helping to finance rearmament, eventually by a sum over two-thirds as much as the total national debt. He was arrested by the Gestapo after the July plot to assassinate Hitler in 1944 and spent nearly a year in various concentration camps. He was put on trial at Nuremberg in 1945 for war crimes, but acquitted – against the Soviet judge's objections – at the insistence of the British.

6 Gustav Stresemann, German foreign minister from 1923 to 1929, signed the Rapallo Pact with the Soviet Union in 1922, including secret military co-operation clauses. With the United States, Germany's main trading partner, he negotiated reduced reparations, first with the Dawes Plan in 1924 and again with the Young

Plan in 1929. With France and Great Britain, he signed the Locarno Treaty in 1925, which offered guarantees for peace on Germany's western border, and soon thereafter accession to the League of Nations. In the same year that Aristide Briand offered 'some kind of federal link' between European states to help bolster peaceful relations, however, he wrote to the German crown prince, 'If the allies had obliged me just one single time, I would have brought the German people behind me, yes; even today, I could still get them to support me. However, they [the allies] gave me nothing and the minor concessions they made, always came too late. Thus, nothing else remains for us but brutal force. The future lies in the hands of the new generation. Moreover, they, the German youth, who we could have won for peace and reconstruction, we have lost. Herein lies my tragedy and there, the allies' crime.'

7 Together with Wilhelm Solf, the first governor of German Samoa and briefly – October to December 1918 – foreign minister, Hans von Seeckt and Walter Simons set up the SiSeSo Society, a private dining and discussion club in Berlin to which RCK would later be invited as a speaker on the eve of the Nazi take-over of power.

8 Joseph Caillaux and his second wife, Henriette, were among the richest couples in France at the time. They had achieved notoriety in 1914 while he was minister of finance and she shot dead the editor of Le Figaro to prevent publication of personally embarrassing letters written to her while Caillaux was still married to his first wife. Henriette was acquitted on the grounds that the murder was a crime of passion, caused by the 'unstable emotions of a woman devoted to her husband'.

9 Giovanni Giolitti was five times prime minister between 1892 and 1921. His centrist Liberal Union led coalitions either with conseratives on the right or with progressives on the left. He initially welcomed Mussolini as an enemy of the extreme Socialists, but withdrew his support in 1924 when Mussolini abrogated press freedom. He remained as a vocal-but-aging liberal critic in the Chamber of Deputies, finally speaking against Mussolini's abolition of elections in 1928, the year in which Giolitti died. Giovanni Amendola was an active politician and journalist, a key leader of the opposition to Mussolini. In December 1924, he published the evidence linking Mussolini to the murder of Giacomo Matteotti, and led the cross-party Aventine Group of one hundred and fifty deputies who boycotted the Chamber that year. He was murdered by Fascist thugs who clubbed him to death while he was on holiday in Cannes in April 1926. Gaetano Salvemini was an academic historian who coined the description of Giolitti as 'Minister for the Underworld' in a critical article published before the war. Elected as an Independent Radical in 1919, he initially admired Mussolini's efforts to reinvigorate Italian society, but in January 1925 he founded a clandestine anti-Fascist newspaper and was put on the Fascist death list. He fled the country, first to France, then England, and finally the United States, where he taught at Harvard from 1934 to 1948.

10 Continuing Vatican interest in RCK's ideas is reflected in the personal dedication to Otto von Hapsburg that Pope John Paul II wrote into a reprint of RCK's Pan-Europa at the height of the Solidarity uprising in Poland in 1983. The copy was

passed on some years later to Graf Rupert von Strachwitz, nephew of Artur Graf Strachwitz, and shown to the author in 2018.

CHAPTER NINE

1 Wilhelm Heile, a member of the Reichstag from 1919 to 1924, called for a United States of Europe at a meeting of the Inter-Parliamentary Union in Vienna in 1922. After this quarrel, however, he was never reconciled with RCK and was instrumental in preventing Pan-Europa's re-establishment in West Germany after 1945 through his support for a rival organization, Europa Union. He died in West Germany in 1969. Pan-Europa was more successful after this, gathering a crowd of fourteen thousand supporters at a demonstration in Berlin in 1979, for instance, in favour of direct elections to the European Parliament.

2 Alfred Nossig, born to Jewish parents in 1864 in Lviv, studied a wide range of subjects – natural sciences, medicine, law, and philosophy – in several universities, receiving his doctorate from Zürich. He lived briefly in Vienna and Paris before settling in Berlin in 1900, and made his name as an artist and sculptor as well as a political agitator working for Zionist causes. He collaborated with Heile during the 1920s, was expelled from Germany to Poland by the Nazis in 1933, and, when Germany invaded Poland, was confined to the Warsaw Ghetto. There he collaborated with the Nazi authorities and was executed by a Jewish resistance organization in 1943.

3 For further details of media and political discussion of this theme in Germany, France, and Britain in the 1920s and 1930s, see Verena Schöberl, *'Es gibt ein grosses und herrliches Land, dass sich selbst nicht kennt … Es heist Europa'* (Berlin: 2008). For a more detailed analysis of the diplomatic relations, see James Wilkie, *Die britische Europapolitik, 1929–1932*, an unpublished two-volume dissertation at the University of Vienna, 1973, and Conan Fischer, *A Vision of Europe: Franco-German Relations during the Great Depression, 1929–1932* (Oxford: 2017).

4 Hanne Dézsy, one of RCK's former secretaries, accepts the Weiss version of events in her insightful monograph on her employer, *Gentleman Europas* (Vienna: 2001). RCK, Arthur Henderson, and Louise Weiss were in their early thirties, and Idel was somewhat older, and this discrepancy in age may possibly have contributed to the heightened tension between the two women. Either RCK's memory was at fault when he wrote his memoirs (unlikely) and Lange was not a debating partner on this tour (equally unlikely), or he intentionally suppressed aspects of the episode that may have caused Idel some discomfort. Perhaps the tour may have been in two parts, each report having some truth?

CHAPTER TEN

1 RCK reports his Czech support as unqualified, but a letter from Beneš to Masaryk, dated 19 September 1926, recommends that Masaryk should not accept the honorary presidency of the Pan-Europa Congress in Vienna, nor commit himself to specific policies, 'because there are a number of practical impossibilities in Coudenhove's

plan with which we cannot agree.' Beneš recommended that Masaryk should simply send a supportive letter and help to fund the event as a gesture, leaving any further action to Beneš. This letter was kindly brought to the author's attention by Lubor Jilek, and can be found in *Korrespondence T.G.Masaryk – Edvard Beneš, 1918 to 1937*, ed. Dagmar Hájková, Vlasta Quagliatová, and Richard Vasek (Prague: 2013).

2   Bruno Birnbaum was dismissed from his post in the Humboldt University when the Nazis came to power for being a Jew. He fled from Germany to the United States and was appointed as a professorial lecturer at the Yeshiva College in New York. He may well have still been there when RCK arrived in 1940.

3   RCK maintained links with many individual Freemasons throughout his life. This may well explain the obituaries that appeared in Masonic publications after his death some forty-five years later. A brief overview of RCK's Masonic connections is contained in an informative article by Otto Zuber entitled 'Richard Graf Coudenhove-Kalergi (1894–1972) als Freimaurer' in the *Jahrbuch der Forschungsloge Quatuor Coronati* (*Yearbook of the Research Lodge Quatuor Coronati*) Nr. 32 (Bayreuth: 1994).

4   Ernst Lothar (1890–1974) was born in Brno and made his name as a writer and theatre director in the interwar years in Vienna. His wife, the actress Adrienne Gesser, a friend of Ida Roland, fled with him into exile in the United States during the Second World War. In *the World of Yesterday*, Stephen Zweig attributed to him the sad quotation: 'Emigration is for a young man with no memories.' Felix Salten (1869–1945) was already an established theatre and art critic in Vienna before the First World War. He married Ottilie Metzl, an actress who was also acquainted with Ida Roland, and they fled at Anschluss to Zürich, where he died just after the end of the Second World War. He is best known internationally as the author of *Bambi*.

5   Edgar Stern-Rubarth, a Jewish journalist from Frankfurt-am-Main, was decorated for bravery in the First World War, converted to Roman Catholicism, and was married in Cologne Cathedral in 1917. He pursued a successful career as a journalist in Weimar Germany, working closely with the Foreign Office when Gustav Stresemann was foreign minister. In 1924 he founded the European Customs Union, a private support group for this policy, and later became president of the semi-official German-French Society. Dismissed by the Nazis from all his posts in 1933, he emigrated to London in 1936, wrote for *The Times* and the *Daily Telegraph*, and took British nationality in 1946. He continued his journalistic career after the war both in Germany and Great Britain, and in 1956 became press secretary in the German embassy in London.

CHAPTER ELEVEN

1   Louis Loucheur, French minister for amaments and recruitment in the First World War, clashed with Jean Monnet when the latter was a junior civil servant in London, co-ordinating Allied supplies across the Atlantic. Offended by instructions from Monnet, whose memos came to him endorsed by President Clemenceau, Loucheur personally insisted that 'young Monnet' be transferred

from civilian to military service, liable for service at the front, where the life expectancy of a new lieutenant was no more than a few weeks. However, Clemenceau, to whom Monnet reported directly, intervened. He agreed that the young civil servant should be enrolled as a lieutenant but – against Loucheur's wishes – insisted that he stay at his post in London. Monnet describes his clash with the minister in the first volume of his *Mémoires* (Paris: 1976). Loucheur became RCK's main business and political supporter in France, which did not endear RCK or Pan-Europa to Monnet.

2 RCK and Idel were personally acquainted with Emile Mayrisch, who also supported European cultural exchanges through an arts programme centred on his country estate at Colpach in Luxembourg. His premature death in March 1928 in a car crash en route to Paris for a meeting of the EIA delayed for a year RCK's plans for a second Pan-Europa Congress, initially scheduled for 1929, at which Mayrisch would have played a leading role. Dannie Heineman would go on to publish his own view of Europe's future in a short book in 1930 entitled *Skizze eines neuen Europas*.

3 The Gruben property and the subsequent parcels of land around it were bought by Idel with her own money. On her death in 1951, she bequeathed it jointly to RCK and to her daughter, Erika. Disposing of it would become a bone of contention between them.

4 Artur Graf Strachwitz, *Wie es Wirklich War: Erinnerungen eines Achtzigjährigen* (Dülmen: 1991).

5 Rolf Italiaander, *Richard N. Coudenhove-Kalergi, Begründer der Paneuropa-Bewegung* (Freudenstadt: 1969).

CHAPTER TWELVE

1 Arthur Salter analysed the Briand Memorandum in an internal note for the League of Nations in 1930, subsequently made public in his collection of essays entitled *The United States of Europe* (London: 1933).

2 For numerous references to RCK in his diaries, see Leo Amery, *The Empire at Bay, 1929–1945* (London: 1988).

3 Article by Winston Churchill in the *Saturday Evening Post*, 15 February 1930, quoted at length by RCK in *An Idea Conquers the World* (London: 1953). For a masterly overview of Churchill's views of Europe, see Allen Packwood, *Churchill and the United States of Europe, 1904–1948* (Churchill College, Cambridge), and for the years after 1945 in particular, see Felix Klos, *Churchill on Europe* (London: 2016).

4 By the end of 1931, RCK had effectively given up hope that the Study Group of the League would deliver any positive conclusions based on Briand's idea of a European federation, as witness comments in his address to Chatham House in June that year. Aristide Briand died in March 1932, and Germany withdrew from the League in September 1933.

5 A common political identity for all subjects of the British Empire was a live issue of academic and journalistic debate, as was a European identity for a prospective political federation on the lines of Pan-Europa. The academic thesis by Herbert

Sartorius, *Panbritannien und Paneuropa: Ein kritischer Vergleich* (University of Cologne: 1934), and the earlier comparative work by Karl Haushofer, *Geo-Politik der Panideen* (Berlin: 1931), bear witness to this.

6 RCK seized on the speech by the Marquis Giorgio Quartara, who spoke encouragingly on European peace through federation. However, Quartara was speaking merely in a private capacity, not representing the Italian government. For more on Quartara, see Louisa Passerini, *Love and the Idea of Europe* (New York/Oxford: 2009). The revised title for the 2012 paperback edition was *Women and Men in Love: European Identities in the Twentieth Century*.

7 Leo Amery, again the highest-ranking British participant and still out of office, reported on the Empire Economic Conference in Ottawa, which had just agreed on Empire Free Trade, which was not really free trade at all, but preference for home producers first, empire producers second, and foreign producers last. RCK suggested that Pan-Europa should propose a comparable economic programme for the continent: Europe first, its colonies second, and then the rest of the world.

8 All RCK's publications were banned in Nazi Germany except two: *Held oder Heiliger* (Vienna/Paris/Leipzig: 1927), a complex essay that deals with ethics and aspects of European identity, and *Stalin & Co.* (Vienna/Leipzig: 1931), a highly critical study of contemporary Bolshevism.

CHAPTER THIRTEEN

1 However well acclimatized, RCK and Idel were nonetheless foreigners in Vienna. Since the end of the First World War they travelled on Czechoslovak diplomatic passports and identified themselves essentially as European. It was easy for nationalists to stigmatize him as Japanese and only half-European, and her as Jewish, or 'cosmopolitan'.

2 At this time, the Austrian Nazi Party had well over a hundred thousand members, while the Austrian Communist Party had only about six thousand members, and in general elections received just twenty thousand votes. The Social Democrats received 1.5 million votes (disproportionally in Vienna) and the Social Christians 1.3 million (largely rural) in the 1930 elections.

3 See article 'Nietzsche und Pan-Europa', in *Pan-Europa Journal* 33 (1930).

4 Leo Amery noted in his diaries a conversation with the Duke of Windsor in the English Church in Vienna after Easter service in 1937. The duke had met RCK a few days previously, and was well informed: 'He seems to have told him all about my interest in Pan-Europa,' wrote Amery. RCK makes no mention in his papers of this meeting. Amery also noted a conversation with RCK in London after Anschluss, when RCK was dining at his invitation with Churchill, Lord Lothian, and Edward Grigg, a Conservative MP who went on to be under-secretary of state for war in 1940: 'All of us [felt] under the impression of Hitler's coercion of Schuschnigg. Most of them [were] strong on the point that, if France and Britain had been prepared to intervene, Hitler would have drawn back. Kept coming back to the point whether we were prepared to see our bluff through.'

5 Details about the economic activities of Pan-Europa are drawn from Anita Ziegenhofer-Prettenthaler's comprehensive study of RCK and the Pan-Europa Union in the twenties and thirties, entitled *Botschafter Europas* (Vienna/Cologne/ Weimar: 2004), especially 271–328.

6 RCK's incisive speech at the memorial ceremony for Dollfuss is preserved in the Austrian national sound-recordings archive, the Österreichische Mediathek, www.mediathek.at

7 John Major was chancellor of the exchequer when the proposal was put forward in July 1990, and Margaret Thatcher was prime minister. The idea had been elaborated in a study group set up in the City of London by Sir Michael Butler, former UK permanent representative in Brussels. The scheme and its ultimate failure are well described in the insightful book by a subsequent UK permanent representative in Brussels, Stephen Wall, published in Oxford in 2008 and entitled *Stranger in Europe*.

8 Many ideas, first broached by RCK in conferences in Vienna and promoted in articles in the *Pan-Europa Journal*, were developed after the Second World War by the Council of Europe and the EEC. These include a charter of human and political rights, a common currency, European driving licences and passports, even a European army. Anita Ziegenhofer-Prettenthaler's *Botschafter Europas* lists all articles published in *Paneuropa* (the *Pan-Europa Journal*) and *Paneuropa-Wirtschaftshefte* (its economic supplement).

CHAPTER FOURTEEN

1 Maximilian Jaeger, Swiss ambassador in Vienna from 1925, was also accredited to Hungary and moved to Budapest after Anschluss. There he played an important role in frustrating the deportation of Jews by the Nazi and Hungarian Arrow Cross parties. He shielded his deputy, Carl Lutz, who set up and supervised many 'neutral' houses covered by Swiss diplomatic status in the capital, thus protecting Jews there during the last years of the war.

2 These incidents are drawn from Richard Bassett's portrait of Julian Amery, published in York in 2015 and entitled *The Last Imperialist*.

3 RCK claimed that he informed the French Foreign Office of his intention to appeal to Mussolini and no objection was raised. He wilfully misconstrued this as an endorsement, though it is unlikely to have been intended as such, given how close the two countries were to open hostilities.

4 There are several parallels between Victor Laszlo, the Resistance hero in *Casablanca* played by Paul Henreid, and RCK, especially his escape from Europe. Both Victor Laszlo and RCK are handsome Czechs (not Czech, but using a Czech diplomatic passport in the case of RCK) in the prime of life, politically alert, and in touch with leading anti-Nazis throughout Europe. They both display an aristocratic detachment from the desperate nature of the situation, confident that, in the end, right and truth will triumph. Victor Laszlo finally escapes beyond the control of the Nazis, together with his wife, Ilsa, played by Ingrid Bergman, and they fly to freedom. RCK and Idel do likewise. It is inconceivable that RCK and Idel failed

to see the film when it was released with a blaze of publicity in New York in 1942, and yet RCK makes no reference to it at all in his memoirs or his letters. The film must have reminded both RCK and Idel of desperately uncomfortable experiences that they would rather have forgotten.

5 In command of a tank regiment in Lorraine, de Gaulle predicted that the German army would initially pursue a 'phoney war' as a tactic before an attack with massive air and ground superiority. He wrote to Prime Minister Paul Reynaud with this analysis of the situation in the autumn of 1939 and was subsequently brought into his government as a junior minister. It was with this very recent political authority that he made his appeal on the BBC on 18 June 1940 for the Free French to continue the war.

6 Marginal notations on RCK's visa application suggest that the Foreign Office in London was aware that the US authorities were 'causing difficulties' with RCK's application, but they do not specify their nature. A letter from Rab Butler at the Foreign Office to Leo Amery, dated 12 July 1940, also reveals that the Foreign Office held 'a biggish file' on RCK and that 'at present his admittance to this country is being prohibited on grounds of security.' It continues, 'We are trying to discover what the security authorities have against the Count; meanwhile the question of granting him a visa has been referred to the Ministry of Information.' Leo Amery persisted, writing to Duff Cooper at the Ministry of Information, adding a request that he might cover RCK's travel expenses to America, as RCK's bank accounts in Paris had been frozen. Eventually, on 18 July, Rab Butler wrote to Leo Amery to say that MI5 had 'relented' and lifted their objections to RCK having visas for the United Kingdom. Instructions were sent to Lisbon to issue them. But the British offer came too late. By then RCK had received visas for America.

7 Ambassador Pell knew Nicholas Murray Butler previously from political and academic circles in America. Murray Butler may have also alerted William J. Donovan to RCK's impending arrival in New York. Although Donovan would not be officially given the post of co-ordinator of information for President Roosevelt until July 1941, he was already the unofficial co-ordinator of a loose grouping of America businessmen, lawyers, and academics who reported strategic intelligence to each other after their journeys abroad. He was also in close contact with William Stephenson, the newly arrived MI6 representative in New York. The two of them were known informally as 'Big Bill' and 'Little Bill', and Donovan relied on Stephenson's expertise when he later went on to create the Office of Strategic Services (OSS), the forerunner of the CIA. For more detail see William Stevenson, *A Man called Intrepid: The Secret War, 1939–1945* (London: 1976), and the more reliable Henry Hemming, *Our Man in New York: The British Plot to Bring America into the Second World War* (London: 2019).

8 Clippers were four-engine seaplanes produced by Boeing, flying longer distances than any other plane at that time. Only twelve were ever built, and the *Yankee Clipper* was the third, serving the transatlantic service between Lisbon and New York from 1939. It offered luxury travel with overnight accommodation for thirty-six passengers. In a separate dining room, white-coated stewards served meals

prepared by a four-star chef. The seaplane had a cruising speed under two hundred miles per hour, and the basic single fare before the war was $375 (about $6,000 in today's prices), higher in refugee-packed Lisbon in 1940. The *Yankee Clipper* crashed and sank when landing in the Tagus in February 1943, killing twenty-four of the thirty-nine people on board. A life-size mock-up is on display at Foynes Flying Boat Museum at the site of the former Irish transatlantic terminal on the River Shannon in County Limerick.

CHAPTER FIFTEEN

1 William C. Bullitt was appointed by President Roosevelt in 1933 as the first US ambassador to the Soviet Union. His initially sympathetic view of the Soviet Union soured on better acquaintance as a diplomat. His Spring Ball of the Full Moon, attended by four hundred guests in April 1935, was the most exotic and lavish party ever held at the ambassadorial residence, and is described by Mikhail Bulgakov in his novel *The Master and Margarita*. Bullitt became US ambassador in Paris in October 1936 and was in daily telephone contact with President Roosevelt. Disobeying instructions, however, he remained in Paris in order to stay near the action when the Nazis invaded France, even though the French government fell back to Bordeaux.

2 The Edgehill Inn has since been demolished, but some of the flats at Palisade Avenue were still standing at the time of writing this biography. A five-bedroom condominium at that address was for sale in 2018 for $1.25 million.

3 Unpublished letter by Miss Lyn Irvine to the editor of *The Times*, written from Cambridge, England, on 6 March 1967.

4 The Nazi-Soviet Non-aggression Pact, signed by foreign ministers Molotov and Ribbentrop on 23 August 1939, defined Germany's and the Soviet Union's spheres of interest in Eastern Europe. It gave Nazi Germany a free hand to invade western Poland, which it did on 1 September the same year. The Soviet Union occupied eastern Poland two weeks later. The pact was amended at the end of September by the new German-Soviet Frontier Treaty, thereby eliminating Poland as a state. On 22 June 1941, Germany broke that treaty and invaded the Soviet Union in Operation Barbarossa.

5 The America First Committee (AFC) had strong bi-partisan support in Congress, and both the *New York Daily News* and the *Chicago Tribune* supported it. At its height it was the largest anti-war organization in American history, with 450 local chapters and over 800,000 paying members. Charles Lindbergh, the aviator, was its most effective broadcaster and spoke at innumerable mass meetings and campus rallies. Yet the AFC lasted little more than a year, winding itself up on 10 December 1941, three days after Pearl Harbor. Lindbergh announced that, now that America itself had been attacked, everyone should join behind the war effort against both Japan and Germany, whatever their previous opinions about Roosevelt's policy. For details of the struggle between America First and efforts to bring America into the Second World War, see Henry Hemming, *Our Man in New York*.

6 Nostradamus was born in Provence in 1503 and died in 1566. His extremely popular *Almanacs* contained over six thousand prophecies or predictions based, he claimed, on his study of astrology. Hitler was known to be credulous about soothsayers in general and Nostradamus in particular. When he was informed that a 'betrayal' – Rudolf Hess's flight to Scotland – had been foretold by Nostradamus, he banned all soothsaying in the Reich on pain of death. *The Prophecies* has never been out of print since they were first written. In 2018 the only known copy of the 1566 edition was offered for sale on the Internet, priced at $21 million.

7 Only some years after the end of the Second World War was Louis Dolivet unmasked as a Romanian communist in the pay of the Soviet Union. Born Ludovici Udeanu, he had operated in the 1920s and 1930s in Germany and France under the alias Ludovic Brecher.

8 Mitsu lived the last seventeen years of her life in a small house that Hansi bought for her in Mödling, a suburb of Vienna. She moved there in 1924 with her daughter Olga, leaving the grand apartment in Hietzing and her country home in Stockau, near Ronsperg. Three years later, Mitsu suffered a stroke which partially paralysed her right arm. She ruefully commented, 'Buddha has punished me for converting to Christianity.' As her health declined, Mitsu kept to her bed for the final years of her life. She died in Mödling in August 1941, thanking Hansi for financial support in her declining years and bequeathing the house to Olga, who had been her carer and companion to the end. From 1945 Mödling was in the Soviet zone of Vienna and, to avoid expropriation, Olga sold the house to her own maid for a very modest price, giving her a loan to be paid off over the next twenty years. It is now partly modernized and occupied by Herr Zottl (the nephew of her maid) and his wife, but visitors can nonetheless still imagine how simple and unpretentious Countess Coudenhove-Kalergi's last home was.

9 A contrary view is presented by Sisley Huddlestone, for many years Paris correspondent for *The Times*, who devoted a section of his lengthy political travelogue, *Europe in Zigzags* (London: 1929), to RCK and his 'practical proposals', publishing a full-page photograph of him to reflect the importance that this seasoned observer of the European political scene attributed to him. Published the same year in New York, Paul Hutchinson's *The United States of Europe* analysed the prospects for Briand's proposal at the League of Nations, primarily from the economic point of view, but with political and social implications also in mind. He explicitly presented Briand's proposal as the culmination of Pan-Europa's 1923 initiative.

10 For an exhaustive analysis of the Austrian Question see Robert H. Keyserlingk, *Austria in WWII: An Anglo-American Dilemma* (Quebec: 1988).

11 RCK's warm relationship with Otto von Hapsburg continued after the end of the war. Otto von Hapsburg became vice-president of the Pan-Europa Union in 1957, and would succeed RCK as president after his death in 1972. Earlier that same year, RCK helped to reconcile the former claimant to the imperial throne and the Austrian chancellor Bruno Kreisky at Pan-Europa's fiftieth anniversary meeting in Vienna.

12 RCK may well have contrasted his fictional representation as Victor Laszlo in *Casablanca* with the picture of 'Wild Bill' Donovan in James Cagney's 1940 film of his First World War experiences in *The Fighting 69th*. Donovan was decorated for valour on more than one occasion, and this retelling of an essentially true story helped to persuade President Roosevelt to call on him to set up the oss, forerunner of the CIA, in 1941.

13 At their meeting in Quebec in August 1943, Churchill suggested to President Roosevelt three councils – Asian, American, and European centres of power – as regional sub-organizations of the yet-to-be-created United Nations. In later tripartite talks in Teheran, Stalin was open to the idea, so long as both the Soviet Union and the United States were also members of the European Council. Roosevelt, however, feared he would not be able to persuade an isolationist Congress to vote in favour of continuing American involvement in European affairs. With Stalin insisting on Soviet involvement and Roosevelt doubtful about delivering American engagement, the idea of a possible European regional power centre at the United Nations was not pursued.

CHAPTER SIXTEEN

1 Opened in 1890, with financial support from the Rockefellers and the American Astors, the Judson Memorial Church served the upper-class area of Washington Square and the poorer neighbourhood immediately to the west. It was conveniently close to the campus of New York University and RCK's office.

2 Paul van Zeeland was Belgian prime minister from 1935 to 1937 and, in exile in London, co-founded and chaired the European League for Economic Co-operation. Milan Hodza was a Slovak proponent of federation for the Austro-Hungarian Empire and advisor to Archduke Ferdinand before the First World War. From 1935 to 1938 he was prime minister of Czechoslovakia, and was thereafter in exile in Switzerland, France, London, and finally the United States, where in 1942 he published *Federation in Central Europe*. Raymond de Saussure was a Swiss psychoanalyst in New York during the Second World War, and returned to Geneva in 1952, where he co-founded the Museum for the History of Science. Oskar Halecki was a distinguished Polish Catholic professor of European history, formerly secretary of the League of Nations Committee on Intellectual Co-operation, and director of the Polish Institute in New York during the war. Victor Cazalet, MP, was secretary of the Westminster parliamentary group for the future of Europe, set up in June 1939, and liaison officer for the British government with General Sikorski. He was on attachment to the UK embassy in Washington when he attended the Pan-Europa Congress in New York in 1943 and was killed with General Sikorski in a plane crash in Gibraltar in July that same year. Despite his anti-communist sentiments, RCK invited the Soviet ambassador to the United States, Maxim Litvinov, to join the panel, knowing that he and Ambassador Bullitt would be interested to meet each other. However, the Russian declined, probably well aware of RCK's opinions about the Soviet Union.

3 Arnold Zürcher, RCK's closest academic collaborator at NYU, published *Experiment with Democracy in Central Europe* in 1933, *Propaganda and Dictatorship* in 1936, and *Governments of Continental Europe* in 1941. Among the other authors were Joseph Hendershot Park, professor of history during RCK's time at NYU, and Richard Schüller, an Austrian Jewish economist, formerly professor of political science at the University of Vienna and chairman of the Economic Committee of the League of Nations. He escaped on foot over the Alps to Italy in 1938 and fled to America in 1940, where he taught at the New School of Social Research. André Istel was an investment banker who represented General de Gaulle at the Bretton Woods Conference in 1944.

4 RCK held a paid position as professor of history in NYU until summer 1946, then was a visiting professor in the restructured Institute of Public Affairs and Regional Studies for two further years. Thereafter he was adjunct professor until 1951, but did not teach after 1948. While in New York, he and Idel found enough funds – possibly through speculation on the stock exchange, suggests one of his post-war secretaries – to buy local Native art and colonial furniture and paintings, which they left in storage when they returned to Europe in 1948. After Idel's death in 1951, RCK auctioned an eighteenth-century French painting and some items of early-American furniture in New York.

5 The most senior member of the State Department open to RCK's arguments during his time in America appears to have been Cavendish Wells Cannon, the assistant chief of the division responsible for South East European affairs. He was the same age as RCK, but his career may have been held back by the fact that he was a Mormon, a church not held in high regard in US government and diplomatic circles. However, he would go on to be US ambassador in Yugoslavia from 1947 to 1949 and in Greece from 1953 to 1956.

6 Details of this accusation are contained in Foreign Office papers in the National Archives, Kew, London, relating to the British embassy in Washington during the war.

7 RCK avoids mentioning any other German or Austrian exiles in New York at the time he was there, except those attending his events, but there were many, among them Ralph and Melanie (Kirschi) Benatsky, good friends from their earlier years in Vienna and near neighbours in Switzerland. Some years later, Kirschi would become RCK's third wife. For brief biographies and a discussion of other exiles, see Erika and Klaus Mann, *Escape to Life: Deutsche Kultur im Exil* (Boston: 1939) in English; and in German (Munich: 1991). Also Katia Mann, *Unwritten Memories* (Frankfurt-am-Main: 1974), with an English translation, published in London in 1975.

8 For the full exchange of letters between RCK and de Gaulle, see *Coudenhove-Kalergi/De Gaulle: Une certain idée de l'Europe* (Paris: 1999) published by the Foundation CDG.

9 *Achtzig Jahre, 1896–1976*, the unpublished typescript memoirs of Gerolf Coudenhove in German. The incident is also reported by RCK's niece (Gerolf's daughter) Barbara Coudenhove-Kalergi in her memoirs *Zuhause ist überall* (Vienna: 2013).

10 For more on the context of Truman's military experience, see H.W. Crocker III, *The Yanks Are Coming! A Military History of the United States in World War I* (Washington: 2014).

11 For a graphic description of the conditions in which Hansi was held in the internment camp in Domazlice, and subsequently in prison in Pilsen awaiting trial, see the novel by Bernhard Setzwein, *Der böhmische Samurai* (Innsbruck/Vienna: 2017).

CHAPTER SEVENTEEN

1 Hansi lived subsequently in Regensburg. His wife and daughter, Lilly and Pixie, returned from hiding in Italy (or possibly Geneva) to live with him, but within a few years the marriage fell apart and he and Lilly formally divorced in 1960. Hansi then married a local actress, Ursula Grosch, but finished his years in reduced circumstances. Embittered, he wrote a pornographic novel, *Ich frass die weisse Chinesin* (*I Ate the White Chinese Woman*) (Hamburg: 1965), the year that he died. Lilly died ten years later in Geneva, and Pixie emigrated to America, dying in California in 2000.

2 The French liner *Oregon*, launched in 1929, was relatively small, only 7,700 gross tonnes. Initially she sailed from the west coast of America to France, but after the war served the transatlantic route for both passengers and freight. She was scrapped in 1955.

3 Churchill stayed three weeks at the Château de Choisi, from 23 August to 18 September 1946, the day before he gave his famous lecture at the University of Zürich. The Château – actually a large villa – was built in 1829 as a neo-classical *maison de maître*, with stylistically harmonious architecture and décor, and statues set in a park with views of Lake Geneva. The only more recent addition to the house was an Art Deco bar in which Churchill doubtless enjoyed his cigars and whisky. His link to the banker who owned the château was through Charles (Carl) Montag, a Swiss national and Churchill's long-standing painting teacher. Personally acquainted with many Impressionist artists, Montag first met Churchill in 1915, and arranged an exhibition for him under the pseudonym Charles Morin at the Galerie Drouet in Paris in 1921. Montag was both a painter and an art dealer in the 1930s and lived in France during the Second World War. Military records in the United States suggest he was 'strongly implicated in German activity in Paris, involved in the "aryanization" of the Bernheim Jeune and Wildenstein firms, and instrumental in the sale of several looted pictures to Swiss clients.' Churchill was presumably ignorant of this.

4 RCK was able to quote to him the quatrain from Nostradamus which he had sent him in 1941, prophesying victory in the war: 'Un jour seront damis les deux grands maistres / Leur grand pouvoir se verra augmenté / La terre neufeu sera en ses hautes esters / Au sanguinaire, le nombre racompté.' And he was equally pleased to translate it for him: 'One day shall be friends the two great masters / their great power shall be the greater for it / Newfoundland shall then come into its own / and numbered be the days of the bloodthirsty man.'

5 The voyage on the *Île de France* was the least luxurious of all RCK and Idel's transatlantic crossings, as the liner had not yet been refitted from her stripped-down state as a wartime troop carrier. None of the Art Deco design elements that had made the vessel exceptional in the 1930s remained, and she now seemed to them a drab and utilitarian people carrier with her human cargo of fourteen hundred passengers leaving war-damaged Europe for New York.

6 Launched in 1938, the *Queen Elizabeth*, at eighty-three thousand tonnes, was the largest ship afloat. She was fitted out as a troopship after her launch in 1939 and converted by the Cunard line for commercial use on the transatlantic route in October 1946. Much larger and faster than the *Île de France*, she carried over two thousand passengers and assured, along with her sister ship, the *Queen Mary*, a regular weekly service to New York from Southampton and Cherbourg. RCK and Idel sailed on her twice.

CHAPTER EIGHTEEN

1 Winston Churchill praised George Marshall as 'the architect of Allied victory' in the Second World War, throughout which Marshall served as US chief of staff. Truman appointed him secretary of state in 1947, and on 5 June that year, in a speech at Harvard, he announced the European Recovery Program, known in brief as the Marshall Plan. Stalin forbade all Soviet satellite states in Eastern Europe from participating in this programme. West-European states that did participate agreed on a key for the distribution of aid, with 26 per cent for Britain, 28 per cent for France, and 11 per cent for the western zones of Germany. Groups of experts in specialist committees dealing with food and agriculture, power, raw materials, machinery, timber, textiles, transport, and manpower quickly reached agreements together on lowering bilateral tariffs and simplifying trade regulations across the Atlantic as key conditions of America's largesse.

2 From 1950, the United States shifted the main channel of aid from the Organisation for European Economic Cooperation (OEEC) and the Economic Cooperation Administration (ECA) to NATO, using the Mutual Security Agency (MSA) as the main conduit for concentrating aid on those countries that were also active in the military alliance. In 1951, NATO set up a core study group consisting of Jean Monnet from France (then president of the European Coal and Steel Community), Averell Harriman from the United States, and Edwin Plowden, a senior civil servant from the United Kingdom (representing Hugh Gaitskell, then Labour chancellor of the exchequer) to study the economic development of NATO states in relation to their economic possibilities.

3 The *Mauretania* was launched in June 1939, crossed the Atlantic only three times before the outbreak of the Second World War, and then served as a troopship until 1946, in total carrying more than a quarter of a million servicemen over half a million miles. After a £1 million refit, the Cunard Line used the *Mauretania* to carry thirteen hundred passengers on a regular fortnightly service between Southampton and New York until the *Queen Elizabeth* and *Queen Mary* jointly

came into service on that same route. The *Mauretania* then cruised in the West Indies and the Mediterranean until she was broken up in 1966.

4 RCK does not name the owners of 4715 Independence Avenue in his auto-biographical works, nor is there a name in any relevant correspondence. Whatever the arrangement, it was a substantial building in a prime location, and it is unlikely that an apartment there would have been affordable for RCK. It is tempting to imagine – but remains unproven – that their good friends Ralph Benatsky and his wife, Melanie Hoffmann, lived there and simply invited RCK and Idel to stay for a few months, since they also did not leave New York finally to return to Europe until late in 1948.

CHAPTER NINETEEN

1 'Sandys's pants' changed colour six months later, when the newly founded International European Movement adopted the same capital E symbol for its flag, but in green instead of red.

2 There is some dispute about the exact numbers attending the Congress of Europe, but most commentators agree there were at least 700 participants and a further 200 or more media representatives. Some 155 participants came from France, led by Paul Ramadier, a former prime minister. The British contingent was next-largest with 145, led by Churchill. There were 68 participants from Belgium and 59 from Italy, 58 from Germany (only from the Western zones of occupation), 40 from Switzerland, and 32 from Denmark. Smaller numbers came from the Netherlands, Austria, Iceland, Greece, Norway, Sweden, Liechtenstein, Ireland, Luxembourg, the Saar, and the Vatican. There were also 'observers' from Bulgaria, Czechoslovakia, Finland, Hungary, Poland, Romania, Spain, and Yugoslavia. At the end of the first day, an emergency motion was passed that upgraded observers from these 'non-democratic' countries to full participant status, allowing them to speak and vote. There were also four observers from the United States and two from Canada.

CHAPTER TWENTY

1 The Interlaken meeting was planned immediately after the Congress of Europe at a co-ordination meeting of the EPU executive committee in the Château d'Ardennes, a nineteenth-century former royal palace situated between Brussels and Luxembourg. It had been converted into a fashionable railway hotel but closed its doors in 1950 and was later destroyed by fire and demolished in 1970.

2 For an insight into the seriousness with which some observers considered the sayings of Kordon Veri at this time, see Dr Ed Bertholet, lauréat de l'Université de Lausanne and president of the Société Vaudoise d'Études Psychiques, *Quelques Expériences avec Fridolin Kordon Veri, medium-psychomètre artiste-inspiré* (Lausanne: 1934).

3 In his letter, Donovan mentions Lord Layton (Liberal politician and former editor of the *Economist* and the *News Chronicle*), Paul Reynaud (former French

prime minister, who resigned in June 1940 rather than surrender to the Nazis), and Harold Butler (leading British representative on the European League for Economic Cooperation – ELEC) as three influential figures all supporting the European Movement. That was quite enough to convince Donovan he was backing the right horse, and he expected to convince RCK, even without quoting by name Churchill, Sandys, Retinger, or Beddington-Behrens.

4   Beside Stephenson's name, Churchill noted in the margin of that year's Honours' list, 'This one is dear to my heart.' Later, in the 1957 honours list, Beddington-Behrens would also be knighted for his services to the European Movement.

5   Before the American Committee was disbanded in 1960 it disbursed over three million dollars in covert support for pro-European activities in Europe, but none of it through RCK's organization. See Richard J. Aldrich, 'The OSS, CIA, and European Unity: The American Committee on United Europe, 1948–1960', in *Diplomacy and Statecraft* 8 (1997): 184–227, and for what did happen to the money, see Frances Stonor Saunders, *Who Paid the Piper? The CIA and the Cultural Cold War* (London: 1999).

6   The first objective – the ECSC – was realized in 1951. The second – the EDC – was blocked by the French senate in August 1954. The third – European political union – remains a goal of the European Union. Barely two months after the failure of the EDC to be ratified by the French Senate, the United Kingdom, France, and the Benelux states signed the Modified Brussels Treaty, which welcomed both West Germany and Italy into the mutual defence treaty they had originally set up in 1948, which created the West European Union (WEU).

The Hôtel du Clos de Sanex lies on the northern shore of Lake Geneva on the route de Lausanne at Prangins. The large private house was converted into a hotel by the widow of the original owner of the property, Gustave Dunand, in 1949, and at the time of Idel's death was managed by his son. It has now reverted to become a private residence again.

CHAPTER TWENTY-ONE

1   The Cantonal archives of Vaud in Lausanne include an earlier exchange of letters from 1941–42 between Alix and her husband's family in Moschen, the large family estate in Silesia, which included a castle with over three hundred rooms. The correspondence was about raising her (monthly?) allowance from 750 Reichsmark to 2,500 Reichsmark. By 1951 it would not have been paid for several years, since the occupation of the area by the Red Army in early 1945. The castle survived the Second World War, was used as a sanatorium for several years under the Polish communist government, and is now a hotel with an associated music festival in early summer each year.

2   At the start of research for this book, RCK's niece, Barbara Coudenhove-Kalergi, suggested to the author that it would be revealing to 'follow the money' when unravelling the story of RCK. This underlying thread certainly helps to illuminate a continuing concern that coloured his personal story.

CHAPTER TWENTY-TWO

1 The October 1951 election brought to power a Conservative government led by Winston Churchill with a majority of twenty-three seats. The outgoing Labour administration had been elected in February 1950 with a majority of just five seats.

2 The Dutch electrical company of Philips was a staunch supporter of Pan-Europa, both before and after the Second World War, and would be instrumental in arranging a positive solution to the financial difficulties of RCK's estate after his death.

3 Walter Keller-Staub was an extremely able lawyer and a 'fixer' with international contacts. The Nazi government in Berlin appears to have made use of his services during the war to arrange the chartering of support ships for the German navy from neutral countries. Later in the war, he also helped the Americans by passing sensitive information to their consulate in Zürich, which was situated conveniently close to his offices.

4 Gaitskill's speech also argued: 'Let me come back to what Britain's role should be. To start with, do not let us confuse the question of whether we think it is good or bad for the Europeans to get together in Western Europe and form their federation with the question whether we should be in it. The first question is their affair and it may well be the answer to their problem. It is not necessarily the answer to ours. For we are not just a part of Europe – at least not yet. We have a different history. We have ties and links which run across the whole world, and for me at least the Commonwealth, the modern Commonwealth, which owes its creation fundamentally to those vital historic decisions of the Labour Government, is something I want to cherish. It comes to this, does it not? If we can associate ourselves with Europe, with the other states in Western Europe, in a larger community with our links with the Commonwealth fully maintained, if by so doing we can achieve that influence upon European development which has so often been urged upon us and which I fully accept as very desirable, this would be a fine ideal: it would be the building of a bridge between the Commonwealth and Europe.'

5 The question of Britain's relations with Europe has continued to bedevil political debate ever since the United Kingdom joined the Economic Communities in 1972. The manifesto of the Labour Party, elected in February 1974, promised treaty renegotiation and a referendum to confirm the result. In April 1975, the House of Commons overwhelmingly approved the renegotiated terms of UK entry to the Common Market, and in June the British public confirmed the result in a referendum by 67 per cent to 33 per cent, with a turnout of 64 per cent. Even this clear result did not end the British debate. The Conservatives returned to power in 1979 under Margaret Thatcher, and initial political enthusiasm for the European adventure slowly turned to euro-scepticism. This spread within the Labour Party in the 1980s, promoted by the radical left-wing movement called 'Militant'. The Social Democratic Party split from Labour on the European issue. Subsequently a referendum in June 2016 surprisingly decided by a small margin (52 per cent to 48 per cent) to leave the European Union. Both the Conservative and Labour parties were divided over how best to respond to the referendum result.

The Conservatives under Boris Johnson won the 2019 election on a manifesto promising to confirm Brexit, and the UK formally left the EU in January 2020. Opinion in the country, however, remained divided about this decision and its consequences. For a carefully nuanced analysis of historical British attitudes to Europe, see Hugo Young, *This Blessed Plot: Britain and Europe from Churchill to Blair* (London: 1998).

CHAPTER TWENTY-THREE

1 The correspondence between the two men is published in Appendix II of *Coudenhove-Kalergi – De Gaulle: Une certaine idée de l'Europe* (Paris: 1999).
2 The United Kingdom and Denmark were the first of the EFTA states to join the European Communities in 1973, followed later by Portugal in 1986 and finally Sweden in 1995. Ireland joined the European Communities at the same time as the United Kingdom, but it was never a member of EFTA. Norway, Iceland, Liechtenstein, and Switzerland remain members of EFTA. The first three of them signed an agreement with the EU on a common European Economic Area (EEA) in 1994. Switzerland rejected the draft EEA agreement in 1992 and has since negotiated a series of specific sectoral agreements.
3 While not politically correct by the standards of contemporary debate, RCK's somewhat brutal assessment of the international scene appears to have been appreciated by the president. For good measure, RCK added: 'If the Russians demand that the Chinese attend, then the West should insist on the Japanese as a balancing factor.'
4 See Gladwyn Jebb (Lord Gladwyn), *The European Idea* (London: 1966). The relevant correspondence is reproduced as Appendix 3 in his book.
5 The United Kingdom declined to join the Euratom Treaty negotiations in part because, in the 1950s, it was well ahead of France in nuclear research for both military and peaceful purposes. The first UK nuclear power station, Windscale, opened in 1956, while the first French nuclear power station was operational only six years later.

CHAPTER TWENTY-FOUR

1 Jean Monnet explains the incident in some detail in his *Mémoires* (Paris: 1976).
2 Preserved and on display in the Maison de Jean Monnet at Houjarray, Bazoches-sur-Guyonne, about thirty miles west of Paris.
3 Monnet's ACUSE was active from 1955 to 1975. Monnet described its activities as implementing 'the Common Market and Euratom treaties, which we had drawn up with men such as Spaak, Beyen, Hallstein, Maurice Faure, and a few others who wanted to revive the movement toward Europe … For twenty years we fought to deepen and widen our European union … In Germany, men such as Brandt, Schmidt, and Kiesinger; in Italy, Pella, Malagodi and Rumor; in Belgium, Tindemans; in Luxembourg, Pierre Werner; in the Netherlands, Roeme; in France Pflimlin, Pinay, Defferre, and Maurice Faure; and finally in

England, Jenkins, Lord Brown and Douglas-Home, were at my side. I have never believed in isolated action, but in collective effort.' See Monnet, *Mémoires*, Vol. 2, 661–9, for his assessment of the role of those who worked with him in ACUSE.

4 Russell Bretherton was subsequently misquoted by a French politician, Jean-Louis Deniau, who asserted that he left the meeting with the following words: 'Gentleman, you are trying to negotiate something you will never be able to negotiate. But, if negotiated, it will not be ratified. And if ratified, it will not work. *Au revoir et bonne chance.*' The quotation is certainly not verbatim, but nevertheless reflected the views of the British government at the time.

5 Correspondence between RCK and Jean Monnet is preserved at the Fondation Jean Monnet pour l'Europe, situated at the Ferme de Dorigny at the University of Lausanne.

CHAPTER TWENTY-FIVE

1 See Hanne Dézsy's description of the travelling entourage and their treatment in various hotels in *Gentleman of Europe* (Vienna: 2001).

2 Elected a member of the European Parliament for a Bavarian constituency in 1979, Otto von Hapsburg gathered a group of like-minded MEPs in Strasbourg to discuss RCK's ideas, and he was instrumental in establishing the Austrian Foundation that would continue RCK's work.

3 RCK's research for *Die Amazonen* comprises several box files of correspondence, notes, and early drafts, as well as a final manuscript of some three hundred closely typed pages, accessible in the Cantonal Archives of Vaud in Lausanne.

4 *The Human Revolution* by Daisaku Ikeda (Soka Gakkai) propounds a variant of Buddhist philosophy that appealed very strongly to RCK. In summary, it reconciled his father's respect for religion with his own political activism.

5 RCK was nominated for the Nobel Peace Prize by European politicians and academics on many occasions: first in 1931 by Erich Koch-Weser, Edvard Beneš, and Johann Schober; then in 1932 by Koch-Weser and Schober, along with Walter Simons and Emil Georg von Stauss; in 1933 by Koch-Weser, Clemens Lammers, Paul Löbe, and C. Becker. He was further nominated in 1934, 1935, 1937, and 1938. In 1940 some British friends, including Leo Amery, suggested his nomination, and in 1941 Kaarel Robert Pusta, the Estonian foreign minister in exile, put his name forward. Another bid in 1946 was headed by Arnold Zürcher with support from Fernando de los Rios, a former Republican minister from Spain, and Waldo Riva, a Swiss jurist. Others followed every year from 1948 to 1952, and again in 1956, 1958, and 1959, 1961, 1963, 1965. A final nomination, in 1967, was made with the support of a British MP, John Biggs-Davison, and a Belgian member of parliament, Arthur Gibson.

6 RCK rejoiced in having two birthdays each year, his Japanese birthday on 16 November and his European birthday, which he considered to be 17 November. His birth in Japan occurred late at night, and the time-zone difference allowed him to think of it as the following day in local time at Ronsperg. His fascination with the practical impact of time zones led him to write a proposal while in exile

in New York, suggesting 'Weltzeit', or world time, with local variants measured as plus or minus in relation to this standard time. He patented the idea and tried to commercialize it in the 1950s, but without success.

7   RCK's asexual disposition in later life was stressed in the author's interview in 2017 with his nephew, Karl-Jakub, who insisted that the older RCK was 'dead from the waist down'. Apart from his three wives, there was only one woman with whom he remained in contact in his later life, a carer for his second wife called Marthe, mentioned by Hanne Dézsy in her memoir. RCK was motivated solely by his respect for her second sight, her ability to assess character and to foretell the future. After Alix's death, he visited her when he was in Schruns, since she was then running a boarding house in a nearby town. He was due to visit her for tea the day after he died.

8   Ralph Benatsky's first two wives were Jewish, but he was a Czechoslovak composer, inaccurately classified as Jewish in a Nazi compilation of Jewish composers just before the Second World War. He and his third wife, Melanie Hoffmann (Kirschi), had a lot in common with RCK and Idel: Vienna, the theatrical world, living in Switzerland, life in exile in America. It is possible that the Benatskys lived on Independence Avenue, and if so, it may have been with them that RCK and Idel lodged on their last visit to New York. RCK and Idel returned to Gruben, while Ralph and Kirschi moved to Zürich in 1948.

CHAPTER TWENTY-SIX

1   The whole party then adjourned to the nearby Hotel Italia for lunch. The area near the chapel has since been developed as a small resort for skiing in winter and mountain walking in summer.

2   Two decades later, in 1990, Ikeda proposed that Coudenhove-Kalergi's favourite song, Beethoven's *Ode to Joy*, by then the recognized anthem of the European Union, should be regularly performed at major Soka Gakkai meetings. This was one cause of the split the following year between the Soka Gakkai, together with its international arm, Soka Gakkai International, and Nichiren Shoshu, the orthodox Buddhist organization, since the traditional priesthood objected to what they saw as the song's 'Christian origins'. Soka Gakkai also appeared heretical by placing greater emphasis on individual action than was acceptable to mainstream Buddhist teaching.

3   Jacques Chaban Delmas was one of the youngest-ever French prime ministers, and among his advisers was Jacques Delors, later president of the European Commission. His government had generously subsidized Pan-Europa events in recent years, and RCK wanted his successor, Pierre Messmer, to do likewise. Messmer was a much older and more conservative military adviser, a previous minister under de Gaulle. Maurice Schumann remained foreign minister at this change of government, but within a matter of months he lost his post in another cabinet reshuffle.

4   Author's interview with Lacy Milkovics in Vienna, summer 2017.

5   RCK's plans for a dramatic mausoleum above the village of Istelwald, overlooking the southern shore of the Brienzer See, led to an exchange of letters with the local commune, but before he could visit to discuss details, Idel had decided to purchase the farmhouse in Gruben.

6   The only person to have died previously at the Hotel Montafon was Ernst Rüdiger Starhemberg, former vice-chancellor of Austria, leader of the Fatherland Front in the 1930s and a friend of RCK. He died there in 1956. His first wife was Nora Gregor, an Austrian Jewish actress and friend of Idel. An Austrian right-wing nationalist, he was fiercely anti-Communist and anti-Nazi, and escaped to Switzerland at Anschluss in 1938. He served briefly in both the Free French and British forces, but emigrated to Argentina in 1941 when the United Kingdom and the United States welcomed the Soviet Union as an ally. He returned to Europe in 1955 when President Juan Peron was overthrown in a *coup d'état*.

7   Author's interview with the undertaker in Schruns, summer 2016. In a codicil to his will, RCK asked that his funeral should be dominated by white, the colour of mourning in Japan, rather than European black, and that flowers should be placed on his grave every year on the anniversary of his death.

8   One of his former secretaries, Hanne Dézsy, suggested suicide in her perceptive memoir, *Gentleman Europas* (Vienna: 2001). However, there appears to be little evidence to support this assertion, beyond Dr Albrich leaving the death certificate, which indicated cause of death as 'heart failure', to be signed by the undertaker. Was Dr Albrich avoiding perjuring himself, or was there another reason for the doctor not signing it?

9   The plot of land where RCK was to be buried was jointly owned by Erika and RCK's estate. To have given away RCK's share to the local commune – as Erika would do with hers – would not have been permitted under Swiss law, since debtors had first claim on all property. Hence the commune was required to pay a notional sum to RCK's executors to buy his half of the plot, while receiving Erika's half as a gift. A final gesture of closure occurred when Erika's grave in the nearby Protestant church in Saanen was cleared in 2015, twenty-five years after her death in 1990. Her headstone was recovered from the clearance and moved to join her mother's and RCK's in the private family graveyard.

Sources and Further Reading

Richard Coudenhove-Kalergi was a prolific writer, publishing primarily in German, and also in English and in French. As further reading, I have first selected books written by RCK himself, and second, books in English which will help readers to explore further the life of this extraordinary man and the turbulent times in which he lived. I have been fortunate to access works in German and in French, which have given this first English biography of the man a more rounded picture than I could have found from English sources alone.

RCK published five books of autobiography: the first, *Crusade for Pan-Europa: Autobiography of a Man and a Movement*, in New York in 1943; the second, *Der Kampf um Europa: Aus meinem Leben*, in Zürich in 1949; and the third (with a preface by Winston Churchill), *An Idea Conquers the World*, in London in 1953. He subsequently published a German translation of this 1953 title as *Eine Idee erobert Europa: Meine Lebenserinnerungen* (Vienna/Munich/Basel: 1958) and then a revised and expanded edition of this volume as *Ein Leben für Europa: Meine Lebenserinnerungen* (Cologne/Berlin: 1966). None of these autobiographies is completely reliable, as a comparison with this biography will reveal, but they each served to promote RCK's name and his cause, and that was essentially what mattered to him. One of his two English autobiographies would be a good place for a reader new to this subject to start, and from that basis to make comparisons with the fuller picture of this passionate European revealed in this biography.

RCK's best-selling seminal work, *Pan-Europa*, was published in Vienna 1923, and he ensured an English translation appeared in New York soon after his visit to America in 1925–26. That presents the core of his message, and it is the key text on which I have based Chapter 7 of this biography.

Three of his other books were translated into English during his lifetime, and another was written by RCK himself in English. *Totaler Staat – Totaler Mensch*, published in Glarus in Switzerland in 1937, shortly before the Nazis annexed Austria, was translated into English by Andrew McFadyean as *The Totalitarian State against Man*, with an introduction by Wickham Steed, and published in London in November 1938. *Kommen die Vereinigten Staaten von Europa?* was published in Glarus that same year, and with the title *Europe Must Unite*, an English translation, also by Andrew

McFadyean, was published in autumn 1939. Soon after the Second World War, RCK wrote *Europe Seeks Unity*, a slim volume of just sixty pages, in English. William Bullitt added an introduction, and it was published by New York University in 1948. *Vom ewigen Krieg zum grossen Frieden* appeared in Göttingen in 1956, was translated by Constantine Fitzgibbon, and published in London in 1959 under the title *From War to Peace*.

The Count published thirty-three books, mostly on political themes, some on more philosophical issues, starting with his 1917 Vienna university dissertation, *Objektivität als Grundprinzip der Moral* (*Objectivity as the Basic Principle of Morality*). I list all published titles at the end of this section on sources and further reading, since they are a precious and substantial legacy. Several titles have been translated into other languages, among them French, Spanish, and Japanese, but only those mentioned above are available in English.

RCK also contributed essays to works edited by other authors and wrote numerous articles, which were published in political journals and newspapers. He spoke at public meetings and broadcast in the German- and French-speaking worlds throughout the 1920s and 1930s, and again in the 1950s and 1960s. Until 1938, the most important outlet for RCK's own articles was the monthly journal *Pan-Europa*, referred to in this biography as the *Pan-Europa Journal* to distinguish it from his seminal work of 1923, also entitled *Pan-Europa*. He edited the *Pan-Europa Journal* and wrote for it almost three hundred articles in German on political issues of the day. These vary in length from just a few pages to thirty or more, and are conveniently listed in chronological order in the major academic study of his work during the interwar years: Anita Ziegenhofer-Prettenthaler, *Botschafter Europas* (Vienna/Cologne/Weimar: 2004). See 541 to 550.

During his Swiss exile, from 1938 to 1940, RCK also wrote a dozen short 'European Letters' in English, French, and German and posted them to his reduced band of Pan-Europa Union members across Europe. In New York from 1940 to 1948, however, he did not write regularly for any single outlet, but numerous articles and letters appeared in various American publications, including the *Washington Post*, the *New York Times*, the *American Mercury*, and *Collier's* magazine. Similarly, in Europe after 1948, he had no regular outlet, but contributed to journals and newspapers in various European countries depending on his theme and his target audience.

Much of his correspondence and many of these articles are well preserved and comprehensively catalogued in the Cantonal Archives of Vaud in Lausanne, both in the extensive files marked Richard Coudenhove-Kalergi (P-1000) and the equally informative files of Vittorio Pons, his literary executor (P-1001). Other archives – in Pilsen in the Czech Republic; in London at the National Archives, the London School of Economics, and the Royal Institute of International Affairs (Chatham House); in Cambridge at Churchill College; in Vienna at the University Library; in Florence in the European University Institute at Fiesole – have also yielded useful insights into the written record, showing the range of his contacts and the issues that concerned him at different stages of his life. New York University Library has been helpful in supplying material relating to his years there on the staff, as has the Fondation Jean Monnet pour l'Europe, situated close to the Cantonal Archive in

Lausanne, as concerns his relations with Jean Monnet. Both the voluminous P-1000 and P-1001 files in Lausanne and the files in the library of the European University Institute at Fiesole hold copies of selected material from the 'lost' Pan-Europa archive of the inter-war years, now held in Moscow. Apart from his published works, these have been the main sources for primary research for this biography – in all three languages – into the man, his life and his times.

Several of RCK's relatives also wrote or published memoirs during their lives, and they reveal aspects of his family history and relations with his parents and siblings. His father's essays on duelling, on anti-Semitism, on the struggle between the Catholic and Protestant strands of Christianity, on aspects of oriental philosophy, and on Schopenhauer, for instance, reveal much about his father and the powerful impression he made on his son. The reminiscences of his brother Gerolf (available only in manuscript: *Achtzig Jahre: 1896–1976*) and of his youngest brother, Ery, published as *Da fällt mir meine Geschichte ein* (Zürich: 1992), his niece Barbara Coudenhove-Kalergi's lively reminiscences, *Zuhause ist Uberall (*Vienna: 2013), and his mother, Mitsu's, fragmentary recollections, published long after her death in a bilingual Czech/German edition, *Memoiren von Gräfin Mitsu Coudenhove-Kalergi, die auf dem Schloss in Ronsperg gelebt hat* (Domazlice: 2006) all add facets to help understand RCK's personality. None of these memoirs is available in English. Nor is an imaginative and insightful novel based on the turbulent life and character of RCK's elder brother, Hansi, written by Bernhard Setzwein: *Der böhmische Samurai* (Innsbruck/Vienna: 2017). Regrettably, the two books that have been published by family members in English – the reminiscences of his 'hermit' uncle, Hans Coudenhove, *My African Neighbours: Man, Bird, and Beasts in Nyasaland* (New York: 1925) and *Broken Lights*, the 1951 to 1959 letters and diaries of his sister, Ida Görres (London: 1964) – add little to a reader's understanding of RCK.

There are several biographies of RCK in German, but some are essentially hagiographic (Rolf Italiaander: *Richard Coudenhove-Kalergi*, 1969) or somewhat uneven and episodic (Walter Göhring, *Richard Coudenhove Kalergi: Ein Leben für Paneuropa*, Vienna: 2016). The most insightful appraisal of the character of the older RCK is to be found in Hanna Dézsy: *Gentleman Europas: Erinnerungen an Richard Graf Coudenhove-Kalergi* (Vienna: 2001), from which I have quoted various episodes. And the more academic approach of Vanessa Conze, *Richard Coudenhove Kalergi: Umstrittener Visionär Europas* (Cologne: 2003) has also helped to interpret his character in the context of his times. The major academic work of Anita Ziegenhofer-Prettenthaler, *Botschafter Europas* (Vienna/Cologne/Weimar: 2004), however, is the key to exploring more about RCK, specifically his pre-war activities. It is both academically comprehensive and balanced in its interpretation. The French equivalent, which also contains an extensive bibliography with an emphasis on works in French, is by Anne-Marie Saint-Gille, *La 'Paneurope': un débat d'idées dans l'entre-deux-guerres.* (Paris: 2003). A slimmer volume with four interesting essays on aspects of RCK's life and work – entitled *Coudenhove-Kalergi: Le Pionnier de l'Europe Unie,* by Morinosuke Kajima, Jacques de Launay, Vittorio Pons, and Arnold Zürcher – was published by the Centre for European Research at the University of Lausanne in 1971.

The years in which RCK lived – from the end of the nineteenth century to the year that Britain joined the European communities – are so richly recorded and reflected in writings of contemporary authors at the time and by historians after the event that no simple list would suffice to reflect both their glory and their horror. Here, however, are a few examples of titles, some of which influenced RCK and the way he responded to the problems of his age, and others that shed light on the context in which he lived and worked.

Oswald Spengler's *Decline of the West* is a seminal work for understanding the spirit of the of the post-1918 age, as is Hitler's *Mein Kampf*. For descriptions of the social and political scene around the early years of Hitler and his political movement, William Shirer, *The Rise and Fall of the Third Reich* (London: 1959), is an ever-useful source. The broader history of Europe in the twentieth century is well told by Ian Kershaw in *To Hell and Back: Europe 1914 to 1949* (London: 2015), as is the story of Hitler in Kershaw's 2008 one-volume biography, simply entitled *Hitler* (London: 2010). All post-war histories of Europe that deal with the integration of the continent are indebted to Walter Lipgens (ed.), *Documents on the History of European Integration*, volumes one and two (Berlin: 1985 and 1986), and his own *History of European Integration, 1945–1947: The Formation of the European Unity Movement* (Oxford: 1982) explores that episode in depth. Efforts to unite the continent after 1945 are well and simply summarized – though with some neglect of the role of RCK – in the early pages of Wilfried Loth, *Building Europe: A History of European Unification* (De Gruyter, Oldenburg: 2015). For a more general idea of the development of Europe as a concept, *The Idea of Europe* by Denis de Rougemont (London: 1966) offers a comprehensive overview of the continent's growing awareness of its own identity in an informatively annotated anthology.

Probing more into the specific story of European integration between the two world wars, the dozen essays contained in *European Unity in Context: The Interwar Period*, edited by Peter Stirk (London/New York: 1989) explore issues more closely related to RCK and his central concern. Philomena Murray and Paul Rich bring that story up to date with ten essays in their edited volume of *Visions of European Unity* (Boulder/Oxford: 1996), starting with the world of RCK and ending with the contemporary debate on cultural politics and European citizenship. Peter Stirk's later book, *A History of European Integration since 1914* (London/New York: 1996), offers an authoritative overview of the period, with an excellent annotated bibliography. A more recent survey entitled *Europe in Crisis: Intellectuals and the European Idea, 1917–1957*, edited by Mark Hewitson and Matthew d'Auria (New York/Oxford: 2012), contains a summary chapter on RCK in English written by Anita Prettenthaler-Ziegenhofer, author of the most thorough German study of the Count and Pan-Europa mentioned above.

The memoirs of contemporaries of RCK shed much light on the common concerns of their time. Stephan Zweig's reminiscences in *Die Welt von Gestern: Erinnerungen eines Europäers*, submitted in manuscript to his publisher the day before he committed suicide, appeared in Stockholm in 1942. It was immediately translated as *The World of Yesterday: Memoirs of a European* (New York: 1943). These reminiscences offer the richest background to the social and intellectual context of the inter-war years.

Felix Klos, *Churchill on Europe* (London/New York: 2016), serves as a reliable and insightful guide to the British war leader's post-war views of this subject. For readers who want an excellent exposé of Churchill's multifaceted relationship with the continent, they could not do better than read Allen Packwood's *Churchill and the United States of Europe, 1904–1948* (Churchill College, Cambridge). For a single-volume biography, they might turn to Andrew Roberts's highly readable *Churchill: Walking with Destiny* (London: 2018).

Other important figures of the period who played a major part in RCK's life also wrote their memoirs, notably Jean Monnet and Charles de Gaulle, and these are a rich source of detail, as are the revealing biographies of each of them which have been written in English: *Jean Monnet: First Statesman of Interdependence* by François Duchêne (New York/London: 1994) and *A Certain Idea of France: The Life of Charles de Gaulle* by Julian Jackson (London: 2018).

Few personal details about RCK are revealed in these books, however. For these, readers will need to explore the Count's extensive correspondence in the archives, of which only the letters to and from Charles de Gaulle have been published: *Coudenhove-Kalergi – De Gaulle: Une certaine idée de l'Europe* (Fondation Charles de Gaulle, Paris: Cahier nr.6: 1999).

To build up the composite picture of the man, English readers can rely on comments by other informed observers of the age. Sisley Huddleston, correspondent of *The Times* in Paris, travelled and wrote extensively about the region in *Europe in Zig-zags* (London: 1929); M.W. Fodor, the *Manchester Guardian*'s correspondent in Vienna, wrote *South of Hitler* (London: 1938); Elisabeth Wiskemann, a British diplomat in Bern with oversight of Central Europe for many years, wrote a memoir entitled *The Europe I Saw* (London: 1968). Last but not least, readers will enjoy the 1929–1945 diaries of Leo Amery, the multilingual politician and friend of Churchill and RCK, which are entitled *The Empire at Bay* (London: 1988).

Sources in German offer even richer information. Verena Schöberl's survey and analysis of media reception of Pan-Europa in Germany, France, and Great Britain between 1922 and 1933, *Es gibt ein grosses und herrliches Land, das sich selbst nicht kennt ... Es heisst Europa* (Berlin: 2008), quotes from close to 150 newspapers and includes various journalists' character assessments of RCK. A key French source for RCK's years of exile is the sympathetic interpretation and masterly overview drawn by Franck Vereecken in his doctoral thesis for the University of Paris (Sciences Politiques), *La Lutte pour les Etats Unis d'Europe: Richard Coudenhove Kalergi en exil (1938–1947)*, published by The Lothian Foundation in Brussels in 1996.

Readers will quickly discover from the following small selection of books in English, listed below in chronological order of publication, those most likely to whet their appetite to learn more about the age in which RCK lived. Others mentioned in the endnotes also point similarly towards the more extended field of politics, international relations and high culture to which RCK related.

Keynes, John Maynard. *The Economic Consequences of the Peace*. London: 1920.

Salter, Arthur. *The United States of Europe and Other Papers*. London: 1933.

Di Madariaga, Salvador. *A Portrait of Europe*. London: 1952.

Selby, Walter. *Diplomatic Twilight, 1930–1940*. London: 1953.

Hay, Denis. *Europe: The Emergence of an Idea*. Edinburgh: 1957.

Brook-Shepherd, Gordon. *Dollfuss*. London: 1961.

Pinder, John. *Europe against de Gaulle*. London: 1963.

Heater, Derek. *The Idea of European Unity*. Leicester: 1992.

MacMillan, Margaret. *The Peacemakers: Six Months that Changed the World*. London: 2001.

Brook-Shepherd, Gordon. *Uncrowned Emperor: The Life and Times of Otto von Hapsburg*. London: 2003.

Liebich, André. *Wickham Steed: Greatest Journalist of His Times*. Bern: 2018.

Thorpe, Benjamin. J. *The Time and Space of Richard Coudenhove Kalergi's Pan-Europe, 1923-1939*. Nottingham University doctoral thesis: 2018. Available on the web.

Bouverie, Tim. *Appeasing Hitler: Chamberlain, Churchill, and the Road to War*. London: 2018.

Hemming, Henry. *Our Man in New York: The British Plot to bring America into the Second World War*. London: 2019.

Emerson, Charles. *Crucible: The Long End of the Great War and the Birth of a New World, 1917–1924*. London: 2019.

Finally, I list the thirty-three monographs written by RCK. They are presented in chronological order of publication and show how, throughout his life, RCK's political writings intertwined his philosophical concerns with the promotion of his political project.

Objektivität als Grundprinzip der Moral. Phil.diss., University of Vienna: 1917.

Apologie der Technik. Leipzig: 1922.

Ethik oder Hyperethik. Leipzig: 1922.

Pan-Europa. Vienna: 1923. English translation *Pan-Europa*. New York: 1926.

Krise der Weltanschauung. Vienna: 1923.

Pazifismus. Vienna/Leipzig: 1924.

Praktischer Idealismus: Adel, Technik, Pazifismus. Vienna: 1925.

Kampf um Europa. (3 volumes). Vienna/Leipzig: 1925–1928

Held oder Heiliger. Vienna/Paris/London: 1927.

Was will Paneuropa? Vienna: 1929.

Gebote des Lebens (German/Japanese dual-language edition). Vienna: 1931.

Los vom Materialismus. Vienna/Leipzig: 1931.

Stalin & Co. Vienna/Leipzig: 1931.

Das Paneuropa ABC. Leipzig/Vienna: 1932.

Revolution durch Technik. Leipzig/Vienna: 1932.

Europa erwacht! Zürich/Vienna/Leipzig: 1934.

Paneuropa kämpft für Friede, Arbeit, Brot! Vienna: 1935.

Zusammenschluss oder Zusammenbruch! Zürich/Wien: 1935.

Europa ohne Elend. Paris/Wien/Zürich: 1936.

Totaler Staat – Totaler Mensch. Glarus: 1937. Translated by Andrew McFadyean as *The Totalitarian State against Man*. Glarus: 1938.

Kommen die Vereinigten Staaten von Europa? Glarus: 1938. Translated by Andrew McFadyean as *Europe Must Unite*. Glarus: 1939.

Europe Seeks Unity (introduction by William Bullitt). New York: 1948.

Ida Roland in Memoriam. Verona: 1951.

Die europäische Nation. Stuttgart: 1953.

Mutterland Europa. Zürich: 1953.

Vom ewigen Krieg zum grossen Frieden. Göttingen: 1956. Translated by Constantine Fitzgibbon as *From War to Peace.* London: 1959.

Der Gentleman. Zürich: 1962.

Die europäische Mission der Frau. Zürich: 1962.

Die Wiedervereinigung Europas. Vienna: 1964.

Totaler Mensch – Totaler Staat. Vienna/Munich: 1965.

Paneuropa, 1922–1966. Vienna/Munich: 1966.

Für die Revolution der Brüderlichkeit. Zürich: 1968.

Weltmacht Europa. Stuttgart: 1971.